Working in a Legal Environment

SECOND EDITION

Diana Collis

Cynthia Forget

emond

Toronto, Canada
2011

Emond Montgomery Publications Limited
60 Shaftesbury Avenue
Toronto ON M4T 1A3
http://www.emond.ca/highered

Printed in Canada.
Reprinted April 2018.

We acknowledge the financial support of the Government of Canada.
Nous reconnaissons l'appui financier du gouvernement du Canada.   Canadä

The events and characters depicted in this book are fictitious. Any similarity to actual persons, living or dead, is purely coincidental.

Contributing editors: Adrian Ho
                          Cynthia L. Chewter
                          Kathlyn Horibe
                          Meghan Clarke
                          Nora Rock
                          Randi Chapnik Myers

Acquisitions editor: Bernard Sandler
Developmental editor: Sarah Gleadow
Supervising editor: Jim Lyons
Copy editor and indexer: Paula Pike
Proofreader: Cindy Fujimoto
Permissions editor: Melody Tolson
Text designer and typesetter: Tara Wells
Cover image: webphotographeer/iStockphoto

Library and Archives Canada Cataloguing in Publication

Collis, Diana, 1957-
    Working in a legal environment / Diana Collis and Cynthia Forget. — 2nd ed.

Includes index.
ISBN 978-1-55239-387-1

    1. Law offices—Canada—Textbooks.   2. Office management—Textbooks.
I. Forget, Cynthia, 1964-   II. Title.

KE352.C64 2011   340.068   C2011-904982-1
KF318.C64 2011

This book is dedicated to

My grandmother and grandfather, Edith Winifred Wilson and Thomas Woodrow Wilson (Woody), who always said I could. They taught me that family, love, integrity, and believing in yourself are paramount in leading a fulfilling and healthy life.

My father Bill and daughter Julie Anne Lynn, who are my angels, helping to guide my path.

My husband, Larry, who always looks after everyone—especially me—and without whose love and support this text would not have been possible.

Our children and grandchildren, who inspire me every day to be the best that I can be.

It is not the hardships in life that shape who we are, but the blessings that we have been given, and I have been truly blessed.

Diana Lynn Collis

With heart-felt dedication to the memory of Counsel Mr. Marty G. Murphy Peterborough's own Perry Mason June 2, 1947 – July 2, 2004

Cynthia Forget

Contents

CHAPTER 12

CHAPTER 13

APPENDIX

INDEX

CREDITS

List of Figures

Preface

The second edition of *Working in a Legal Environment* delves into every aspect of office administration, and continues to provide orientation and instruction in specialized legal procedures in a concise and student-friendly manner. The revisions to the second edition reflect feedback from users of the first edition, and include:

- Expanded coverage of non-verbal communication, including differences across cultures

- Strategies for communicating effectively with clients whose first language is not English

- Techniques for enhancing your electronic communication skills

- Additional instruction on how to conduct legal research online

- New information on client identification and verification procedures

- Updated discussion on time-management and scheduling systems, including the benefits of smart phones as organizational tools

- Quick-reference charts and tables

- New and updated sample documents, precedents, and screenshots

- Expanded sidebars featuring interesting contemporary and historical notes

- Discussion of co-op placement, job search, and interview strategies, and resumé and cover letter writing, to help you launch your career

- A new Writing Guide appendix that reviews the basics of proper punctuation, grammar, and style.

The text begins with the roles and responsibilities of various professionals found in the legal setting. Successive chapters explore the inner workings of the court system, time and financial management, organizational skills, communication skills, the production and processing of legal documents, and legal terminology and citation. Also included are chapters on legal documents and commonly used legal forms. The final chapter discusses your future career as a legal professional and focuses on program placements, resumés, portfolios, interviews, and potential career paths. Each chapter concludes with review questions and practical activities to ensure that you understand and are able to apply the concepts covered in the chapter.

We hope that you find this text to be an excellent educational resource, and that you will continue to use it as a desk reference in your career as a legal professional.

Acknowledgments

First and foremost, gratitude is extended with heartfelt appreciation to Diana's students and colleagues past and present at Fleming College for their advice and contributions to the text material.

The first and second editions of *Working in a Legal Environment* would not have been possible without the insight, suggestions, and support provided by the following contributors and reviewers: Paul Atkinson, Bob Burgis, Linda Brankston, Julie McFadden, Barbara Moyle, Amy Maycock, Abi Aduesi, Trevor Burgis, David McFadden, Janice Miller, Kelly MacDonald, Kelly Johnson, Shannon Michel Smith, Tanya Dunford, Joanne Merchant, Giselle Piper, Jane Clarke, Linda Badiali, Lorraine Thomson, Lyne Durocher, Lynn Berry, Marion Haythorne, Nicole Ayotte, Virginia Harwood, Suzanne Louiseize, Tracy Ryder, Trevor Schindeler, Donna Traynor, Natasha Bruce, Jennifer Collis, and Jennifer McPhee.

Diana would like to especially thank her husband Larry, her children and their partners, William and Tanya, Sarah and Shane, and her grandchildren, parents, and siblings for their patience and understanding when delays, deadlines, rewrites, and excessive workloads made it impossible to participate fully in family activities. A very special thank you goes to Paul Atkinson, Bob Burgis, and Sarah Gleadow for their guidance, patience, support, and good humour. Diana is also grateful to Cindy Fujimoto, Tara Wells, and everyone at Emond Montgomery for their support and guidance.

Cynthia thanks her husband Paul and her children, Nicolas and Renée, for missing her so much; her mom, for always being there and cheering her on every step of the way; Ann Douglas, for being her personal writing guru; Diana Collis, for keeping her focused; and Emond Montgomery, for this opportunity and their patience and understanding throughout.

The Legal Office Environment

We are what we repeatedly do. Excellence, therefore, is not an act but a habit.

—Aristotle

Introduction

Presumably, if you are using this textbook you are enrolled in a legal program, studying to become a paralegal, law clerk, or other professional in the legal field. Your goal is to be employed in a law office. A law office can be an intimidating place. The air of status and prestige may at first shake your confidence a little, and you might even feel out of place. But really, a law office is no different from any other office setting. You want to make a positive first impression on your employer *and* you also want to feel confident that you chose the right career. This chapter will guide you through the workings of a law office. It will give you the tools you need to make a good impression and give you the confidence that comes from knowing what to expect in your position.

Roles and Relationships

Roles

There are a variety of roles in a legal office. In large firms you will likely find a division of work by department—accounting, file management, human resources, legal research, etc. For example, one person may be responsible for managing client files, another person may perform secretarial duties and finance administration, and another may conduct legal research for a specific case. Most law firms also have a receptionist who greets clients, answers telephones, routes incoming and outgoing mail, and assists other staff with their workloads. In a smaller law firm, you will likely have more than one role.

Often, people with the same qualifications and training will have different titles such as "legal assistant," "legal secretary," or "law clerk."

Some law firms employ an office manager who oversees all staff. An office manager usually works to improve areas of the firm such as advertising, marketing, protocols and procedures, and human resources.

CHAPTER OBJECTIVES

After reading this chapter, you will understand:

- the various roles within the legal office environment
- what types of orientation and training you can expect
- the importance of acting with integrity, courtesy, and professionalism
- the difference between hard skills and soft skills
- the benefits of office ergonomics

Lawyers You May Encounter in Your Firm

Managing partners: Lawyers who have an ownership interest in the firm, and who are given special management responsibilities by other owners

Senior partners: Lawyers who have an ownership interest in the firm and have been with the firm for a long time

Junior partners: Lawyers with an ownership interest in the firm but not as much seniority as senior partners

Associates: Lawyer employees of the firm

Articling students: Law school graduates who work under the supervision of fully licensed lawyers until they qualify for admission to the bar society

Finally, there are the lawyers (and in Ontario, paralegals). Law societies in each province and territory throughout Canada govern the law profession. In Canada there are 14 law societies, one for each province and territory. Quebec has two law societies. Figure 1.1 lists the addresses and websites for Canada's provincial and territorial law societies. In Ontario, both lawyers and paralegals are governed by the Law Society of Upper Canada (LSUC).

Paralegal Regulation in Ontario

In 2007, the LSUC began licensing and regulating paralegals—making Ontario the first province to do so. Paralegals in Ontario owe obligations to their clients, the general public, and the administration of justice, as outlined in the LSUC's *Paralegal Rules of Conduct* and the *Paralegal Professional Conduct Guidelines*. These documents, and others, are available on the LSUC website (http://www.lsuc.on.ca).

In Ontario, paralegals differ from law clerks in various regards. While law clerks must work under the supervision of a lawyer, paralegals can open their own practices and work independently. To practise, paralegals must obtain a class P1 licence; this enables them to provide legal services within the permitted scope of practice.

This text refers to "lawyers" and those that work under their supervision. Readers should be aware that in Ontario, many of the references that apply to lawyers apply equally to paralegals.

In order to become a lawyer in Ontario, candidates must graduate from a recognized Canadian law school and complete the LSUC's licensing requirements. In Ontario there are three components to the licensing process: the Skills and Professional Responsibility Program, the licensing examinations, and a ten-month articling term. Candidates who successfully complete the licensing process are eligible to apply and be called to the Bar of Ontario. The process is similar in other provinces and territories.

FIGURE 1.1   Provincial and territorial law societies

Province/Territory	Contact Information	Link
Alberta	Law Society of Alberta Suite 500 919 - 11th Avenue S.W. Calgary, AB T2R 1P3 Tel: 403-229-4700 (Calgary) or 780-429-3343 (Edmonton)	http://www.lawsociety.ab.ca
British Columbia	Law Society of British Columbia 845 Cambie Street Vancouver, BC V6B 4Z9 Tel: 604-669-2533 Fax: 604-669-5232 Toll-free in B.C.: 1-800-903-5300	http://www.lawsociety.bc.ca
Manitoba	Law Society of Manitoba 219 Kennedy Street Winnipeg, MB R3C 1S8 Tel: 204-942-5571 Fax: 204-956-0624	http://www.lawsociety.mb.ca
New Brunswick	Law Society of New Brunswick Suite 206, 1133 Regent Street Fredericton, NB E3B 3Z2 Tel: 506-458-8540 Fax: 506-451-1421	http://www.lawsociety-barreau .nb.ca/emain.asp
Newfoundland and Labrador	The Law Society of Newfoundland and Labrador 198 Water Street P.O. Box 1028 St. Johns, NL A1C 5M3 Tel: 709-722-4740 Fax: 709-722-8902	http://www.lawsociety.nf.ca
Northwest Territories	Law Society of the Northwest Territories P.O. Box 1298 Yellowknife, NT X1A 2N9 Tel: 867-873-3828 Fax: 867-873-6344	http://www.lawsociety.nt.ca
Nova Scotia	Nova Scotia Barristers' Society 1101-1645 Granville Street Halifax, NS B3J 1X3 Tel: 902-422-1491 Fax: 902-429-4869	http://www.nsbs.org
Nunavut	Law Society of Nunavut Bldg. 917, 3rd Floor, Unit B Iqaluit, NU X0A 0H0 Tel: 867-979-2330 Fax: 867-979-2333	http://lawsociety.nu.ca

Province/Territory	Contact Information	Link
Ontario	The Law Society of Upper Canada 130 Queen Street West Toronto, ON M5H 2N6 Tel: 416-947-3300 Toll-free: 1-800-668-7380	http://www.lsuc.on.ca
Prince Edward Island	The Law Society of Prince Edward Island P.O. Box 128, 49 Water Street Charlottetown, PE C1A 7K2 Tel: 902-566-1666 Fax: 902-368-7557	http://www.lspei.pe.ca
Quebec	Barreau du Québec 445, boulevard Saint-Laurent Montréal, QC H2Y 3T8 Tel: 514-954-3400 Toll-free: 1-800-361-8495 Chambre des notaires du Québec 1801 avenue McGill College, bureau 600 Montréal, QC H3A 0A7 Tel: 514-879-1793 Fax: 514-879-1923 Toll-free: 1-800-NOTAIRE	http://www.barreau.qc.ca http://www.cdnq.org/en
Saskatchewan	Law Society of Saskatchewan 2nd Floor, Court House 2425 Victoria Avenue P.O. Box 5032 Regina, SK S4P 3M3 Tel: 306-569-8020 Fax: 306-569-0155	http://www.lawsociety.sk.ca
Yukon	Law Society of Yukon Suite 202, 302 Steele Street Whitehorse, YT Y1A 2C5 Tel: 867-668-4231 Fax: 867-667-7556	http://www.lawsocietyyukon.com

NOTES:

All lawyers in Canada are licensed to practise law. They can act as barristers, solicitors, notaries public, and commissioners. In Ontario there are two categories of licences: L1 and L2. These are established by LSUC bylaw 4, section 2. Historically, a lawyer's role was split into two distinct subprofessions—barrister (legal advocate) and solicitor (legal adviser). With the exception of Quebec, today, in almost all common-law jurisdictions, the distinction between barristers and solicitors is blurred and most lawyers perform a variety of roles:

- Barristers advocate on behalf of their clients in court.

- Solicitors process legal business outside the courtroom.

- Commissioners take affidavits and administer oaths to those swearing a document to be true.

- Notaries public draft or certify deeds, contracts, and other legal documents and validate their authenticity (for example, stating that a document is a true copy).

Under LSUC regulation in Ontario:

- The holder of a class L1 licence is entitled to practise law as a barrister and solicitor.
- The holder of an L2 licence is entitled to practise law in Ontario as a barrister and solicitor in the employ of the Attorney General for Ontario or, if appointed under the *Crown Attorneys Act*, as a Crown attorney or as an assistant Crown attorney.
- The holder of a class P1 licence is entitled to provide legal services within the permitted scope of practice for paralegals.

A lawyer's work varies depending on the area of law in which he or she practises. Your job is to make the lawyer's job easier. Lawyers will have their own requirements and expectations of you. You will need to stay in tune with your employer's needs by having frequent, detailed conversations. The better you know the lawyer's working style, the better a team member you will make, and therefore the better the firm will serve its clients.

NOTES:

Relationships

Managing relationships with your colleagues is challenging. If you become close friends with your co-workers, keep in mind that your working relationship can be affected if the friendship sours. You should avoid forming a clique by becoming too close with two or three co-workers and isolating others. Cliques can have a negative impact on the office. Strive to establish and maintain a professional relationship with your co-workers at all times.

You should be prepared to work with a variety of different personalities throughout your career, including:

- a chatty neighbour

- a slanderer

- someone who is always negative

- an emotionally needy person who seeks an audience on personal matters

- someone who does not carry their workload

- someone who does not follow office protocol.

In most situations, your best strategy is to control what you can, and learn to ignore what you cannot. For example, you can cut short a chatty or needy neighbour by limiting eye contact with the person, filing something out of the immediate area, or stating that you are on a tight deadline. Most people will pick up non-verbal or indirect cues and respond accordingly. If your neighbour doesn't, you may have to resort to an honest, open conversation. Keep in mind that if this is going to be a long-term position, you do not want to be distracted by this person every day.

If a colleague's behaviour is out of your control, such as someone not pulling his or her weight or not following office protocol, you have two choices: ignore the situation and focus on your own job, or speak with your supervisor. Always consider the possible ramifications of any decisions you make regarding co-workers.

In conclusion, you should treat every person who works in the firm with respect, regardless of their title or status. Everyone's goal should be to provide excellent service to the firm's clients. Without satisfied clients, the law firm will not thrive.

NOTES:

Orientation and Training

Ideally, your employer will provide you with an orientation plan when you begin your job. An effective orientation plan provides answers to your questions and reassures you that you are not missing critical information. A detailed plan consists of three elements:

1. a broad introduction and orientation to the organization/firm

2. a training manual and/or procedures and protocol manual

3. a training schedule that covers everything an employee needs to know.

If you start a job and discover that there is no orientation plan, ask for a job description (if you didn't receive one during the hiring process) and a list of short-term and long-term goals. Your employer may refer you to an experienced staff member who can answer all your questions. This may not be as helpful as a well-prepared plan, but it will suffice. Your employer might also assign you a mentor who can provide advice and assistance about even the smallest details of your position.

You should create an orientation checklist. This checklist serves two purposes. First, it familiarizes you with and focuses you on the immediate learning requirements of your job. Second, it forms part of your personnel file to prove that you received adequate orientation.

Figure 1.2 shows a typical orientation checklist. Depending on the nature and dynamics of the office, your checklist may vary.

There is a significant difference between an orientation plan and a training plan. As you can see from the checklist, an orientation plan is your guide to the office, but it does not train you on how to do your job. You should also follow a detailed training plan, which will teach you the particular functions and responsibilities of your position as well as how the firm operates.

If your employer does not provide a training plan, draft one yourself:

- Keep a notebook with you at all times.

- Ask yourself what daily activities you need to accomplish to successfully complete your duties.

- When receiving instructions related to your duties, take notes, review them, and ask for clarification when necessary.

> **PRACTICE TIP**
> - The **orientation plan** is your guide to your office.
> - A **training plan** teaches you the functions and responsibilities of your position.

NOTES:

FIGURE 1.2 Orientation checklist

❏ Get a clear explanation of the schedule for the first week on the job.

❏ Be introduced to all staff members and learn their roles and titles.

❏ Identify a staff member who will act as mentor for the first week or two.

❏ Obtain an organizational chart of the firm with full names and titles of everyone in the firm.

❏ Understand the dress code and firm image.

❏ Get an overview of the department and/or firm.

❏ Learn general office goals and objectives.

❏ Get a full description of your position and responsibilities, as well as what is expected of you.

❏ Get your email, phone, and voicemail set up.

❏ Learn mail and telephone procedures, as well as policies on the personal use of email, the telephone, and other equipment.

❏ Understand parking arrangements—where you can park, costs, passes, etc.

❏ Learn how to order supplies and request particular desk accessories.

❏ Choose a calendar and other organizational tools.

❏ Set up your own workstation (subject to office rules).

❏ Get a nameplate for your desk or office.

❏ Complete your hiring documentation as required.

❏ Get a tour of the building and your work area, and learn the location of washrooms, staff rooms, other work areas, and departments.

❏ Be briefed on working hours, breaks, sick leave, and annual/vacation leave, as well as on overtime and after-hours procedures.

❏ Obtain pay date and payroll information and overtime policies.

❏ Receive information on employee benefits (in print or online).

❏ Receive resources such as directories, protocol manuals, computer program manuals, dictionaries, and staff lists.

❏ Obtain necessary keys, passes, alarm codes, and personnel identification.

❏ Learn end-of-day routines regarding lights, telephones, doors, computers, and alarms.

❏ Learn safety, security, and emergency procedures.

❏ Be introduced to office organization, including files, supplies, and resources.

❏ Learn correspondence styles and standardized practices.

❏ Learn where office equipment is located and how to use it.

❏ Receive information on travel policies regarding mileage, meals, expenses, etc.

❏ Be informed of the format, participation, and frequency of staff meetings.

❏ Obtain union information (if relevant).

❏ Understand performance standards and the evaluation process.

❏ Obtain policies on accountability, customer service, confidentiality, and ethics.

❏ Obtain the firm's conflict-of-interest policy.

❏ Obtain an employee handbook (if there is one).

❏ Develop a detailed training plan.

NOTES:

When you have time, organize this information along with corresponding precedents. For example, place a sample retainer letter with your notes on how to create a retainer letter. Keeping the information together will make your job easier.

During your first week, you may be provided with a custom-designed work schedule to help phase you into the new office. If a schedule has not been prepared, you may wish to discuss one with your supervisor.

Expectations, Codes/Rules, Policies, and Etiquette

Employer Expectations

Legal professionals place a great deal of importance on etiquette, protocol, and conduct. As discussed, provincial law societies regulate the legal profession. The law society's responsibility is to ensure that a person who practises law or provides legal services meets standards of learning, competency, and professional conduct.

Lawyers and paralegals in Ontario are governed by the LSUC's *Rules of Professional Conduct*. Figure 1.3 lists the web links for the provincial and territorial law society rules and codes of professional conduct in Canada.

The rules and codes are typically organized under a variety of headings:

- Relationship to clients

- Practice of law

- Relationship to the administration of justice

- Relationship to students, employees, and others

- Relationship to the society and other lawyers

- Professionalism

- Advocacy

- Fees and retainers

- Practice management.

Law clerks, legal office assistants, and legal secretaries work directly under the supervision of a lawyer. Although you may have autonomy

NOTES:

FIGURE 1.3 Provincial and territorial law society rules and codes of conduct

Province/Territory	Rules and Codes of Conduct Links
Alberta	http://www.lawsociety.ab.ca/files/regulations/Code.pdf
British Columbia	http://www.lawsociety.bc.ca/page.cfm?cid=383&t=Professional-Conduct-Manual
Manitoba	http://www.lawsociety.mb.ca/lawyer-regulation/code-of-professional-conduct/documents/english-version/code_of_conduct.pdf
New Brunswick	http://www.lawsociety-barreau.nb.ca/assets/documents/CODEOFPROFESSIONALCONDUCT_February_2009.pdf
Newfoundland and Labrador	http://www.lawsociety.nf.ca/code/code.asp
Northwest Territories	http://www.cba.org/CBA/activities/pdf/codeofconduct.pdf
Nova Scotia	http://www.nsbs.org/legalethics/toc.htm
Nunavut	http://www.cba.org/CBA/activities/code/
Ontario	Lawyers: http://www.lsuc.on.ca/with.aspx?id=671 Paralegals: http://www.lsuc.on.ca/WorkArea/DownloadAsset.aspx?id=2147484090
Prince Edward Island	http://www.lspei.pe.ca/pdf/code_of_professional_conduct_CBA1987.pdf
Quebec	http://www2.publicationsduquebec.gouv.qc.ca/dynamicSearch/telecharge.php?type=2&file=%2F%2FB_1%2FB1R1_A.htm http://www.cdnq.org/cgi-bin/carteEn.php
Saskatchewan	http://www.lawsociety.sk.ca/newlook/Publications/Code2003/CodeCompleteNov03.pdf
Yukon	http://www.lawsocietyyukon.com/pdf/codeofconduct10.pdf

PRACTICE TIP

In Ontario, LSUC rules impose an obligation on lawyers and paralegals to properly delegate and supervise staff. The relevant rules are set out in bylaw 7.1, rule 5.01 of the *Rules of Professional Conduct* for lawyers, and rule 8.01(3) of the *Paralegal Rules of Conduct*.

when important tasks are delegated to you, it is the lawyer who is ultimately responsible for a breach of the rules. Under law society rules, it is important that you understand the scope of information you can provide. You must be careful not to give advice or provide information that requires the legal judgment of a lawyer (and in Ontario, a paralegal).

Three common breaches of the rules relate to breach of confidentiality, misuse of trust funds, and a non-lawyer giving legal advice.

Confidentiality is paramount to the protection and service of the client. If you breach confidentiality, the lawyer you are working for can face serious consequences. To avoid any indiscretions, never leave client files and documents in a public area, or in an area where other clients can access them. Safely store files when the office is closed. Never discuss the details of any client-related matter outside the law firm or within earshot of other clients. It is even unacceptable to tell anyone, including your own family or friends, that a particular person is a past or present client of your firm. You will likely be asked to sign an oath of confidentiality or a confidentiality agreement similar to the one shown in figure 1.4 to ensure that you comply with this protocol.

Trust moneys belong to the client. There is a legal and ethical obligation to account for every penny at all stages of a client matter. Failure to live up to that responsibility can have serious consequences for the lawyer or paralegal.

Non-lawyers (and in Ontario, non-paralegals) should never provide legal advice because it could cause serious problems for the client and the lawyer/paralegal. This rule sounds simple, but it is easy to forget when a client asks, "What do you think I should do?" In an attempt to help, non-lawyers sometimes answer the question in a way that leads the client to believe they are receiving a legal opinion or legal advice.

Some firms have policies of behaviour that dictate employee conduct and the employer's expectations. You may be required to sign a form to indicate that you received and understand the policies. If you do not receive a copy of the policies, you should inquire into the availability of one.

A policy will address a number of the issues outlined in the orientation and training section of this chapter, such as dress code, conflicts of interest, and personal use of the telephone, email, and Internet. Employers often complain that staff members spend too much time surfing the Internet or sending personal email. Find out your employer's policies, and stick to them. An employer generally has other basic expectations as well, such as punctuality, dependability, loyalty, and teamwork.

Employee Expectations

Expectations go both ways. Employees as well as employers have rights and expectations. Employee rights are protected by the *Human Rights Code* (for example, freedom from sexual harassment and discrimination) and the *Occupational Health and Safety Act* (the right to refuse unsafe work, protection from workplace harassment and violence). You should also be treated fairly and with respect, and your health-related needs should be accommodated. You are entitled to receive the salary and benefits you were promised in your contract, and your employer should provide you with regular feedback to help you improve your job performance.

NOTES:

FIGURE 1.4   Sample confidentiality agreement

To: Christopher Maher

From: Jo-Anne Merchant

Re: Confidentiality

I acknowledge a moral and professional obligation not to disclose client information directly or indirectly except as authorized by you.

I agree not to disclose the names of clients, the nature of legal matters, personal information, or any other information gained in this office to unauthorized persons.

I shall not deal carelessly with any information so as to cause it to be disclosed.

This acknowledgment will bind me even after my position ends, and applies to all current and past clients.

I have read the foregoing and discussed it with my employer. I understand and agree to comply with the terms of this agreement.

I understand that any breach of the terms of this agreement may be just cause for the termination of my employment.

Employee name: *(please print)* _____

_____   _____
Employee signature   Date *(dd/mm/yy)*

Witness: *(please print)* _____

_____   _____
Witness signature   Date *(dd/mm/yy)*

NOTES:

Once you feel secure in your role, you can ask your employer about ongoing training. There may be changes in certain areas of law or technology, or you may simply want to explore new positions in your firm. Other sources of training include local bar associations, law societies, and colleges and universities. Your employer may give you time off work and/or cover the costs of your training.

If an opportunity to advance becomes available in your office, your employer should fill the vacant position impartially.

Communicating

Legal jargon and slang develop naturally, and can be unique to your office. You should avoid using legal jargon and slang when you speak to clients. Even when clients are not around, you should limit your use of slang because it does not set a professional tone.

It is human nature to gossip—at the water cooler or elsewhere—but this habit can be detrimental to your career. Gossip can break down a team and create an unproductive office. Also, beware of becoming too friendly with the office gossip. If you align yourself with this person, your reputation may suffer.

Finally, use humour in the office cautiously. When used appropriately, humour can reduce stress, alter negative thinking, improve communication, increase empathy, defuse difficult situations, and increase productivity. However, demeaning humour such as sexist, racist, or crude comments can destroy an office environment. Avoid insults, sarcasm, and cynicism. You may think you're being funny, but others may not see it that way. To ensure that your humour is a hit, consider your audience and the situation. The same comment in two different situations will have two different outcomes. Also, remember that preceding a comment with a phrase like "I hope this does not offend anyone" does not excuse what comes next. Be sensitive when telling jokes and always remember that you are working in a professional environment.

Soft Skills

What is the difference between hard and soft skills? The easiest way to explain the difference is that hard skills can be learned by following a set of instructions, whereas soft skills are developed through practical work and life experiences.

More and more employers are recognizing the value of soft skills. Creativity, ambition, critical thinking, and communication and leadership skills are all examples of soft skills. Any number of people can prepare and type a document, but not everyone can take the initiative and improve office procedure or lead a committee. These are the skills that will get you the position you want. And most soft skills are transferable, which means you can apply them to numerous positions, even those outside your field.

As you develop your soft skills, be sure to incorporate them in your resumé, either by listing examples of tasks or by creating a summary of "other abilities." Just because soft skills cannot be quantified in the same way as hard skills does not mean they are less important.

Setting Out and Moving Up

When you graduate with a legal secretarial, law clerk, or paralegal diploma you have made an excellent start on your path to career opportunities in the legal field. Nevertheless, few employers will be prepared to give you much responsibility for client files or dealing with complex legal issues until you have proven that you can apply the knowledge you have acquired in a responsible and professional manner. Don't be surprised (or discouraged) if your career path starts in the mail room, or as a receptionist or file clerk.

However, a job well done is highly valued in a legal environment, no matter what task you have been given. As you prove your worth, you will be given increasing responsibility. Over time, you will find that you can advance within the original work environment and will also become increasingly aware of other opportunities in the legal field that may require both the practical experience you are acquiring and additional education or certification. Some of the wide range of possibilities that will open up to you are listed in chapter 13 in figure 13.1.

Equipment and Ergonomics

Selecting Furniture and Equipment

It is important to be acquainted with the types of furniture and equipment commonly found in an office, because you may be the person responsible for purchasing equipment or furniture for yourself and others in the office.

Before you purchase any furniture or equipment, identify your needs, space, and budget and get your employer's approval. In some cases it may be more economical to lease or rent furniture and equipment. Make sure you crunch the numbers before you decide which option is best for your office. You should also consider whether or not

NOTES:

the equipment requires a service contract. Some equipment, such as photocopiers and printers, may benefit from this more than others. If your equipment is leased, service may be included in the contract.

If you are changing the set-up of your office, consider which equipment you use most often, how noisy the equipment is, how much space it occupies, and how you use it. Always set up your equipment in a way that will be most convenient for you. Figure 1.5 contains a list of equipment that you're likely to find in a law office, or that you may have to purchase or lease at some point.

Ergonomics

Poor ergonomics leads to a number of physical injuries. Some of the more common complaints include back, neck, and shoulder pain, repetitive strain injury (usually in the wrists), and headaches or migraines. Well-adjusted or ergonomically designed equipment can reduce the discomfort caused by routine daily tasks. Not every office can afford to be fully ergonomic, but you can identify the equipment and furniture that causes you the most trouble and request a change. You may also be able to make simple adjustments to your existing work set-up that will

The Mayo Clinic defines **ergonomics** as the science of designing the job to fit the worker rather than physically forcing the worker's body to fit the job.

FIGURE 1.5   Office equipment and furniture

- Desks (for lawyers, support staff, conference rooms)
- Chairs (for lawyers, support staff, conference rooms, reception area)
- Filing cabinets
- Supply cabinets
- Bookcases
- Fireproof cabinet
- Computers (hardware and software)

- Printers (black and white, colour, laser)
- Facsimile machine (fax) (special features)
- Photocopier (standard, colour, special features)
- Legal reference materials
- Office signs
- Scanner
- Postage meter
- Adding machines/calculators

- Cheque-writing machine
- Electric pencil sharpener and electric stapler
- Binding machine
- Dictation and transcription machines
- Telephones and telephone equipment
- Numerous smaller office and desk tools

NOTES:

improve your comfort. Figure 1.6 lists some common office equipment and ergonomically ideal ways to set it up.

If your budget is limited, you can always improvise ergonomic solutions. For example, place a package of paper under your computer monitor to make it higher, or use a flat box filled with waste paper to simulate a foot rest. Try out various tools to alter the set-up of your work area, such as organizational stands or caddies to hold frequently used items, thereby reducing the reaching and stretching you're forced to do.

Evaluate the way you sit, stand, and reach in relation to your equipment and furniture, and adjust your positioning to maximize ergonomic effect. You should end up being more comfortable—and more productive as well.

NOTES:

FIGURE 1.6   Ergonomic office equipment

Equipment	Ideal Set-up/Body Position
Chair	The armrests should be low enough to allow your elbows to rest comfortably. The chair should support your posture, its seat height should be adjustable, it should be able to swivel, and it should have wheels. Add a lumbar cushion or backrest if necessary. Sit with your hips and knees at right angles; if necessary, use a foot rest or adjust the height of your chair. Do not cross your legs. Keep your head and neck in an upright position and your shoulders relaxed. Keep your elbows close to your body and at right angles to your hips.
Computer monitor	Keep the monitor about an arm's length from your eyes (with the keyboard pulled out). Ensure that the monitor's contrast and colour settings are easy on your eyes. Keep the monitor directly in front of you (rather than angled to the side). Reduce glare on the monitor surface by moving the monitor, restricting the source of light (e.g., by drawing the blinds), or using an anti-glare screen.
Document stand	Position the stand as close to the monitor as possible, at the same height and distance. Minimize your eye, neck, and head movements when looking from the monitor to the document stand.
Keyboard and keyboard tray	Use a keyboard with good key accessibility, or use a split keyboard. Key lightly; do not forcefully pound the keys. Use a soft, gel-filled wrist pad. The keyboard tray should be adjustable and should slope away from you at a downward angle. Keep the keyboard close to you—roughly above your knees.
Lighting	Use task lights that are flexible and that can be focused on document stands, screens, or desk work. Use task lights in combination with indirect lighting (on the wall or ceiling) to avoid strong contrast between dark and bright areas of your workspace. Too little or too much light can contribute to headaches and eyestrain. Eliminate glare by using anti-glare computer screens or drawing the blinds.
Mouse	Use a mouse pad with a built-in wrist rest. Add a mouse extension tray to the keyboard. Keep your wrists in a neutral position and your elbows close to your body. You should not have to reach for the mouse, and your forearms should be supported.
Telephone	Use a telephone headset or a speaker phone. Position the phone within easy reach.

REVIEW QUESTIONS

1. What is the difference between a senior partner and a junior partner?

_____

_____

_____

_____

_____

_____

_____

2. What can you do if there is no orientation plan?

_____

_____

_____

_____

_____

_____

_____

3. Name five difficulties that you could encounter with your co-workers.

_____

_____

_____

_____

_____

4. What is the key to a successful working environment in a law firm?

_____

_____

_____

_____

_____

_____

_____

5. What is the most critical way of protecting the client?

_____

_____

_____

_____

_____

_____

_____

6. Can you give legal opinions? Take instructions from clients? Prepare legal documents?

_____

_____

_____

_____

_____

_____

_____

7. Why should you not gossip in the office?

_____

_____

_____

_____

_____

8. When is humour appropriate in the office? When is it inappropriate?

_____

_____

_____

_____

_____

_____

_____

9. What are soft skills? What are hard skills? Give an example of each.

_____

_____

_____

_____

_____

_____

_____

10. What is ergonomics? Why is it important?

_____

_____

_____

_____

_____

_____

_____

11. What should you consider before purchasing furniture or equipment?

_____

_____

_____

_____

_____

12. What can you do to ensure that the client receives quality service and is happy with the firm?

_____

_____

_____

_____

_____

_____

CAREER AWARENESS ACTIVITY

To fully understand the education, knowledge, skills, responsibilities, and expertise needed to become a professional in a legal office setting, it's helpful to speak to someone with experience in the field.

Arrange an interview with a person working as a law clerk, legal assistant, paralegal, or lawyer. Before the interview, do your research. Know the type of law practised by the office you are visiting. If you are interested in becoming a litigation assistant, interviewing someone in a corporate law office will be less useful to you than visiting an office that deals primarily in litigation. If you don't know anyone who works in a legal environment, ask your instructor for a possible interviewee.

Once you've found your subject, arrange an interview for a specific time and place. If the person does not have time to meet in person, conduct your interview by telephone or email.

Prepare your questions before the interview. Format your list of questions so that you have space to write the subject's response beside each question. Sample questions are provided below. You may wish to change these questions and add your own.

Once the interview is complete, send a note to the interviewee, thanking them for taking time out of their busy schedule to help you with your research. Prepare a three- to four-page report outlining what you have learned about potential positions that might be available to you. Attach the interview sheet to your report. Be prepared to present the report to your class.

Sample Questions

1. What are the major responsibilities of an employee in the field?
2. What education and training do I need to gain a position in this field?
3. What other characteristics or traits should one possess or develop in order to succeed?
4. What are the entry-level positions in this field?
5. What is the position's salary range?
6. What are the opportunities for growth?
7. What will I need to do in order to advance?
8. What type of in-house training is available?
9. What are the working conditions like in this field?
10. Is travel required?
11. What do you find most rewarding about your job?
12. What frustrations, if any, do you experience?
13. What is the employment outlook?
14. Are you satisfied in your position?
15. If you could change something about your position, what would it be?

Canada's Justice System

Courts offer a venue for the peaceful resolution of disputes, and for the reasoned and dispassionate discussion of our most pressing social issues.

> —The Right Honourable Chief Justice of Canada,
> Beverley McLachlin, P.C.

Introduction

The mandate of law societies across Canada is to promote public confidence in the legal system and to protect the public interest in the administration of justice. If you work in the legal field, you need to be familiar with court and board proceedings, and the way in which business is conducted in these forums. This chapter will give you a sound understanding of the roles and responsibilities within courts and boards, which will help inform and improve your day-to-day interactions.

The Courthouse: Then and Now

The courthouse is full of history, symbolism, protocol, and respect for the law. The courthouse is where the fruits of your labour are presented and decided on. Whether it's a $100 Small Claims Court action, a family matter, or a first-degree murder jury trial, this is where all the proceedings occur.

Entire books have been written on the evolution of courthouse architecture, its symbolism, and various construction styles over the years. The most important aspects, however, are those that have remained constant. Generally, courthouses reflect the political ideals, religious and cultural beliefs, and tenor of the times in which they are built. Today's courthouse can be an elaborate monument to an architect's vision, or it can be a one-room building with a few carefully positioned desks and a makeshift bar. What matters most is one's respect for the convened court and the application of the law in the administration of justice.

In the Middle Ages, court proceedings were conducted outdoors, not within the confines of architecturally grand buildings. However, certain foundations and conventions were established in these open-air courts. The judge sat under a "tree of justice," generally an ancient tree that represented years of wisdom and justice. Tree branches were placed on the ground to form a ring around the judge. Court took place within this area, with observers standing outside the ring of branches.

In the 12th century, buildings began to be constructed—often in the centre of town—to house the court. Generally, the prison was located on the ground floor and the court on the second floor. A symbol of Christianity (such as a crucifix) above the judge's bench came to replace the "tree of justice," and the ring of branches was supplanted by a short wooden fence.

By the 16th and 17th centuries, as the separation between church and state became more distinct and entrenched in constitutional law, Christian symbolism in the courtroom was replaced with emblems of state, and the division between judges and lawyers grew wider. Offices were gradually added for administrative functions as courts became more active and formal.

By the 19th century, many new courthouses were built as European nations expanded to the western world. Detention cells were moved to locations separate from courthouses. The judge's bench or dais was raised, the jury were placed off to the side, and the defence and prosecution were positioned equally before the judge. The wooden fence that was once a ring of branches became the bar. Only accredited barristers and solicitors were permitted inside the bar. This practice is still observed today: After law students have completed all required courses, articles, and exams, they are "called to the bar," presented with their diploma, and invited to proceed inside the bar.

Today, the courthouse generally includes not only courtrooms but also offices for all stakeholders in the justice system. Stakeholders use or require access to courthouse facilities and therefore have a vested interest in these facilities, which include:

> **DID YOU KNOW?**
>
> **Court** (n.) Taken from the "King's court," which included the king's residence and the functionaries who assisted the King. The first law "courts" in England were decision-making processes presided over by the King's representative, who would travel on a circuit to enforce the "King's peace."

FIGURE 2.1   The Annapolis Royal Court House in Annapolis, Nova Scotia is the oldest operating courthouse in Canada. It was rebuilt in 1836–37 after the original building was destroyed by fire.

- Crown offices and judges' chambers
- barristers' and duty counsel offices
- interview rooms and holding cells
- police and community agency offices
- a law library
- offices for numerous administrative services such as justice of the peace intake, filing, and trial coordination
- public waiting areas and washrooms.

Aside from the physical aspects of a courthouse, one of the most significant tenets of today's courts is *judicial independence.* This concept is quite complex, and encompasses many aspects of the court. In essence, judicial independence ensures that the presiding judicial officer, usually the judge, arrives at a decision freely and independently without government interference. Inside the courtroom doors, the judge makes a ruling guided by fact and laws such as the *Courts of Justice Act,* current legislation and regulations, and the rulings of higher courts on similar issues. This fundamental concept is paramount in the Canadian justice system. Unlike some judges in the American system, Canadian judges do not seek election from the public at large; rather, they are appointed by federal or provincial/territorial governments. In order to be eligible to become a judge, a person must practise law for at least ten years, and then proceed through a strict selection process run by a special appointments committee. Appointments are announced by the justice minister of Canada for federal courts, and by the attorney general of the relevant province or territory for provincial/territorial courts.

FIGURE 2.2 The interior of the Supreme Court of Canada, Ottawa. Nine justices typically preside over this court.

Organizational Structure of the Court System

The Canadian government is divided into three *branches*: legislative, executive, and judicial. The legislative branch creates the laws, the executive branch implements government policy, and the judicial branch oversees the court system.

There are several levels of courts in Canada. The Supreme Court of Canada occupies the highest level. It is an appeal court that can choose to review the important or controversial cases from the provincial/territorial courts of appeal and from the Federal Court of Appeal. The Federal Court of Appeal and the provincial/territorial courts of appeal hear appeals from trial-level courts in their respective areas of jurisdiction. There is a trial division of the Federal Court that has a very narrow jurisdiction, dealing with lawsuits against federal government employees, intellectual property disputes, and admiralty cases. Each province or territory has two levels of trial court, one considered a superior court and the other a provincial/territorial court. The way civil cases are allocated between these courts varies somewhat from province to province. The superior level of trial court deals only with the more serious, or indictable, criminal cases and then only if the accused person chooses this court. Provincial or territorial trial courts are the busiest criminal courts, handling all quasi-criminal charges under provincial and territorial laws, and a great many *Criminal Code* cases as well.

Administrative boards are agencies created by special statute to settle disputes between individuals and/or companies, or between individuals or companies and the government. In making their decisions, administrative boards are required to follow procedures similar to those of courts. Boards are discussed in more detail on pages 35 to 38.

Figure 2.3 illustrates the structure of the federal and provincial/territorial courts.

The names of the courts and divisions vary by province and territory; however, their responsibilities remain largely the same. Figure 2.4 lists the websites for Canada's provincial and territorial courts.

The Courtroom

Standard Elements and Layout

There are numerous styles of courtrooms—some more casual or formal than others—but they all consist of the same standard elements. Figure 2.5 shows a typical courtroom and identifies the key features. To meet the demands placed on court facilities and resources, temporary or makeshift courtrooms are sometimes set up; their layout and elements may differ from those shown here.

At one end of the courtroom is a table or desk on a raised dais for the judge or judicial officer. In front of the dais are tables or desks for the courtroom clerk and the court reporter. In the middle of the courtroom

FIGURE 2.3   Structure of the federal and provincial/territorial courts

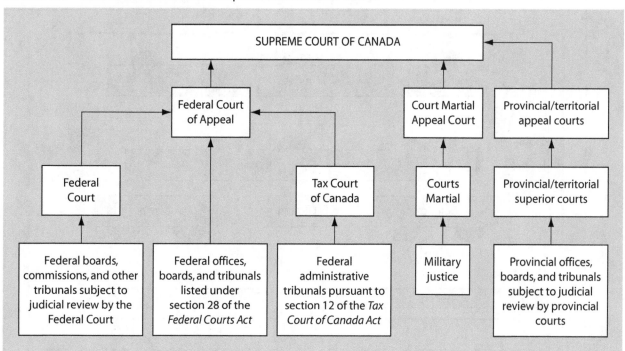

FIGURE 2.4   Provincial and territorial courts

Province/Territory	Link
Alberta	http://www.albertacourts.ab.ca
British Columbia	http://www.provincialcourt.bc.ca
Manitoba	http://www.manitobacourts.mb.ca
New Brunswick	http://www.gnb.ca/justice/asrlste.htm
Newfoundland and Labrador	http://www.court.nl.ca
Northwest Territories	http://www.nwtcourts.ca
Nova Scotia	http://www.courts.ns.ca
Nunavut	http://www.nucj.ca
Ontario	http://www.ontariocourts.on.ca
Prince Edward Island	http://www.gov.pe.ca/courts
Quebec	http://www.gouv.qc.ca
Saskatchewan	http://www.sasklawcourts.ca
Yukon	http://www.justice.gov.yk.ca/prog/cs/courts.html

are two tables of equal size for defence and Crown counsel. Generally, defence counsel sits facing the judge on the left-hand side of the court and the Crown attorney sits on the right. In some courts or sometimes for special reasons, these positions are reversed. Between the two counsel tables is a lectern from which defence and Crown counsel conduct

FIGURE 2.5   A typical courtroom

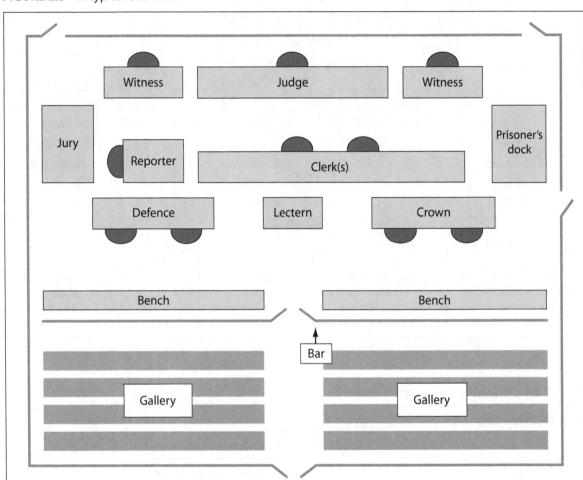

their questioning and deliver their arguments to the court. Behind the counsel tables are benches or chairs for defence counsel awaiting their matters. One or two witness boxes are situated to the left and/or right of the judge. In the Superior Court of Justice, a jury box with 12 chairs is located off to one side. On the wall behind the judge is often found the coat of arms for the court. Most courtrooms are also equipped with a secure prisoner's dock where accused persons appear before the court.

Courtrooms have seating areas for the public, known as the gallery (or the body of the court), with capacity based on the size of the court-room. The gallery is separated from the rest of the courtroom by a short wooden fence (the bar). In newly constructed courtrooms, judges or judicial officers enter the courtroom through a private door, which court staff are also permitted to use. Counsel, police officers, security personnel, and other participants such as witnesses enter the courtroom through the public door. These separate entrances underscore judicial independence.

The court docket lists all matters scheduled before the court for that particular day. In today's technological world, these dockets are comput-erized and made available to counsel and other court officials. They are also posted outside the courtroom for the information of the general public. A sample court docket is shown in figure 2.6.

FIGURE 2.6   A sample court docket

COURT DOCKET — CRIMINAL

COURT 1311	ROOM 1	JUDGE	PROVINCIAL CROWN	TIME 09:00 AM
DATE 28 June 20--	PAGE 1	JP	DUTY COUNSEL	RECESS

NO	INFO #	DOB	BADGE #	DATE OF ARREST	NAME	OFFENCE	ACTION	✔	PLEA	FINDINGS	COMMENTS
1	0024	12 MAY 58	169	7 JAN --	DOE, JOHN	ASSAULT					
2	2979	21 OCT 62	131	23 DEC --	SMITH, STEVE	THEFT UNDR $5,000.00					
3	0090	22 AUG 74	104	15 APR --	MASSEY, JANE	CARELESS DRIVING					
4	0090	22 AUG 74	104	15 APR --	MASSEY, JANE	OVER 80 MG					
5	0972	21 JAN 81	110	16 AUG --	GREEN, JENNIFER	ASSAULT					
6	0972	21 JAN 81	110	16 AUG --	GREEN, JENNIFER	BREAK & ENTER W/INT					

Protocol and Decorum

Many rules and practices govern conduct within a courtroom, but one word captures them all: respect. The object or focus of respect is not so much the judge as it is the court as a whole. When the judge enters the courtroom, the clerk stands and says, "All rise," and with these words the court is declared open. The judge steps up to the dais and bows to counsel before sitting down. Counsel and other officers of the court bow in tandem, as a mutual sign of respect. When the judge sits, all others then take their seats, bringing the court into session. It is significant that each and every time a court convenes or reconvenes, this act of mutual respect is displayed. In addition, while court is in session, any time an officer of the court enters or exits the courtroom, he or she bows to the bench.

Start times for court vary depending on the jurisdiction and the nature of the court's business. Generally, most Ontario Court of Justice courts commence sitting at 9:30 a.m., with some starting at 9:00 a.m. Most Superior Court of Justice courts start at 10:00 a.m. Most courts take a morning recess of approximately 15 minutes, and rise for an hour lunch break at 1:00 p.m. Not all courts take an afternoon recess. In addition to these scheduled breaks, the court often recesses when there is a lull in business and counsel are not yet able to deal with their matters.

With no specific end time, court sittings conclude at the discretion of the presiding judicial officer. It's not unusual for a court to sit into the evening so that a particular witness can finish delivering evidence. The judge dictates all procedures that take place in the courtroom and exercises some discretion over how it is run.

When you enter a courthouse, you may be subjected to a weapons search. You might walk through an electronic gateway, or security personnel might sweep hand-held wands over your body. Specific rules dictate behaviour or decorum inside the courtroom. Many courthouses post these rules on the outer courtroom doors. Whether the rules are posted or not, you should know and observe the following:

- No food

- No gum

- No drinks (those inside the bar are permitted to drink water from a plastic or paper cup)

- No sunglasses

- No hats (This is not as cut-and-dried as it sounds. Men and boys cannot wear hats. Women and girls cannot wear baseball caps, but they can wear dress hats. Anyone can request permission to wear a religious headdress. Such requests are typically granted where the presiding justice acknowledges the headdress as an expression of an accepted religion.)

- No shirts with inappropriate printed messages, and no tank tops, halter tops, or bare midriffs

- No reading of books, magazines, or newspapers (legal publications are allowed)

- Turn off all cellphones, pagers, laptop computers, and other electronic devices

- Maintain silence at all times when court is in session

- Enter and exit the courtroom quietly

- Stand when addressing the court or when the court addresses you

- Keep your hands out of your pockets when standing before the court

DID YOU KNOW?

The neck tabs (or bands) that lawyers and judges wear were adopted by the legal profession in the middle of the 17th century. Although the tabs may have evolved from the broad collars of the time, it is generally accepted that they represent the two tablets of the Ten Commandments, symbolizing the responsibility to uphold justice.

Restricted Access: In Camera Hearings and Publication Bans

Although courtrooms are public forums and are therefore generally open to the public, there are some exceptions. For example, all Family Court cases are closed to the public, with only those people directly involved in a case permitted inside the courtroom. In criminal trial cases, the judge will sometimes close the courtroom and order the proceedings to be carried on "*in camera*," which means that no observers are permitted. An *in camera* order is usually made when the case involves extremely sensitive witnesses, such as young children or emotionally distraught victims. If a judge orders a courtroom closed, the courtroom clerk posts the order on the courtroom door.

Further restrictions exist in criminal youth court. The *Youth Criminal Justice Act* (which applies to youths aged 12 to 17 years) dictates that no accused person's name can be published. In addition, the complainant's name must be withheld if publication of their name would identify the accused.

Judges can apply publication bans to hearings if they think that the integrity of the hearing or future hearings is at risk. For example, preliminary hearings are often banned from publication to ensure that potential jurors at upcoming trials are not prejudiced by media reports about the preliminary hearing.

NOTES:

Players and Their Roles

Adjudicator	The person who presides over a board.
Applicant	The person who starts an action by filing an application with the court.
Arbitrator	The decision-maker in a hearing.
Children's Lawyer	The government agent who represents children in Family Court in matters where the court feels their participation is required—for example, when parents are unable to come to suitable custody and access arrangements and the court requires an independent third party to represent the child's best interests.
Clerk or registrar	The court official who runs the administration of the court and assists the judge. The clerk swears in witnesses, arraigns the accused, maintains exhibits, completes and processes all court documentation, and ensures decorum in the court.
Clerk/monitor	The court official who performs the duties of both a clerk and reporter; a dual role in less administratively busy courts.
Community agency representatives	Representatives from various community agencies at the courthouse who assist accused persons before the court (for example, the John Howard Society or the Elizabeth Fry Society).
Counsel	The formal term for lawyer.
Court security	Civilian personnel hired by local police to guard prisoners and to provide security to the court building and its occupants.
Court services officer (CSO)	The court official responsible for segregating the jury and responding to its needs. A CSO is also assigned to a judge of the Superior Court of Justice for miscellaneous tasks such as photocopying, errands, and court escort.
Crown attorney	Counsel appointed by the Queen in right of Ontario to prosecute accused persons for the province. Generally, there is one Crown attorney per county and several assistant Crown attorneys.
Defendant	The accused person in Criminal Court, or a person being sued in civil court.
Deputy judge	The adjudicator who presides over Small Claims Court.
Duty counsel	A lawyer paid by the province to assist anyone who, for any number of reasons, is unable to retain a lawyer of their own.
Federal prosecutor	A lawyer contracted by the federal government to act as its agent to prosecute charges that fall under federal jurisdiction.
General public	People not employed by or involved in the judicial system. Courts are open to the public to observe court proceedings, unless the judge orders the proceedings closed.
Interpreters	Translators hired by the court when an accused person or other key player in the case does not speak or understand English well enough to participate in their own defence; also sign language interpreters for the hearing-impaired.

Investigating officer	The police officer in charge of the case. During a trial or preliminary inquiry, the investigating officer usually sits beside the Crown attorney to assist with the evidence.
Judge	The judicial officer of a provincial/territorial or federal court, appointed by the respective government.
Judicial officer	The decision-maker in a courtroom, such as a judge, justice, justice of the peace, deputy judge, or adjudicator.
Justice	Part of the official title of a judge of the Ontario Court of Justice and Superior Court of Justice (for example, Justice McPhee).
Justice of the peace	The judicial officer who presides over Bail Court, First Appearance Criminal Court, and Provincial Offences Court. The justice of the peace, who is also a notary public, issues search warrants and swears criminal informations put before the court.
Master	An official in the Superior Court for civil matters who is not a judge but who performs judge-like functions to determine matters on motions.
Municipal prosecutor	A lawyer hired by a municipality to prosecute part I offences under the *Provincial Offences Act*. Penalties for these offences are fines capped at $500, with no jail sentences.
Ontario Association of Children's Aid Societies (OACAS)	A non-governmental agency that acts as the applicant in child protection cases regarding neglect, abuse, unfit living conditions, etc. The OACAS also works with families to connect them with community resources (for example, food voucher programs and counselling) and to ensure that children are properly cared for, sometimes through court orders for a set period of time.
Plaintiff	The person who files a claim by way of application in civil proceedings and Small Claims Court in the Superior Court of Justice.
Probation officer	An employee of the Ministry of the Solicitor General and Correctional Services who supervises convicted offenders who are placed on probation.
Provincial prosecutor	A lawyer hired by the province to prosecute part III offences under the *Provincial Offences Act*. Penalties for these offences are fines in excess of $500, with the possibility of a jail sentence.
Reporter	The court official responsible for maintaining the formal record of the court. The reporter operates court recording equipment, maintains a manual log book, and prepares verbatim transcripts on request.
Respondent	The person who responds to an application in Family Court, Civil Court, or Small Claims Court.
Trial coordinator	The court official responsible for setting court schedules, assigning judges to courts, and assigning cases to judges.
Victim Witness Assistance Program (VWAP) representative	An employee of the Ministry of the Attorney General whose mandate is to provide support and services to victims of crime.
Witness	A person who testifies under oath before a court to offer evidence relevant to the case at hand.

Court Staff and Services

In most matters, with the exception of meeting with your client, court staff are your first point of contact at the courthouse. They are bound by the rules of procedure applicable to each type of court matter. They are not free to determine what they will or will not accept or with whom they will or will not deal. Court staff are not allowed to provide an opinion or give advice on what content should be included or complete forms on your behalf. The rules applicable to a particular court process in Ontario are listed in figure 2.7. Use the links in figure 2.4 to research court rules in other provinces and territories.

Civil Matters

In order to make efficient use of your time when submitting documents to the court, you should understand and appreciate the role of and restrictions on court staff. It is important to develop a positive, effective, and professional working relationship with court staff.

Court staff offer administrative assistance to both professional and un-represented members of the public. The responsibilities of court staff include, but are not limited to, the efficient processing of a wide variety of court-related documents, including signing, sealing, and issuing documents; adherence to court rules and relevant statutes; and accuracy and technical completeness (for example, ensuring that all necessary boxes and sections on a form are completed).

Timeliness in the filing of documents is extremely important. Court staff are required to refuse any document that is filed late; they have no discretion to accept late documents. In order to avoid problems and ensure a speedy process, you, as the law clerk, should be prepared to give court staff basic information when arriving at the counter (for example, your client information and what documents are being filed). Give the staff time to review the court documents to ensure that they are acceptable.

FIGURE 2.7 Ontario court processes and applicable rules

Process	Rule
Civil matters	*Rules of Civil Procedure* http://www.e-laws.gov.on.ca/html/regs/english/elaws_regs_900194_e.htm
Criminal law matters	*Rules of the Ontario Court of Justice in Criminal Proceedings* http://laws-lois.justice.gc.ca/eng/regulations/SI-97-133
Family law matters	*Family Law Rules* http://www.e-laws.gov.on.ca/html/regs/english/elaws_regs_990114_e.htm
Small claims matters	*Rules of the Small Claims Court* http://www.e-laws.gov.on.ca/html/regs/english/elaws_regs_980258_e.htm

Criminal Matters

In a criminal matter, in addition to the processes mentioned above, most communication with the court passes through the Crown's office and the trial coordinator. The Crown's office must provide the defence with full disclosure before a trial begins. "Disclosure" is the term used for the compilation of documents or other evidence in the Crown attorney's possession. This usually includes a synopsis of the Crown's case, police reports, witness statements, the accused's criminal record (if any), and police officers' notes.

Administrative Board Proceedings

To help ease the backlog in the courts, agencies, boards, tribunals, and commissions—referred to here as "administrative boards" for ease of reference—were created to resolve legal disputes between parties and apply government policy outside the traditional court system. The body of legal rules and principles that applies to these boards is known as administrative law.

There are over 1500 federal and provincial boards across Canada. Boards are created by statute. For example, the *Residential Tenancies Act, 2006* establishes the Landlord and Tenant Board (formerly the Ontario Rental Housing Tribunal) to hear and decide landlord–tenant and rent disputes. The Board has exclusive jurisdiction to determine all questions of fact or law that arise. Some well-known boards include:

- Canadian Human Rights Commission (federal)
- Canadian Human Rights Tribunal (federal)
- Canada Industrial Relations Board (federal)
- Citizenship and Immigration Commission (federal)
- Conservation Review Board (provincial)
- Environmental Appeal Board (provincial)
- Environmental Assessment Board (provincial)
- Financial Services Commission of Ontario (provincial)
- Hazardous Materials Information Review Commission (federal)
- Liquor Control Board of Ontario (provincial)
- Municipal Board (provincial)
- National Energy Board (federal)
- Ontario Human Rights Commission (provincial)
- Landlord and Tenant Board (provincial)
- Ontario Securities Commission (provincial)
- Pay Equity Commission (provincial)
- Workplace Safety and Insurance Appeals Tribunal (provincial).

DID YOU KNOW?

Tribunal (n.) Adopted from the word "tribune" (Latin *tribunes*), a title given to government-appointed decision-makers in ancient Rome.

A board operates in many ways like a court. It is an impartial body that must provide all parties with fair process. In most cases, the board operates independently from the government and the courts. However, the courts do have some supervisory authority over boards to ensure that they are not acting beyond their jurisdiction. Courts can also review board decisions on questions of law, though not on questions of fact. The laws governing boards specify how board decisions can be appealed, as well as identify those who may launch an appeal.

Within boards, the essential players are chairs, vice-chairs, panel members, and administrative or counter staff. The term "adjudicator" is used here to include all adjudicative positions that assist the parties in coming to a decision. The government appoints adjudicators based on their experience and knowledge in the required area.

Like court staff in civil and criminal matters, board staff are not permitted to provide a legal opinion or complete any required documents for a client. Counter staff perform the following tasks:

- receive and review applications and other documents for completeness and timeliness

- schedule hearings

- respond to public inquiries

- provide information to the public regarding procedures for completing and filing forms according to specific board practices.

Board matters are dealt with either through mediation or a hearing process by a single member or a panel of members.

Mediation

Depending on the legislative authority relating to the dispute, parties may be given the opportunity to resolve their issues through mediation prior to a hearing. Mediation is a process where the parties of an action meet with an objective third party to clarify issues, discuss options, and work toward a mutually acceptable resolution of the dispute.

The benefits of mediation are:

- it is a time-efficient process

- it is the least expensive and most amicable way of dealing with a dispute

- it takes place in a private and confidential environment

- it results in a settlement that is suitable to the needs of all involved parties.

If at the end of mediation it appears that an agreement will not be reached, the matter will then proceed to a hearing or arbitration. Only civil matters can be dealt with under the arbitration process. The parties involved agree to a settlement through mediation and then an arbitrator decides on a settlement based on a set of legal ground rules that are subject to Canadian law.

Hearings

Board hearings are conducted much like court proceedings, although the process is less formal and rules of evidence are not applied as strictly. In Ontario, the *Statutory Powers and Procedures Act* (SPPA) provides a framework for the conduct of hearings—much like the *Courts of Justice Act* regulates court proceedings. Section 25.1 of the SPPA provides that "a tribunal [board] may make rules governing the practice and procedure before it." A board can also adopt guidelines that offer appropriate interpretations of the SPPA and applicable regulations.

The hearings are similar to court hearings in a number of respects. Standard protocol and decorum required in court are expected in board hearings. Hearings are open to the public unless dictated by the policy or procedure of a specific board, or unless a party requests that they be closed due to the nature of the proceeding. The law governing a board will specify the geographical location of hearings as well as their start time. In most circumstances, hearings are conducted in the board building or office nearest to the municipality in which the application was filed. Hearings can also be held in, among other places, church basements and community centres. Applicants and/or respondents can represent themselves or be represented by a lawyer, agent, friend, or relative. Some boards have rules or requirements that dictate who may act as an agent and represent a party. If a party chooses to represent himself or herself, the board's staff and adjudicators are not allowed to provide legal advice during the hearing.

Hearing Rooms

Board hearing rooms are not as elaborate as courtrooms. Participants may sit at one large table, boardroom style, or the room may be set up in a square or U-shape configuration, with a table for the adjudicator at the front of the room. Tables for the parties are set up along the sides and/or at the end of the room. Other participants, including support staff, are situated as necessary, depending on the nature of the board and the

NOTES:

FIGURE 2.8   A typical board hearing room

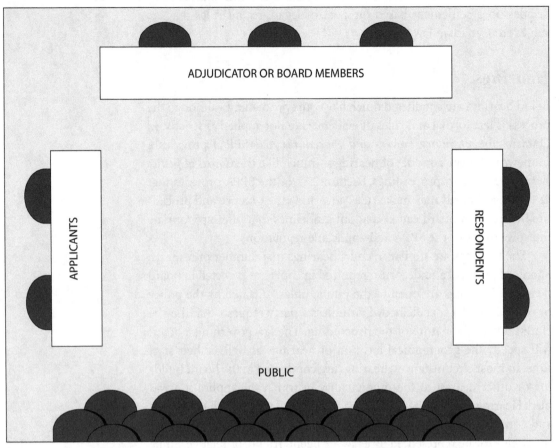

discretion of the chair. The adjudicator or the lead board member is addressed by name as Mister or Madam Chair. Where the board has more than one member, the members are addressed by their name or as Member X. The set-up of a board hearing room is illustrated in figure 2.8.

Conduct of a Hearing

Both the applicant and the respondent present their evidence, including documentation and witness evidence, to the adjudicator. The adjudicator explains the applicable rules and the issues that will be discussed. The adjudicator can ask any party to affirm or take an oath to tell the truth. Each party makes an opening statement. The applicant presents their case ("the application") first. Both the respondent and the adjudicator can ask questions of the applicant and their witnesses. The respondent presents their case ("the response") next. Again, both the adjudicator and the applicant can ask questions of the respondent and their witnesses. The parties then make closing statements. The board considers the issues as expressed in the application and response, hears evidence, and considers the parties' legal submissions. On this basis, the decision-maker, in a timely manner, issues an order, with reasons. The decision may be oral or written. An oral decision will be followed up by a written one.

Technology in the Justice System

The pace at which electronic technology is integrated into Canada's justice system is influenced by a number of factors. Changes of this sort require the endorsement and cooperation of all court stakeholders, which makes the introduction of new technologies and methods a gradual process. Obtaining sufficient funding for software, hardware, courtroom and office wiring, and training continues to be a challenge. Other factors include users' comfort levels with technology, and confidence that important court information can be stored securely in electronic form.

It was not that long ago that all accused persons subject to a criminal proceeding were required to appear in court every time their matter was scheduled to be dealt with. Corrections and police officers were required to transport people on remand (in custody while awaiting trial) to and from the court for insignificant court appearances. Now, most courthouses and correctional facilities are equipped with technology that allows an accused person to appear before the courtroom on video while remaining in secure custody. Similarly, the courtroom can be seen on screen in the correctional facility. Direct telephone lines and sound-proof rooms allow the accused and their lawyer to speak privately and confidentially. "Video remand" has reduced the costs and security risks associated with transporting prisoners, and the court is no longer delayed while inmates are brought from holding cells.

Several programs designed for use within court and board proceedings by representatives and other persons with a vested interest in a proceeding allow for enhanced case organization, document searching, timeline and flowchart development, image processing, real-time transcripts, and computer animation. These tools greatly benefit all stakeholders. For example, a lawyer or agent can create timelines and flowchart diagrams depicting the events of a crime, which can be used by all players in the proceeding as a reference point, to raise doubt, establish facts, and so on.

Programs such as Microsoft's PowerPoint are used for electronically presenting case exhibits such as photos, drawings, and scanned documents. Images can be viewed by all parties simultaneously and can be easily sorted and retrieved. Digital audio recording systems can record and play back on multiple channels, and include the options of bookmarks and text explanations to aid in quick playbacks. Other programs perform electronic word searches, eliminating the need to manually skim paper documents and resulting in huge savings in time.

A growing number of judges and adjudicators now enter notes on laptops instead of in hardcover books, traditionally referred to as "bench books" or "bench notes." This allows case information to be organized, searched, and retrieved efficiently. More and more lawyers, Crown counsel, and agents, especially younger lawyers in large urban centres, are also using laptops for note taking, reviewing materials, watching and showing visual presentations, and organizing and storing all information relating to a particular case.

PRACTICE TIP

The effective use of technology results in a more efficient system for managing documents, because fewer documents are lost, and in better case organization, because all information related to a case can be made secure and accessible.

Most courtroom clerks and board staff now access and update court databases and dockets with the outcome of cases as they are heard. Staff can thus view changes as they are happening and pass the new information along to parties. This system also allows staff to create computer-generated documents used by courts and boards.

E-filing of documents has streamlined communication. Various forms are routinely completed on a computer and "filed" on a dedicated database web server that is accessed by the court clerk and board staff. Law offices can also use this system to send and retrieve documents, pay filing fees, notify parties, and receive court notices and other information. E-filing is used in most jurisdictions across Canada.

The use of technology has also resulted in savings of government money by reducing paper waste and streamlining many procedures, from the presentation of material in court to the answering of inquiries by counter staff. The ever-changing nature of technology will also lead to newer hardware and software that will coexist with or replace what is currently available. Ultimately, technology will help those working in the justice system to provide better service.

REVIEW QUESTIONS

1. What does "called to the bar" mean?

_____

_____

_____

_____

_____

_____

_____

2. What is judicial independence and why is it so important?

_____

_____

_____

_____

_____

_____

_____

_____

3. Who can enter the courtroom and watch the proceedings?

_____

_____

_____

_____

_____

4. What is a court docket?

_____

_____

_____

_____

_____

5. What are some of the security precautions you can be subject to in some courthouses?

_____

_____

_____

_____

_____

_____

6. What is a publication ban and when is it used?

_____

_____

_____

_____

_____

_____

7. What is the role of the Crown attorney?

_____

_____

_____

_____

_____

8. What is a "quasi-judicial agency" and what purpose does it serve?

_____

_____

_____

_____

_____

_____

9. What is an adjudicator and how are adjudicators appointed?

_____

_____

_____

_____

_____

_____

_____

10. When would the courts get involved with a board decision?

_____

_____

_____

_____

_____

_____

_____

_____

_____

11. What tasks do the counter staff for a board perform?

_____

_____

_____

_____

_____

12. What piece of legislation provides the framework for the conduct of a board hearing?

_____

_____

_____

_____

_____

_____

ACTIVITY

Advocacy is the ability to effectively argue your position to a court or board, and it is a large part of the court and board process. One of the best ways to learn about the topics covered in this chapter and gain an appreciation for your chosen field is to observe advocates in action.

Attend and report on a court or board proceeding. The choice is up to you. Confirm with your instructor the various local court and board locations and the best days to attend.

Prepare a report of three to four pages based on your instructor's directions. Be sure to approach the court staff and parties involved and talk to them. You will be surprised how friendly, interesting, and helpful everyone will be. Do not be afraid to ask to meet the judge or arbitrator. Be like a sponge and get as much as you can out of your court attendance.

You must answer the following questions:

- What was the full name of the court or board?

- What were the correct names of the judge or adjudicator, the court staff, and the parties involved, including the lawyers, agents, and plaintiffs/applicants and defendants/respondents?

- What was the outcome? If it was a civil case, summarize the issues and the outcome.

- Most importantly, comment on the process itself. Were the lawyers or agents good advocates, or did they seem to be just going through the motions?

- How were the participants dressed?

- Would you want any of them to represent you? Why or why not?

- What did you think was done well?

- Were the parties treated fairly?

- Did you agree with the result? Why or why not?

Time Management

A task expands to fill the time allowed for it.

—Parkinson's Law

Introduction

The business of time is relentless. Even when you stop working, the clock keeps ticking. It's impossible to stop time, so it's crucial to learn to manage your time effectively. Poor time-management skills can affect your ability to perform your job, and eventually damage your reputation at the office. Employees who lack time-management skills tend to lose important documents and miss appointments and deadlines. They are also more likely to spend evenings and weekends at the office, struggling to catch up.

Good time managers are proactive. They plan and monitor their time so that they have enough flexibility to handle unexpected situations. They stay ahead of the game. In contrast, people who do not manage time well tend to be reactive. They spend their time reacting to crisis after crisis. They are less productive, and more frazzled and exhausted by the end of the day. The good news is, it's possible to learn time-management skills. It may take some effort initially, but it will make your life much easier in the long run.

Tracking Your Time

Before you implement any time-management system, conduct a time study of your work to determine how you spend your time and where you need to improve. A time study does not have to be a burden. Select a typical day, log your tasks, and record how much time each item required. Use the sample log in figure 3.1 or create your own log based on your daily activities. Be thorough and record all time-eating tasks such as answering phone calls, greeting visitors, replying to email, engaging in discussions with employers or colleagues, searching for files, dealing with other interruptions, and, of course, performing all your other duties throughout the day.

CHAPTER OBJECTIVES

After reading this chapter, you will understand:

- the importance of tracking where time is spent

- how to plan and organize schedules to optimize efficiency

- the best use of scheduling systems, dockets, and tickler/reminder systems

- when multitasking is required and when it's better to focus on one task at a time

- the difference between task management and project management

- how to identify the symptoms of stress and strategies for coping with stress

FIGURE 3.1 Time log

Hours	Telephone	Drop-in Visitors	Client Meetings	Time w/ Lawyer	Time w/ Co-workers	File Opening/ Closing	Gen. Filing	Corres./ Email	Preparing Legal Docs	Client Acctg.	Misc.
8:30											
9:00											
9:30											
10:00											
10:30											
11:00											
11:30											
12:00											
12:30											
1:00											
1:30											
2:00											
2:30											
3:00											
3:30											
4:00											
4:30											
5:00											
5:30											
6:00											

After this exercise, you will have a picture of a typical day. You may wish to keep a log for a full week to get a more complete record of your time. Review the log to identify where your time is not being optimized. These are the areas where you should focus your efforts and implement time-management practices.

This exercise will also help you identify your personal "prime time"—the period of the day when you are most productive. For many people this may be early in the day, but for others it may be right after lunch. By recognizing your high- and low-energy times, you can plan your work accordingly. For example, demanding tasks should be done while you are at your peak, while less challenging or low-energy tasks should be reserved for your less productive hours. The sections that follow break time management into categories to help you learn to recover lost or misspent time.

Organization Basics

Managing anything well requires organization, and time management is no exception. In its simplest terms, organization is the ability to find what you need when you need it. Being organized will maximize your productivity by reducing the amount of time you waste searching for misplaced items, and relieve the frustration and stress caused by not being able to find things.

Where you decide to store items is critical. Start with your desk surface. Ensure that you have enough free space to work on a file or project without having to move other items off your desk. Do not clutter a limited working space with personal items such as photographs or office supplies; such things are more appropriately stored elsewhere. The outer areas of your desk are ideal for in/out trays, standing file sorters, calendars, pens, and other frequently used items.

A lower desk drawer is suitable for storing high-priority, active files, ongoing projects, confidential information, or frequently used reference material. Top drawers can be an invitation to hoard. Avoid having a top drawer where you stuff everything but can find nothing. Group similar items together, and use small dividers, trays, or boxes to keep the drawer free from clutter.

Keep regularly used items or files within easy reach—a slide of your chair at arm's length. For example, a side cabinet with shelves or file drawers can house routine project files, monthly statistics, phone books, and so on. Reserve space beyond your immediate work area for storing office supplies, recently closed files, and less-used reference material.

In all of your organization decisions, keep in mind that you want things to be logical, labelled, user-friendly, and ergonomically correct. Design your workspace so that you can put your fingers on a specific piece of paper exactly when you need it, and can easily access all required materials, tools, and information.

Planning and Organizing

Many law clerks and assistants are assigned the duty of managing the office schedule. Because lawyers are paid for their time, scheduling errors and inefficient scheduling cost money, and you must be able to schedule time efficiently. For example, should appointments be booked in 15-minute intervals or 30-minute intervals? Does your employer see clients Monday through Friday, or only on Wednesdays and Thursdays? Once you have these parameters, set up your system accordingly.

You should also seek direction or determine from experience how much time should be allotted for various types of appointments and for other tasks, such as returning phone calls, preparing documents, and preparing for court dates. This information will help when you are speaking with a client who wants to make an appointment. When filling in the employer's schedule, keep your mind on time management. For example, don't create sporadic schedules that result in chunks of unscheduled

DID YOU KNOW?

Sir Sandford Fleming, in whose honour Fleming College was named, is considered to be the inventor of standard time zones.

The Evolution of the Day-Timer®

We are all familiar with the Day-Timer®. It is a time-management product that allows you to keep track of appointments, expenses, and a host of other details. But where did it begin?

In 1947, Morris Perkin, a lawyer from British Columbia, devised a specialized calendar system, which he called Lawyer's Day, that could hold more information than a typical calendar. In 1952, Perkin needed a commercial establishment to handle the printing of his product. He approached the Dorney brothers, and this arrangement changed their lives. Initially, the Dorneys simply printed Lawyer's Day, but when Perkin's customer list became too large, the Dorneys took over shipping and marketing. Perkin and the Dorneys merged their companies and were very successful. As time passed and the product developed and was further marketed, it was rebranded as the Day-Timer®.

time. Instead, attempt to fill mornings before scheduling afternoons. This won't always be possible for a number of reasons, including accommodating clients, but it's important to be aware of the impact of the schedule on the daily operation of the office.

As the law clerk or assistant, meet regularly with your employer and be available when they are in the office. Be proactive by predicting what they will need. For example, if your employer has a meeting with a client, bring them the client file and relevant notes at least 15 minutes before the meeting. If your employer has a court attendance coming up, make sure that he or she is equipped with a complete, organized file and that all critical information is easy to retrieve. Listen carefully during meetings with your employer, take notes, and be ready to provide information or suggestions.

Scheduling Systems

There are more scheduling tools available today than you'd probably care to look at, but they all serve the same purpose: to assist you in planning your time. The operative word here is *assist*, because even the best system is only as good as the user. Some commonly used scheduling systems include:

- traditional calendars

- daily diaries

- electronic time-management programs.

If you are given the option of choosing a scheduling system, the first step is to assess your needs. If your workplace consists of one lawyer and yourself, clearly you do not need a large, complex system designed to accommodate multiple users. When choosing a system, consider what type of items you need to schedule or track, and what level of detail is required. For example, do you have to record the appointments of clients at 15-minute intervals, or does your employer see just a few clients per day? What other information is required in your schedule of appointments? Such information includes file numbers, phone numbers, and upcoming court dates. Obviously, the more detail you include, the more space you require. Items that should find their way into your schedule include meetings and appointments, task deadlines, and personal obligations that will affect your work day or take you out of the office, such as a doctor's appointment.

You may also use your scheduling system to track and record important information such as expenses, notes from phone conversations, your work log, and travel mileage.

If you want to use one scheduling system for everything, you'll need a system with a lot of space. Alternatively, use a smaller or simpler system and supplement it with reminders, brief to-do lists, and notes to yourself.

A popular communication and organizational tool is a smart phone, such as a BlackBerry or iPhone. A smart phone is a cellphone that operates wirelessly, offering Internet and email access. It functions as a personal digital assistant (PDA), allowing the user to store contact information, date books, reminders, alarms, task lists, and memo pads, as well as to edit documents. This technology allows lawyers to input data and transfer information to the office computer system and keep in touch with law clerks, legal secretaries, and other employees while away from the office. This often improves communication between lawyers and their staff, and reduces the amount of time that law clerks or other employees spend inputting data from the lawyer when he or she returns to the office.

No matter what scheduling system you settle on, it will be of little value if you can't rely on its contents. Remember this: Record everything, revise often, and refer to it always. With practice, your schedule will become something you can rely on with confidence.

Figure 3.2 shows a sample page from a daily paper diary.

DID YOU KNOW?

The use of a smart phone can save a lawyer approximately four hours per week in new billable hours.

Dockets

Most lawyers (and in Ontario, paralegals) bill clients based on the time it takes to carry out work for them. The recording of this information is referred to as docketing. Do not confuse docketing with scheduling. The docket and the schedule perform two entirely different functions. It is true that lawyers may use their schedules to docket time; however, the schedule sets out appointments, meetings, and other obligations, while the docket documents the billable and non-billable hours spent on tasks relating to clients. Tracking time or docketing is essential in order to produce an accurate statement of account for each client. Lawyers also track non-billable time, which is time spent doing work for which they cannot or choose not to bill clients. For example, a client *cannot* be billed for time spent on professional development; a lawyer may *choose* not to bill a client for time spent on an initial consultation.

FIGURE 3.2 Daily paper diary

Monday, October 19, 20--	
7:30–8:00	Jonnie Walker—Impaired (new client)
8:00–8:30	Prepare for Jones sentencing
8:30–9:00	Return telephone calls
9:00–9:30	Smith, Joan, review will—File #1002/05
9:30–10:00	Hoggett, Jim and Paula—Sign real estate documents—File #331/05
10:00–10:30	Court Jones—Sentencing
10:30–11:00	--
11:00–11:30	--
11:30–12:00	Lunch—April Corp—Re new share offer
12:00–12:30	--
12:30–1:00	--
1:00–1:30	Telephone calls
1:30–2:00	Prepare docs for April Corp
2:00–2:30	--
2:30–3:00	--
3:00–3:30	Teleconference call pre-trial Adams v. Roe
3:30–4:00	Review file re: Barbie Cole
4:00–4:30	Prepare tomorrow's to-do list
4:30–5:00	Adams Jones—Assault (new client)—Next court date Nov 21
5:00–5:30	Barbie Cole—Divorce—sign application—File #DC-123-11
5:30–6:00	Dictation—Smith will ... Brown real estate

NOTES:

It is important to track non-billable time in order to monitor where all time is spent.

The law clerk, assistant, lawyer, or paralegal may be responsible for docketing. Docketing is discussed in more detail in chapter 5, Client File Management, and even more specifically in chapter 6, Client Accounts.

Tickler/Reminder Systems

In the legal environment, missing an appointment, deadline, or limitation period can have serious ramifications. Law society rules and the Lawyer's Professional Indemnity Corporation require lawyers to be diligent, efficient, and prompt in fulfilling all commitments. For this reason, the LSUC promotes the use of a tickler system, which helps ensure that critical dates are not overlooked. The system can take the form of a desk calendar, dates written on the outside of a client file, reminder cards, or an electronic reminder system.

A manual tickler system is simply a box of index cards or NCR (no carbon required) forms used to remind the law firm about upcoming deadlines, court dates, or other appointments. Ideally, one person files these cards, checks them daily, and pulls the relevant cards to give to the appropriate person for action. To further ensure the reliability of the system, most firms designate someone to look after the tickler system when the regular person is away from the office. There may be one central system for the entire office, or there may be separate systems for each lawyer or area of law. Many law firms also keep a duplicate tickler card system on the appropriate lawyer's desk, or diarize the reminder dates in a desk calendar.

The actual tickler cards and details of the system vary somewhat from firm to firm. However, LSUC guidelines recommend the following materials for a well-organized tickler system.

Basic tickler system supplies:

- an index card box
- index cards (3 × 5 inches) to fit the box
- a set of index cards with tabs to separate each month
- a set of index cards with tabs numbered for each day of the month (1 through 31).

ADDITIONAL READING

Stanley P. Jaskot and Charinjit Gill, "What to Docket and the Art of Worry-Free Docketing," online: http://www.jaskotfamilylaw.ca/pdf%20files/docketing.pdf.

NOTES:

Optional supplies:

- a separate box for statute-of-limitation dates (dates after which it's too late to issue a claim)

- a colour-coding system (for example, a different colour card for each area of law)

- additional tabs to be used for filing into the next year.

When setting up your tickler cards, decide what information is necessary and where it should go on the card. This is an important decision because you want the cards to be consistent and predictable. When pressured by deadlines, lawyers or their staff should not have to search all over the card for the file number. If the file number is always placed in the upper right corner of the card, everyone will know where to find it. This can be a real time saver.

The most common information included on a tickler card is shown in figure 3.3.

Keep in mind that the tickler or reminder system is designed to help lawyers meet their obligations. It is not helpful to pull the current date's card, only to find that a huge task is due the next day. To plan for this, cards should be filed so that they are pulled before the actual due date.

Depending on the task, a reminder card could be filed so that it is pulled 30 days in advance, one week in advance, and then again two or three days in advance. The sample card shown in figure 3.4 outlines the dates that the clerk has determined are relevant to a small claims matter. The law clerk needs to prepare the statement of claim by March 14th. The card is filed either one week before the 14th or on the 14th. If the card is filed on the 14th, it should be pulled at least one week prior to the due date on the card. In this case, the card and the file should be pulled by March 7th. Upon completion of the task at hand, the card is

FIGURE 3.3   Contents of a tickler card

- Date file/card opened
- Name of client
- Description of subject matter or service required
- File number (always locate it in the same position)
- Name of lawyer responsible for the matter (if more than one lawyer in the firm)
- Next tickler date (when the lawyer is to be reminded)
- Dates of required actions
- Dates of interim actions
- Date the matter is to be attended to (lead time)
- Any dates or notes for follow-up or confirmation
- Any other information helpful to the lawyer or the keeper of the tickler system

FIGURE 3.4 Sample tickler card used in a small claims matter

Williams, Ronald Harold Mr.

201103-001
Small Claims/Construction
Court File: COB 123/11

Date	Event
March 1, 20--	Demand letter sent by mail
March 11, 20--	Response to demand letter due
March 14, 20--	Prepare statement of claim/file
March 15, 20--	Service made on defendant—statement of claim
April 4, 20--	Defence to claim due
March 31, 20--	Extension for defence requested and granted
April 11, 20--	Defence due (extended date—received April 10, 20--)
April 8, 20--	Defence served on client

re-filed for the next action date. When no further action is required, the tickler card is placed in the client file.

By following this procedure, you will eliminate surprise tasks and last-minute work that you have not planned for in your day.

Figures 3.5 and 3.6 are sample tickler cards from a family law matter and a real estate transaction, respectively.

In addition to this more typical tickler card system, some legal offices choose a preprinted tickler card, as illustrated in figure 3.7. This type of tickler is available in duplicate. The card itself is more generic than other tickler cards, but can easily be used to accommodate most needs. The extra copy is usually kept in the client file or with the responsible lawyer.

Electronic versions of legal software such as PCLaw and Amicus Attorney offer tickler or reminder systems. These systems operate on the same theory as manual systems, but they remove the need for filing and

FIGURE 3.5 Sample tickler card used in a family law matter

Cole, Barbie
Re: Divorce

File # DC-123-11

Jan 20, 20--	File opening letter and retainer agreement sent	Rec'd Jan 23
Jan 25, 20--	Draft and review application	
Jan 26, 20--	Issue application (served by mail today)	Rev March 1—No answer
Mar 2, 20--	Draft affidavit and order (filed March 7)	
Mar 14, 20--	Divorce order (31-day effective date)	
April 15, 20--	Certificate for divorce obtained	
April 30, 20--	File closed	

FIGURE 3.6   Real estate transaction tickler card

Lodge, Mike   File #: 1211/12

Re: Purchase from Meadus

763 Brown Street, Peterborough

Requisition Date—November 15, 20--

Closing—December 5, 20--

November 3—Check tax certificate

- Building clearance
- Review search
- Prepare requisition letter

November 30—Review the file

- Prepare the closing memo

FIGURE 3.7   Sample preprinted tickler card

Date of Incident: *12/Dec/10*

Limitation Date: *12/Dec/12*   File #: *1289/LIT*

Client Name: *Bruce, N.*

Re: *(Motor Vehicle Accident (MVA))*

B.F. Schedule:

File review: *09/Dec/11*   File progress: *15/June/12*   Issue claim: *01/Oct/12*

Caution Time Up:

Responsible Lawyer:

storing paper cards. One designated person, often referred to as an administrator, typically maintains electronic tickler systems. Each system has its own rules and requirements, so it may take some time to familiarize yourself with the program your office uses. As with any computer file, it's critical to back up the system daily in the event that it is corrupted or lost due to computer malfunction.

Figures 3.8 and 3.9 show the electronic calendar features found in PCLaw and Amicus Attorney, respectively.

Many firms use electronic programs such as Microsoft Outlook and Novell GroupWise. These are marketed primarily as email products, but they also have useful calendars that can be used as an office tickler system. Simply by keying details into the calendar function of the program and

FIGURE 3.8 The electronic calendar feature in PCLaw

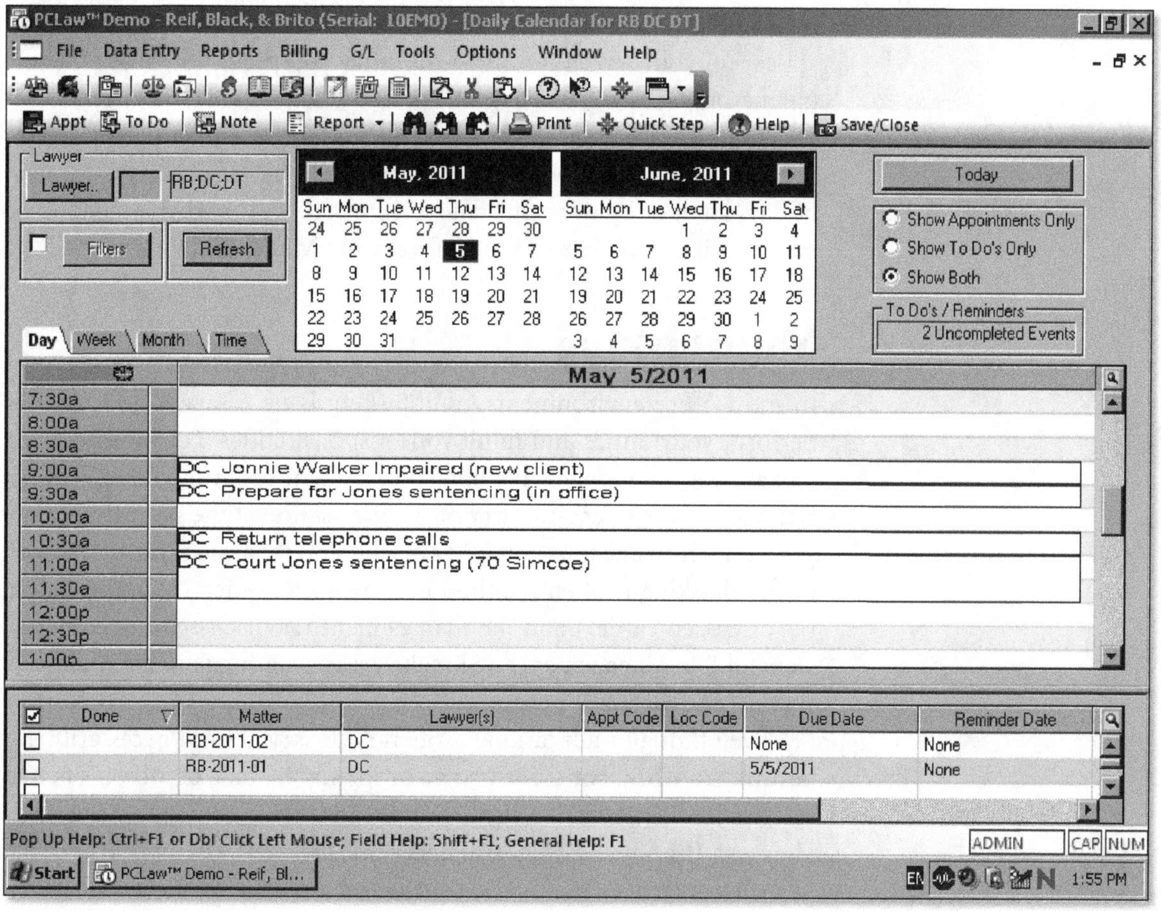

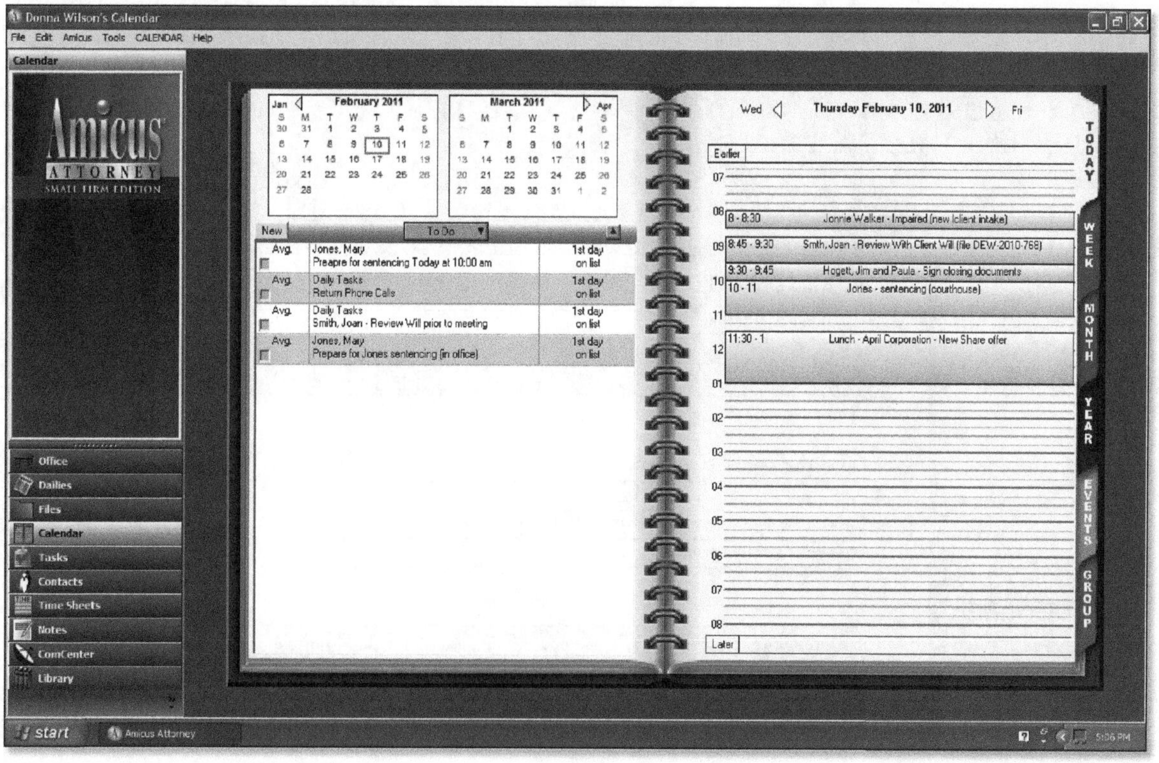

FIGURE 3.9 The electronic calendar feature in Amicus Attorney

marking the entry for a reminder, you can dictate what time and date you require the reminder. Then, at that specified time, a message box will appear on your screen outlining the entry you previously made. When the message appears, you have the option of dismissing the reminder or selecting a snooze function, which will cause the reminder to reappear at another time specified by you—whether an hour later or some number of days later, or on a specific date. Figure 3.10 shows what a scheduling system might look like in a law office using Microsoft Outlook.

Multitasking

In most office environments, multitasking is necessary to successfully perform your duties and fulfill your responsibilities. For example, can you answer the phone while filing a document or jotting down a note? Can you type a letter and carry on a conversation at the same time? Can you jump from one task to another quickly and then back again? This sort of multitasking is often required in a law office. Effective organization (as discussed earlier) and file management (as discussed in chapter 4, General File Management) will make it easier to juggle tasks while still performing each task properly.

Even though multitasking is often necessary, it's not necessarily the best way to work. For some people or for some kinds of jobs, it's better to focus on one task at a time, complete it, then move on to the next. However, it's not always possible to work this way. The opportunity to work on only one task can be considered a luxury. When you do have

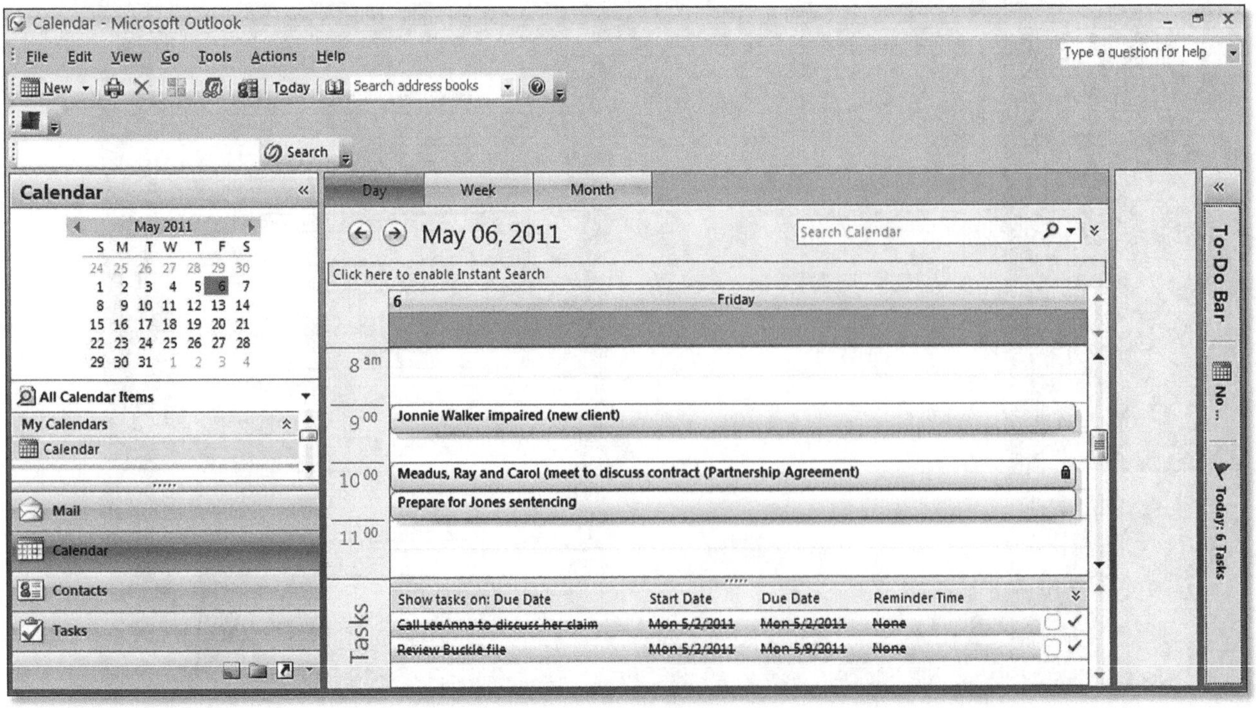

FIGURE 3.10   The electronic calendar feature in Microsoft Outlook

this luxury, use it to work on larger projects or matters that require greater concentration.

Task Management

The to-do list, which itemizes specific tasks to be completed, is a very common time-management aid. As with any tool, its usefulness depends on whether or not you are using it in the most effective way. Simply listing tasks to be done is not enough. Prioritize or rank your tasks to ensure that important or urgent matters are dealt with first. You can prioritize your tasks in various ways. Commonly, a numbered list is used, with the most pressing matters at the top. Another common system takes the numbered list a step further by using an alphabetized or coded approach. For example, "A" items need to be completed today; "B" items need to be completed soon, but not necessarily today; and "C" items require attention, but can be performed at a later date. Figure 3.11 shows an example of this approach.

You could also prioritize items with colour: "Urgent or important" items could be highlighted in red, and "other today" and "future date" items in green and yellow. Or you could compile multiple lists instead of one list, labelling them according to their deadline: "today," "this week," and "sometime in the future."

FIGURE 3.11   Prioritized to-do list

TASK LIST October 18, 2012				
#	Priority	Task	Due Date	Completed Date and Initials
1.	A	Open new client files, including all correspondence, forms, etc.	18 Oct 12	18 Oct 12 celE
2.	C	Move closed files to completed storage file	24 Oct 12	
3.	B	Make phone calls reminding clients of their appointments tomorrow	18 Oct 12	18 Oct 12 celE
4.	A	Type dictation letters left on tape from lawyer	18 Oct 12	
5.	B	File correspondence related to client files	19 Oct 12	
6.	B	Enter client docket times in files for this week	22 Oct 12	
7.	A	Prepare legal documents for client as per lawyer's instructions	18 Oct 12	18 Oct 12 celE
8.	C	Shred confidential information	22 Oct 12	
9.	B	Return calls from yesterday per lawyer's instructions	18 Oct 12	18 Oct 12 celE
10.	A	Pull tickler cards for today's date and tomorrow's date—take necessary action	18 Oct 12	18 Oct 12 celE

As you might expect, a number of computer programs have a task list or to-do list feature. Some people find the computerized assistance ideal, while others need the kinetic and visual aid of a handwritten list. Many law clerks and legal assistants simply record task lists on a notepad and keep it on their desk. The notepad is an inexpensive and easy way to keep all the basic task information in one place, so you can refer to it quickly and check your progress when necessary.

The system you choose is not as important as being consistent with your lists and procedures and referring to them regularly. Keep your lists realistic. Don't overload today's list with so many tasks that you could never complete them. This is self-defeating and can cause you to feel pressured, stressed, and unsuccessful. Rather, keep your goals attainable. It is reassuring and uplifting when you start crossing items off your list.

The 80/20 Rule

In 1906, Italian economist Vilfredo Pareto created a mathematical formula to describe the unequal distribution of wealth in his country. This formula, now known as "Pareto's principle" or the "80/20 rule," has been applied successfully in many fields ever since.

This powerful "natural law" basically states that, in any given situation, there are usually a "vital few" factors whose overall influence far surpasses the importance of the rest of the "trivial many" factors.

For example, 80 percent of a firm's income often comes from 20 percent of its products, and 20 percent of its income comes from 80 percent of its products. The lesson for business is simple: Focus on what's important.

But what does this have to do with time management? Think of it this way: About 20 percent of your workload consists of high-priority items. According to the 80/20 rule, you should spend 80 percent of your time on these tasks, and spend the remaining 20 percent of your time on the less important 80 percent of your tasks.

In other words: Spend 80 percent of your time on the important 20 percent of your work, and spend the rest of your time on the work that remains.

Another common organizational tool is the sticky note. These brightly coloured notes help keep urgent or important tasks on your to-do list from escaping your memory. A word of caution: If you overuse sticky notes, they will eventually defeat their purpose. They are meant to catch your attention. If your work area is overloaded with sticky notes, you won't even notice them. Reserve these types of reminders for must-do items or for tasks that can be easily overlooked.

One final piece of advice regarding your task lists: Prepare tomorrow's to-do list the day before. If you review your in-basket and determine tomorrow's work in advance, you will be better prepared when you sit down at your desk in the morning. Preparation is another time saver.

Invention of the Sticky Note

In the early 1970s, Art Fry was in search of a bookmark for his church hymnal that would neither fall out nor damage the hymnal. His colleague, Dr. Spencer Silver, had developed an adhesive strong enough to stick to surfaces but that left no residue after removal. Fry solved his bookmark problem by applying some of this adhesive to a piece of paper and sticking it on his hymnal.

Fry soon realized that this product could be used for other purposes when colleagues started dropping by and asking him for some of his "bookmarks."

In 1977, test marketing failed to ignite consumer interest. However, in 1979, the 3M Company implemented a massive consumer sampling strategy and the Post-it® note took off. Today we see them everywhere—colourful flags stuck on files, computers, desks, and doors, in the office and at home. Post-it® notes have changed the way we work.

Source: Adapted from "Post-It Notes—Art Fry and Spencer Silver," http://inventors.about.com/library/inventors/blpostit.htm.

Project Management

Large or special projects require more management than routine jobs. They can quickly become daunting and all-consuming, and small yet important duties can easily be overlooked. With such projects, the best approach is to break down the project into a series of steps. By doing this, you not only manage your project more effectively, but you also receive a sense of satisfaction as you complete each step. Set clear deadlines for every step of your project and monitor your progress regularly, making adjustments to schedules and timelines as necessary.

If you are working on a project as part of a team, the management of the project is usually fairly formal. The various aspects of the project tend to be broken down and assigned to team members, and deadlines are given. There are also usually regular team meetings at which members report on their progress, unexpected challenges, the next steps required, and so on. Someone, either a team member or an assistant, will prepare minutes to ensure that nothing is overlooked. When working as part of a team, be sure to keep all members up to date on new developments in your assigned area. For example, copy important emails to team members. Be prepared to update the team on your progress at each meeting and to discuss any further issues.

With any type of project, the key to success is planning and organizing. If your plan is clear, logical, and well developed, and you keep all your work related to the project well organized, you will stay on track, be focused, meet deadlines with less stress, and, ultimately, effectively manage your project.

Time Stress

Stress is most commonly described as a state of frustration that generates the "fight or flight" response. It is a strain on emotions, nerves, and self-control. Fundamentally, stress is an internal response to external events. You cannot control all events, but you can control the way you react and respond to the stress.

A moderate amount of stress is healthy and is actually beneficial in keeping you alert and engaged in your daily life. Positive events such as getting married, moving homes, having a baby, or getting a new job can cause stress. Other stresses result from negative events such as increased demands and pressure, unrealistically high expectations for yourself, conflicts with colleagues, new management, change in procedures, difficult clients, heavy workload, and tight deadlines.

One of the most common symptoms of stress is procrastination, the act of putting off a task to some time in the future. Why do we procrastinate? There are a number of reasons, including:

- you don't like the task at hand

- you find the task daunting or overwhelming

- you don't have enough time to complete the task, so you avoid getting starting

- you have other things you would rather do

- you don't have all the information or direction you need.

Figure 3.12 identifies typical symptoms of stress. Review the list and be mindful of the signs. Identifying stress before it becomes unmanageable is the best way to keep it in check.

Identifying your stress is the first step. The next step is learning how to accept it, cope with it, and take effective action to manage it.

Despite having many calendars, lists, and reminders, people often hold information in their minds. If you do this, it will create even more stress because you'll worry about the items on your mind and you'll put additional pressure on yourself to remember them. Writing or typing out what is on your mind helps relieve the stress on your memory. Similarly, when having face-to-face or telephone conversations, you should take notes of what is said and file the notes appropriately. Stress is created when you try to remember a specific discussion, especially if someone asks for clarification or proof of dialogue.

Even seemingly minor practices can help you reduce stress. For example, returning items to their designated place after using them will reduce the stress caused by not being able to find something that you "need right now." This point will be discussed further in chapter 4, General File Management.

Constantly rushing around in a frazzled state of mind, trying to get everything done on time, can be both stressful and counterproductive. It can actually decrease your productivity by overwhelming your mind

FIGURE 3.12   Typical symptoms of stress

Physical Signs	Thought Signs	Action Signs
Headaches	Brooding, worrying	Withdrawn
Irregular breathing	Frustration	Irritable
Increased heart rate	Resentment	Emotional
Tense muscles	Negative thoughts:	Shaking, trembling
Sweating	• "Not again"	Aggressive
Face turns red	• "That's it, I give up"	Less efficient
Sleep disturbances	• "I can't handle this"	Losing things
Anxiety	• "I don't have enough time for this"	Memory problems
Low energy	• "They don't do as much work as I do"	Procrastination
Change in appetite		Increased illness
Depression		Poor concentration
Weight loss or gain		More errors

and making you prone to error. Don't book your schedule so full that you have no room for flexibility. It is inevitable that unpredictable events will occur, but if you slightly pad your time allotments, you'll be able to adjust your time accordingly. If you find yourself with so many deadlines that you simply can't meet them, ask your supervisor to prioritize your tasks. Your supervisor will decide which tasks are urgent and which deadlines can be extended. When discussing your workload with your employer, don't complain, whine, or blame other people. Instead, bring up your concerns in a positive and professional way.

Continual pressure on the mind and body under stress leads to poor judgment, reduced creativity, irritability, errors, emotional burnout, and more. Figure 3.13 outlines both mental and physical ways that you can be proactive and reduce the effects of stress.

FIGURE 3.13   Coping with stress

Mental Methods	Physical Methods	
Use positive self-talk:	Take breaks	Organize
• "Stay calm, don't overreact"	Stretch or walk	Slow down
• "You can do this"	Get fresh air	Follow established systems
• "One foot in front of the other"	Eat healthy snacks	Follow time-management tips and guidelines
• "You're doing the best you can—keep going"	Create more privacy	Plan and simplify
Problem-solve	Reduce clutter	Get enough sleep
Reprioritize	Be flexible	Drink plenty of water
Use lists and notes to relieve memory stress	Try deep breathing	Exercise
Be realistic	Follow routines	
Leave work at work		

Best Practices and Pitfalls

This chapter has focused on time management in the workplace, but you should also realize that what happens at work is often carried over to the rest of our lives. Following best practices and avoiding pitfalls can help you reduce stress through good time management.

Do	Don't
Prioritize. Identify high-priority items and work on them first. Your task lists should indicate high-, medium-, and low-priority tasks. If your workload becomes so heavy that you risk missing deadlines, ask your supervisor to identify what must be done now and what can wait.	*Don't procrastinate.* Putting off tasks that you dread will lead to greater stress down the road. Unfortunately, avoiding difficult tasks does not make them go away. If you procrastinate by abandoning high-priority tasks for trivial ones, you'll end up being behind on large projects.
Do one thing at a time, if possible. Focusing on one task allows you to concentrate and do your best work.	*Don't multitask to excess.* Although it is often necessary, multitasking affects your concentration and can actually be a form of procrastination.
Get organized and develop good habits. Keep your organization systems logical, labelled, user-friendly, and ergomically correct. Make use of the array of organization products and tools available, including software programs. Use precedents and templates for routine letters and forms. When you receive a document that requires little action, deal with it quickly and file it away.	*Don't drown in clutter.* When your workspace is cluttered, you waste time because you end up handling the same documents and papers over and over.
Manage your mail. Open, sort, and file or dispose of email and snail mail. Be ruthless about what you keep and what you throw out. Store messages and documents that you'll need later. As a general rule, your email inbox should be no longer than one viewing page.	*Don't let your mail pile up.* By not promptly opening and dealing with email or snail mail, you are inviting problems. Action deadlines could be missed or important data overlooked. Mail piles up quickly and can become a chore.
Schedule time for preparation. Schedule time to organize and review lists, and to prepare for the coming days or weeks. Prepare tomorrow's to-do list the day before. This way, you will be organized for the next morning.	*Don't overschedule.* The unexpected is bound to occur. If there's no flexibility in your schedule, surprises will cause panic. Build some breathing room into your schedule to accommodate unplanned changes and work, and to give you time for organization and self-management.
Use a scheduling system. When you use a scheduling system well, you can rely on it with confidence. The system will prevent you from overlooking important dates.	*Don't overlook reminder systems and task lists.* Using sticky notes for everything defeats their purpose, because items will no longer stand out. Reminder systems and lists complement your scheduling system. They stop you from depending on sticky notes and scrap pieces of paper to remind you about everything.
Write everything down. Keep a steno pad next to the phone to make notes on all conversations and instructions regarding tasks. This way, you'll know exactly where to find what you're looking for.	*Don't hold information in your mind.* Trying to remember everything without writing it down causes stress and anxiety and depletes your energy. You'll constantly worry that you may forget something.

Do	Don't
Use a tickler system. Law societies require lawyers (and in Ontario, paralegals) to maintain tickler systems. Check tickler cards daily, pull the current date's cards, and ensure that they are given to the appropriate person.	*Don't allow your tickler system to surprise you.* Avoid the feeling of dread caused by pulling out a card that tells you a large project is due that day. Use the system to remind you of large projects by filing an additional card an appropriate amount of time in advance.
Discover your own "prime time." This is when you are most productive. Use this time for high-energy tasks; use your lower-energy time for less demanding tasks.	*Don't overload task lists.* Overloading yourself with work is self-defeating and demoralizing. Don't add so much to the list that you could never accomplish it all.
Control interruptions. Manage phone calls, visitors, and other interruptions. Use non-verbal cues, such as reducing eye contact, to let co-workers know when you don't have time to chat. Identify stress before it becomes unmanageable. You can't control all the events in a day, but you can control how you react and respond to stress.	*Don't let stress take over.* Constantly existing in panic mode is counterproductive because it creates anxiety and leads to exhaustion. You are also more likely to make mistakes and overlook small details.
	Don't take work stress home with you.

NOTES:

REVIEW QUESTIONS

1. What is the first thing you should do when examining your time-management habits? Why?

    _____

    _____

    _____

    _____

    _____

    _____

    _____

2. What are the benefits of organization?

    _____

    _____

    _____

    _____

    _____

    _____

    _____

    _____

    _____

3. What is the most important factor in any scheduling system?

    _____

    _____

    _____

    _____

    _____

4. What items are typically recorded in a scheduling system?

    _____

    _____

    _____

    _____

    _____

5. What is a personal digital assistant and in what ways can it help a law clerk?

_____

_____

_____

_____

_____

_____

_____

6. What is a tickler system, what information is recorded on it, and why is it so important?

_____

_____

_____

_____

_____

_____

_____

_____

7. What should you consider when using sticky notes?

_____

_____

_____

_____

_____

8. Besides simply noting items on a to-do list (or task list) what else must be considered?

_____

_____

_____

_____

_____

9. What is personal prime time?

_____

_____

_____

_____

_____

_____

_____

_____

10. What are the pros and cons of multitasking?

_____

_____

_____

_____

_____

_____

_____

_____

11. What can you do to handle general office stress?

_____

_____

_____

_____

_____

_____

_____

12. What are the best methods of reducing wasted time?

_____

_____

_____

_____

_____

_____

ACTIVITY

You arrive at work and find the following:

- a note from the lawyer indicating that she had to leave the office and won't be back for the rest of the morning

- phone messages for the lawyer (one regarding a meeting this afternoon)

- a draft document you gave the lawyer that is marked up with changes to be made (the document needs to be filed in court tomorrow morning)

- a dictation tape from the lawyer with letters to clients

- a client in the waiting room who has an appointment with the lawyer this morning

- client information sheets requiring new files to be opened.

Prioritize these items, indicate any specific action required, and give your reasoning.

General File Management

Effective file management provides the basis or infrastructure for timely, effective client service and appropriate management of client matters.

—LSUC, "File Management" Guideline

Introduction

You land a great job. You have the education, skills, and ability to do it—and you do it well. The problem is that you can never find what you need when you need it, which can make you look like you don't know what you're doing. The real problem could be the filing system: either it is not effective or you need to take some time to become familiar with it and understand it.

A file management system is more than a bunch of folders stuffed alphabetically into a drawer. A well-designed and well-managed system is the cornerstone of every efficient office, and should help you locate any document you need in half a minute or less.

Identifying Problems in the Existing System

If you're having trouble with a system, take a closer look at it before deciding that it is inadequate and in need of a complete overhaul. Perhaps it is suitable, but you simply need to become more familiar with it. Every filing system has some common objectives. A well-designed filing system should

- ❑ make filing easier, quicker, and less tedious
- ❑ facilitate the retrieval of items in 30 seconds or less
- ❑ use clear, logical, and simple file categories and labels
- ❑ be practical and functional
- ❑ be expandable and flexible for office growth
- ❑ save money

❏ ensure the integrity of the system, even with changes in personnel

❏ outline practices and procedures in a manual or list of rules to ensure standardization

❏ allow for easy identification and purging of inactive records in accordance with a retention schedule

❏ provide improved service to clients and accommodate internal requests for files

❏ protect vital records and maintain client confidentiality

❏ comply with jurisdictional legal requirements

❏ include cross-filing where applicable.

Developing the File Plan

Even if you conclude that the existing system isn't the most efficient arrangement possible, it may be that the system is too elaborate, or the office too big, for it to be completely restructured. In that case, you may simply have to adapt to the status quo. Before you start restructuring an existing filing method, check with the people who use the system every day and ask the lawyer or lawyers in the firm for permission to rework it.

If you are given permission to redesign, rebuild, or enhance an existing filing system, there are a number of considerations to take into account. The primary consideration and guiding principle is that the system should be simple.

Figure 4.1 lists a number of aspects that need to be considered in designing a new system.

Designing and organizing a new filing system can be daunting. Rest assured, however, that it is well worth the time and effort. When you have a system that efficiently addresses the needs of the office, your job will become much easier.

A word of caution: Do not immediately run out and buy numerous filing supplies. Wait until you have settled on the appropriate system and figured out the best way to set up the files. Buy supplies only when you know what you need to make the system work.

Filing Tools

You must evaluate the type of files used in the office and the manner in which they are usually retrieved. This should help you determine suitable filing tools that are best for your office. The right tools for the job can make all the difference. There is a vast array of supplies and equipment available. This section explains the various filing tools available to fine tune your system.

FIGURE 4.1   Designing a filing system

Consideration	Explanation
Accessibility	Centralized—one system in the office that all employees access
	Decentralized—separate systems maintained by each employee or department
	Portable—a system that is mobile, in wheeled carts or carry cases
	Direct access—files are immediately retrievable without need of further assistance from indexes or directories
	Indirect access—reference to an index or directory is necessary to identify a file's location
Space	Filing space—available area in the office for the number of cabinets/drawers the system will require
	Storage space—a separate location for dormant or closed files
	Expansion space—enough room in the filing system to accommodate growth (e.g., new files can be added without having to reorganize the system)
Security	Confidentiality—files need to be kept in a location away from public access or view
	Locks—to protect confidentiality and prevent theft
	Fire protection—certain files need to be safeguarded in fireproof cabinets (i.e., wills, powers of attorney, client property, deeds and securities)
Usage	Reference—staff may refer to files based on names, permit numbers, geographical areas, date, subject, etc.
Volume	Number of records—limited paper files may dictate a simple alphabetical system, whereas high-volume document production offices may require a multi-segmented alphabetical or numeric system
	Number of staff—the more staff there are, the more hands are in the files, and therefore there is greater need for standardization, logical organization, ease of retrieval, out cards, etc.
Legal requirements	Law society rules regarding retention schedules, conflict checking, limitation periods, tickler systems, etc., must be followed
Costs	Initial equipment (cabinets, file folders, etc.)
	Employee time to set up system

NOTES:

Filing Equipment

Once you have assessed the space you need for your files, browse through a few office-supply catalogues to become familiar with your options and to determine costs. You will also have to pay close attention to aspects of the existing system that might affect the choices that are available to you. For example, if you have file tabs on the sides of your folders rather than the top (as in some numerical systems), it would not be practical to have standard file drawers where the sides cannot be seen. Instead, you should have sliding filing shelves.

Also keep in mind that there are smaller storage needs that may be less obvious parts of the filing system. Many law firms, for example, receive trade magazines and association newsletters. These are best kept in large binders or magazine holders. Wall racks, which consist of a number of file slots, can be useful for storing frequently accessed reference material or holding files for each lawyer with documents for review.

The famous in/out basket, another small storage need, is often misused. In fact, the "out" tray is not commonly used in smaller offices. Rather, the documents more often move from the top ("in") basket to the bottom basket. The top is usually reserved for truly "in" matters (matters that need to be dealt with), and the bottom generally holds materials that have been reviewed and need further action but are not urgent. However, lawyers usually operate with a separate "out" basket, which you may be required to retrieve regularly.

Other smaller systems are often useful for specific needs. For example, mobile filing carts on wheels can be a space solution in some offices. Perhaps there is a certain set of files that you access only once a week. The cart can be stored out of the way, and rolled over to your desk when needed.

When selecting and organizing your filing equipment, make the best use of all space. Do not forget to go vertical. There is often a lot of wasted space that could be used for less frequently accessed materials. If files grow so large that they cannot be accommodated in an accordion file, specialty cardboard boxes (often referred to as banker's boxes) can house files in either a legal-size or a letter-size format and are ideal for storing high-volume files or closed files. It is not uncommon to see lawyers and police officers walking into a courtroom carting numerous banker's boxes filled with all necessary client-related documents.

NOTES:

File Folders

The most commonly used and familiar filing tool is the simple paper file folder, the practical foundation to office organization. When purchasing file folders, make sure to check their weight. Some are made of a thicker cardstock than others, which gives them a longer life. Most standard folders will hold about 75 sheets of paper, and can be expanded by scoring the bottom. This prevents files from sliding below each other and below the sightline of filing cabinet guides and tabs.

Typical file folders.

Hanging folders have become popular aids to organization, browsing, and retrieval. Although they are visually appealing, they are expensive and take up considerably more space in the cabinet. Be careful not to accidentally put files away in the space between hanging files. When files go missing, that is often where they went.

Hanging file folders.

File folders can also be purchased with brads attached. A brad is a two-pronged fastener made of flexible metal that is attached to a file folder. A document is two-hole-punched along the top or the side and secured to the folder with a brad. Alternatively, you can purchase the brads separately and simply punch holes in the folder. Self-adhesive brads are available as well. Documents filed in such folders can be neatly stored and organized, but the process can become more time-consuming.

Accordion files are useful when files become too large for a standard folder. They expand to various widths to accommodate more paper. Often, more than one accordion file may be needed. In that case, take care to label folders that belong together, indicating, for example, "one of three," "two of three," and so on.

Accordian file folders.

Filing boxes are used either when the files are too large for accordion file folders or for maintaining closed files during regulatory document retention periods. There are several different types of file boxes. What you choose will depend on file folder size and storage capacity. The front of each file box should have a label listing the documents or files enclosed in the order they are filed.

Banker's box.

Guides, Tabs, and Labels

File guides are filing cabinet dividers used to separate various groups of files. Whether your files are organized by subject, year, or lawyer, the guides create easily identifiable divisions, which aids in retrieval. Guides are available in both top and side versions. Generally, top-cut guides start at the left and subsequent guides move positions toward the right for ease of visibility. Side-cut tabs typically start at the bottom and move upward.

The tab is the part of the folder that protrudes from either the top or the side, and is where you attach name labels. Folders are usually placed in order with the tabs to the right. This way, your left hand can locate guides, while the right hand locates the tab.

Labels provide the naming surface for guides, tabs, and specific file folders. Consistency in labelling is important. Labels should be typed from the left edge of the label. In this way, when folders are placed in the cabinet, all tabs will line up in an orderly fashion, enhancing ease of retrieval. Labels are available in various sizes and with coloured bars across the top and/or side.

The human eye distinguishes colour more rapidly and easily than it does words. Various forms of colour-coded systems are becoming increasingly popular in offices. As with any system, a colour-coded system can be simple or complex. Some systems will use coloured folders to identify various sections of the system. For example, purple folders might be used for criminal matters, yellow for family matters, and blue for civil matters. Law offices that service various jurisdictions may distinguish geographical areas by colour. Colour coding can also be combined with other filing methods to optimize the efficiency of the overall system.

A colour-coded system that is ideal for very high-volume folders uses side-wrap stickers. Each letter has an associated colour. When a file is opened, the first few characters of the file name are adhered to the side of the folder with individual stickers. The number of letters that are shown is variable; three or four are usually sufficient. For example, the last name "Smith" may have three stickers—a red "s," a blue "m," and a white "i." When the folders are filed, a colour pattern is instantly recognizable. This system virtually eliminates the possibility of misfiling because errors will be easily seen.

Other filing supplies include hole punches, adhesive pockets, binders, sorters, page protectors, literature display stands, desktop organizers, and filing cards for various uses (including tickler systems). Virtually any such item that enhances organization and retrieval is a filing supply option.

Filing Practices

Most offices usually devise their own hybrid filing system that combines the most appropriate or effective aspects of different filing methods.

Figure 4.2 identifies and describes the most commonly used systems, and provides examples of what each method is most suited for.

Maintain a Filing Manual

Regardless of which system, or combination of systems, is used in your office, there should be a record or manual of office filing procedures. This manual will help maintain continuity and consistency when, for example, a new or temporary colleague needs to learn how to retrieve or replace a file.

Retention Schedules

Retention schedules outline the length of time that files are to be stored. Different types of files have different retention periods. Each office will usually set its own policy regarding most general files, and will follow regulatory policies for particular kinds of files. Tax laws, for example, regulate the retention of accounting documents, and law societies

DID YOU KNOW?

It is estimated that the human eye can distinguish 11,000 different colours.

DID YOU KNOW?

The most famous decimal filing system, used in 90 percent of the world's libraries, is the Dewey Decimal System, developed in 1876 by Melvin Dewey. This system was developed to unify library cataloguing of books. The system is divided into 10 classifications, which are further divided into 10 divisions, which are further divided into subdivisions. The Fleming College call number for the first edition of *Working in a Legal Environment* used the Library of Congress system of cataloguing and was KE.352.C64 2007.

FIGURE 4.2   Filing system arrangements

ALPHABETICAL		
System	**Description, Uses, and Examples**	**Advantages and Disadvantages**
Dictionary style (also known as the topical system)	*All files are ordered alphabetically by file name* • general files are often maintained this way Examples: Accounts, Correspondence, Memos, Research	• simplest system • direct access to files • very flexible and easy to expand • careful consideration is required to maintain logical assignment of names • related subjects are not grouped • often requires cross-filing

Encyclopedia style (also known as the classified system)	*Subjects are grouped under broad categories*
	• legal file management can be maintained using this style
	• categories are alphabetized according to major headings
	• subjects (secondary headings) within each category are also alphabetized
	
	Example:
	Case Law
	    Impaired Driving, Toxicological Evidence
	       Roadside Breath Demand
	          Evidence to the Contrary
		• very flexible: major headings can be created to suit particular uses (e.g., files may be organized by lawyer, geographic area, type of law)
		• often indirect access to files

NUMERIC		
System	**Description, Uses, and Examples**	**Advantages and Disadvantages**
Straight numeric	*Files are arranged by number (e.g., file or matter number), in ascending order* • best for files where numbers have already been assigned (e.g., permits invoices, serial numbers) • in larger systems, numbers replace major headings found in subject files Example: Human Resources 100 Finance 200 Policy Directives 300 • under each major heading, individual files are numbered within the series Example: Human Resources—Benefits, 101; Recruiting, 102; Job Descriptions, 103	• easy to expand by adding files to the end of the system, but difficult to insert files in the middle • indirect access to files • requires an index

NUMERIC		
System	**Description, Uses, and Examples**	**Advantages and Disadvantages**
Chronological	*Files are arranged by date* • suitable for small systems where documents have a short life span • dates can be major headings • separate dividers for years (2009, 2010, 2011) • secondary dividers for months Example: A real estate matter would be filed according to the closing date	• ideal for tickler systems and limited time frames • an index may be required
Numeric/duplex	*System of two or more number segments used to classify files* • used for high-volume files in large offices Example (year 2011, lawyer code 01, subject code 24): 2011-01-24	• flexible • can greatly increase productivity • requires an index • indirect access to files • can be expensive
Numeric/decimal Dewey Decimal System	*Files are arranged numerically using two or more segments of numbers—the middle number sequence is the major subject heading identified numerically* • used where a large number of records needs to be organized by subject	• groups similar subjects • convenient for browsing • unlimited expansion • restricted to ten major divisions • requires an index

ALPHANUMERIC		
System	**Description, Uses, and Examples**	**Advantages and Disadvantages**
Alphanumeric	*Uses a combination of letters and numbers* • client files are often filed this way • the system could use a combination of letters and numbers representing various elements of the matter • the alphabetical code could represent the type of law (CR for criminal matter, FA for family law matter, etc.), or the applicable lawyer or location • the middle number could represent the year the file was opened, followed by the client number for that year Example: CR-2011-61, or FA-11-219 A complete client file name with a primary, secondary, and tertiary label might look like this: Smith, Ann CR-2011-61 Re: Breach of Probation	• identifiers composed of letters and numbers are more effective if they mean something, rather than being arbitrarily assigned • misfiling is more common and difficult to correct • if files are filed numerically rather than alphabetically, the system goes from smallest to largest number • requires an index

specify rules that relate to client file retention. Ensure that you adhere to the appropriate rules for your jurisdiction.

Naming Files

Your whole filing system is only as good as your system for naming files. You can have the best system in the world, but if files are not logically or correctly named and labelled, no one will be able to find anything. The way you name a file will be different with each system, but is always important. The key is to be consistent. A file name should be clear to everyone in the organization accessing the file. Numeric systems are easier to name in that they follow a specific assignment of numbers. Alphabetical systems require more consideration because the file names are subjective and the integrity of the system must be externally managed.

When naming a file in an alphabetical system, be logical. Review the documents and the purpose of the file and determine how it is most likely to be requested. File names should not start with descriptive words. Use nouns. Declarative words can follow. For example: "Blue Houses" should be named "Houses, Blue." "Houses, Red" and "Houses, Yellow" would then follow. Although this is a simple example, it demonstrates the point. People are not going to look for the blue houses file under "Blue." As well, naming with nouns allows you to group subjects together for better organization. Just as you should have a filing manual, consider setting up some guidelines for naming files, such as what the core files will be, and then what principles to adhere to in setting up non-standard files.

Your file names will often require more than one simple title. The first line of your file name is called the primary heading; the second line is called the secondary heading; and the third line is called the tertiary heading. For example, the labels of general subject files may look like the labels in figure 4.3, while the labels of particular client files may look like those in figure 4.4.

Naming your folders in this manner aids in browsing and retrieving files. In addition, it makes the job of adding new files to the system straightforward and ensures that they are added in a consistent way.

Client files differ from general office files. The naming of client files is discussed in detail in chapter 5, Client File Management, but the following is an example of how client files may be named and ordered.

NOTES:

FIGURE 4.3   General subject file labels

FIGURE 4.4   Client file labels

NOTES:

Rules for Naming and Ordering Files

When determining how to name and order files, observe the following rules.

	File Name	Naming and Filing Rule
1	Names	Alphabetize according to the last name, then the first name, then any initial. Edith R. Wilson would be named and filed as: Wilson, Edith R.
2	Initials	Alphabetize a name containing an initial before a name beginning with the same letter. J.W. Collis would be named and filed as: Collis, J.W. Collis, Jeffery
3	Names with prefixes (with and without spaces)	Treat a last name with a prefix (such as "Le" the same as any other surname. Rob LePlante and Douglas LePointe would be named and filed as: LePlante, Rob LePointe, Douglas Treat surnames with spaces as a single word: De Grace, Adam De Grave, Allison De Greef, Tyren
4	Abbreviated names	Alphabetize as though the name were spelled out. Wm A. Carpenter and Wilma Carpenter would be named and filed: Carpenter, Wm. [William] A. Carpenter, Wilma
5	Hyphenated names	Alphabetize hyphenated last names as a single name. Ignore hyphens. Phyllis Lamrock and Cynthia E. Lamrock-Forget would be named and filed as: Lamrock, Phyllis Lamrock-Forget, Cynthia E.
6	Professional titles with a name	Ignore titles when alphabetizing. Dr. Ted Rathwell would be named and filed as : Rathwell, Ted (Dr.)
7	Personal titles	Alphabetize after other units in the name: Keates, Lawrence R., Jr. Keates, Lawrence R., Sr. Keates, Lawrence Ross

	File Name	Naming and Filing Rule
8	Single letters in business names	Alphabetize each letter as a single unit, disregarding prepositions and conjunctions. R & R Carwash Rent Anything Company Resting Beds Ltd.
9	Married titles	Alphabetize according to the name provided. Mrs. Carol Wilson and Mrs. Patricia Wilson would be named and filed as: Wilson, Carol, Mrs. Wilson, Patricia, Mrs.
10	Abbreviations in business names	Alphabetize as though abbreviations were spelled out. Ignore punctuation. John Smith Hardware Ltd. [Limited] St. [Saint] John, Denis John Smith Hardware Loading Co. Smith, Elizabeth
11	Articles and prepositions such as "the," "an," "of," and hyphenated business names	Disregard small words and symbols when alphabetizing. Call-A-Cab Ltd. Parkhill on Avenue Call-A-Cab Parcel Delivery Parkhill Enterprises Callaghan, George Parkhill on Hunter
12	Hyphenated business names	Alphabetize hyphenated names as one unit. Ignore hyphens. Trent Entertainment Limited Trent-Porter Computers Trent-Gordon Delicatessen Trentsaw Cutting Co.
13	Compound business and geographic names	Alphabetize each word in a compound name as one unit. Newfoundland Groceries New York Groceries
14	Possessives	Disregard apostrophes when alphabetizing. Cole Drugs Coles Bookstore Cole's Business Store
15	Numbers in names	Order in numerical sequence. Numbers precede letters (e.g., "4th Line" before "Dixon Donuts"). 4th Line Theatre 6th Avenue Book Store 38 Degrees Restaurant
16	Numbered corporations	Alphabetize in numerical sequence. 123 Dental Equipment Rentals Inc. 12568 Arlington Books Inc. 228978 Brockford Towers Inc.

File Indexes

A file index is a useful tool that is usually recommended for any type of filing system. An index is simply a listing of all established file folders. Some systems make an index mandatory. For example, a straight numeric system definitely requires an index to locate a numerically organized file if you begin a search with only a client name or subject topic.

A file index should list files in the exact order that they are placed in the cabinets. Essentially, the listing is a paper plan of the file arrangement. It should be clearly categorized by all headings and subheadings. A file index should also be organized alphabetically if a numeric system is used. For example, if client files are organized numerically, the file index should list all clients alphabetically and indicate the corresponding numeric title.

As with filing systems in general, a file index will only be useful if it is maintained. When files are added or removed from the system, the index needs to be updated accordingly. An electronic version of the index should be stored and updated on computer, and a printed version should be kept at the beginning of the files or displayed nearby for easy reference.

Cross-Filing

You will have to make decisions about where to file a document and how to name a file. Though you do need to be decisive, it is often appropriate to cross-file documents, files, or both. Cross-filing occurs when a document or file could logically be located in two different categories. For example, a document distributed at a stakeholders' meeting regarding court security would be filed in the specific "Court Security" file. However, since it was the topic of a committee meeting, a copy of the document should also be placed in the "Stakeholders' Meetings" file. Someone seeking this document may refer to it specifically by topic, or they may simply ask for "the form that was handed out at the last meeting." In addition to these two cross-filings, there could be an additional file location. If the document is a new form, for example, you may want to place a copy in a "Forms" file. Cross-filing should not be overused, but when appropriate it can be very beneficial.

Subdividing and Purging

In maintaining a filing system, you should take care to ensure that the system does not become bulky or unspecific. File folders should generally not grow to more than five centimetres (two inches) thick. Once a folder gets that thick, it should be subdivided. For example, a management or shareholders' meeting file could be subdivided into sections such as minutes of meetings, agendas, correspondence, and general information. All documents in a file should be organized chronologically, with the most recent document on top or at the front.

A miscellaneous folder grows just like the junk drawer in a kitchen.

One of the biggest traps in a subject filing system is the miscellaneous folder, where many people will file a document when they're in doubt as to where it should go. Using the miscellaneous folder in this way solves the problem of getting a document off your desk, but does it help you in retrieval? When there is no logical place in the system for a document, it can come to rest in the miscellaneous file. But use this approach with care. As a general rule, once there are five related documents in the miscellaneous folder, you should open a new folder for the topic.

Even before deciding where to file a document, you should consider whether or not you need to keep it. Is it useful now? Could it be useful in the future? Does it form part of a paper trail that needs to be maintained? If you answer yes to any of these questions, keep it. But there is a fine line between keeping extensive files and hoarding. Choose carefully.

Maintenance of an effective and efficient filing system requires diligence. You may be tempted to throw documents into the ever-growing bin of "to be filed." Not only does this approach inhibit the efficient retrieval of those documents while they sit there, but you are also creating a procrastinating environment. It is far easier to condition yourself to allocate ten minutes out of your day to file. Better yet, place each document in its appropriate place once you no longer need it on your desk.

Purging files also benefits maintenance. Purging relates to general office files, not client files. To purge is to review files and determine what is no longer necessary or is outdated. This in itself could take days if performed just once a year, but is barely a chore if it is done routinely. As part of your standard filing procedures, consider vetting one file per day or week (depending on the volume). While reviewing files, ensure that you follow all dictated or established rules regarding file retention.

The Out Card

Because retrieval is the key purpose to a filing system, you need to be able to identify borrowed files. Various members of your office will work with files, and you need a way to locate files that are in use by lawyers or other staff. A simple solution is the "out card." An out card resembles a file folder, has red trim, and has a tab succinctly labelled "Out." The outside of the folder has preprinted lines where the borrower identifies the name of the file, the date, and their name. The card is inserted in place of the missing file. When the file is returned, the out card is removed, and the return date is recorded either by the user or the file manager. It is often the case that different out cards are used for separate areas of the system.

Name	File	Date taken out	Int	Date returned	Int
Renée Forget	2011/98	23/01/12	rf	27/01/12	rf

Hot Files

Some law staff devise what are often called "hot files." These are a few files kept within short reach of the working desk, such as current files with a high volume of action, frequently needed forms, or regularly used reference materials. Keep these files to a minimum and make sure they are easily identifiable so that they do not clutter the desk.

Filing Using Technology

The days of strictly manual document and file management are almost past. Most documents are now generated electronically, either through dedicated legal programs such as DivorceMate, Conveyancer, Estate-a-base, Amicus Attorney, and Summation iBlaze, or through word-processing programs such as Microsoft Word and Corel WordPerfect. When setting up your electronic files, your objectives should be organization and ease of retrieval, just as they are in your manual system.

When deciding on an organization system for your electronic files, consider how you overcame the challenges of an unorganized, inconsistent paper system. You should apply the same approach to your computer files. Whether your paper filing system is organized alphabetically, numerically, or chronologically, your electronic files should reflect the same structure. This not only addresses issues that likely underlie your entire system, but a similarity between paper and electronic filing systems also makes it easier for users in your office to understand how documents are filed and where to find them. Create a plan or map of your computer folders; tree diagrams are often effective for illustrating this. In figure 4.5, main folders under "Woodrow and Perry" are named by year and subfolders are named in accordance with your manual system (for example, year of intake, file name, client name, document type). As you enter a new year, ensure that your subfolders are consistent with those of the previous year. This, again, contributes to efficient retrieval. The key, remember, is to be consistent and diligent.

Computers can be our best friends and our worst enemies. It can be frustrating when files appear to be lost. In some cases, accidents will happen and documents will be damaged or deleted. To minimize the impact of technological mishaps, make sure your electronic files are backed up. It is especially important to back up files before you install any new hardware or software.

Develop a regular schedule for backing up. Some offices may already have protocols in place requiring that you back up daily, weekly, or monthly. If your firm has an information technology (IT) department, consult the specialist for instructions and information.

If your firm does not have a file backup procedure already in place, establish one as soon as possible. Key issues to consider when designing a backup procedure include the amount of data to be backed up, the frequency with which backups are made, the required stability of storage media, and ease of use. Depending on your requirements, the types of

FIGURE 4.5 Electronic file storage structure

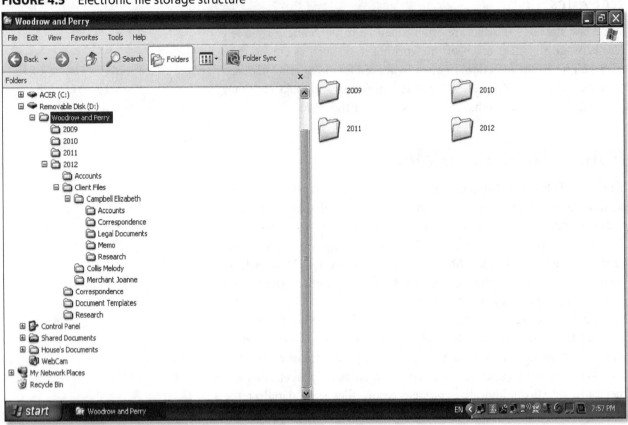

backup and archival devices available include tape drives, hard drives, Zip drives, CD burners, and flash media (USB and thumb drives).

Best Practices and Pitfalls

Finally, you know what they say about best-laid plans. Despite all your efforts, you may find your filing system to be less than perfect. If it is, go back to basics. Assess your needs, evaluate your existing system, and identify problems. Knowing the cause of your problem is half the solution. Always keep in mind that the purpose of your filing system is efficient retrieval. Ensure that your filing guide or manual depicts the procedures you intended, then follow it. The table on the next page outlines some of the key factors in maintaining an effective filing system.

Remember: A file that cannot be retrieved is useless. By implementing the best system for your office based on the suggestions above, you will be able to rely on your records and provide information to others on a timely basis.

Do	Don't
File often and regularly. Maintain a sorting folder for items yet to be filed.	Don't procrastinate. Don't let the "to be filed pile" build up. Not only will filing become a time-consuming task, but locating unfiled documents will be difficult.
Ensure that your filing system is flexible enough to allow for growth and the addition of new files.	Don't forget to plan ahead. A lack of planning can leave documents without a logical home. Reviewing your needs carefully will limit this problem.
Allow three to four inches of extra space in drawers for easy access.	Don't allow bulging folders. They slow down filing and can make tabs and dividers more difficult to see.
Subdivide files as they grow. Use categories that will make retrieval easier (e.g., correspondence, memos to file, lawyer's notes, docketing). This is especially important in client files.	Don't misfile. Misfiling will result in lost documents, stress on you, discontent on the part of the lawyer, and numerous other potential problems.
Periodically evaluate your filing system. It may need to be tweaked to maintain efficiency.	Don't disperse responsibility for file management. Having too many people responsible for filing can lead to inconsistency in naming and placement. Assign a file manager, or identify specific sections for each person to manage.
Maintain an up-to-date index that clearly outlines your filing system.	Don't place loose papers like sticky notes or paper-clipped items on the outside or inside of the folder. It is too easy to lose them that way.
Ensure that files are protected for confidentiality.	Don't allow folders to become unruly and disorganized. Use brads to store similar items together. Only certain documents should remain loose.
Maintain consistency by referring regularly to your filing manual.	
File in chronological order, with the most current date on top or in the front.	
Uphold legal requirements and practise consistent retention procedures.	
Establish and follow checklists as needed to ensure that steps are not omitted.	
Use cross-filing where appropriate.	

REVIEW QUESTIONS

1. Why should you have a file plan? What considerations should be taken into account in a file plan?

2. Describe a typical alphabetical filing system.

3. What is the purpose of a filing system?

4. What are retention schedules and what dictates their structure?

_____

_____

_____

_____

_____

_____

_____

_____

_____

_____

5. What key factors should be considered when creating a file label?

_____

_____

_____

_____

_____

_____

_____

_____

_____

_____

6. When is it appropriate to cross-file documents into two or more categories?

_____

_____

_____

_____

_____

_____

_____

_____

_____

_____

_____

7. What is a filing index, and why do you use it? Give an example of when you would use one.

_____

_____

_____

_____

_____

_____

_____

_____

8. What are three major types of filing systems? For each system, give an example of when it would be appropriate to use.

_____

_____

_____

_____

_____

_____

_____

_____

9. What problems can be caused by misfiling?

_____

_____

_____

_____

_____

_____

_____

_____

10. How do you maintain consistency when there are numerous people doing the filing?

_____

_____

_____

_____

_____

_____

_____

_____

11. What is the most common numeric system?

_____

_____

_____

_____

_____

_____

_____

_____

12. How do you refer to the first, second, and third lines of a file label?

_____

_____

_____

_____

_____

_____

_____

_____

ACTIVITIES

1. You are given a number of files. Name and organize them in alphanumeric order.

   a. David A. Smith, 192/05, Re: Separation Agreement

   b. D.B. Smith, 112/04, Re: Adoption

   c. D.B. Smith, 125/05, Re: Purchase 274 Braidwood Avenue, Peterborough

   d. Windover Plumbing and Gravelle, 92/04, Re: Debt Collection

   e. Windover Plumbing and Carpenter, 92/04, Re: Debt Collection

   f. Angela Williams, 63/06, Re: Estate Planning

   g. Northview Church, 113/05, Employment Contract

   h. North Shore Computers, 111/05, Re: Debt Collection

   i. Cavan Carpentry 12/06, Re: Partnership Agreement

2. You are given the following list of matters for which new files must be opened. Suggest file names that conform to correct alphabetical filing and proper punctuation rules.

   a. City of Peterborough, Peterborough Square Lease Agreement, Client City of Peterborough, Received in office January 3, 2012

   b. Millbrook Bowling Centre, Preparation of Partnership Agreement, Client Owner Lawrence Keates, Received in office December 3, 2011

   c. John Smith Hardware Limited, Purchase of 10 King Street, Peterborough, ON, Client Bryan Traynor, Received in office February 14, 2012

3. Devise a file map for your program. Make sure you include a folder for each semester. Within each semester, create folders for your courses. Once you have created all necessary folders, move course materials into the applicable folder.

Client File Management

The way to gain a good reputation is to endeavour to be what you desire to appear.

—Socrates

Introduction

Lawyers (and in Ontario, paralegals) have an ethical duty to maintain client files in an organized manner, protect client confidentiality, and respond to client inquiries in a timely manner. An important aspect of meeting this obligation is knowing the procedures for opening, managing, and closing client files. This includes what information needs to be collected, when it should be collected, and how it should be organized.

Identification and Verification

Law society rules across Canada set out the requirements for lawyers (and in Ontario, paralegals) with regard to identifying and verifying the identity of their clients. The requirements differ depending on whether the client is an individual or an organization. In Ontario, the requirements for lawyers and paralegals are set out in Part III—Client Identification and Verification of LSUC bylaw 7.1. You should check the rules and bylaws in your province to determine what requirements apply.

Identification of a client means obtaining basic information at the beginning of a retainer about the client and any third parties that may be providing direction or instructions to the client. Much of this information is the same information that would be collected on the initial contact with the client (such as name, address, etc.). Lawyers and paralegals in Ontario are required to identify all of their clients unless one of the exemptions outlined in bylaw 7.1 applies.

Verification of a client's identity means confirming who a client or third party says they are by looking at an original identifying document from an independent source. A copy of the document is placed in the client file along with a record of the type, reference number, and place of issue. Source documents for individuals include a birth certificate, driver's licence, provincial health insurance card, and a passport or

CHAPTER OBJECTIVES

After reading this chapter, you will understand:

- the importance of client identification, verification, and conflict of interest checks

- the difference between a retainer letter and agreement

- the purpose of new client information sheets and client consent forms

- what time docketing is and how often it should be done

- the steps in managing a client file from opening to closing similar document. For an organization, source documents include a certificate of corporate status issued by a public body, a trust or partnership agreement, articles of association, or any other similar record that confirms the organization's existence.

Lawyers and paralegals in Ontario are only required to verify the identity of clients and third parties if they engage in or instruct with respect to a funds payment, receipt, or transfer; bylaw 7.1 contains certain exemptions.

Section 23(1) of LSUC bylaw 7.1 requires all licensees retained to provide professional services to a client to obtain the following information. If the client is acting for or representing a third party, the relevant information must be obtained for the third party.

Individual	Organization
• Full name • Business address and business telephone number • Occupation(s)	• Incorporation or business identification number, and the place of issue of the number* • Nature of the type of business(es)/activities engaged in* • Name, position, and contact information for each individual who gives instructions with respect to the matter • In addition to the above, the licensee must make "reasonable efforts" to obtain (1) the name and occupation(s) of each director, other than an organization that is a securities dealer, and (2) the name, address, and occupation of everyone who owns at least 25 percent of the organization or its shares.

* For organizations other than a financial institution, public body, or reporting issuer.

The following guidelines will help determine whether compliance with client identification and verification requirements is necessary:

1. Is the lawyer/paralegal being retained to provide legal services to a client? (If so, she must identify the client and any third party who may instruct/direct the client unless an exemption applies.)

2. Is the lawyer/paralegal engaging in or instructing with regard to funds receipt, payment, or transfer? (If so, he must verify the identity of the client and any third party who may instruct/direct the client unless an exemption applies.)

3. Is the lawyer/paralegal required to verify the identity of an organization? (If so, she must also verify the identity of the individual acting on the organization's behalf.)

4. Is the lawyer/paralegal meeting the individual whose identity he or she is required to verify in person? (If not, an agent must verify the individual's identity on behalf of the lawyer/paralegal, or an attestation must be obtained from an oaths commissioner/guarantor.)

Figure 5.1 shows an identification and verification form.

Conflict-of-Interest Checks

A law firm cannot represent clients with conflicting interests—for example, applicant and respondent in a matrimonial matter, or plaintiff and defendant in a lawsuit. A law firm also cannot act against a former client unless the new matter is wholly unrelated to the previous representation. A single consultation by an opposing party can prevent a firm from taking on a new client, even if the opposing party did not retain the firm.

Under law society rules, before a law firm can accept a new client, the firm must search a list of clients and related parties to ensure that there is no conflict of interest. The search is generally performed before the first meeting. That way, if a conflict is discovered, it does not affect the firm's representation of any existing clients. Conflict searches may need to be performed several times—typically, after the first meeting,

FIGURE 5.1   Identification and verification form

VERIFICATION OF IDENTITY

Client Name: _____

Client Home Address: _____

Alternate Mailing Address: _____

Phone No.: _____ Alternate Phone No.: _____

Verification Document Reviewed — Copy Attached

❑ Driver's Licence

❑ Passport

❑ Other (provide details): _____

First Meeting Date Identity Verified: _____

Identity Verified By: _____

Assigned Lawyer/Paralegal: _____

Assigned File Name and Number: _____

PRACTICE TIP

In Ontario, the rules governing conflicts of interest are LSUC rule 2.01 for lawyers and rule 3.04 for paralegals.

when more information about opposing parties is available, and any time a new party is added to the matter.

Conflict-of-interest searches may be performed manually or electronically. Figures 5.2 and 5.3 show the conflict search function in PCLaw and Amicus Attorney—legal software packages used for file management, accounting, and document production.

Retainer Agreements

When you hear the term "retainer" in a legal environment, it can mean one of two things:

- an advance payment held in trust by a lawyer for future services, or

- a written agreement setting out the terms of the lawyer–client relationship.

Retainer agreements and/or letters (also referred to as engagement letters) are prepared at the beginning of the lawyer–client relationship. The particulars of the agreement will vary depending on each lawyer's preferences, the type of law involved, and who is responsible for payment. However, most retainer agreements include the following information:

- the client's name and the firm name

- the nature of the work to be performed

- the initial retainer (payment) required, with an acknowledgment that the retainer has been received and placed in trust

- the name and hourly rate or fee of the primary lawyer responsible for the file

- the names or titles of other lawyers or staff who may assist with the file and their respective hourly rates

- the firm's fee and billing policies (these may also be set out in a separate billing memorandum referred to in the retainer agreement).

The retainer letter or agreement may be long and detailed, as illustrated in figures 5.4 and figure 5.5, or more succinct, as illustrated in figure 5.6. Retainer agreements are usually signed by the client to show agreement with the terms of the lawyer–client relationship. A copy of the agreement is given to the client and the original signed retainer agreement is kept in the client file. The contents and details are changed based on the type of law and fee arrangements.

If a prospective client does not retain the firm, this should be confirmed in writing with a non-engagement letter explaining that the firm does not act for the client and will take no action on the client's behalf.

FIGURE 5.2   PCLaw's conflict search function

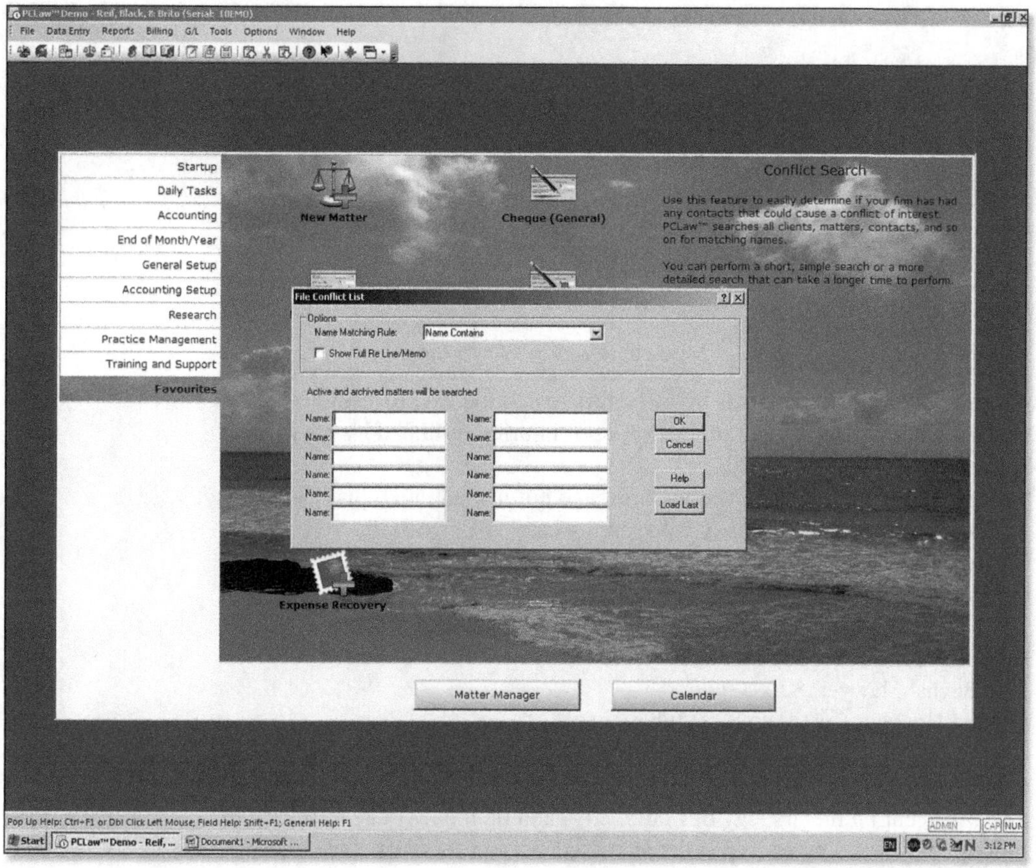

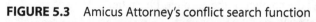

FIGURE 5.3   Amicus Attorney's conflict search function

FIGURE 5.4   Detailed retainer agreement between solicitor and plaintiff (may or may not include a letterhead)

DATE: September 16, 20--

CONTRACT OF RETAINER

BETWEEN:

Buchan & Buchan, Barristers and Solicitors

and

Monica Tassie

1. I, Monica Tassie, retain you as my solicitors to commence proceedings against Fred Lutz and Lutz Motors Ltd. in respect of injuries sustained by me in an accident on September 14, 20--.
2. I understand that I have retained the firm, and not just an individual lawyer, and that other lawyers and staff may work on my case.
3. I understand that the hourly rates of those who may work on my file are as follows:

    P.R. Buchan, lawyer: $250.00/hour
    S.B. Buchan, lawyer: $200.00/hour
    Edward Nguyen, law clerk: $75.00/hour.

4. I understand that the hourly rates of office staff may increase by no more than 5 percent on the first day of March 20--, and on the first day of March in subsequent years. I agree to pay the increased amount for work done after the date on which the rates change.
5. I understand that if I am dissatisfied with the amount of the account, I have the right to have that account assessed by the court.
6. I understand that before work begins under this retainer, I am required to pay a deposit of $3,000.00 to be credited against accounts when rendered. I understand that I may be required to furnish future deposits from time to time to cover future fees and disbursements.
7. I understand that I must pay accounts promptly when they are rendered and that interest is chargeable on overdue accounts at the rate of 18 percent per year.
8. In the event settlement funds are received, I direct that they be paid to P.R. Buchan in trust, and that you may deduct any fees or disbursements owing at the time settlement funds are received, on rendering an account to me, and that the balance of the settlement funds will then be paid to me.
9. I understand that it is my obligation, on receiving advice and being asked for instructions, to provide you with instructions as requested.

Signed: *Monica Tassie*   *September 16, 20--*

Source: Adapted from Laurence Olivo and Mary Ann Kelly, *Civil Litigation*, 2d ed. (Toronto: Emond Montgomery, 2009), 65.

FIGURE 5.5 Detailed retainer letter between solicitor and plaintiff in a criminal matter

WOODROW & PERRY

Barristers & Solicitors

1605 Treetop Road
Peterborough, Ontario
K9K 1G2
Telephone: 705-743-5796
Facsimile: 705-749-3492

woodrow.perry@shaw.ca

File # DW/20--/398

January 23, 20--

Tryren Pepper
12 Maher Drive
Peterborough, ON
K9K 1Y3

Dear Mr. Pepper

RE: Section 266, CCC and Dangerous Operation of a Motor Vehicle, Section 249, CCC

Thank you for considering Woodrow & Perry for your legal services. We look forward to working with you. As discussed at our meeting on December 12, 20--, I am confirming that you have asked me to advise you and act on your behalf with respect to the criminal charges as noted below.

I further confirm that you have retained me in connection with all aspects of conducting a defence of the charges of Assault, Section 266, CCC and Dangerous Operation of a Motor Vehicle, Section 249, CCC

(a) in Superior Court of Justice, or
(b) any proceedings in any court.

I will keep you informed about matters that arise and discuss with you any significant decisions you must make. I will give you my best legal advice, but you will make the final decisions. Significant decisions may require your written consent.

Communication is important. I can only do my best job if I have your trust and am fully informed. In particular, as this matter proceeds, I ask you to give me all information you have, or have access to, that could help me in working on your matter.

We will report to you from time to time in person, and by letter, telephone, and email. You will also receive copies of correspondence sent and received and documents prepared that are relevant to your matter.

As indicated at our meeting, we require payment to us of a deposit of $5,000.00 on account of legal fees and disbursements. This deposit will be placed in our trust account, which does not bear interest. We are authorized to transfer from the deposit money any amounts owing to us on account of our fees and disbursements. You may be asked to replenish the deposit from time to time.

You will be billed for disbursements and fees. Fees are based on factors such as the difficulty and importance of the matter; special circumstances such as urgency; whether special skill or service is required and provided; the value of the subject matter; the results obtained; and on the time and effort involved, calculated on the basis of time spent at our current hourly rates. The billable rates for the lawyer and law clerk who will be involved in your matter are as follows:

Lawyer: **$500.00 per hour**

Law Clerk: **$95.00 per hour**

Accounts will be rendered to you on an interim basis. All accounts are to be paid within 20 days. Any account unpaid within the 20 days will bear interest at the rate of 12% annually until paid.

At all times you have the right to terminate before your matter is completed subject to your paying the balance of our fees and disbursements owing to us.

We may terminate our services at any time in circumstances where:

(a)   you did not cooperate with us in any reasonable request;
(b)   continuing to act for you would be unethical or illegal;
(c)   your instructions conflict with our duties under the *Code of Professional Conduct,* or if we feel our advice to you is being disregarded;
(d)   your accounts are not paid on a timely basis and you do not make other arrangements for payment.

We would also have to withdraw our services if we learned of a conflict of interest that would make it unethical for us to continue to act for you. A conflict of interest occurs when what is best for one of our clients adversely affects another of our clients.

In any of these circumstances we will request that you sign a non-engagement letter stating that we no longer act for you. We will render a final account and you will have to pay this account. We will release your file to you once all accounts have been paid, except in unusual circumstances as set out in the *Code of Professional Conduct.*

I agree to provide these services on your behalf once I have received the attached retainer agreement signed, dated, and witnessed within 7 (seven) days from the date of this letter. A self-addressed, stamped envelope has been included for your convenience.

If you have any questions or concerns regarding the fee as set out or any other matter, please feel free to call or email me at any time. The office is open from 9:00 a.m. to 12:00 p.m. and 1:00 p.m. to 4:30 p.m. Thank you for providing me with this opportunity to represent you. I am looking forward to working with you and bringing this matter to a close as quickly as possible.

Regards

Donna Woodrow

DW:kk

Enclosure: Retainer Agreement

FIGURE 5.6 Succinct retainer agreement between solicitor and plaintiff (may or may not include a letterhead)

WOODROW & PERRY
Barristers & Solicitors

1605 Treetop Road
Peterborough, Ontario
K9K 1G2
Telephone: 705-743-5796
Facsimile: 705-749-3492

woodrow.perry@shaw.ca

To: Stephen Buckle, Paralegal
3969 Wallace Point Road
Peterborough, ON K9J 6Y3

Re: Ayden Watts, Debt $15,000.00

I Elizabeth Campbell hereby retain you to take all necessary steps to collect the overdue
account of Ayden Watts, 10 Wallace Point Road, Peterborough, Ontario. You are further
authorized to take whatever court proceedings you consider necessary and proper and to
employ such agents as you consider advisable.

I agree to provide you instructions as required. I further agree to pay your accounts as
rendered and I understand that in addition to disbursements I will pay a flat rate of $500.00.

Dated February 26, 20--

_____   _____
Elizabeth Campbell   *[Key in name of witness below signature line.]*

FIGURE 5.7   Non-engagement letter

WOODROW & PERRY
Barristers & Solicitors

1605 Treetop Road
Peterborough, Ontario
K9K 1G2
Telephone: 705-743-5796
Facsimile: 705-749-3492

woodrow.perry@shaw.ca

File # 169/20--

January 23, 20--

Noah MacKay
41 Black Road
Peterborough, ON
K9J 2Y2

Dear Mr. MacKay

RE: Mackay Litigation

This letter is further to our initial meeting on January 15, 20--. As indicated to you at that time, we are unable to represent you in connection with this matter.

If you do not a have another representative in mind I would suggest contacting the Law Society of Upper Canada, because they maintain a list of lawyers and paralegals that may be able to handle your matter.

Note that there may be strict time limitations within which you must act in order to protect your rights in this matter. It is important that you retain a legal representative as soon as possible to ensure your matter is dealt with appropriately and in a timely fashion. I recommend that you immediately take steps to obtain legal representation.

I confirm that we do not have any documents belonging to you. All documents were returned to you at the end of the initial meeting.

Regards

Donna Woodrow

New Client Information Sheets

A new client information sheet should be completed when the client file is opened. It is the first document placed in the new file. The sheet serves as a quick reference for information about the client and opposing parties. Legal software packages such as PCLaw and Amicus Attorney can generate new client information sheets, as illustrated in figures 5.8 and 5.9. Figure 5.10 illustrates a generic new client information sheet. Figure 5.11 shows a more detailed new client information sheet used in a civil matter. The content of new client information sheets varies based on preference and the type of law involved in the client matter.

FIGURE 5.8 New client information sheet generated from PCLaw

MATTER: DC-11-234   CLIENT: 3   OPENING DATE: September 9, 20--

NAME: Cole, Barbie

ATTN: Barbie

RE: Separation Agreement

ADDRESS: 12 Albert Street
           Peterborough, ON K9K 1G2

BUS PH: FAX: CELL:

OPPOSING LAWYER:

OPPOSING FIRM:

PH: FAX:

NOTES:

FIGURE 5.9 New client information sheet generated from Amicus Attorney

Client/Matter Information for: Walker, Jonnie
Date: Sun, Feb 6, 20--

Matter Name: Walker, Jonnie
Matter Number: DEW-2011-036
Client Number: 36
File Type: Criminal
File is: Active
Billing status: Billable
Lawyer: Donna Woodrow

Parties:

Name: Mr. Jonnie T Walker

Other:
Address:
10 Dublin Street
Peterborough Ontario
Canada K9K 3T5

Lawyers Assigned: Donna Woodrow

FIGURE 5.10 Generic new client information sheet

NEW CLIENT INFORMATION SHEET

Client Name: Cayden Roberts   File #: 215-11-CR

Address: 58 Tallwood Drive, Peterborough, ON K9J 3R4

Telephone #: 705-698-2578

RE: Criminal, Break and Enter Charge

Responsible Lawyer: Joanne Harding

Dated File Opened: March 16, 2011

Date File Closed:

Notes:

FIGURE 5.11   Detailed new client information sheet

NEW CLIENT INFORMATION SHEET

File #: 785-11-RE   Court File #:

Matter Type: Civil

Client Name: Ryelan Edwards

Address: 589 Simcoe Street,   Client DOB and SIN #: 1974/11/03
              Peterborough, ON K9J 4R5   187 258 369

Primary Contact Information: Home # 705-743-3659

Alternate Contact Information: Cell # 705-745-2659

Opposing Party Information: Debora Cunningham Lawyer # 705-748-2356

Medical Information: Broken left leg in three spots—requires pins and has had several surgeries

Rate: $250.00/hr

Trust Amount Held: $500.00

Legal Aid Certificate:

Limitation Date: January 01, 2013

Notes: _____

_____

_____

_____

_____

NOTES:

Client Consent Forms

A **third party** is someone who is not a party to an agreement or transaction. A third party can also mean a party added to a lawsuit by a defendant.

Lawyers often need to gather or give information about their clients, such as medical, educational, or employment records. If this information is in the possession of a third party or if it is being sent to a third party, law society rules regarding confidentiality and disclosure provide that a client's written consent or authorization is required before the third party can release the information to the lawyer. The third party may charge a fee for gathering or photocopying the information. In Ontario, the rules governing confidentiality are rule 2.03 of the *Rules of Professional Conduct* for lawyers, and rule 3.03 of the *Paralegal Rules of Conduct*.

If the third party does not provide his or her own consent form, the law firm can prepare a consent form. A consent form must

- identify the third party

- identify the client

- set out the information required

- direct the third party to release the requested information to the lawyer

- be signed and dated by the client (the client's signature may be witnessed).

If information is required from more than one source, an individual consent form is prepared and signed by the client for each third party. The original consent form is sent to the third party, with a cheque from the firm for the applicable fee (if any). Copies of the consent form are made for the client and the file. Figures 5.12 to 5.14 illustrate three sample client consent/authorization forms.

FIGURE 5.12   Client consent to release documents/information form

CONSENT TO RELEASE DOCUMENTS/INFORMATION

I, John L. Jones, born September 25, 1957, hereby authorize and direct All Skills Technical School to release to Linda Brankston, Barrister and Solicitor, any documents or information concerning/arising from any contact with me.

_____
John L. Jones

Date _____

FIGURE 5.13   Client request access to personal health records form

Physician's Name: Dr. Allan White

Address and Phone Number: 984 Willowdale Drive, Peterborough, ON K9V 7R4; 705-648-3111

REQUEST ACCESS TO PERSONAL HEALTH RECORDS

I, Sarah Elizabeth Evans   ,

(print full name of patient)

of 41 Cardine Street, Peterborough, ON K9J 4T6

(address)

hereby consent to the disclosure or transmittal to or the examination or discussion by

Robert Burgis

(name of lawyer)

of the clinical records compiled in a Civil Suit resulting from a car accident

(nature of matter)

in respect of Sarah Elizabeth Evans, born December 03, 1970   .

(patient's name) (date of birth)

Jim Clancy	*Sarah Elizabeth Evans*
Jim Clancy	Sarah Elizabeth Evans
(Witness)	(Client's signature)

Date: April 16, 2011

NOTES:

FIGURE 5.14   General client authorization

AUTHORIZATION

TO: Dr. Aaron Vance

FROM: Virginia Harwood

DATE: November 4, 20--

RE: Virginia Harwood personal injury

I, Virginia Harwood, authorize you to release any and all records, reports, and X-ray films pertaining to the injuries I sustained as a result of a motor vehicle accident that occurred on May 1, 20--, in Peterborough, Ontario to my solicitors of record, Woodrow & Perry, 1605 Treetop Road, Peterborough, Ontario K9K 1G2.

This is your full and sufficient authority to do so.

Dated at Peterborough, Ontario on November 4, 20--.

_____

Virginia Harwood

Time Dockets

Lawyers record all time spent on legal work, distinguishing between billable and non-billable hours. Law clerks and legal assistants may also have to record their time if it will be billed to the client. As discussed in chapter 3, Time Management, the action of maintaining these records is called docketing. Time dockets form the basis for client bills.

Time dockets break each hour into ten segments of six minutes. A task completed in half an hour would be docketed as 0.5, and a task completed in one hour as 1.0. Tasks taking six minutes or less are docketed as 0.1. Time is generally rounded up to the next 0.1 increment, so a task completed in 45 minutes would be docketed as 0.8. Docketing time is discussed in more detail in chapter 6, Client Accounts.

Billable work is time spent on activities for which the client will be billed. It includes meetings, telephone calls, the preparation of legal documents, research, and court time.

Non-billable work is time spent on activities that will not be charged to a client. It includes client work that a lawyer decides not to bill for, such as a free consultation, or research performed by an articled clerk. It also includes general office work not performed for a specific client, such as staff meetings or continuing legal education.

A **counsel fee** is a special daily rate applied for time spent in court or at settlement conferences.

Time docketing should be done several times a day—ideally, each time you work on a different file. If you docket only at the end of the day or every few days, you will inevitably fail to capture a great deal of billable time. Poor docketing habits result in a loss of income to the lawyer or law firm.

Time may be docketed manually, electronically, or by a combination of the two. In some firms, a client matter docket sheet is fastened to the inside front cover of the client file. Other firms use a daily time-tracking sheet for each lawyer to record file-related activities. If time is docketed electronically, the entries must be keyed in using a system such as PCLaw. Examples of each of these methods of tracking time can be found in Figures 6.2, 6.3, and 6.4 in chapter 6.

Whatever method is used, the recorded information will include:

- the client's name or file number, or both

- a detailed explanation of the services performed

- the amount of time spent, in 1/10th of an hour increments.

In a small office, you may be responsible for preparing the client matter docket sheet or the daily time-tracking sheet and setting up the accounting record when you open the file. In a larger office, the completed docket sheet or daily time sheet has to be sent to the accounting department in order for a client accounting record to be established.

Opening Client Files

A client file is opened whenever a new client retains the services of the firm. In most law firms, new client files are opened every week, so this task will become a regular part of your work. Figure 5.15 sets out the usual steps for opening files in the order that they are performed.

Using Technology

Part of your duties will include opening files within a dedicated electronic program. There are many software packages specifically designed for today's busy legal office. These packages have a wide range of capabilities, including tools for the efficient entry of new data and information. They also include file management, document production, and account-processing functions. Some law firms design their own systems using spreadsheet, word-processing, and database programs.

Three common software packages used in law offices are PCLaw, Conveyancer, and DivorceMate:

- PCLaw is general file management and legal accounting software.

- Conveyancer is file management, document production, and accounting software used in real estate law.

- DivorceMate is software for the creation and management of family law forms in Word or WordPerfect.

FIGURE 5.15   File-opening procedures

Step	Details
✓ Take the incoming phone call from the potential client.	Collect relevant information, including the client's full name and contact information, the nature and urgency of the matter, and the full names of all opposing parties.
✓ Schedule the initial appointment.	Check the lawyer's diary for the next available appointment time. Some lawyers distinguish between appointment times for meeting new clients and appointment times for meeting existing clients. The initial meeting may be with a paralegal or a senior administrator rather than a lawyer.
✓ Perform a conflict-of-interest check.	Check the names of the client and any opposing or related parties against the firm's conflict-of-interest list.
✓ Meet with the new client.	The lawyer/paralegal meets with the client to identify and/or verify the client's identity and obtain background information related to the matter. The firm's billing and retainer requirements are explained to the client in this meeting.
✓ Name the file.	Use the client's last name followed by first name, and indicate the type of matter. For example: SMITH, John Re: Separation Agreement
✓ Assign a file or matter number.	Following the filing system used in your office, assign the file a matter number. If you are using a legal software package such as PCLaw or Amicus Attorney, a matter number will be assigned when a new client record is created (see figures 5.8 and 5.9).
✓ Prepare the file label.	Create an identifying label. Typically, this includes the file name, number, and type of law. For example: RATHWELL, John CR-2011-160 Re: Small Claims If you are using PCLaw or Amicus Attorney, a label can be printed directly from the software. Place the initial documents and notes inside the folder and create any subfolders that will be needed.
✓ Prepare a file-opening sheet/card.	Insert the new client information sheet (see figures 5.8 to 5.11).
✓ Create a tickler card.	As described in chapter 3, a tickler card notes the client name, matter number, and type. It sets out all critical activities and limitation periods and other deadline dates for the matter.

	Step	Details
✓	Prepare a docket sheet or time-tracking sheet.	Prepare a docket sheet or time-tracking sheet and forward a copy to the accounting department if necessary (see chapter 6, pages 132-37).
✓	Prepare a retainer letter and/or agreement.	On receipt of retainer moneys, prepare a retainer letter/agreement for the client's review. A retainer agreement will be signed by the client and kept in the client file. A copy is given to the client.
✓	Prepare client consent forms (if needed).	Prepare client consent forms (if needed). An original signed consent form is forwarded to each third party and copied to the file. A copy is given to the client.
✓	Double-check tasks and file the new client folder.	Double-check that all initial steps are complete and place the file in your filing system with an appropriate bring-forward date.

Figures 5.16 to 5.21 illustrate the data entry process for opening a file in PCLaw, Conveyancer, and DivorceMate.

Once opened, a client file will look something like the file pictured in figure 5.22.

FIGURE 5.16   Screen view of a new matter in PCLaw

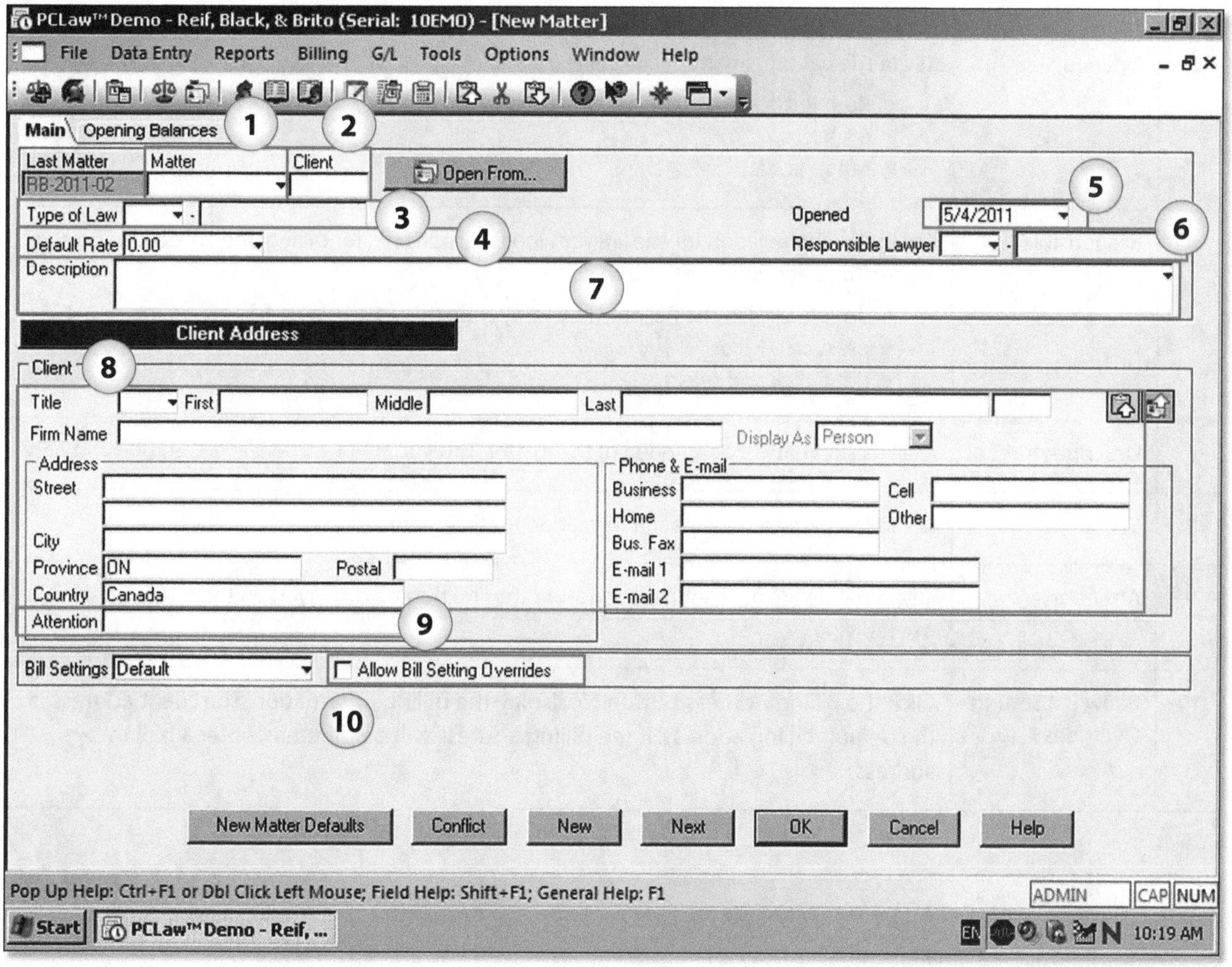

FIGURE 5.17 Data entry of a new matter into PCLaw

	Element	Details
1	Matter	A default file number may appear: • accept; or • type in a new matter number.
2	Client	Accept the client number or key in an existing client number. To select from a list of clients: • double-click in the Client box; • press ctrl+F1; or • right-click and select.
3	Type of Law	Key in the abbreviation for the type of law. To select from a list of types of law: • double-click in the Type of Law box; • press ctrl+F1; or • right-click and select.
4	Default Rate	Key in the rate to be used by default on all time entries for this matter. To select from a list of rates: • double-click in the Default Rate box; • press ctrl+F1; or • right-click and select.
5	Opened	Key in the date the matter was opened. To select from a list of dates opened: • double-click in the calendar box; • press ctrl+F1; or • right-click and select.
6	Responsible Lawyer	Key in the abbreviation for the lawyer who is responsible for billing and collections on this matter. To select from a list of lawyers: • double-click in the Responsible Lawyer box; • press ctrl+F1; or • right-click and select.
7	Description	Key in a summary or description of the matter. This information appears on pre-bills and bills.
8	Client	Key in the name and contact information for this client.
9	Attention	Key in the text (e.g., client name and/or other text) to be displayed on the attention line when billing.
10	Allow Bill Setting Overrides	Click the Billing Address button to display the billing information. The client address is the default billing address. If the billing address will be different, enter a billing address.

FIGURE 5.18 Screen view of a new matter in Conveyancer

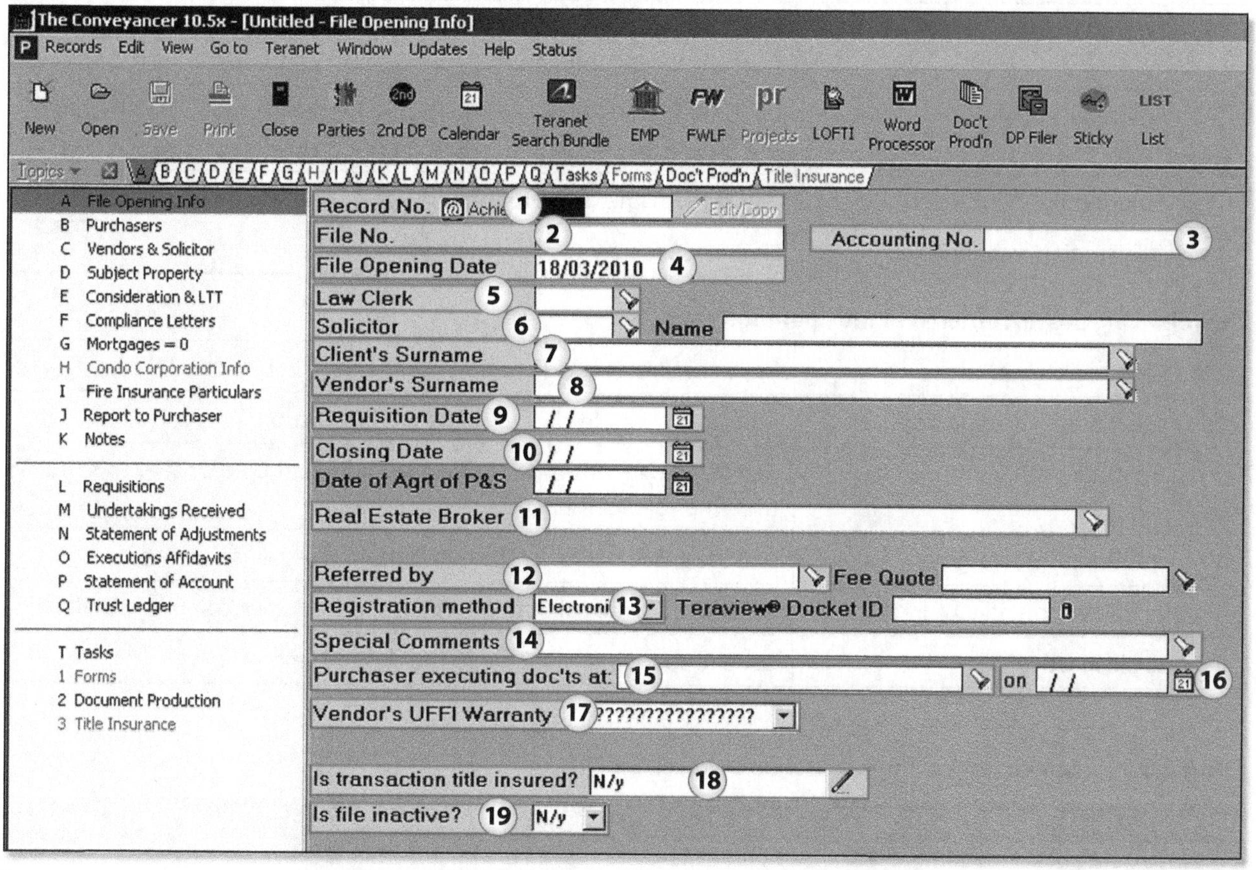

FIGURE 5.19 Data entry of a new matter in Conveyancer

	Element	Details
1	Record No.	Key in the name or number under which the transaction record will be saved.
2	File No.	Key in the file number assigned by your office to this transaction.
3	Accounting No.	Key in the accounting number assigned by your office to this transaction.
4	File Opening Date	Key in the date the file was opened, or select the date from the calendar function.
5	Law Clerk	Key in the initials of the law clerk assigned to the file, or press F8 to select from the database.
6	Solicitor	Enter the initials of the solicitor assigned to this file, or press F9 to select from the database.
7	Client's Surname	Press F9 or double-click to select from the Parties database or add the party to the database.
8	Vendor's Surname	Press F9 or double-click to select from the Parties database or add the party to the database.
9	Requisition Date	Key in the date on which the requisition period ends, or select the date from the calendar function.

	Element	Details
10	Closing Date	Key in the date on which the transaction closes, or select the date from the calendar function.
11	Real Estate Broker	Press F9 or double-click to select the client's real estate broker from the Brokers database or to add the broker to the database.
12	Referred by	Key in the name of the referral source if applicable.
13	Registration method	Use the space bar to toggle to the desired response.

The following are not entered at file opening:

14	Special Comments	Key in reminder dates or other information required for follow-up.
15	Purchaser executing doc'ts at:	Press F9 or double-click to select the jurisdiction.
16	on [date]	Key in the date on which the documents are signed, or select the date from the calendar function.
17	Vendor's UFFI Warranty	Use the space bar to toggle to the desired response.
18	Is transaction title insured?	Press F9 or double-click to select the title insurance company database.
19	Is file inactive?	Use the space bar to toggle to the desired response.

FIGURE 5.20   Screen view of a new matter in DivorceMate

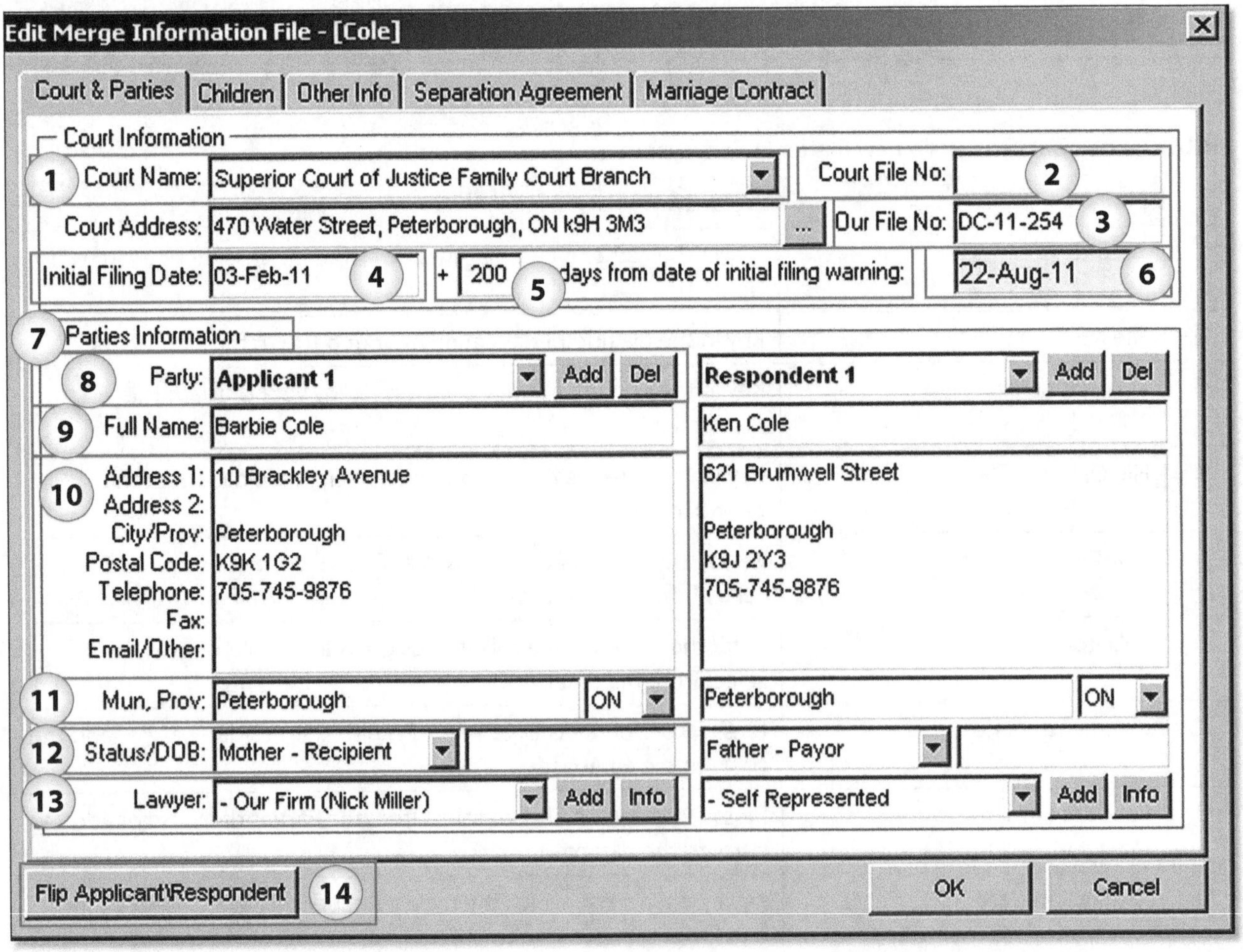

FIGURE 5.21   Data entry of a new matter into DivorceMate

	Element	Details
1	Court Name:	Accept the default court information or use the drop-down menu to select one of the three most common court locations.
2	Court File No:	Key in the file number assigned by the court.
3	Our File No:	Key in the office file number.
4	Initial Filing Date:	Accept the default date given or key in the filing date if it is different from the default date.
5	[Number] days from date of initial filing warning:	Accept the default date or key in any number of days needed.
6	Date box	This date is calculated by adding the warning number of days to the Initial Filing Date.
7	Parties Information	Enter detailed information for each applicant and respondent, including their name, contact information, and date of birth.
8	Party:	Accept the default, Applicant 1 or Respondent 1. To add another party, click Add (Family Court Forms only).
9	Full Name:	Key in the party's full name in proper format.
10	Address:	Key in complete contact information.
11	Mun, Prov:	Key in the municipality. Select the province code from the drop-down menu.
12	Status/DOB:	Confirm status or select from the drop-down menu. Key in the date of birth.
13	Lawyer:	Select at least one lawyer from the firm in the drop-down menu.
14	Flip Applicant\Respondent	If you need to move information from one screen to the other, click here.

NOTES:

FIGURE 5.22   Client file (opened)

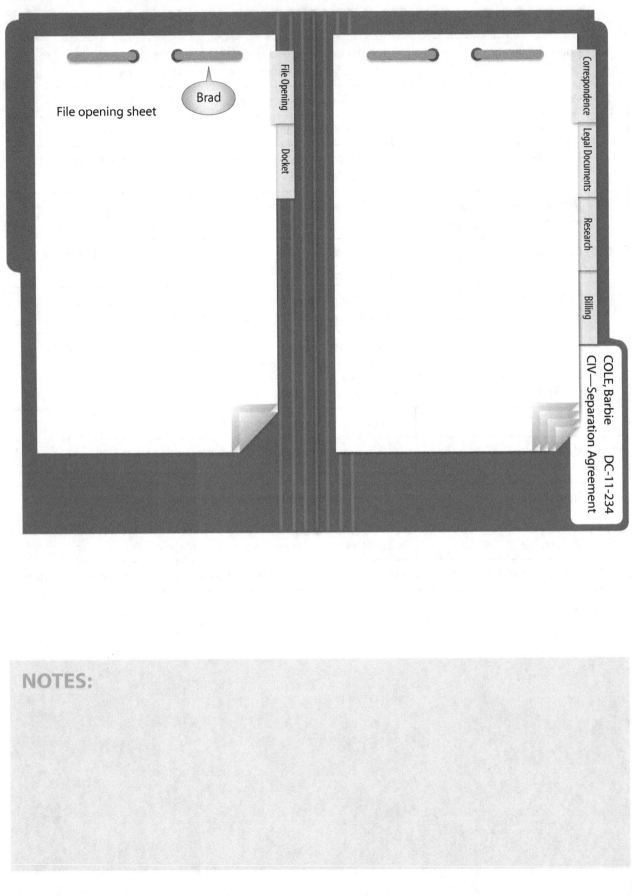

Managing Client Files

Client files can quickly outgrow slim file folders and require boxes, so it is important to devote regular time to maintaining them. There are three keys to keeping client files organized:

1. Keep different types of documents organized chronologically in labelled subfolders appropriate to the type of matter. The LSUC's Practice Management Guidelines suggest that all client files should include the following common subfiles: correspondence (including memorandums to file, telephone messages, and notes made by lawyers and staff); original documents; retainer letter; firm accounts and billing information; and legal research.

2. Complete your filing promptly so that client files are always up to date. File documents chronologically in the proper subfiles, with the most recent document on top or in the front.

3. Expand the file to accordion folders or boxes as soon as the file becomes too large for a single folder. Make sure to list the contents on the label (for example, "SMITH, John. Re: Personal Injury Claim. Box 1 of 3—Affidavits of Documents, Discovery Transcripts, Legal Research").

Client files should always be stored separately from general office files. Unless the file is in active use, it should be returned to the proper spot in the cabinet. A lost or misplaced file can hurt a client's case and result in liability on the part of the lawyer or law firm.

Closing Client Files

A client file is closed when all matters have been completed and the final payment has been received from the client. Law society guidelines and regulations regarding closing, storage, and retention of client files must be observed. Storage and destruction methods should protect client confidentiality. The LSUC's *Guide to Retention and Destruction of Closed Client Files* for lawyers and paralegals, available on the Law Society's website, outlines the requirements in detail.

The first step in closing a client file is to purge it of unneeded material. Documents belonging to the client are bundled and returned to the client. These include original documents provided by the client, documents received from opposing parties, medical or other reports, and any court or legal documents not previously provided to the client, such as pleadings, affidavits, orders, and transcripts. If necessary, copies can be made for the closed file. The client may be asked to sign an acknowledgment confirming receipt of the documents.

All documents belonging to the lawyer should remain in the file. These include correspondence, memos, notes, and evidence of the client's instructions, including authorizations and draft agreements. Electronic files should be archived in a retrievable format.

The checklist shown in figure 5.23 is a general guide for determining what documentation in the file belongs to whom. However, what is kept or returned does vary and depends on the type of file, the risk of possible claim, and each lawyer's preferences. If there is any doubt about what material should be retained in the file, returned to the client, or destroyed, confer with the lawyer responsible for the file. Figures 5.24 and 5.25 show a sample closing letter and document receipt acknowledgment, respectively.

It is also the responsibility of the lawyer to review each client file on closing to determine whether the file should be kept indefinitely or destroyed at a later date. Files that should be kept indefinitely should be marked "DO NOT DESTROY."

Closed files should be stored separately from active files. Recently closed files are usually stored at the law firm, while older files may go to offsite storage. The front of each box or cabinet containing closed files should have a list of enclosed files affixed to it. Some firms maintain the existing naming and labelling format when closing files; others renumber the closed files sequentially and use a cross-reference index.

FIGURE 5.23   Law Society of Upper Canada guidelines for ownership of documentation

Category	Example of Documents	Belongs to Client	Belongs to Solicitor
Client's property Prepared by solicitor for client's benefit Solicitor has been paid	Copies of case law	✓	
	Instructions to counsel by the solicitor	✓	
	Briefs	✓	
	Document drafts and copies	✓	
	Originals of all documents prepared for client	✓	
	Copies of letters received by solicitor (if paid for by client)	✓	
	Copies of letters from solicitor to third parties kept in the client's file	✓	
	Originals of letters from solicitor to client	✓	
	Memoranda of law (preparation paid for by client)	✓	
	Pre-trial notes and tapes of conversations with witnesses	✓	
	Trial preparation documents (chambers and trial briefs, document books, trial books, etc.)	✓	
	Copies of any other documents prepared by the solicitor for which the client has paid	✓	

Category	Example of Documents	Belongs to Client	Belongs to Solicitor
Solicitor's property Prepared by solicitor for own benefit Client has not been billed	Copies of letters (not paid for by client)		✓
	Copies of letters from solicitor to third parties kept in filing system of all letters written in the solicitor's office (and not paid for by client)		✓
	Entries of attendance		✓
	Working notes, summaries of evidence, and submissions to the court		✓
	Pre-trial notes and tape recordings of conversations (other than with witnesses)		✓
	Inter-office memoranda (non-legal)		✓
	Entries in diaries		✓
	Time sheets		✓
	Office journals		✓
	Books of account		✓
	Computerized records		✓
	Notes and documents prepared for the solicitor's own benefit/protection at his or her own expense		✓
Solicitor's property Sent by client to solicitor; ownership intended to pass	Originals of letters from client to solicitor		✓
	Instructions from client to solicitor		✓
	Authorizations from client to solicitor		✓
	Documents sent by client to solicitor with the intention that they become the solicitor's property		✓
Client's property Third-party documents sent to solicitor	Letters received by solicitor from third parties	✓	
	Vouchers and receipts for disbursements made by solicitor on behalf of client	✓	
	Experts' reports	✓	
	Discovery and trial transcripts	✓	

NOTES:

FIGURE 5.24 Closing letter to client

WOODROW & PERRY
Barristers & Solicitors

1605 Treetop Road
Peterborough, Ontario
K9K 1G2
Telephone: 705-743-5796
Facsimile: 705-749-3492

woodrow.perry@shaw.ca

File # DM-2011-398

January 23, 20--

Tyren Keates
12 Maher Drive
Peterborough, ON
K9K 1Y3

RE: Anderson MVA

Dear Mr. Keates

Thank you for allowing me to represent you in this matter. Your case is now concluded and we are closing our file. We will retain our file for a period of ten (10) years.

I wish to confirm that I am enclosing original documents you gave to us in connection with this matter:

[Documents belonging to the client that have not been previously sent to the client—e.g., original documents.]

You should keep all your information concerning this matter in a safe place in case you need it in the future. If you would like to have anything else from our file, please let us know as soon as possible.

We hope this matter was concluded to your satisfaction. If we may be of assistance in the future, please let us know.

Regards

Donna Woodrow

DW:ak

Enclosures *[List documents enclosed.]*

FIGURE 5.25   Acknowledgment from client for receipt of documents

ACKNOWLEDGMENT OF RECEIPT

To: Tyren Thain

RE: Anderson MVA

I, Tyren Thain, hereby acknowledge receipt of the following documents from Woodrow & Perry:

1.

2.

[List documents sent to the client.]

3.

4.

_____   _____

[Key in name of client.]   Date

REVIEW QUESTIONS

1. A retainer agreement is:

    a. an advance payment to a lawyer

    b. prepared at the beginning of a lawyer–client relationship

    c. a binding contract between a lawyer and client

    d. b and c

2. What information is included in a retainer agreement?

    _____

    _____

    _____

    _____

    _____

    _____

    _____

    _____

3. What is the purpose of a client consent form?

    _____

    _____

    _____

    _____

    _____

    _____

    _____

4. Using one of the consent forms from this chapter, prepare a consent for release of your high school records to your instructor.

    _____

    _____

    _____

    _____

    _____

    _____

    _____

5. Explain the difference between billable and non-billable hours.

_____

_____

_____

_____

_____

_____

_____

_____

_____

6. Briefly distinguish between methods used to track billable hours in a law office.

_____

_____

_____

_____

_____

_____

_____

_____

_____

7. What information must be included on time dockets?

_____

_____

_____

_____

_____

_____

_____

_____

_____

8. What are the most common subfolders found in a client file?

_____

_____

_____

_____

_____

_____

_____

_____

9. When may a client file be closed?

_____

_____

_____

_____

_____

_____

_____

_____

_____

10. When a file is closed, what documents belong to the client?

_____

_____

_____

_____

_____

_____

_____

_____

_____

11. Should documents of uncertain relevance be destroyed when closing a file? Explain your answer.

_____

_____

_____

_____

_____

_____

_____

_____

12. How is the retention period for a closed file determined?

_____

_____

_____

_____

_____

_____

_____

_____

ACTIVITIES

1. Law society rules provide that a conflict-of-interest check must be done before a lawyer can accept a new client. Why is a conflict check necessary? Using the Internet, find the applicable conflict-of-interest rule for your province's law society.

2. Assume that you are a law clerk working for a firm in Peterborough, Ontario. The lawyer you work with met with two new clients yesterday and you have been asked to open files for each client. Prepare a new client information sheet, tickler card, and client matter docket sheet for each client, then update the file using the appropriate software.

Client #1

Thomas Elliot—recently charged under sections 253(a) and 253(b) of the *Criminal Code* of Canada.

Mr. Elliot's address is 1214 Parkhill Road, Peterborough, ON K9K 1G2, telephone number 705-745-3845.

Set up reminders for the following:

- A first appearance date in court for [two weeks from today's date].
- A meeting with the Crown within one week of the first appearance date.

Prepare a retainer agreement using one of the retainer agreement templates found in this chapter. The lawyer's hourly rate is $250.00 per hour, the counsel fee is $1,500.00 per day, and the law clerk's fee is $100.00 per hour. Your instructor will provide additional information.

Client #2

Shannon Tomkins—Separation

Ms. Tomkins's address is 761 Brown Street, Peterborough, ON K9J 1V5, telephone number 705-876-9281.

Her husband is Ian Tomkins. His address is 6 Aylmer Street, Peterborough, ON, telephone number 705-876-3121. The client does not know his postal code.

Set up reminders for the following tasks (request appropriate timelines from your instructor):

- Obtain financial disclosure from the client and the opposing party.
- Prepare a draft separation agreement.
- Meet with the client to review the draft separation agreement.

Prepare a retainer agreement using one of the retainer agreement templates found in this chapter. The lawyer's hourly rate is $300.00 per hour and the counsel fee is $1,800.00 per day. Your instructor will provide additional information.

Client Accounts

The financial management of a law practice requires attention to sound business practices and adherence to governing regulatory provisions.

—LSUC "Financial Management" Guideline

Introduction

Although lawyers (and in Ontario, paralegals) choose to practise law or provide legal services for many different reasons—for example, to protect individual rights, or to help people navigate the justice system—the reality is that being in the legal profession is a business. They charge for their services and, like all business people, try to cover their expenses and ultimately make a profit.

A number of financial transactions take place from the time the client enters the office to retain the services of a lawyer until the client is billed and the file is closed. The maintenance of accurate financial records can be tedious and time-consuming, but it is essential. Having an accurate and up-to-date record of a law office's financial position at your fingertips will help you and your employer make sound decisions, and meet the firm's goals and obligations.

Besides offering business advantages, accurate financial management is compulsory. The law society in each province sets out minimum requirements for the maintenance and retention of records related to money collected from or paid on behalf of clients as well as property belonging to and held on behalf of clients. Bookkeeping guides for Ontario lawyers and paralegals are available on the LSUC's website.

By following standard accounting practices, you can ensure that the lawyer (and in Ontario, paralegal):

- accurately manages client accounts

- conducts accurate transactions with financial institutions such as banks and trust companies

- pays bills

- meets payroll obligations

- calculates and remits GST/HST and provincial sales tax

CHAPTER OBJECTIVES

After reading this chapter, you will understand:

- the importance of maintaining accurate financial transactions

- the purpose and types of accounting systems

- how fees are structured

- the use and type of bank accounts

- the collection, disbursement, and reconciliation of trust funds

- the purpose and importance of accurate docketing

- client disbursements

- maintenance of petty cash funds

- the application of GST/HST to client accounts

- the process involved in client billing

- an overview of Legal Aid in Canada

- remits income taxes

- submits required documentation to the law society.

In Ontario, LSUC bylaw 9, made under subsections 62 (0.1) and (1) of the *Law Society Act*, sets out the legal requirements with regard to financial transactions and records. This chapter will give you a solid understanding of those requirements.

Accounting Practices and Systems

In larger law practices, accounting functions are often centralized in a dedicated accounting department. Some smaller practices also have an accounting department, but many lawyers prefer to use a decentralized system in which law clerks, legal assistants, legal secretaries, and other support staff are directly or indirectly involved in the accounting process. Decentralized accounting requires that more attention be paid to the financial details of account management.

In order to facilitate the accounting process and satisfy law society reporting requirements, law offices must implement and maintain some type of accounting system. There are a wide variety of available systems, including

- manual double-entry systems

- manual one-write systems

- spreadsheet software

- general accounting software

- legal accounting software.

Law offices generally choose an accounting system on the basis of cost, familiarity, ease of use, and capabilities. Although some small law firms continue to use manual accounting systems, most firms now use either generic accounting software (QuickBooks, MYOB, etc.) or dedicated legal accounting programs (PCLaw, Amicus Attorney, etc.).

PCLaw is a billing and accounting system designed for law offices. The software program tracks time and fees, manages accounting books, prints and records cheques, and produces bills and receipts. The illustrations in this chapter are screenshots of PCLaw software.

Fees

Lawyers perform professional legal services in exchange for financial compensation. How much they charge generally depends on their expertise, experience, and reputation, as well as the demand for their services. The geographic area and type of law they practise can also affect the rate they charge. Those in urban areas often receive higher fees than those in rural areas because of supply and demand, higher expenses, and/or the number of years of experience.

DID YOU KNOW?

Blaise Pascal (1623–1662) was only 17 years old when he invented the first adding machine. It was a wooden box with 16 dials that, when turned, quickly performed addition and subtraction calculations. Pascal's father, a clerk who had to do a lot of calculations and all of them by hand, was the first person to benefit from his son's invention.

Fees are compensation given in exchange for legal services.

Fee Structures

The typical billing arrangements that a lawyer (and in Ontario, a paralegal) can offer are hourly fees, flat fees, block fees, and contingency fees (with some restrictions).

Hourly Fees

The most common type of fee is a fee charged by the hour. For this method of billing, the lawyer charges for work at an hourly rate until the case is resolved. Time spent on a client matter is referred to as billable time.

Flat Fees

A fixed, flat fee is usually charged when a matter is fairly routine and the average amount of time can be easily estimated. Types of matters that can be appropriate for flat-fee billing include uncontested divorces, real estate transactions, the preparation of wills and powers of attorneys, and simple criminal matters.

Block Fees

A block fee is charged for specific services when the matter is broken down into stages. At each stage of the process, the client is billed a predetermined amount. For example, in a civil matter, pleadings, discovery, and the pre-trial hearing are all different stages of one end result. Block fees make it easy to bill for matters that settle before trial, and can encourage prompt settlement.

Contingency Fees

Contingency fees are fees whose amount and terms of payment are contingent on (dependent on) the success of a case. Very strict rules govern contingency-fee agreements. Details must be thoroughly discussed with the client. A number of factors are taken into consideration when determining the fee, such as the likelihood of success, related expenses, and the complexity of the case. The arrangement must be in writing and must set out the method by which the fee is to be determined. For example, a contingency fee is usually the method of payment in a civil matter, such as personal injury matters.

Note that contingency fees are permitted only in some provinces, including Ontario; some provinces prohibit them.

Billing for Non-Lawyer Time

Lawyers (and in Ontario, paralegals) generally bill for all the time spent on a client matter. This includes time spent on research, the preparation of court documents, correspondence, meetings, and phone calls to discuss

> **DID YOU KNOW?**
>
> A lawyer or paralegal in Ontario is not permitted to receive or accept cash from a client in an aggregate amount of more than $7,500.00 (bylaw 9, Part III, subs. 4(1)).

the case. Reduced hourly rates are usually charged for services performed by associate lawyers, law clerks, or legal assistants. However, they cannot charge a client for time spent on a file by a secretary. Such time is considered overhead, or part of the cost of running a business.

Docketing

Docketing is the tracking of time spent on a client matter.

So that clients can be accurately billed, a time-tracking method commonly referred to as docketing is used. Docketing practices, which can vary from office to office, were also discussed in chapter 3, Time Management, and chapter 5, Client File Management. The objectives of docketing are:

- to maintain a record of client-related activities
- to provide details related to time spent on a client file
- to communicate time-related activities to the accounting department
- to produce an accurate statement of account to the client.

Billable time spent is expressed in six-minute (one-tenth of an hour) increments. Docketed time is always rounded up to the next six-minute increment. Ten minutes is recorded as 0.2, 13 minutes as 0.3, and so on.

For example, using the chart in figure 6.1, if a lawyer spent 1 hour and 20 minutes on a file at an hourly rate of $450.00, the client would be billed as follows: $450.00 (hourly fee) × 1.4 (docketed time) = $630.00.

Lawyers use a number of methods for recording time, including:

- file-specific dockets
- daily time sheets
- computerized time sheets
- diaries.

Time docketing should take place each time any activity occurs on the file.

NOTES:

FIGURE 6.1   Billable time increments

Minutes	Billable Hour
1–6 minutes	1/10th (0.1) of a billable hour
7–12 minutes	2/10th (0.2) of a billable hour
13–18 minutes	3/10th (0.3) of a billable hour
19–24 minutes	4/10th (0.4) of a billable hour
25–30 minutes	5/10th (0.5) of a billable hour
31–36 minutes	6/10th (0.6) of a billable hour
37–42 minutes	7/10th (0.7) of a billable hour
43–48 minutes	8/10th (0.8) of a billable hour
49–54 minutes	9/10th (0.9) of a billable hour
55–60 minutes	10/10th (1.0) of a billable hour

Most docketing methods and forms incorporate the same basic elements, including:

- the lawyer's name
- the date of service
- the client name and matter number
- a description of the activity
- an activity code
- the time spent on the activity.

Detailed dockets are essential as a record of the services provided to the client. A properly completed docket not only makes it easier for the client to understand the billing summary, but also ensures that there is an accurate listing in the client file in case the client disputes the bill. Ineffective docketing can cost your lawyer substantial time and money.

The activity code assigned to docketed time is usually alphabetical or numeric, or a combination of the two. For example, an alphabetical code might be "mwc" for "meeting with client" or "rd" for "reviewed documents"; a numeric code might be 122 for "memo to file" or 140 for "attend Land Registry office." Many computerized software programs have standard billing codes built into their programs for ease of use. These codes can be useful for your lawyer and the data entry clerk because they save time, but they don't provide the detail required in the event of a disputed bill, or the detail the client needs to understand the bill.

Full explanations should be used in addition to billing codes. For example, "meeting with client to discuss draft separation agreement" ensures clear and understandable records for both the firm and the client alike.

File-Specific Docket Sheet

A file-specific docket sheet is opened when the client retains your lawyer's services. The docket is kept in the client file. Update it each time a file-related activity occurs, and add up the total time entered on the docket either at regular monthly intervals or when the account is rendered for billing. Figure 6.2 illustrates a docket.

Daily Time Sheet

A common method of tracking time on client-related activities is a daily time sheet, as illustrated in figure 6.3. If a manual system is used, you will likely be asked to enter the information into a computerized system at the end of each day. Following the completion of these steps, stamp the time sheet as "posted" and file it in a designated area by date.

FIGURE 6.2 File-specific docket

Barbie Cole	Ken Cole
CLIENT	OPPOSITE PARTY
20 Queen Street, Millbrook	16 King Street, Millbrook
ADDRESS	ADDRESS
Family	Linda Brankston
TYPE OF MATTER	SOLICITOR
[name of court]	[address of the court]
COURT	ADDRESS

Date (2011)	Code	Details	Time Spent/ $250.00	Amount Charged	Amount Paid	Total
July 15	mc	Interview with you; received instructions	1.0	250.00		250.00
July 18	dr	Draft claim	0.7	175.00		425.00
July 18	tc	Call to respondent's lawyer	0.5	125.00		550.00
June 23	pymt	Rec'd on account			500.00	50.00

FIGURE 6.3   Daily time sheet

WOODROW & PERRY

Daily Time Record for John Brown

Today's Date: August 28/20--

File/Matter #	Client/File Name	Code	Details	Time Hours	Time 1/10
2011/645	Jones ats Smith	drd	Draft defence for Jones	1	2
2010/310	Broll/divorce	dc	Dictate Divorce Petition FLA claims	2	1
2011/600	Sims pf Roy	ro	Review Sims offer to purchase	1	5
2011/432	Fox sale to Kim	mt	Sign up Fox Mtge		5
2010/690	Real v. Twit	int	Direct clerk to issue Claim and Direction to sheriff to serve Twit	1	2
2011/190	Tweedy Inc.	rw	Review share offer details	2	
2011/645	Jones ats Smith	pr	Prepare for discovery of Jones call to client re Aff. of documents	1	
2011/375	Brooker v. Trent	mt	Meet counsel for Trent to discuss settlement	1	2
2011/375	Brooker v. Trent	mt	Travel to Trent and return		5
2011/375	Brooker v. Trent	tc	Call and discussion with client re settlement offer		6
2011/432	Fox sale to Kim	tcl	Call to Kim's lawyer re requisitions		5
Daily Total				12	3

NOTES:

Computerized Time and Fee Sheets

Computerized time and fee sheets are a time-efficient and accurate way to log billable time, non-billable time, and flat fees. Time spent is directly entered into the database, either during a task or after the task is completed. This procedure eliminates duplication of time entries.

In PCLaw, when you enter a matter number into the program time sheet, the lawyer and billing-rate information is automatically retrieved, and the billable amount is calculated. The time spent is automatically recorded against the associated client matter. When you enter the matter number into the program fee sheet, the lawyer information is automatically retrieved. You can then enter the applicable flat fee and description to the associated client matter.

Figure 6.4 shows a computerized time sheet in PCLaw.

FIGURE 6.4 PCLaw time sheet

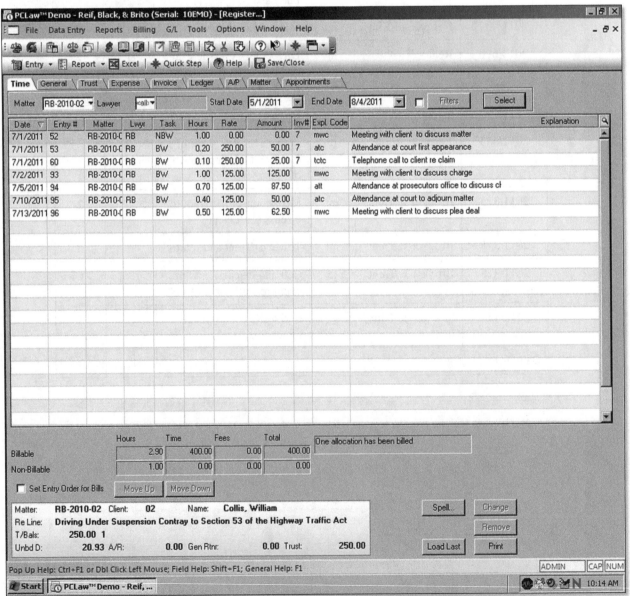

FIGURE 6.5   PCLaw fee sheet

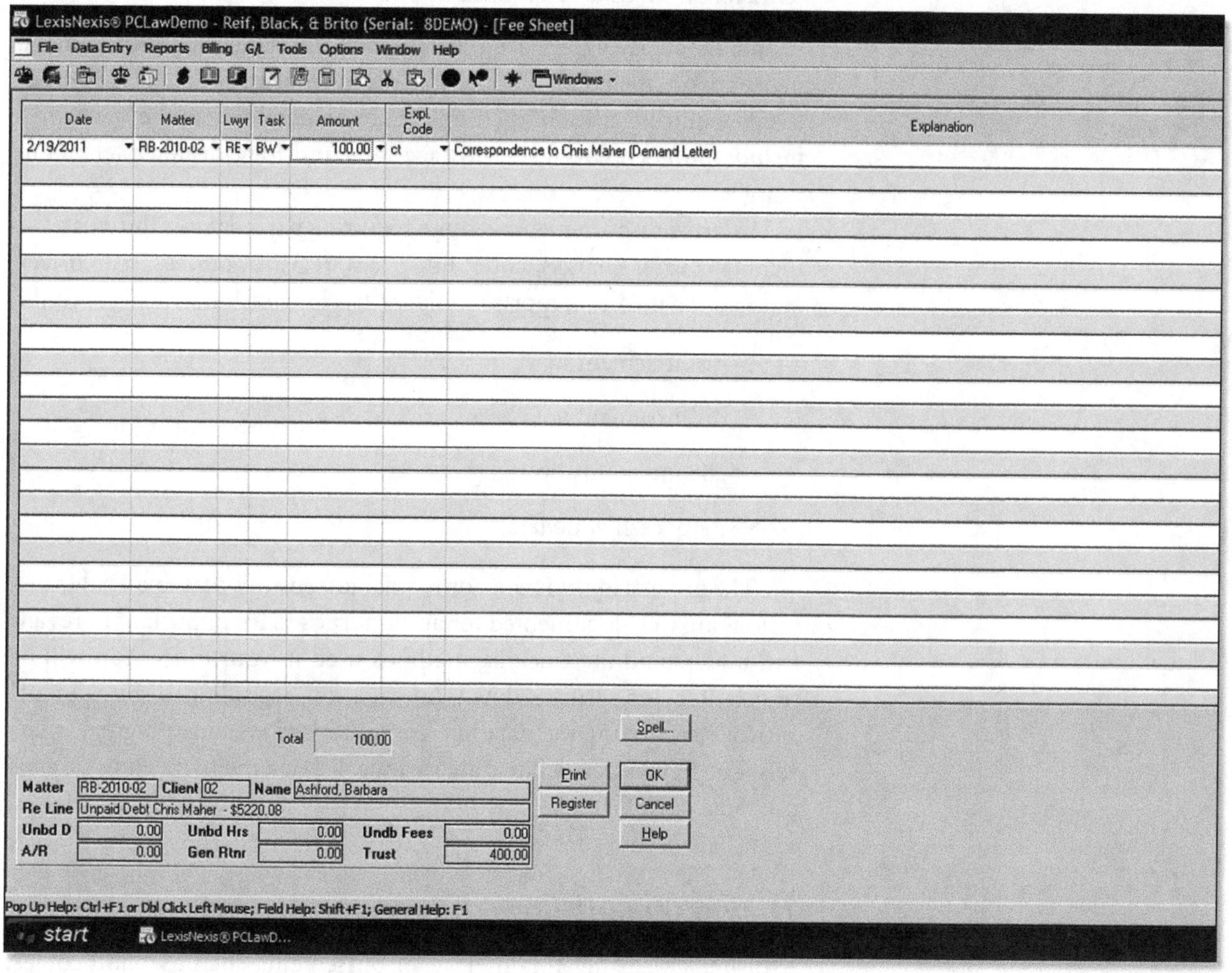

Diary

Lawyers often use desk diaries or appointment calendars to docket time spent on client activities. Some offices maintain duplicate diaries, one belonging to the lawyer and the other at the front desk. At the end of each day, photocopy the lawyer's diary page and enter the information into a computerized system. As with the time sheet, stamp the diary page as "posted" and file it in a dedicated area by date.

NOTES:

Client Disbursements

Disbursements are fees the lawyer pays on behalf of the client.

In addition to paying legal fees, clients reimburse lawyers for disbursements incurred on their behalf. Internal disbursements—that is, disbursements requiring tasks to be completed by an employee in the law firm—include photocopies, faxes, postage fees, and long-distance telephone charges.

External disbursements—those requiring payment to a third party—include courier charges, court filing fees, registration fees, search fees, and fees for medical reports. Tools for tracking disbursements include:

- disbursement logs

- disbursement vouchers

- cheque requisitions

- petty cash vouchers.

The use of a log, voucher, or requisition ensures that financial transactions are well documented for audit purposes. It's important to review and understand the tracking methods used in your office. You will be responsible for writing down information regarding disbursements and/or for entering the data in a computerized system at regular intervals. The figures below illustrate various disbursement-tracking systems used in a law office.

Disbursement Logs

A disbursement log for internal disbursements such as photocopies, faxes, and postage is an effective means of tracking these costs.

A manual log for photocopies (shown in figure 6.6) includes

- the date

- the file name

- the matter number

- the number of copies

- the initials or signature of the person making copies.

A fax log (shown in figure 6.7) includes

- the date

- the file name

- the matter number

- the fax number called

- the initials or signature of the person sending the fax.

FIGURE 6.6   Photocopy log

	PHOTOCOPY LOG			
Date	File Name	Matter #	# of Copies	Initials
July 10/2011	French, Patrick	11-201	8	DC
July 11/2011	Miller, Janice	10-113	2	JM

FIGURE 6.7   Fax log

	FAX LOG			
Date	File Name	Matter #	Fax To	Initials
July 10/2011	French, Meghan	10-228	705-939-1657	DC

Many law practices have photocopiers, fax machines, and telephone systems that require the entry of a matter number before use. Fax and copy machines with this feature allow you to print a report, either on request or at predetermined intervals. The report contains disbursement details that can be allocated to individual matters. In the case of long-distance calls, the invoice from the phone company identifies the client for each call.

Disbursement Vouchers and Cheque Requisitions

Other methods of tracking disbursements are disbursement vouchers for internal disbursements and cheque requisitions for external disbursements. A disbursement voucher includes

- the date

- the matter number

- the type/description of disbursement

- a disbursement code (for example, ps = postage,
  ph = photocopies, fx = facsimile)

- the initials or signature of the person logging the information.

Figure 6.8 is an example of a disbursement voucher used in a law office.

In most cases, external disbursements are paid by cheque. A cheque requisition includes

- the date

- the matter number

- the reason for request

- a disbursement code

- the dollar amount

- a notation with respect to GST/HST applicability

- the signature of the person requesting the funds

- the signature of the person authorizing the funds.

Figure 6.9 is an example of a cheque requisition used in a law office.

Using Technology for Disbursements

The information recorded on logs, vouchers, and requisitions is entered into a computerized system for payment and billing purposes. In a large firm, this process is completed by an accounting department; in a small firm, it is usually performed by a designated person.

Client expenses are entered in a number of different ways. Figure 6.10 shows how PCLaw enables you to bill the client for a charge before paying the expense. Figure 6.11 shows how PCLaw enables you to write a cheque to Bell Canada and allocate a portion of the invoice to a specific matter. Both the client ledger and the bank journal are automatically updated when a cheque is entered.

NOTES:

FIGURE 6.8   Disbursement voucher

DISBURSEMENT VOUCHER

Date: _____   Matter #: _____

Type/Description of Disbursement: _____

Photocopies: _____   Fax: _____

Long Distance: _____   Other: _____

Code: _____

Initials: _____

FIGURE 6.9   Cheque requisition

CHEQUE REQUISITION

Date: _____   Matter #: _____

Requisition #: _____

Invoice #: _____

From: Trust Account _____   General Account _____

Payable to: _____

Reason: _____

Date Cheque Required: _____

Code: _____   Amount: _____

GST/HST: _____

Total Cheque: _____

Requested by: _____

Authorized by: _____

FIGURE 6.10 PCLaw expense recovery

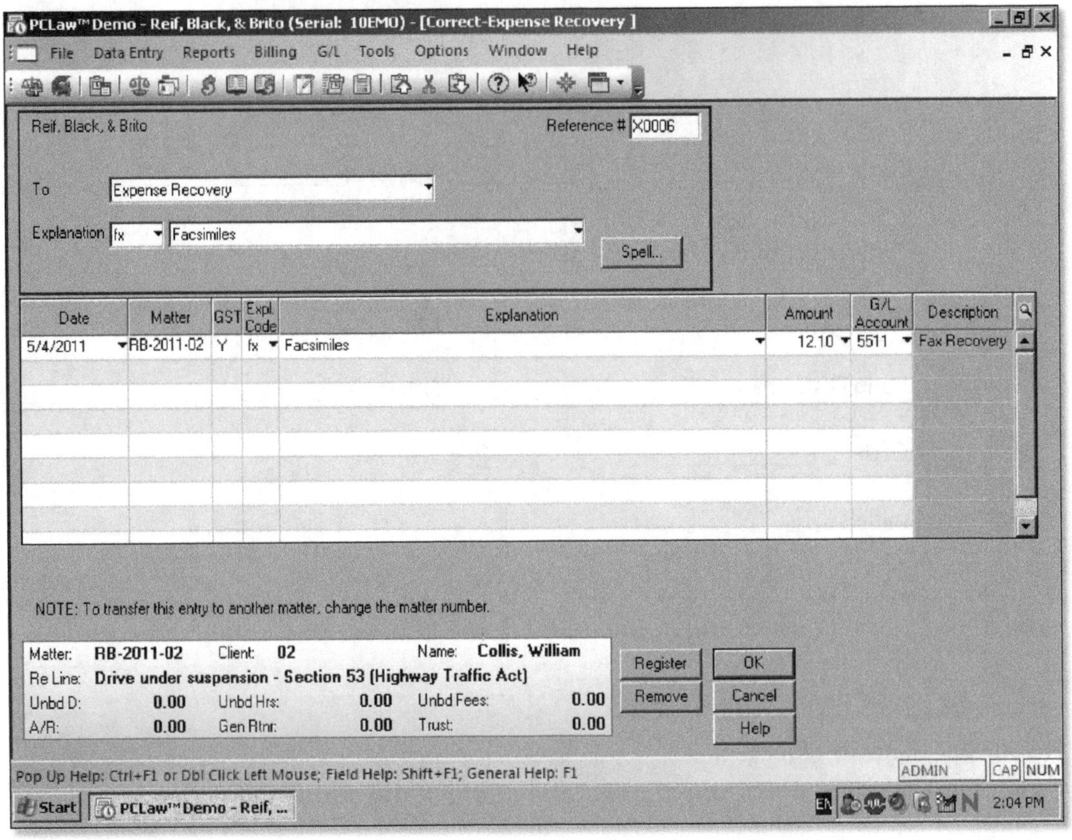

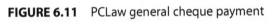

FIGURE 6.11 PCLaw general cheque payment

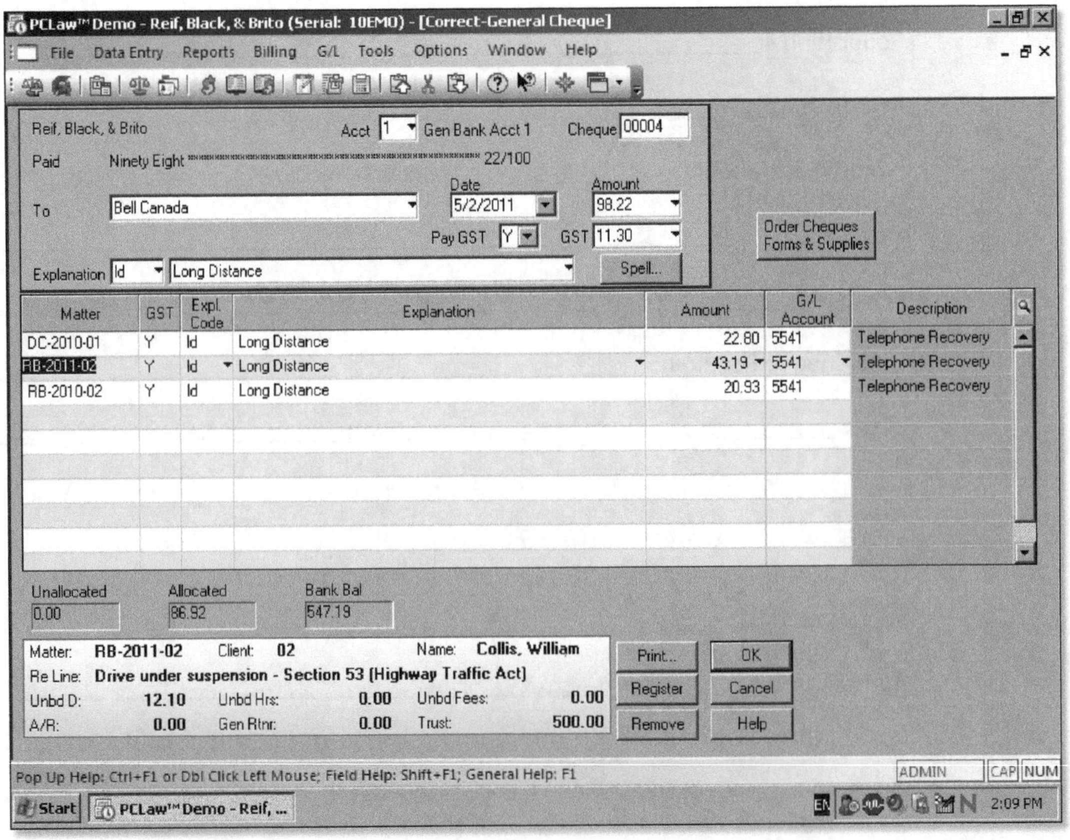

Petty Cash

Usually, business expenses are paid by cheque or electronic funds transfer. However, there are situations where immediate access to cash is necessary. Petty cash provides quick access to funds required for items such as postage, miscellaneous business supplies, or a COD (cash on delivery) expense.

A petty cash fund is established by the withdrawal, by cheque, of a predetermined amount of money from the firm's general bank account. Most law practices have an established policy of acceptable expenditures for petty cash disbursements. A designated person in the office maintains control and administration of the fund and keeps the cash in a locked metal cash box. If you need funds from petty cash, you should provide a receipt. Keep the receipt in the petty cash box as evidence that the funds were withdrawn. If you cannot provide a receipt, a petty cash voucher is required for approval and audit purposes. At all times, the amount of the vouchers or receipts and the amount of the remaining cash should equal the original amount of the petty cash fund.

Basic petty cash vouchers are available at any office supply store, or can be created with word-processing software. Figure 6.12 shows an example of a petty cash voucher. A completed voucher includes

- the date of the voucher

- the associated matter number (if applicable)

- the name of the person requesting payment

- the reason for the payment

FIGURE 6.12 Petty cash voucher

PETTY CASH VOUCHER

Date: _____ Matter #: _____

Paid to: _____

Reason: _____

Code: _____ Amount: _____

HST: _____

Total: _____

Requested by: _____

Authorized by: _____

- the accounting or disbursement code

- the amount of the payment including HST

- the signature of the person requesting the payment

- the signature of the person who authorized the payment.

Reconcile the petty cash fund each month and replenish it either on an as-needed basis or on an established monthly protocol.

Bank Accounts

Law societies have strict rules regarding the collection, retention, and disbursement of "trust money," which is money received from clients. This money can take various forms—retainers, funds from the distribution of estates, conveyance funds, settlement funds, etc. Any money received from or on behalf of a client is considered trust money and must be deposited into a trust account (often called a "mixed" or "pooled" trust account). These funds belong to the client and cannot be withdrawn or disbursed without client consent.

Law society rules require that lawyers (and in Ontario, paralegals) who handle trust moneys maintain at least two bank accounts: a trust account and a general account. The rules specify that trust accounts must be kept at one of the following kinds of financial institutions:

- a chartered bank

- a registered trust company

- a credit union.

Trust funds are moneys that belong to the client.

General funds are moneys that belong to the lawyer (and in Ontario, the paralegal).

Trust accounts are covered by LSUC bylaw 9, part IV, subsections 7(1), (2), and (3).

The general account is the lawyer's bank account for operating the business.

Lawyers must maintain a separate set of books for each account—one for the general account and one for the trust account. In order to avoid confusion, some use cheques of different colours for each account.

Law firms must also maintain separate deposit books and receipt books for each account. These books are clearly labelled to avoid confusion.

General Bank Account

A general account is set up to pay for the lawyer's business expenses such as rent, mortgage payments, office supplies, and payroll. Money deposited into this account is money that is

- collected from a client for legal services that have been billed

- received from a client to reimburse the lawyer for expenses paid on the client's behalf.

Depending on your employer, you may be given signing authority on general accounts. That is, you may be authorized to deposit funds into the general account and to sign cheques to pay for expenses out of the account.

Trust Account

A trust account, also referred to as a mixed or pooled account, is set up for the money that belongs in whole or in part to a client. If you do not receive funds from, or for, clients for any reason except as payment for your billed and delivered fees and disbursements, you need not maintain a trust account.

Money that is deposited into this account is money that is

- advanced as a retainer for fees or disbursements not yet billed

- held on behalf of a client

- held on a client's direction or order

- paid to the lawyer where it is not practical to split the payment of money in part to the client and in part to the lawyer.

Law society rules prohibit a non-lawyer (and in Ontario, a non-paralegal) from having signing authority on trust accounts.

However, a law clerk or assistant may be asked to co-sign cheques. A second signature of a non-lawyer is often employed as an internal audit control.

Lawyers have a *fiduciary obligation* to protect client funds and keep them separate from their business assets. A fiduciary obligation is a legal duty of a lawyer to look after the well-being of a client. The client relies on the lawyer to perform his or her duty in the client's best interests.

If the funds of more than one client are maintained in the same trust account, you should create and maintain a record of all trust transactions in and out of the account—that is, of trust receipts and disbursements, respectively. Figure 6.13 illustrates a trust receipts journal and figure 6.14 illustrates a trust disbursements journal.

You must also create account journals to track all transactions in and out of the trust account.

Figure 6.15 illustrates a trust bank journal in PCLaw, showing both receipts and disbursements for three clients.

Separate client trust ledgers must also be maintained for each client. A client ledger is a chronological record of all trust transactions for a particular client. Figure 6.16 illustrates a client trust ledger in a manual system. Figure 6.17 shows a client ledger in PCLaw, illustrating all legal activity related to one client.

DID YOU KNOW?

The word **fiduciary** is Latin for trust.

FIGURE 6.13 Trust receipts journal

Donna Woodrow			
Barrister & Solicitor			
TRUST RECEIPTS JOURNAL			
Date (20--)	Received from: *[Source of funds]*	Client	Amount
February 20	Camden Carpenter	Carpenter re: purchase 1193 Grandview	800.00
March 1	Elizabeth Campbell	Campbell re: Will	750.00
April 5	Ryder Hadwyn	Hadwyn re: Adoption	400.00

FIGURE 6.14 Trust disbursements journal

Donna Woodrow				
Barrister & Solicitor				
TRUST DISBURSEMENTS JOURNAL				
Date (20--)	Method/ No.	Paid to: *[Person money paid to]*	Client	Amount
February 28	Chq. 313	Land Registry	Carpenter re: Purchase 1193 Grandview	300.00
March 30	Chq. 314	Donna Woodrow	Campbell re: Will	750.00
April 30	Chq. 315	Donna Woodrow	Hadwyn re: Adoption	400.00

NOTES:

FIGURE 6.15 PCLaw trust bank journal

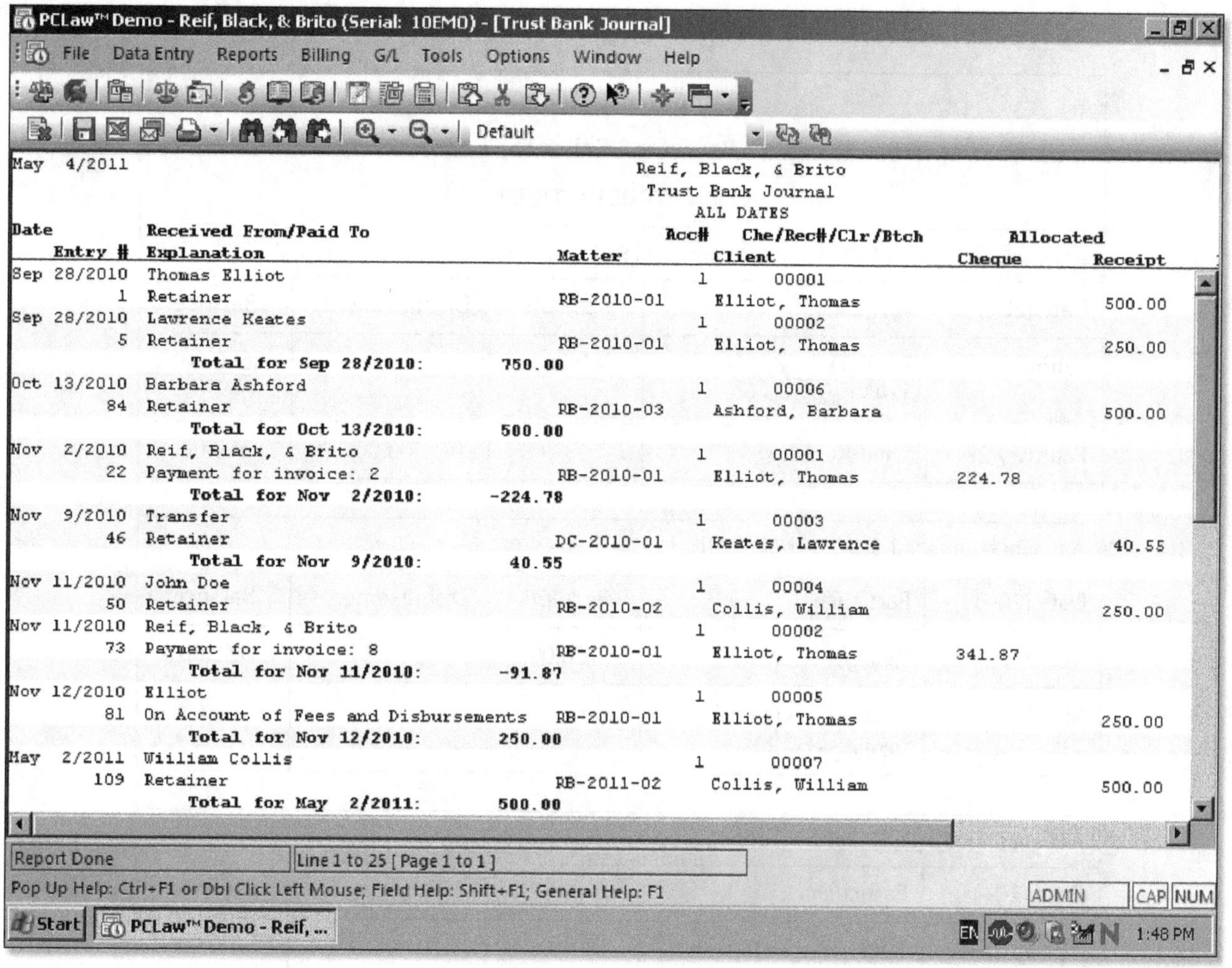

May 4/2011

Reif, Black, & Brito
Trust Bank Journal
ALL DATES

Date / Entry #	Received From/Paid To / Explanation	Matter	Acc# / Client	Che/Rec#/Clr/Btch	Allocated Cheque	Allocated Receipt
Sep 28/2010	Thomas Elliot		1	00001		
1	Retainer	RB-2010-01	Elliot, Thomas			500.00
Sep 28/2010	Lawrence Keates		1	00002		
5	Retainer	RB-2010-01	Elliot, Thomas			250.00
	Total for Sep 28/2010:	**750.00**				
Oct 13/2010	Barbara Ashford		1	00006		
84	Retainer	RB-2010-03	Ashford, Barbara			500.00
	Total for Oct 13/2010:	**500.00**				
Nov 2/2010	Reif, Black, & Brito		1	00001		
22	Payment for invoice: 2	RB-2010-01	Elliot, Thomas		224.78	
	Total for Nov 2/2010:	**-224.78**				
Nov 9/2010	Transfer		1	00003		
46	Retainer	DC-2010-01	Keates, Lawrence			40.55
	Total for Nov 9/2010:	**40.55**				
Nov 11/2010	John Doe		1	00004		
50	Retainer	RB-2010-02	Collis, William			250.00
Nov 11/2010	Reif, Black, & Brito		1	00002		
73	Payment for invoice: 8	RB-2010-01	Elliot, Thomas		341.87	
	Total for Nov 11/2010:	**-91.87**				
Nov 12/2010	Elliot		1	00005		
81	On Account of Fees and Disbursements	RB-2010-01	Elliot, Thomas			250.00
	Total for Nov 12/2010:	**250.00**				
May 2/2011	William Collis		1	00007		
109	Retainer	RB-2011-02	Collis, William			500.00
	Total for May 2/2011:	**500.00**				

NOTES:

FIGURE 6.16   Client trust ledger

Donna Woodrow

Barrister & Solicitor

CLIENT TRUST LEDGER

Account: Carpenter, Camden re: Purchase 1193 Grandview

Date (20--)	Particulars	Receipts	Disbursements	Balance
February 20	Retainer re: Purchase 1193 Grandview	800.00		800.00
February 28	Land Registry		300.00	500.00

Account: Campbell, Elizabeth re: Will

Date (20--)	Particulars	Receipts	Disbursements	Balance
March 1	Retainer re: Will	750.00		750.00
March 30	Transfer to General Invoice #1212		750.00	0.00

Account: Hadwyn, Ryder re: Adoption

Date (20--)	Particulars	Receipts	Disbursements	Balance
April 5	Retainer re: Adoption	400.00		400.00
April 30	Transfer to General Invoice #1268		400.00	0.00

NOTES:

FIGURE 6.17   PCLaw client ledger

Receipt of Trust Funds

When trust funds are received, you must complete a trust receipt. The trust receipt provides the client with proof of payment. The funds are then posted to (deposited in) the correct client account. The receipt identifies

- the name of the person who provided the money
- the date received
- the file name and matter number.

Give the original receipt to the client and put a copy of the receipt in the client file. A second copy stays in the receipt book or is forwarded to the accounting department for data entry purposes. Figure 6.18 shows the format of a handwritten receipt.

Some computerized systems allow you to enter the amount of funds received from a client directly into the particular client ledger and then print a receipt. Figure 6.19 shows this function in PCLaw.

Trust money must be deposited to the trust account as soon as possible. If the funds cannot be deposited on the day they are received, keep the cheque (or cash) in a safe or locked cabinet. Write "for deposit only" on all incoming cheques and place a photocopy of the cheque in the client file. When preparing the deposit slip, note the date and the matter number on the slip. For confidentiality purposes, do not include the client name. When using an automatic teller, attach the ATM receipt to the duplicate deposit slip. An example of a deposit slip is shown in figure 6.20.

FIGURE 6.18 Handwritten receipt

No. *20--/13* *September 19*, 20*--*

Received from *Barbie Cole DC-11-234*

Two Hundred Fifty *xx/100* Dollars

$ *250.00* *Linda Reif*

FIGURE 6.19   PCLaw trust receipt

NOTES:

FIGURE 6.20   Detailed duplicate trust account deposit slip

DEPOSIT SLIP
Current Account
TD CANADA TRUST

CREDIT ACCOUNT OF:
Woodrow & Perry
Barristers & Solicitors
Trust Account

Date:

20--	01	10

Transit

5 4 3 2 1

Account Number

1 2 3 4 5 6 7 8 9 0

TELLER STAMP

Depositor's
Initials
Teller's
Initials

Cheques and Credit Card Vouchers			Details		Cash	
File #98/20--	1000	00	×	$5		
			×	$10		
			×	$20		
			×	$50		
			×	$100		
			×			
			×			
			coin			
			Cdn Cash Total		nil	
TOTAL	1000	00	Credit Card Vouchers and Cheques Forwarded		1000	00

Disbursement of Trust Funds

Dealing with trust funds is subject to law society rules. It is important to protect the funds from loss or the appearance of impropriety. Lawyers (and in Ontario, paralegals) must never withdraw funds from a mixed or pooled trust account unless the client for whom the withdrawal is made has sufficient funds in the account. That is, funds cannot be borrowed from one client to pay another client's expenses. If a client has not advanced any funds, any disbursements made on their behalf are paid from the general account and are reimbursed by the client at the time of billing.

You can disburse trust fund money by cheque or by an account-to-account transfer. A lawyer must sign the cheques for this transaction. Never make a cheque payable to "cash" or "bearer" or withdraw cash from the trust account.

Pursuant to law society rules, only the following funds may be disbursed or withdrawn for the trust account:

- money required for payment to a client or the person acting on behalf of a client

- money to reimburse the lawyer for money expended on behalf of a client

- money received in payment of fees for services performed for which a client has been billed

- money directly transferred into another trust account and held on behalf of a client

- money that should not have been paid into a trust account but was inadvertently paid into the trust account

- other money authorized by the law society—for example, interest earned from the trust account.

With regard to the last point, the client and the lawyer do not receive interest on the money deposited in the trust account. Your lawyer must write a letter directing the bank or financial institution where the trust account is kept to periodically remit interest earned on the money to the provincial law foundation. Figure 6.21 shows a sample letter of direction provided by the LSUC. If more than one mixed trust account is maintained, a separate direction must be given for each one.

Service charges on the trust account are paid from the general bank account.

FIGURE 6.21 Letter of direction

LETTER OF DIRECTION

To: The Manager

Name of Bank: *[Name of chartered bank or financial institution]*

Branch:

Address:

Re: The Law Foundation of Ontario and Account No. _____

The above account is _____ in my name.

_____ in the name of the firm with which I am associated.

In accordance with section 57 of the *Law Society Act*, I direct you, until further notice, to compute the amount earned by applying to the balance in the above account the rate of interest approved from time to time by the Trustees of the Law Foundation of Ontario. Please pay into an account held in your main office in Ontario in the name of the Law Foundation of Ontario amounts so calculated and give written notice to me at the address shown on the above account and to the Law Foundation of Ontario, 20 Queen Street West, Suite 2210, Box #19, Toronto, Ontario, M5H 3R3, when each such payment is made. This notice should show, as applicable, the amounts of the payment, and the amounts of the daily/monthly balances, and the rates of interest used in computing the payment.

Dated the _____ day of _____, 20___

_____

[Signed]

Firm Name: Woodrow & Perry, Barristers & Solicitors

Address: 1605 Treetop Road
Peterborough, Ontario
K9K 1G2

Trust Reconciliation

As explained, lawyers (and in Ontario, paralegals) have a responsibility to comply with law society rules regarding trust accounts. Those who improperly handle client trust funds may be reprimanded, fined, suspended, or even disbarred from practice. The law society recommends preparing a trust reconciliation by the 25th of each month. Once satisfied with the reconciliation, it must be signed and dated by the lawyer (and in Ontario, the paralegal).

To complete a bank reconciliation:

1. Compare the balance of your bank account in your bank statement to the balance according to your accounting records.

2. Identify the cause(s) of any difference that exists between the two records.

3. Adjust your accounting records to reflect the transactions since the reporting date.

4. Correct any errors made by you or the bank in recording transactions.

You must reconcile trust accounts monthly—that is, you must check your record of each client trust balance against the bank's trust account balance. These two amounts must be the same. You must also reconcile your trust journal with the client ledgers to make sure they agree. Beware: Incidental errors are bound to occur; no amount of training can eliminate them. However, regular reconciliations can prevent costly errors that could affect your lawyer both financially and professionally. Figure 6.22 is an example of a trust reconciliation report.

NOTES:

FIGURE 6.22   Trust reconciliation report

Woodrow & Perry
Barristers and Solicitors
Trust Reconciliation
March 31, 20--

Mixed Trust Account
Balance per Bank Statements March 31, 20--:

Balance per bank statements	$29,925.19
Add outstanding deposits	2,000.00
Minus outstanding cheques	3,831.08
Adjusted balance per bank statement	**$28,094.19**

Outstanding Cheques:

Cheque #	Date	Amount
126	Mar 29, 20--	1,000.00
127	Mar 29, 20--	2,831.08
Total Outstanding Cheques		$3,831.08

Woodrow & Perry
Barristers and Solicitors
Trust (Listing) Ledger Trial Balance
March 31, 20--

File Name	Matter No.	Last Activity Date	Amount
Batten	DC-10-312	Feb 4, 20--	6,110.74
Burgis	AK-10-80	Dec 24, 20--	5,687.96
Carpenter	AK-10-111	Jan 3, 20--	940.00
Collis	DC-11-05	Jan 5, 20--	750.00
Guerin	DC-10-202	Nov 17, 20--	1,710.00
Hadwyn	KK-11-31	Feb 20, 20--	2,500.00
Keates	KK-11-59	Jan 17, 20--	5,000.00
Miller	DC-11-297	Mar 15, 20--	2,000.00
Rathwell	KK-10-428	Mar 20, 20--	2,395.49
Thain	AK-11-258	Mar 1, 20--	1,000.00

Total funds held in trust as per Trust Ledger:	$28,094.19

TRUST COMPARISON
AS AT March 31, 20--

Total Reconciled Trust Bank Balance	$28,094.19
(See Trust Reconciliation above)	
Total of unexpended balances per Clients' Trust Ledger	$28,094.19
(See Trust (Listing) Ledger Trial Balance above)	

Law Practices and GST/HST

All Canadians pay 5 percent goods and services tax (GST) and a provincial sales tax (PST). The PST percentage amount varies from province to province. Harmonized sales tax (HST) is payable in British Columbia (12%), Ontario (13%), Nova Scotia (15%), New Brunswick (13%), and Newfoundland and Labrador (13%). These provinces have harmonized their GST with their provincial sales tax (PST). In all other provinces and territories, GST is paid separately from PST. GST or HST is charged on most purchased goods and services, and the tax collected is periodically remitted to the federal government.

Note that figures 6.23, 6.24, and 6.25 assume an HST rate of 13 percent.

Because lawyers provide legal services to their clients and charge fees for those services, they must collect GST/HST on those services. Lawyers also pay disbursements on behalf of their clients. Under the *Excise Tax Act*, some disbursements are subject to GST/HST while others are not.

If a lawyer pays GST/HST on behalf of a client, the lawyer is entitled to collect the GST/HST from the client.

General disbursements such as postage, long-distance telephone calls, and faxes are subject to GST/HST. However, some offices choose not to charge these costs back to their clients, viewing them simply as a cost of doing business.

Other disbursements are subject or not subject to GST/HST depending on whether they are "incurred as agent" or "not incurred as agent." "Incurred as agent" means that the disbursement is incurred or disbursed in the lawyer's capacity as an agent for a particular client.

In GST/HST Policy Statement P-209R (July 7, 2004), the Canada Revenue Agency describes how a lawyer's disbursements are treated in relation to GST or HST. The policy statement outlines the various areas of practice and the guidelines applicable to GST or HST collection. It's available online at http://www.cra-arc.gc.ca/E/pub/gl/p-209r.

Disbursements Not Subject to GST or HST

Generally, any fees that a government body charges to register, issue, and file documents or to obtain information are not subject to GST or HST. These fees are referred to as agency disbursements because the lawyer has acted as an agent on behalf of the client. Examples of such disbursements include fees paid

- for zoning and development permits
- to a Land Titles office or Registry office
- to file an application for registration of intellectual property
- to incorporate or register a business
- to register, change, or discharge an encumbrance

- for licences and permits to use, occupy, sell, and operate property and shares
- to start legal proceedings such as originating process (statement of claim or application for divorce)
- to file a defence or a notice of intent to defend
- to obtain a writ of possession
- to file an application for probate.

Disbursements Subject to GST or HST

Generally, disbursements subject to GST or HST are on funds paid on behalf of a client to a third party. Examples include fees paid for

- medical reports
- title searches
- municipal searches, including information related to tax arrears, outstanding work orders, and permit violations
- utility searches, including details related to outstanding debts
- patent searches
- trademark searches
- a witness's services (witness fee)
- transcripts
- service of a document
- expert opinions
- birth, death, and marriage certificates.

Client Billing

Accounts are billed to clients at regular intervals or when work on the file is complete. The billing process varies from office to office and its details are determined by established practices and procedures. Billing procedures can also vary depending on the type of accounting system that is used by the law firm. In some firms, the accounting department completes all billing; in other firms, you will be responsible for preparing the bill and giving the accounting department a copy of the bill. The steps in a typical billing procedure in a legal office are as follows:

1. produce a report
2. produce a pre-bill (also called a sample or draft bill)
3. review the pre-bill
4. adjust the client account
5. produce the bill in final format
6. produce the accompanying statement of account cover letter.

Regardless of the type of legal accounting system that is used in your office (manual, electronic, or a combination of the two), the billing process begins with the creation of a report that indicates billable time and disbursements allocated to the client. Check the report for any obvious data entry errors.

The report shown in figure 6.23 is produced in PCLaw; other systems produce reports with similar data.

Once you are satisfied with the report information, you are ready to move on to the next step.

Print a draft bill, review it for missed entries, double entries, or entries posted to an incorrect file. Also check for any spelling or typographical errors and make notes of any questionable information on the pre-bill. This is your opportunity to make any necessary amendments to the information.

The lawyer responsible for the file should then review the amended pre-bill for any further adjustments. It is the responsibility of the lawyer who handled the matter being billed to determine the fees to charge the client. Lawyers often make a handwritten notation of adjustments that are needed on the draft bill.

FIGURE 6.23 PCLaw billing journal

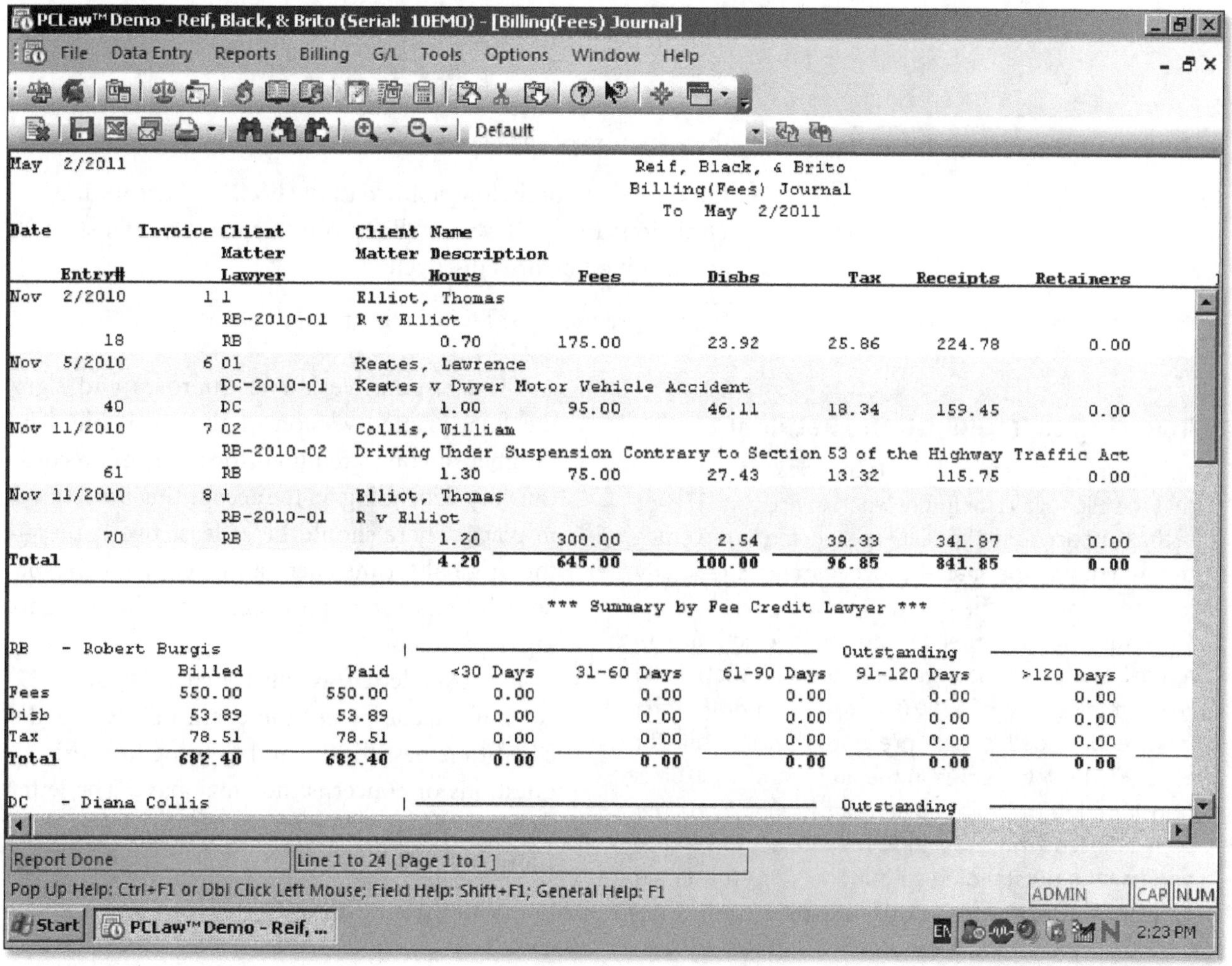

After the lawyer's review, adjust the pre-bill as necessary using the appropriate procedures. It is quite common to produce a second or third pre-bill for a final check before the bill is considered final.

Once you are satisfied with the information, print the bill in its final format on the firm's letterhead. Figures 6.24, 6.25, and 6.26 show examples of client bills in various formats. There are many acceptable formats for client bills. A client bill may include some or all of the following elements:

- the date of the account at the top or at the end of the bill

- the name and address of the client

- the file number

- the billing period

- the file name

- an introductory paragraph ("For professional services rendered …")

- the amount of fees charged plus GST/HST

- the amount of taxable disbursements plus GST/HST

- the amount of tax-exempt disbursements

- a list of payments on account received during the billing period

- a trust transfer amount, if applicable

- the signature of the lawyer

- the errors and omissions abbreviation (E&OE—"Errors and Omissions Except"), which allows you to correct or adjust an account if an error is discovered

- the law practice's GST/HST registration number.

Invoicing to Replenish the Retainer

As discussed, a "retainer fee" is an advance payment that the client pays for future legal services, and is kept in the trust account. The client is expected to replenish the retainer as the matter proceeds, and is regularly invoiced while the file is in progress. For example, assume that Jacob Pepper has just retained your firm in a legal matter. The lawyer has requested that Jacob pay a retainer fee of $300.00. At the end of the first invoice period, Jacob is presented with a bill for $255.90. The retainer fee in the amount of $300.00 is transferred to the invoiced amount, leaving a retainer of $0.00. Jacob must replenish the retainer to $300.00 and pay the outstanding amount of $255.90, totaling $555.90, before he receives his next invoice.

The responsible lawyer approves and signs the final printed version of the client bill. The number of copies required for the firm's records can vary depending on the accounting procedures in place. There should be at least two copies—the original for the client and a copy for the file. Some offices also require a copy for the accounting department.

A cover letter, as illustrated in figure 6.27, generally accompanies the client bill. It asks the client to review the bill and to bring forward any questions or concerns they may have. The letter shown in figure 6.28 requests the client to replenish trust funds.

FIGURE 6.24   Client bill trust not transferred

WOODROW & PERRY

Barristers & Solicitors

1605 Treetop Road
Peterborough, Ontario
K9K 1G2

woodrow.perry@shaw.ca

Telephone: 705-743-5796
Facsimile: 705-749-3492

File # RB-2011-02

May 30, 2011

William Collis
10 Grammy Drive
Peterborough, ON
K9J 1L2

RE: Drive Under Suspension Contrary to Section 53 (*Highway Traffic Act*)

DATE	DESCRIPTION	HOURS	AMOUNT	LAWYER
May-02-11	Meeting with client to discuss charge	1.00	95.00	DC
	Attendance at prosecutors office	0.70	66.50	DC
	Attendance at court to adjourn matter	0.40	38.00	DC
	Meeting with client to discuss plea options	0.50	47.50	DC
	Totals	2.60	$247.00	
	Total HST on Fees		32.11	

DISBURSEMENTS

	Long Distance	43.19		
	Totals	$43.19		
	Total HST on Disbursements	5.61		
	Total Fee & Disbursements		**$327.91**	
	Balance Now Due		**$327.91**	
Total HST	$37.72			

TRUST STATEMENT

		Disbursements	Receipts
May-02-11	Received From: William Collis		500.00
	Retainer		
	Total Trust	$0.00	$500.00
	Trust Balance		**$500.00**

FIGURE 6.25 Transferring trust

WOODROW & PERRY

Barristers & Solicitors

1605 Treetop Road
Peterborough, Ontario
K9K 1G2

woodrow.perry@shaw.ca

Telephone: 705-743-5796
Facsimile: 705-749-3492

February 1, 20--

Jacob Pepper
12 Maher Drive
Toronto, ON
M3C 2V6

RE: Criminal Charges

DATE	DESCRIPTION	HOURS	AMOUNT	LAWYER
Jan-02-20--	Meeting with Client (Initial Interview)	0.50	100.00	TB
Jan-05-20--	Attend Adjournment	0.50	100.00	TB
Jan-15-20--	Meet with Crown	0.80	160.00	TB
Jan-28-20--	Report to Client	0.50	100.00	TB
	Total	2.30	460.00	TB
	Total HST on Fees		59.80	

DISBURSEMENTS

Photocopies	$22.00	
Long Distance/Fax	9.95	
Total Disbursements	31.95	
Total HST on Disbursements	4.15	
Total Fees and Disbursements		**555.90**
Amount transferred from trust		−300.00

AMOUNT DUE WOODROW & PERRY   **$255.90**

TRUST STATEMENT

Date	Details	Amount	Balance
Jan-02-20--	Received from you	300.00	300.00
Feb-01-20--	Paid to Woodrow & Perry	−300.00	0.00

E&OE
HST No. 1222611811

FIGURE 6.26   Client bill showing flat fee

WOODROW & PERRY
Barristers & Solicitors

1605 Treetop Road
Peterborough, Ontario
K9K 1G2

woodrow.perry@shaw.ca

Telephone: 705-743-5796
Facsimile: 705-749-3492

June 1, 20--

Barbara Ashford
1301 Charlotte Street, Unit 1
Peterborough, ON
K9J 7Y4

INVOICE

Date:	May 10, 20--
Court Location:	Belleville Provincial Court – Room B
Reason:	Adjournment of **Ashford** matter
Results:	Matter set for trial – August 5, 20--, 10 a.m. – Courtroom A
FEE:	**$100.00**
HST:	13.00
Total	**$113.00**

Thank you for choosing Woodrow & Perry.

_____
Donna Woodrow

FIGURE 6.27 Client bill cover letter

WOODROW & PERRY
Barristers & Solicitors

1605 Treetop Road
Peterborough, Ontario
K9K 1G2
Telephone: 705-743-5796
Facsimile: 705-749-3492

woodrow.perry@shaw.ca

File # 20--/238

October 30, 20--

Jacob Pepper
12 Maher Drive
Toronto, ON
M3C 2V6

RE: Criminal Charges

Please find enclosed my statement of account, in the amount of $255.90 for the professional services I have rendered on your behalf. I trust you will find it satisfactory. However, please review it carefully. If you have any questions or concerns, feel free to call me. According to the terms of our Solicitor–Client Agreement, this invoice is due upon receipt. For your convenience, I have enclosed a stamped self-addressed envelope.

Thank you for your time and attention to this letter. If you have any questions, please do not hesitate to contact me.

Yours truly,

WOODROW & PERRY

Donna Woodrow

DW/dc

Encl. Statement of Account

FIGURE 6.28   Sample statement of account letter requesting replenishment of trust funds

WOODROW & PERRY
Barristers & Solicitors

1605 Treetop Road
Peterborough, Ontario
K9K 1G2
Telephone: 705-743-5796
Facsimile: 705-749-3492

woodrow.perry@shaw.ca

File # 20--/238

October 30, 20--

Jacob Pepper
12 Maher Drive
Toronto, ON
M3C 2V6

RE: Criminal Charges

Please find enclosed my statement of account for the professional services I have rendered on your behalf. I trust you will find it satisfactory. However, please review it carefully. If you have any questions or concerns, feel free to call me. According to the terms of our Solicitor–Client Agreement, this invoice is due upon receipt. For your convenience, I have enclosed a stamped, self-addressed envelope.

Also as per our Solicitor–Client Agreement, trust funds are to be maintained at $300.00. As you can see, your current Trust Fund balance is $0.00. I would appreciate it if you would include a payment of $300.00 to bring your trust account up to date, for a final total payment of $559.50.

Thank you for your time and attention to this letter. If you have any questions, please do not hesitate to contact me.

Yours truly,

Donna Woodrow

DW/dc

Encl. Statement of Account

Legal Aid in Canada

In Canada, everyone is entitled to representation in court. This principle is supported by the Legal Aid system. If a litigant cannot afford to pay for a lawyer, the governing body of the system—either the provincial government or the provincial law society—will review an application to determine his or her eligibility for financially assisted representation.

Qualifying

Eligibility for Legal Aid differs from province to province, but generally applicants are required to demonstrate their need by providing financial records. The various Legal Aid plans generally cover criminal law, family law, and immigration law matters.

If the reviewing agency determines that a person is eligible for financial assistance, and that the legal matter involved is covered by the particular Legal Aid plan, assistance is granted.

The person then selects a lawyer, provided that the chosen lawyer accepts Legal Aid clients. In some provinces there are on-staff Legal Aid lawyers who are assigned to deal with client matters. A lawyer who agrees to take a case will generally provide the local Legal Aid office with any required documentation. For example, in Ontario the responsible lawyer submits the signed Legal Aid certificate. The lawyer then proceeds to represent the client. The province pays the lawyer directly for the services provided, based on tariffs set in each particular province. The tariffs are a schedule of fees paid to lawyers for standard legal services. Figure 6.29 shows an example of correspondance confirming representation with a Legal Aid certificate.

Duty Counsel

Many provinces provide duty counsel lawyers to assist people who appear before a court without any representation. Duty counsel representation is funded through the Legal Aid Plan. This service is generally provided for matters in criminal court (for example, young offenders, bail hearings, guilty pleas, and sentencing). Duty counsel are also available in Family Court to help clients prepare and review documents and to offer representation at various hearings and settlement meetings.

It is the responsibility of duty counsel to provide on-the-spot legal advice. However, duty counsel cannot represent someone after the first day of the case. In complex or more serious matters, duty counsel will often recommend and request a court adjournment on behalf of the individual so that the person has time to retain formal counsel.

FIGURE 6.29   Retainer agreement for Legal Aid client

WOODROW & PERRY
Barristers & Solicitors

1605 Treetop Road
Peterborough, Ontario
K9K 1G2
Telephone: 705-743-5796
Facsimile: 705-749-3492

woodrow.perry@shaw.ca

BY HAND

August 24, 20--

John Jones
1193 Braidwood Avenue
Peterborough, ON
K4J 1V0

Dear Mr. Jones

RE: Our Matter #AK/20--/259 – Breach of Probation

Thank you for asking me to assist you with your case. I am writing to confirm my
understanding of the facts of your case and to set out what you have asked me to do.

Facts of the Case

On August 10, 20--, you were charged with possession of a controlled substance and breach of
probation. You are to appear in court at 70 Simcoe Street, Peterborough, Ontario on August 30,
20--. As discussed, I will meet you at the court and will have your matter adjourned. We are
scheduled to meet on September 6, 20-- at 4:30 p.m.

Legal Aid Certificate

I would like to confirm that I have received a certificate from the Ontario Legal Aid Plan
(OLAP) to cover the cost of my fees and disbursements in this matter. Please note that the
certificate limits the amount of time I can spend on your case. It is therefore important that
we use the time wisely. In order to keep you up to date on the developments of your case and
to control the time I spend on your case, I will send you copies of all outgoing and incoming
correspondence and other documents.

Contact Information

I have a confidential voice-mail system. You can leave messages 24 hours a day. I make every
effort to return calls within 24 hours. Also, I am now online and you are welcome to send me
an email message at woodrow.perry@shaw.ca. Please note that the email is not confidential.

… /2

Woodrow & Perry
Page 2
August 24, 20--

Office Hours

The office is open Monday to Friday from 9:00 a.m. to 12:00 p.m. and from 1:00 p.m. to 5:00 p.m. We close for lunch between 12:00 p.m. and 1:00 p.m. If you need to see me between 12:00 p.m. and 1:00 p.m., please call ahead.

Again, thank you for providing me with this opportunity to represent you. I am looking forward to working with you on this matter. If you have any questions, please do not hesitate to contact me.

Yours truly

Allicia Keates

Submission of Legal Aid Accounts

In many provinces, a Legal Aid certificate is a lawyer's statement of account to Legal Aid. Requirements for submission of Legal Aid accounts differ across provinces and territories. Figure 6.30 provides the URL for the various Legal Aid plans. The Internet links direct you to specific information related to Legal Aid availability, financial criteria, and submission of accounts for each of the provinces and territories.

FIGURE 6.30   Legal Aid in Canada

Province/Territory	Details
Alberta	http://www.legalaid.ab.ca
British Columbia	http://www.lss.bc.ca
Manitoba	http://www.legalaid.mb.ca
New Brunswick	http://www.sjfn.nb.ca/community_hall/L/lega6030.html
Newfoundland and Labrador	http://www.justice.gov.nl.ca/just/legalassist/legalaid.html
Northwest Territories	http://www.justice.gov.nt.ca/legalaid
Nova Scotia	http://www.nslegalaid.ca
Nunavut	http://www.povnet.org/node/3104
Ontario	http://www.legalaid.on.ca
Prince Edward Island	http://www.gov.pe.ca/infopei/index.php3?number=46064
Quebec	http://www.csj.qc.ca/english/plandusite.asp
Saskatchewan	http://www.legalaid.sk.ca
Yukon	http://www.legalaid.yk.ca

REVIEW QUESTIONS

1. When a lawyer determines her fee, what does she take into consideration?

2. What is a retainer fee?

3. What is the difference between billable work and non-billable work?

4. What is a mixed or pooled bank account?

5. When can a lawyer disburse trust funds?

_____

_____

_____

_____

_____

_____

_____

6. Once an account has been rendered to a client, into which account would you deposit moneys received in payment of the account?

_____

_____

_____

_____

_____

7. What is a docket? When is it opened?

_____

_____

_____

_____

_____

_____

8. What are the objectives of maintaining an accurate time log?

_____

_____

_____

_____

_____

_____

9. What is a disbursement?

10. Why is it important to know which services and disbursements are subject to GST/HST and which are exempt from GST/HST in relation to lawyer–client activities?

11. What steps are involved in billing a client?

12. What is the purpose of Legal Aid in Canada?

ACTIVITIES

1. Docketing

Following your instructor's direction, docket your school-related activities. Your instructor will provide you with an electronic version of this docket. Your docket must adhere to the norm and be typewritten. Once you complete the docket, print it and submit it with a cover page.

LEGAL PROFESSIONAL DOCKET SHEET
FOR YOUR COLLEGE

NAME: _____

Date	Course Name	Activity Code	Description (describe activity in detail)	Docketed Time
July 12	Legal Research	Lec	Statute & Case Citation	1.8

Legend

Time		Activity Codes*					
6 mins = 0.1	36 mins = 0.6	Lecture	Lec				
12 mins = 0.2	42 mins = 0.7	Seminar					
18 mins = 0.3	48 mins = 0.8	Homework					
24 mins = 0.4	54 mins = 0.9						
30 mins = 0.5	60 mins = 1.0						

* Complete with applicable activities and their corresponding codes.

2. Receiving Trust Funds

You have recently opened a file for Mr. Thomas Elliot. He has left the following cheque as a retainer. Using the appropriate software (for example, PCLaw), deposit the funds to trust and prepare a receipt for Mr. Elliot. Place a photocopy of the cheque in Mr. Elliot's file.

Mr. Thomas Elliot   No. 218
1214 PARKHILL ROAD
PETERBOROUGH, ON K9K 1G2   Date _____
Tel. 705-745-3845

PAY TO
THE ORDER OF *Mr. Bryan Perry* $ *500.00*

Five hundred ——————————————————— xx/100 Dollars

TD Canada Trust   *Thomas Elliot*
Lansdowne Branch

ıı⍩ ᴸ23ıı⍩ ⍩:ᴸ234 5ııⷫ6 78ᴸ: ᴸ2ııⷫ 345ıⷫ67ᴸⷫ

---

3. Billing

Continue working with Mr. Thomas Elliot's file. Ensure that all hours to date have been recorded in PCLaw. Update the manual docket and the PCLaw time sheet. Activities and times are as follows:

- Lawyer attended first appearance. 15 minutes.
- First court date set for [get date from your instructor]. Update your tickler.
- Lawyer met with Crown to discuss charges. 20 minutes.

Prepare a disbursement voucher to photocopy the disclosure ($0.10 each). Update PCLaw's client costs data entry screen.

Produce a pre-bill. Ensure that no entries are missed.

Produce a bill and a client ledger.

DISBURSEMENT VOUCHER

Date: _____   Matter #: _____

Type/Description of Disbursement: _____

Photocopies: _____   Fax: _____

Long Distance: _____   Other: _____

Code: _____

Initials: _____

---

4. Handling Client Receipts

While opening the daily mail you find that Mr. Thomas Elliot has submitted a cheque in the amount of $420.00 to be applied against his outstanding account.

He has also requested that any future payments be drawn from his trust moneys. He will update trust funds on a regular basis. You have spoken with the lawyer and he has agreed.

Update PCLaw's Client Receipts data entry screen to reflect Mr. Elliot's payment. Change the system settings to automatically transfer the trust moneys at billing.

Select "File" from the menu bar.

Select "Matter."

Select "Open matter."

Select "Client."

Select the Sections tab.

Select "Auto transfer from trust at billing."

While in that screen you realize that you omitted a quote amount of $2,000.00. Include this now.

Mr. Thomas Elliot   No. 325
1214 PARKHILL ROAD
PETERBOROUGH, ON K9K 1G2   Date _____
Tel. 705-745-3845

PAY TO
THE ORDER OF *Mr. Bryan Perry* _____ $ 420.00

Four hundred and twenty _____ xx/100 Dollars

TD Canada Trust   *Thomas Elliot*
Lansdowne Branch   _____

⑈123⑈ ⑈12345⑈678⑈   12⑈345⑈67⑈

Communication

We take communication for granted because we do it so frequently, but it's actually a complex process.
—Joseph Sommerville, PhD

Introduction

Communication is an integral part of everyday life. When you communicate with others, you are seeking to convey your intent, ideas, emotions, and opinions. In addition to your words, it is also tone, body language, and ability to listen that will influence how well you are understood.

In a legal environment, you will communicate with lawyers, paralegals, co-workers, clients, opposing representation, court officials, and others on a daily basis. Being able to communicate effectively both verbally and in writing with everyone you come into contact with is one of the most important skills for working in the legal field. Maintaining a written record of those communications is equally important.

Not only do clients expect professional representation when they retain a legal team, but law society rules across Canada dictate that lawyers (and in Ontario, paralegals) must act honourably and with integrity and civility through all stages of the client matter. This includes being sensitive to the needs of the client and others in order to determine the best approach to communicating in a timely and effective manner.

By acquiring the right tools, you will be able to get your message across—in person, in writing (including email), and on the telephone. Effective communication is a lifelong learning process.

What Is Communication?

Communication is not simply responding to and/or understanding what another person said. It is the exchange of information between at least two people. One person, the sender, sends a message and the other person, the receiver, receives it. For the message to be correctly understood, its words and intent must have the same meaning for both the sender and the receiver. As the sender, you run the risk of being misunderstood if you do not tailor your message in a way that is appropriate to the receiver and if you do not use appropriate non-verbal cues, among other things.

CHAPTER OBJECTIVES

After reading this chapter, you will understand:

- how we communicate, and the barriers to effective communication
- how to listen effectively
- how to use and understand non-verbal forms of communication
- the importance of effective telephone skills
- how to deal with clients face to face
- how to handle difficult clients
- the advantages and disadvantages of email communication
- how to plan productive meetings

In most areas of the law, lawyer/client communication problems are the number one cause of complaints, followed by basic deadline and time-management issues. (*LAWPRO Magazine*, Summer 2008)

If the receiver does not understand your message, you cannot be said to have communicated, and therefore the receiver cannot respond appropriately.

Barriers to Communication

When working in a law office, you must be sensitive to the communication needs of the individuals with whom you are communicating, and determine the best communication approach in each circumstance. The LSUC recommends that legal representation should clarify with the client the preferred method of communication—for example, written, phone, facsimile, email, in-person meeting, and so on.

Anything that interferes with the understanding of a message is a barrier to communication. Barriers may be present regardless of how skilled individuals are at communicating, and regardless of how good the communication system is in a particular environment. They may also be present at the sender, the receiver, or along the path the message travels.

Figure 7.1 summarizes the most common barriers.

FIGURE 7.1   Barriers to effective communication

Barrier	Details
Psychological factors	People's state of mind will differ depending on the levels of stress and anxiety that affect their ability to concentrate and comprehend.
Attitudinal barriers	A message may be distorted by the effects of people's past experiences, their prejudices, and biases.
Physical barriers and environmental factors	Background noise, poor lighting, uncomfortable temperature, frequent interruptions, and odours can be distracting.
Physiological factors	Poor health, impaired vision, and impaired hearing, as well as hunger, stress, and fatigue, can interfere with the ability to communicate or comprehend messages.
Cognitive barriers	Individuals may be unable to comprehend a message because of factors such as their age and/or cognitive limitations that may result from mental health issues, cognitive/intellectual disabilities, etc.
Linguistic ability and language differences	From a language standpoint, the receiver of a message may not be equipped to understand the message (unfamiliar words, misunderstood nuances).
Cultural barriers	Different cultures attach different meanings to verbal and non-verbal cues.
Presentation of information and word choice	Incomplete or unorganized thoughts and poor/unclear word choice can make comprehension difficult.

The Communication Cycle

The communication cycle involves a series of steps. First, the sender needs to define the message, encode it, and consider the most effective means of conveying it to the receiver. The sender sends the message via the appropriate channel (oral, written, or visual). The receiver then receives the message, decodes it, and responds as appropriate. When the receiver responds, the roles of sender and receiver become reversed: the receiver is now the sender and the initial sender becomes the receiver.

The communication cycle is illustrated in figure 7.2. Figure 7.3 describes the elements involved in each step.

FIGURE 7.2   The communication cycle in action

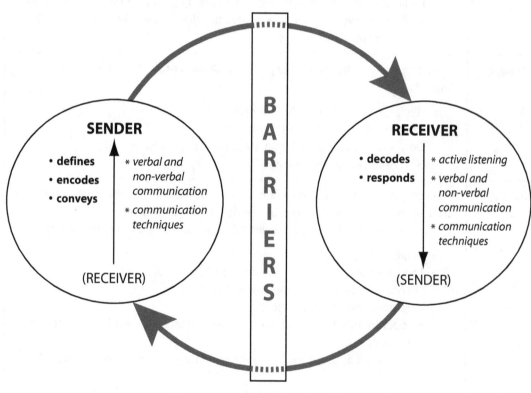

NOTES:

FIGURE 7.3 Elements of the communication cycle

Step	Details
Defining	Before you send a message, think about and determine the following: • What is the purpose of the communication? • What needs to be contained in the communication? • Who is your audience, and what barriers may be present? • What is the most effective method of conveying this information? • When is the best time to communicate with the receiver?
Encoding	The process of encoding a message involves choosing the most effective verbal and non-verbal means of communication. Consider the following: • Does the receiver have any prior knowledge of the subject matter? • What assumptions may the receiver or you (the sender) have about the subject matter? For example, if a client (the receiver) comes to your office to begin divorce proceedings and has a parent who had a bad experience with a different lawyer in a divorce matter, the client may believe that she will encounter the same problems.
Conveying the message	When determining the method of communication, consider the following elements: • What barriers may exist for the receiver? • Do you require immediate feedback? • Do you require written documentation of the communication? • Is technical accuracy necessary?
Receiving (decoding)	Receivers can be influenced by a number of elements. With verbal communication, careful listening is critical. Immediate feedback may be required. Remember the following when listening or reading written communications: • Avoid distractions. • Pay attention to and try to understand non-verbal cues. • Do not rush or interrupt the person speaking. • If appropriate, ask for clarification. • Be open-minded. Your experiences, beliefs, and attitude influence the way you listen. • Take notes if appropriate. They may enhance your ability to understand the message.
Responding	When responding (as a sender), consider all of the above elements.

NOTES:

FIGURE 7.4   Communication techniques

Element	Details	Example
Paraphrasing	Restate the message in your own words.	"Let me see if I understand …" "In other words …" "I gather that …"
Clarification	Make sure you understand the message in better detail by asking specific questions, perhaps with applications to hypothetical situations.	"But what happens when …" "So what would you do if …"
Direct questions	Focus on specific topics. They invite a "yes" or "no" answer or a more detailed response.	"Do you like the program you are in?" "When would you like to come and speak with me?"
Open-ended questions	Encourage a person to share their thoughts and feelings.	"What do you like about the program you are enrolled in?" "What are your career opportunities?"

Tools for Effective Communication

Although barriers to communication cannot be eliminated, there are a number of tools you can use to promote communication. Figure 7.4 outlines some techniques that will help to ensure that you are listening, demonstrating your understanding of the message, promoting discussion, and responding to the message appropriately. Two other important tools for communicating effectively—listening and non-verbal communication—are discussed in the following sections.

Working with Language Barriers

Many clients, particularly in larger urban areas, may have a language other than English as their first language. When communicating with these clients, the most important element is your attitude: be patient and cooperative, and be aware that you will need to spend extra time to ensure that both you and the client understand each other.

The following are some other useful tips for communicating more effectively where a language barrier is present:

- Make a conscious effort to speak more slowly than usual, and to pronounce words more clearly.
- Speak loudly enough to be heard, but do not yell. Raising your voice will not make it easier to understand you.
- Use common, simple words, and try to keep your sentences short.
- Check for verbal and non-verbal cues that indicate understanding, and ask for feedback to confirm that you have been understood.
- If you have not been understood, try repeating your message. If the person still does not understand what you are saying, try rephrasing and using different words.
- Use gestures, and a pencil and paper if necessary.

Listening

Many people believe that hearing and listening are the same thing. Hearing is the physical process of receiving the sounds around you, including words. Listening is the mental process of paying attention to what those sounds mean—decoding them. There are two kinds of listening: passive and active. Passive listening is the act of hearing with little or no overt action on the part of the receiver. During active listening, the receiver

- shows sincere interest in what is being said
- faces the speaker
- makes appropriate eye contact
- does not interrupt
- ignores distractions
- focuses on what is being said
- interjects comments such as "I see," "mmm," or "uh huh" every now and then
- looks for non-verbal cues
- takes notes if appropriate
- keeps an open mind
- does not judge or criticize
- responds appropriately.

Effective listening is an art that requires concentration and practice.

Non-Verbal Cues

Non-verbal cues transmitted through body language and the tone of the sender's voice or writing are powerful cues that can either strengthen or weaken a message, depending on how they are used. For example, if you say, "I am more than happy to handle that matter for you," with your arms crossed and with a sarcastic tone, although your words may communicate an eagerness to help, your non-verbal cues imply otherwise. Your eye contact, facial expressions, and posture can either help or hinder the way you communicate. To be convincing, your verbal message and your non-verbal communication must say the same thing.

Our facial expressions convey emotions such as happiness, sadness, fear, anger, disappointment, and surprise. Figure 7.5 describes familiar facial and eye expressions associated with various emotions. These expressions have the same meaning in most parts of the world, and understanding them is useful when interpreting messages. For more information on differences in non-verbal communication across cultures, see the box feature on page 182. It is important to note that individuals may not always be aware of their expressions from moment to moment, or of the impression that their expressions are creating in others. Furthermore, individuals with certain conditions cannot always control their facial expressions.

A person's posture can also communicate information about how the person is feeling. Figure 7.6 describes some of the meanings typically associated with different postures. It is important to note that the message that is commonly perceived—for example, the perception that an individual who is standing with her arms crossed is angry—may not be what the individual intended, and there could be other reasons for the posture (for example, this could be a comfortable resting position for some individuals).

If you are communicating with an individual with a physical or mental health issue, including a physical disability, impairment, or mental illness, the "message" typically associated with a particular posture, expression, or other non-verbal cue may not apply. Be sensitive to the fact that you may misinterpret non-verbal cues in such cases, and so might they; be aware of the potential for miscommunication.

FIGURE 7.5 Messages typically conveyed by facial expressions

Message	Details	Expression
Happiness	Enjoyment, pleasure, joyfulness	Eyes open, lips turned upward
Sadness	Loss, depression, distress	Eyes downcast, lips lowered
Fear	Apprehension, anxiety, panic, distress, nervousness	Eyes wide open, raised eyebrows, mouth tense with lips drawn back
Anger	Rage, hostility, exasperation, irritability	Eyes fixed in a hard stare, upper lips lowered
Disgust	Dislike, contempt, loathing, scorn	Eyes narrowed, upper lips curled, nose moving
Surprise	Shock, amusement, alarm, astonishment	Direct gaze with raised eyebrows

FIGURE 7.6 Messages typically conveyed by posture

Message	Details	Posture
Sadness	Loss, depression, distress, melancholy	Slumping or sitting with head bent forward, shaky voice, crying
Illness	Sickness, poor health, physical or mental malaise	Favouring or protecting an affected body part, slow or strained movements
Nervousness	Agitation, anxiety, tension, diffidence	Fidgeting or repetitive movements, darting eyes, tentative gestures
Interest	Attentiveness, alertness, curiosity, avidity	Leaning toward a person, encouraging facial expressions
Lack of interest	Boredom, annoyance, indifference, apathy	Leaning or turning away from a person, attention elsewhere
Impatience	Irritability, restlessness, brusqueness, annoyance	Drumming fingers, short sighs, sudden gestures
Anger	Rage, hostility, exasperation, irritability	Sitting or standing with arms crossed, or standing with hands on hips

Cultural Differences in Non-Verbal Communication

Culture plays an important role in non-verbal communication. To the extent that it can create misunderstanding or even offence between individuals who come from different cultural traditions, it can be a barrier to effective communication.

For example, in Western cultures, eye contact is a positive element that can indicate openness, interest, and honesty, whereas avoidance of eye contact can indicate lack of interest, shyness, embarrassment, guilt, or deception. However, in certain cultures, it is considered rude or aggressive to make direct eye contact, and between members of the opposite sex, direct eye contact is seen as inappropriate.

Different cultures and religions also vary with regard to physical contact in public—for example, among orthodox Jews, touching members of the opposite sex that are outside of the immediate family is considered improper. This restriction is shared by a number of cultures and religions. The appropriate degree of assertiveness, too, can vary. For example, while many Canadians consider raised voices in a conversation to be a sign of disagreement or anger, in other cultures an increase in volume signifies excitement or lively discussion.

Proxemics—the study of distances between individuals as they interact—is another area of cultural variation, with differences in what is considered an appropriate amount of space in various situations. For example, in Canada and the United States, the acceptable distances in social settings are much greater than in Saudi Arabia and Japan, where a smaller distance is considered comfortable. In practice, in a conversation between individuals from these different cultures, this could result in some of the individuals perceiving others as pushy or even aggressive, and those individuals in turn viewing the others as aloof or distant.

A greater understanding of cultural differences in non-verbal communication will be an asset to your ability to communicate with individuals from other cultures. The Centre for Intercultural Learning, part of the Canadian Foreign Service Institute of Foreign Affairs and International Trade Canada, maintains detailed information on cultural practices by country in the "Country Insights" section of its website, at http://www.intercultures.ca.

Telephone Skills

The telephone is an extremely important communication tool in any business. At a law office, it is often the first point of contact with clients. Generally, clients call when something has happened and they need a lawyer's advice: perhaps they have dreaded making the call; they may be feeling uncomfortable, angry, or distraught. Your telephone manner not only reflects on the firm, but in this case must also help put the client at ease. The client needs to feel that they are being listened to and understood by someone competent. Only then will they be able to communicate with you properly.

When speaking with the caller, first identify yourself using a pleasant, personable tone. Keep a notepad handy and jot down the caller's name as well as other details related to the call. Use their proper name during the conversation. Be considerate of the caller's time. Gather information courteously and efficiently, keeping the conversation simple by avoiding the use of legal jargon. Keep background noises and other communication barriers within your control to a minimum.

You can learn a great deal about a client, such as their frame of mind and personality, by listening "between the lines." Pay attention to changes in voice tone and inflection.

Quite often lawyers or colleagues are away from the office, in meetings, or on another line when a client calls. If this is the case, ask the caller whether you may be of assistance. If the caller wants to speak with the individual directly, or if you are unable to answer the caller's inquiry, offer to take a message. An appropriate response is, "I'm sorry, but Ms. Guerin is unavailable. May I be of assistance, or would you like to leave a message?" Do not inform the caller of the individual's whereabouts.

Most callers want to be assured that they will be called back within a period of time. If the individual the caller is trying to reach is not available to return the call in a timely manner, phone the caller back with an explanation and a new time to expect a return call.

When a lawyer or colleague is away from the office for an extended period, another individual will be designated to handle their calls and/or clients. If this is the case, take a message and let the caller know who will be returning their call.

Whoever handles both incoming and outgoing calls represents the entire firm and its philosophy of effective client service. Familiarize yourself with the office protocol and procedures. Details of all client-related calls must be documented accurately, clearly, and concisely, because they form part of the client file. Combine this knowledge with the techniques described in figure 7.7 for excellent telephone conduct.

Placing Calls on Hold

There are a number of reasons why you may need to place a client call on hold. This is often the case in a busy office. You may have to retrieve information in order to answer an inquiry or transfer the client to someone who can assist them. If you have a multiline system, it may simply be that another line is ringing. Whatever the reason, when you put a caller on hold, be courteous.

A client's time is valuable to them. Do not assume that the individual is able or willing to have their call placed on hold. Ask permission first and wait for a reply. If you are given permission to put the caller on hold, check back periodically (every 30 to 40 seconds) to confirm that they would like to continue to hold, and offer to take a message. For example, "I'm still checking that for you, Mr. Hadwyn. Do you mind holding, or would you prefer to leave a message?"

PRACTICE TIP

Treat every caller equally—the last caller of the day deserves just as much courtesy, patience, and respect as the first.

DID YOU KNOW?

The first answering machine was invented in 1898 by Valdemar Poulsen (1869–1942). He called it a telegraphone.

FIGURE 7.7 Telephone techniques

Element	Details
Food	Do not eat, drink, or chew gum while speaking on the telephone.
Information	Keep a notepad handy. Write down the caller's name and other relevant information as the caller is speaking. If you are unclear about anything, ask for clarification.
Enunciation	Speak directly into the mouthpiece. Your voice can sound muffled if you are performing other tasks while on the telephone. Consider using a headset.
Promptness	Answer the telephone within three rings. Prompt answering helps to build a reputation for efficiency.
Identification	Callers like to know that they have reached the number dialed. State the name of the firm and your name. For example: "Woodrow and Perry, Quintin speaking, may I help you?" "Woodrow and Perry, Quintin speaking."
Professionalism	Be courteous. Your telephone voice should be positive, friendly, and professional. Your tone says a lot about your attitude.
Smile	A smile can be detected over the telephone and makes you sound friendlier.
Interest	Make sure the caller does not feel that they have interrupted you. Do not interrupt the caller when they speak. Demonstrate interest in what they are saying with your tone.
Accuracy	When providing information to the caller, check for accuracy. This may entail retrieving information from a file or another member of the office. Verify all information before passing it on.
Efficiency	Do not keep a caller waiting. When retrieving documentation, do it quickly. If information is not readily accessible, offer to call the individual back. If you are not able to provide the needed information, refer the person to someone who can.
Closing	Let the caller end the call. Do not assume that the call is over simply because you have provided all the requested information. If the caller is chatty, try ending the call by recapping the next course of action. End the call with courtesy. Thank the caller for calling. For example, "Thank you for calling, Ms. Collis. We will see you on Friday at 2:00 p.m. Goodbye." Never say "bye-bye" or "bye now" or use other slang phrases.

NOTES:

Give the caller an idea of how long you may be away from the telephone. If you are going to be a while or the caller says they do not want to be on hold, ask if you can call them back with the information. Make sure to thank the caller for holding after you return to the call.

Transferring Calls

Transferring calls is routine office practice. Unfortunately, if a transfer is not handled well, it can leave an unpleasant impression with the caller. First, learn how to transfer a call properly on your telephone system. Do not inadvertently disconnect a caller. Find and understand your office protocol for call transfers. Callers should never be transferred more than once.

Make sure the caller knows the reason for the transfer and explain what you are about to do. For example, "Mr. Traynor will be able to answer your questions, Ms. Hardy; I'll transfer you to his line" or "Mr. Traynor is at extension 1224. I'll transfer your call now."

When transferring calls, you also need to request permission from the person receiving the transfer. If they can take the call, give them the caller's background information, including their name, the purpose of their call, and any other useful information.

If the caller must be placed on hold before the transfer is completed—for example, if the individual sought is on another line—let the caller know in advance. Give the caller the option of holding. You might say, "Mr. Carpenter is on another line at the moment. Would you care to hold, or would you prefer to leave a message?"

Check back with the caller periodically. Apologize for the delay and ask whether they would like to continue waiting. If they are unable to hold or have been holding for a while, offer to take a message or ask if they would like their call forwarded to the individual's voicemail.

Handling Multiple Lines

If you have a multiline telephone system and a second call comes in, you may have to put the first caller on hold. Let the first caller finish their sentence, then politely tell them you need to answer another line. For example, ask, "Do you mind holding?" or "May I put you on hold?" Abrupt statements such as "Hang on" or "Just a sec" are rude and make the caller feel that their call is unimportant. Answer the second call and ask that caller whether they will hold. Return to complete your conversation with the first caller. Periodically check back with the second caller. If they are unable to continue holding, offer to take a message.

Taking Messages

All telephone messages must be complete and accurate. This cannot be emphasized enough, because this documentation forms part of the client file. Use a self-duplicating, no carbon required (NCR) telephone message slip. Some offices have an electronic telephone message system. During the call, determine the particulars of the message as well as its urgency. The lawyer will then be able to prioritize callbacks and have the appropriate file or information at hand when returning the call.

Make sure you include on the message slip the following information:

- the name of the caller

- the caller's contact number

- the date and time of the call

- the action required (for example, "Please call," "Will call back," or "URGENT")

- details of the message

- your signature or initial on the telephone message slip.

Verify the recorded information with the caller. Confirm the spelling of names as well as the return telephone number. If the caller's name has a difficult or unusual pronunciation, spell the name out phonetically next to the proper spelling. If the name is particularly difficult to pronounce, either leave the message on the individual's voicemail or deliver it personally. This way, you are able to give the correct pronunciation verbally. Not pronouncing a caller's name correctly on a return call can leave the caller with a bad impression of the individual.

Remember that messages are confidential. Do not leave them sitting on your desk for others to see. Deliver the message personally to the lawyer as soon as possible, with a copy placed in the client's file. Follow up to make sure the lawyer has returned the call. If there has not been a return call, you may be instructed to call on the lawyer's behalf. This will ensure that your clients receive the best client service possible.

Figure 7.8 shows a standard message form.

Voicemail

Voicemail is an excellent tool to help catch those calls that you miss. But it can be extremely frustrating for clients if they think you are using it to screen their calls. To avoid giving the wrong impression, be sure to return calls within 24 hours. Even if you're not able to answer their questions right away, give them a call to tell them you're working on it.

When setting up your voicemail, make sure it's your voice that callers hear on the greeting, and determine what you will say before you record it. Greetings are usually pretty standard, but it helps to have it written down in advance. Your message should sound something like: "This is the office of … Sorry we are unable to answer your call." Include office hours or, if you are going to be away for an extended period of time, indicate when you will return and who clients are to contact in your absence.

Check and remove messages regularly. A good habit of checking your voicemail will also prevent client messages from being lost or going

FIGURE 7.8 Message form

MESSAGE

Date: _February 14, 20--_   Time: _10:30 a.m._

To: _Noah Keates_

WHILE YOU WERE OUT

From: _Anita Perron_

Telephone: _705-932-3070_

Telephoned		Please call	✓
Called to see you		Will call again	
Wants to see you		Returned your call	

MESSAGE: _Ms. Perron would like you to call regarding the settlement conference. She has some concerns regarding her witness's statements._

Operator: _DT_   URGENT ✓

---

unreplied. When listening to your messages, have a pen and notepad ready to write down the details of the message, just as you would when talking to a live caller. A copy of these written details should be placed in the client's file.

Handling Difficult Calls

Occasionally, you will have to deal with telephone calls from unhappy clients. Stay calm and patient, and keep your tone friendly and approachable. Do not take what the caller says personally. They are not taking issue with you but with the situation they are in. In most cases, a caller will calm down once they have vented.

Listen carefully to the caller and do not interrupt. Interrupting may only serve to frustrate the caller further, thus increasing their discontent. Avoid putting the caller on hold, but if you have to, do so politely and reassure them that you will return as soon as possible.

When appropriate, calmly ask the caller questions. Try to get a clear understanding of what is bothering them. Let the caller know you appreciate their concerns and ask them how they would like to proceed.

Offer solutions and alternatives, if you can, and end the call on a positive note by confirming the solution, making sure the caller is in agreement.

Do not confuse angry calls with abusive or offensive calls. In the heat of the moment, it can be difficult to think of an effective manner to deal with these calls. For this reason, most offices have a standard protocol to defuse such situations. Learn this protocol and follow it. If your firm does not already have a protocol for dealing with abusive calls, discuss it with your employer and assist in putting one in place.

Face-to-Face Client Service

As part of your duties, you will be required, at one time or another, to deal with the general public. Every time you interact with a visitor, you have an opportunity to create and maintain a positive impression of your firm. Watch for non-verbal cues—and be aware of your own—while actively listening, to ensure a positive experience for both you and the visitor.

Most visitors to your office are there for an appointment. Remember, they are not only clients or potential clients, they are also your guests, and as such they deserve your courtesy and respect. Do not let their appearance or attitude influence the way you deal with them. Treat everyone in a friendly, courteous, and interested manner.

Acknowledge everyone coming into your office with a smile and a greeting. Not acknowledging someone is the equivalent of ignoring them, which creates an anxious atmosphere. For example, if the individual is unknown to you, an appropriate greeting would be, "Good morning, may I help you with something?" Assist them accordingly. If you recognize the individual and know that they are in the office for an appointment, an appropriate greeting would be, "Good morning, Mrs. Lodge. Mr. Keates will be available in a few moments." If the lawyer is available, inform the lawyer by intercom that the client has arrived for their appointment. If there is a delay—perhaps the lawyer is in court, on a call, or in another meeting—advise the client and give them an idea of when they can expect to be seen. Keeping a client waiting without an explanation is uncomfortable for both them and you. If there is going to be a very long delay, politely explain the situation and ask the client whether they would like to continue waiting or schedule another appointment. If they wish to leave, make sure you schedule an appointment for them in the next available time slot. This may mean that you have to adjust the lawyer's calendar.

NOTES:

Difficult Clients

Some clients coming into your office may be rude, angry, or abrupt. Quite often these people are that way with everyone. Do not take it personally. Many of the techniques for dealing with difficult telephone callers apply here as well.

Acknowledge the individual politely. Stay calm. Do not be rude, angry, or abrupt in return—doing so will only create a more volatile situation. Even if your words are polite, be aware of the non-verbal cues you may be giving the client, and adjust these as necessary to avoid antagonizing the individual further. Do not talk across your desk. Come around to the individual and ask them to have a seat. You need to be sitting as well. Sitting side by side can have a calming effect, which may help defuse the situation. If the individual is extremely agitated, you may have to take them to another area to talk with them. This will give them added privacy and attention, but also prevent them from causing a commotion in the public spaces of the office.

When talking with the individual, try to put yourself in their position. Perhaps they just had a bad experience in court, or are fearful of what might happen in court later. Perhaps they are involved in a contentious or hurtful situation. Listen to what they are saying, and make sure they see that you are listening. Try not to interrupt; wait for a natural break in their dialogue. You do not want to appear impatient. Use positive body language to try to defuse the situation. Be empathetic. Statements such as "I understand what you are saying" or "Let's see if we can figure out where to go from here" are effective in these types of situations.

Remember that pursuant to law society rules, a non-lawyer (and in Ontario, a non-paralegal) cannot give legal advice. You can only determine what the next appropriate step is, such as scheduling an appointment, gathering information from the individual, or providing them with information. It is not your job to change an individual's position on a particular matter. The best you can hope for is that they calm down and behave reasonably.

In some cases, even if you have used all the correct techniques, the individual may remain difficult. If this is the case, you may need your employer or a colleague to intercede. If you handle the situation calmly and correctly, you will leave a positive impression with the individual.

Figure 7.9 lists some more tips when dealing with clients face to face.

PRACTICE TIP

When dealing with difficult clients, your personal safety should be your first concern. In general, try to ensure that you are never alone with an agitated individual. If for some reason you must be, stay within a colleague's line of sight. Only go into a separate room if you feel comfortable doing so, and leave the door open. Sit close to the door, and do not sit with your back to an inside wall. If for any reason you do not feel safe, remove yourself from the situation. Ensure that you are familiar with office protocols and procedures for potentially unsafe situations.

NOTES:

FIGURE 7.9   Client service tips

- Acknowledge individuals when they walk in.
- Greet everyone pleasantly with a smile.
- People are often uncomfortable in a lawyer's office. Put them at ease by offering a cup of coffee or glass of water, and by offering to hang up their coats.
- Don't call clients you've just met by their first names. Older clients in particular may be offended if you do.
- If an individual looks confused or as if they would like assistance, offer it.
- If an individual is elderly or disabled, try to accommodate their needs (for example, offer a chair).
- Treat all visitors equally.
- Use active listening skills.
- Sound interested.
- Ask for clarification as needed.
- Never show boredom or frustration.
- Do not be drawn into a battle.
- Identify and promptly meet the individual's needs.

Email

Email is now used every day, almost everywhere, to communicate with others. It shares many of the same characteristics of conventional print mail, but is much faster for communicating and eliciting a quick response, eliminating the need for costly mail service and long-distance calls. However, this added efficiency often makes email much more susceptible to errors and oversights, so some of its advantages and disadvantages deserve special mention here.

DID YOU KNOW?

The carrier pigeon is an ancient means of communication. Because of their strong homing instinct, these pigeons can deliver messages from sender to receiver and back again. The messages (often written on cigarette paper) are rolled and inserted into a small tube attached to the bird's leg. The recorded use of carrier pigeons dates to 12th-century Baghdad. Since then, they have been used to deliver news and stock prices by Reuters press agency founder Paul Reuter; for secret communication during wars; and until recently, for emergency communication services in India. The world's first "airmail" stamps were issued to commemorate the Great Barrier Pigeon-Gram Service, which operated from 1898 to 1908.

The advantages of email include:

- It enables the immediate delivery of information (barring problems with Internet speed/connectivity).

- Follow-up information can go back and forth quickly.

- The same message can be sent to multiple people at the same time.

- A record of communication is automatically created.

- It is easy to use, cost-effective, and reduces the use of paper.

- It gives recipients the opportunity to read and understand messages before responding.

The disadvantages of email include:

- Recipients do not have the benefit of hearing or seeing the writer (and the writer's non-verbal cues), which makes it difficult for recipients to fully understand the writer's intent.

- Email can be easily misinterpreted.

- Email is not readily available to everyone.

- Email might be forwarded inadvertently to others without knowledge of the writer.

- Messages deleted from the inbox often remain on the hard drive, which creates a potential security/privacy issue (just as you would use a shredder for discarding sensitive documents, find out how to permanently delete files from your computer and email program).

- Email can easily transmit computer viruses.

The format and setup of an email are discussed in detail in chapter 8, Legal Correspondence. However, there is more to an email than structure. Most people tend to be too informal in email, often including off-the-cuff comments. When using email, as with any print format, remember that your words and how you use them are your only ways of conveying meaning. Because email cannot convey tone of voice or body language, humour or sarcasm can be easily misinterpreted. Use an active rather than a passive voice, and keep your message short, personal, and direct. Be clear and accurate. Remember that your message may be read by individuals other than the intended recipient, so ensure that it contains nothing that could have negative consequences for your career.

To avoid sending an incomplete or unedited email unintentionally, it is good practice to leave the recipient field blank while you compose your message. When you finish writing your message, proofread it to ensure that spelling and grammar are correct. Errors can cost you and your firm a client's confidence and trust in your work, and can even cost you a client's business. When you're finally ready to send the message, enter the recipients into the recipient field, and double-check them to ensure that you're sending the message to the appropriate individuals.

When replying to an email, make sure that you understand the original message. If you are unclear about anything, ask the sender for clarification. Do not respond hastily. Before sending your reply, double-check all recipient fields to ensure that you're sending the message to the appropriate individuals. If the original message was copied to a number of recipients, make sure your reply is going to everyone it should. It may not be necessary for everyone to know your response.

Follow the guidelines in figure 7.10 when using email.

FIGURE 7.10   Email tips

• Be concise and to the point.	• Do not write in CAPITALS unless you REALLY NEED EMPHASIS, because capitals often imply that you are yelling.
• Respond to all inquiries within the email.	
• Request clarification if needed.	• Do not use abbreviations and emoticons.
• Use proper spelling, grammar, and punctuation.	• Do not send or forward chain letters or jokes.
• Maintain a professional tone.	• Do not send or forward offensive emails.
• Respond promptly.	
• Proofread your email before you send it.	• Do not reply to spam.
• Use "Reply to All" with caution.	• Do not copy a message or attachment without permission.
• Use a meaningful subject line.	
• Use an active rather than a passive voice.	• Do not use email to discuss confidential information.
• Avoid long sentences.	• Find out what your office policy says about personal email protocol and follow it.
• Do not attach unnecessary files.	

Meetings

Meetings that are unproductive leave people feeling like they have just wasted half their day. In contrast, well-planned, necessary, and time-sensitive meetings are quite effective. If you are asked to organize a meeting, use the following tips to ensure its success.

Determining the List of Invitees

You may be asked to invite key players, or you may simply be told what the meeting is about and be expected to determine who should be present. In the latter case, you need to examine the purpose of the meeting and decide who would have valuable input or who should be asked to attend as a courtesy for their information.

Scheduling the Meeting

Depending on the nature of the meeting, you may be asked to organize a meeting for a particular date or to ensure the attendance of particular people. A meeting that is scheduled for a certain time may be a regularly convened meeting or one that is needed to deal with a time-sensitive issue. In any case, the timing of the meeting is considered to be more important than attendance by all parties.

With a meeting where the attendance of particular people is required, you will have to contact each person to determine their schedule and coordinate a date that best suits each invited party. Scheduling such a meeting is obviously more difficult than scheduling a meeting for a settled-upon time. To find a suitable time for the meeting, determine three or four dates that work for your lawyer, contact each invitee, and ask whether they are available to attend on each of the potential dates. Review all responses and select the date that is most convenient. It may not be possible to accommodate all people, but unless a significant player is unavailable, go ahead and set the date.

Booking the Room

Before formally setting the date and time, ensure that you have a suitable location for the meeting. Perhaps your office has a boardroom that can accommodate everyone. In other situations, you may have to arrange for space outside the office. Allow time to set up the meeting space and enough time to close the meeting.

Announcing the Meeting

When the meeting space has been confirmed, announce the meeting to all invited people. Be sure to mention in your announcement who has called the meeting, the purpose of the meeting, the time, date, and location of the meeting, and the expected length of the meeting. Also ask invitees to reply to your announcement with their contact name and number. Within the announcement, depending on the nature of the meeting, it may be appropriate to request agenda items from the participants and to indicate that a finalized agenda will be forwarded with a reminder notice prior to the meeting.

Preparation and Distribution of the Agenda

The chair of the meeting will usually provide you with the contents of the agenda. Prepare the agenda in a formal manner, and include items such as the title or description of the meeting (this could be the purpose of the meeting or the name of the group that is convening), as well as the time, date, and location of the meeting. Following this information, itemize and number the agenda items and, if appropriate, note who will be addressing each point. Figure 7.11 shows a sample agenda.

Certain standard items are typically included on the agenda for any meeting. The first item is usually an introduction of the participants and their role, followed by the chair's own introduction (if he or she is not already known to all members). If there had been a previous meeting

FIGURE 7.11 Sample meeting agenda

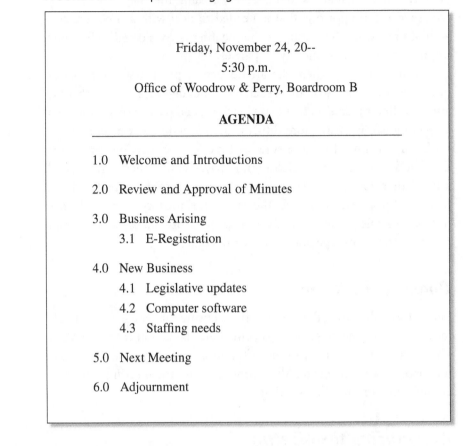

Friday, November 24, 20--
5:30 p.m.
Office of Woodrow & Perry, Boardroom B

AGENDA

1.0 Welcome and Introductions

2.0 Review and Approval of Minutes

3.0 Business Arising
    3.1 E-Registration

4.0 New Business
    4.1 Legislative updates
    4.2 Computer software
    4.3 Staffing needs

5.0 Next Meeting

6.0 Adjournment

on the same subject, the minutes from that meeting (which all attendees should have received soon after the previous meeting) are reviewed and approved. Before the meeting moves on to particular agenda items, there may be an opportunity for members to raise additional agenda items. After all agenda items have been discussed, any new business should be noted. The agenda concludes with the date of the next meeting (if required).

Preparing the Meeting Room

Before the meeting starts, you have to prepare the room. This could simply mean ensuring that there are enough chairs, or it could entail much more. The agenda will dictate the requirements. Items to consider include: technical equipment (laptop for PowerPoint presentations, overhead projector, whiteboard, etc.), podium, and copies of various documents. Ensure that there are extra copies of the agenda and minutes of the previous meeting (if applicable). Plenty of drinking water should also be available.

In more lengthy meetings, you may be asked to arrange for break snacks or even lunch. If this is the case, you will have to decide on what is appropriate, how much to order, when to have it delivered, budget considerations, and how to serve it. All of these matters should be co-ordinated in advance.

Minute Taking

The minute taker has an important and challenging job. He or she must actively listen to the discussions of the meeting and record accurate and substantial minutes. Minutes of a meeting are not verbatim notes; they do not need to outline every thought or question presented. Rather, they summarize each topic with the key points made, the recommendations or decisions made, and the action(s) required. Minutes also note the dates or times scheduled for future meetings.

Cleanup

When the meeting adjourns, it will be your responsibility to ensure that the meeting room is left the way you found it. Dispose of garbage, remove extra copies of documents, and restore chairs, tables, and other furniture to their original positions. If you borrowed equipment for the meeting, return it.

Preparation and Distribution of Minutes

You should prepare the minutes of the meeting as soon after the meeting as possible. Although the minutes may not actually be needed for days, weeks, or even months, the longer you put off writing them up, the less you will recall of the meeting. If you do procrastinate, you'll likely find the writing stressful—facing a deadline with poor recollection.

You should set up the heading of meeting minutes like the heading of the agenda, showing date, time, and location. Then indicate the names and titles of those present and those who sent regrets. Your meeting notes should summarize items in the order they were addressed at the meeting. Begin each section with the topic and the speaker, followed by your summary. At the close of the minutes, indicate the time, date, and location of any future meeting, and indicate the time the meeting concluded. Finally, indicate "Minutes prepared by," followed by your name. When you have completed the minutes, forward them to the chair for review and approval. Make any amendments as directed. Once you have received approval, the minutes are ready for distribution. Send a copy of the minutes to each participant and each absent invitee, and place a copy of the minutes in the meeting file. Figure 7.12 shows a sample minutes page.

NOTES:

FIGURE 7.12 Sample minutes page

Minutes of Bimonthly Meeting
Friday, November 24, 20--
Office of Woodrow & Perry
Boardroom B

Present: Phyllis Perry (Chair)

Donna Woodrow

Ken Woodrow

Katie Lodge

Todd Knowles (Guest)

Regrets: Sarah Hadwyn

Tanya Guerin

1.0 Welcome and Introductions

Phyllis Perry welcomed everyone to the meeting. Introductions were made.

2.0 Minutes of the Previous Meeting

Motion

Moved by Donna Woodrow, and seconded by Katie Lodge, to approve the minutes of September 29, 20-- as distributed.

CARRIED

3.0 Business Arising

3.1 E-Registration: Electronic registration is to start locally in March 20--. Ken Woodrow has made arrangements to get the software and instructions on its use by January 20--.

4.0 New Business

4.1 New legislation: Regulations pertaining to paralegal regulation under the *Access to Justice Act* are expected to be announced soon.

4.2 Computer software: The newest version of DivorceMate will be shipped in March. Staff training will be provided.

- Todd Knowles, a representative from Amicus Attorney, discussed the effectiveness of using Amicus Attorney. Amicus Attorney is an integrated practice management software program that organizes client files, schedules appointments, and manages to-do lists, contacts, phone calls, etc.
Mr. Knowles provided an overview of the features and benefits of Amicus Attorney. Donna Woodrow requested that staff review the proposed implementation of the program and discuss at the next meeting.

4.3 Staffing needs: There are no staffing needs at this time.

5.0 Next Meeting

Thursday, January 25, 20--

6.0 Adjournment

Meeting adjourned at 7:45 p.m.

REVIEW QUESTIONS

1. List five methods of communication.

   _____

   _____

   _____

   _____

   _____

   _____

   _____

2. List six barriers to effective communication, and give an example of each.

   _____

   _____

   _____

   _____

   _____

   _____

   _____

   _____

   _____

   _____

   _____

3. For a message to be correctly understood, the
   _____ and the _____
   of the message must have the same meaning for the sender and
   the receiver.

4. In your own words, explain the difference between passive and active listening.

   _____

   _____

   _____

   _____

   _____

   _____

   _____

5. Which of the following elements can be used as a guideline to ensure that you are listening, show you understand the message, promote discussion, and enable you to respond to the message appropriately?

   a. paraphrasing

   b. clarification

   c. open-ended questions

   d. direct questions

   e. none of the above

   f. all of the above

   g. some of the above

6. List the types of non-verbal communication mentioned in this chapter. What should you remember when interpreting non-verbal cues?

   _____

   _____

   _____

   _____

   _____

   _____

   _____

   _____

   _____

7. The telephone is an important communications tool. Which of the following statements are not true?

   a. It is okay to have the radio on loudly when you are on the telephone.

   b. Clients often telephone just to chat.

   c. It is not necessary to identify yourself.

   d. Tone and attitude do not matter.

   e. All clients deserve courtesy, patience, and respect.

   f. There is no need to let a caller know that an individual is unavailable to call back in a timely manner.

8. Office protocol and procedures should always be followed. The text details eleven telephone techniques. Describe five of them.

_____

_____

_____

_____

_____

_____

_____

_____

_____

9. List four important points to remember when a caller is put on hold.

_____

_____

_____

_____

_____

_____

_____

_____

_____

10. You can leave a lasting impression with a client by acknowledging individuals when they walk in. List three more ways.

_____

_____

_____

_____

_____

_____

_____

_____

11. List five important tips to remember and apply when using email.

_____

_____

_____

_____

_____

_____

_____

_____

_____

_____

_____

_____

_____

_____

_____

_____

12. There are a number of steps that should be completed to ensure a successful meeting. List seven.

_____

_____

_____

_____

_____

_____

_____

_____

_____

_____

_____

_____

_____

_____

_____

_____

_____

ACTIVITIES

1. You are a law clerk in a busy office. This afternoon it is your turn to handle reception and incoming calls.

   A client, Mr. Card, has arrived at the office at 1:45 p.m. for a 2:00 p.m. appointment. There are two other clients already waiting to meet with the lawyer, Mr. Woodrow, who has been delayed at court. One of the clients, Mrs. Wilkins, has been waiting for over an hour. She is happily knitting a sweater for her grandson. Mrs. Wilkins is quite content to continue waiting. The other client, Mr. Hardy, is pacing back and forth in the office and barking into his cellphone. He has been waiting for about 45 minutes. At this point, you have no idea where the lawyer is or when he will return. You have already rescheduled two other appointments. What course of action do you take? Briefly explain your response.

2. Mr. Woodrow has asked you to check his email while he is out of the office. You notice that there is a message from a client, Mr. Goodwin. The message was sent about an hour ago, advising Mr. Woodrow that Mr. Goodwin will be late to court this afternoon for his first appearance. Mr. Woodrow has already left for court. What do you do?

3. The lawyer is out of the office this afternoon. Prepare the appropriate telephone messages for the following calls and outline the next steps to be taken in each case.

a. Mrs. Cole (705-745-5815) called at 1:00 p.m. to advise that she has received her draft will and has some questions about some of the clauses, especially the guardianship clause. She would like Mr. Woodrow to call her back as soon as possible. Mrs. Cole will not be available between 2:00 p.m. and 4:00 p.m. this afternoon. During the call, you remind Mrs. Cole that she has an appointment on Friday at 10:00 a.m.

MESSAGE

Date: ....   Time: ....

To: ....

WHILE YOU WERE OUT

From: ....

Telephone: ....

Telephoned		Please call	
Called to see you		Will call again	
Wants to see you		Returned your call	

MESSAGE: ....
....
....
....
....
....

Operator: ....   URGENT ____

_____

_____

_____

_____

_____

b. Mr. Burgis of Moldaver, Burgis and McFadden (705-740-9283) called at 2:20 p.m. to discuss the particulars related to a direction in favour of his client. Mr. Burgis indicates that the direction should have been on his desk by now because the transaction closes in two days. Mr. Burgis would like Mr. Woodrow to call him back.

MESSAGE

Date: .... Time: ....

To: ....

WHILE YOU WERE OUT

From: ....

Telephone: ....

Telephoned		Please call	
Called to see you		Will call again	
Wants to see you		Returned your call	

MESSAGE: ....

....

....

....

....

....

Operator: .... URGENT _____

Legal Correspondence

The skill of writing is to create a context in which other people can think.

—Edwin Schlossberg

Introduction

Why do lawyers write so many letters? The primary reason is that there is a legal obligation to do so. As discussed in chapter 7, law society rules mandate that lawyers (and in Ontario, paralegals) communicate with clients in a timely and effective manner. The rules also state that this must be done conscientiously, diligently, and in a cost-effective manner. Depending on the type of law practised or legal service provided, letters may include advice, explanations, or information to clients. Types of letters include retainer letters, demand letters to other parties, and letters to opposing counsel and others.

If written clearly, concisely, and effectively, letters can be easily understood. Letters also provide a written record, or paper trail, of client-related activities, which is equally important to the legal representative and to the client. Letters that are disorganized, too long, or riddled with errors will make a terrible impression that can influence how quickly the correspondent will respond.

CHAPTER OBJECTIVES

After reading this chapter, you will understand:

- the importance of being familiar with a client matter before drafting legal correspondence

- the appropriate structure and content when drafting legal correspondence

- the importance of using proper titles in order to present your correspondence

- the formatting requirements when drafting multipage letters

- the best use of templates when drafting correspondence and other documents

- the proper use and structure of internal memorandums and of emails

PRACTICE TIP

The first step to producing polished and professional correspondence is a solid grasp of the fundamentals of grammar, spelling, punctuation, and style. Ensure that you are familiar with the proper usage of all of the elements described in the Writing Guide appendix. In addition to the Writing Guide, a full-length reference text will serve you as a valuable reference throughout your career.

Christopher Sholes, a mechanical engineer, invented the typewriter with his partners S.W. Soule and G. Glidden in 1868. The Remington Arms Company manufactured the first model in 1873. However, the keys on the original typewriter jammed easily. To solve this problem, James Densmore, another business associate, suggested that the keys for letters commonly used together be separated, in order to slow down typing. The resulting pattern of keys became today's standard "QWERTY" keyboard.

Say all you have to say in the fewest possible words, or your reader will be sure to skip them; and in the plainest possible words, or he will certainly misunderstand them.

—John Ruskin (1819–1900)

Standard Correspondence

Background Information and Research

Before sitting down at your computer to compose a document, make sure you have at hand all the information you'll need to begin writing. Pull the client file so that you can refer to certain information such as dates, names, and addresses. Familiarize yourself with the tone and style of past correspondence. If you are responding to a letter, you also need to have a copy of the letter you received in front of you. This is your background information; without it, you won't be able to write an effective letter.

Doing your research is also important. Good research makes the difference between an adequate letter and a superior one. Know what you want to say. Be observant. Make note of such details as copies sent to others, deadline dates mentioned, and previous action taken. Your success in letter writing will increase with proper preparation.

Structure and Content

Business letters commonly have a three-part structure, and in many instances each part will be just one paragraph long. The first part introduces you and states the purpose of the letter; the second part provides information, answers questions, and makes requests; and the third part summarizes or concludes by reiterating important dates, offering further assistance, and thanking the recipient. Letters that need to convey more information than can fit into three short paragraphs will still have the same three-part structure, but the middle part will be expanded to include as many additional paragraphs as necessary.

That said, however, it is not uncommon for an office to send or receive a letter that is just one sentence long. Such letters are used in part because of time constraints, but there is a more important reason: Sending a letter, even one that is only one sentence long, provides the required information to the client and creates a clear paper trail of communication.

As with any document you may be writing, be careful when choosing your words and avoid using legal jargon that the recipient may not understand. Remember, it is best to be factual, clear, and concise.

Figure 8.1 illustrates a letter written in the three-paragraph format.

Figures 8.2 to 8.5 illustrate letters that are only one or two sentences long.

FIGURE 8.1   Three-paragraph letter

WOODROW & PERRY
Barristers & Solicitors

1605 Treetop Road
Peterborough, Ontario
K9K 1G2

woodrow.perry@shaw.ca

Telephone: 705-743-5796
Facsimile: 705-749-3492

April 27, 20--

TD Canada Trust
Landsdowne Street
Peterborough, Ontario
K9H 2N9

Dear Sir/Madam:

**Re: Cody Carpenter
1451 Glenforest Avenue, Peterborough
Mortgage No. 456231-963**

Paragraph 1: introduces yourself and the purpose

I wish to advise you that I have been retained by Cody Carpenter with respect to the sale of his property at 1451 Glenforest Avenue, Peterborough. This transaction is scheduled to close **June 17, 20--**.

Paragraph 2: offers information, answers questions, or makes requests

Please forward to me by fax as soon as possible a statement setting out the amount required to discharge this mortgage on the closing date, assuming that all payments due in the interim are made in a timely fashion.

Paragraph 3: may summarize purpose, reiterate important dates, thank the receiver, offer further assistance, etc.

Should you require further documentation, please do not hesitate to contact me.

Yours very truly,

WOODROW & PERRY

Donna E. Woodrow

DEW/dc

FIGURE 8.2 Letter requesting reply

WOODROW & PERRY

Barristers & Solicitors

1605 Treetop Road
Peterborough, Ontario
K9K 1G2

Telephone: 705-743-5796
Facsimile: 705-749-3492

woodrow.perry@shaw.ca

April 27, 20--

VIA FAX

Collis and Collis
Barristers & Solicitors
Lindsay, Ontario
K10 2J0

Attention: Mr. Collis

Dear Mr. Collis:

Re: Hadwyn v. Guerin, File #108/11

May I please have a reply to my letter dated April 11, 20--, a copy of which I enclose.

Yours very truly,

WOODROW & PERRY

Nicolas P. Perry

NPP/dc

Encl. 1

cc Client

FIGURE 8.3   Letter requesting that payment on account be made

WOODROW & PERRY

Barristers & Solicitors

1605 Treetop Road
Peterborough, Ontario
K9K 1G2

woodrow.perry@shaw.ca

Telephone: 705-743-5796
Facsimile: 705-749-3492

File #2011/298

April 27, 20--

Mr. Ayden Hadwyn
11 Nash Road
Peterborough, ON
K9K 1Z2

Dear Mr. Hadwyn:

Re: Outstanding Account

My account dated February 1, 20-- in the amount of $2,298.52 remains outstanding.
Please arrange to make payments or I will have no alternative but to have my account
assessed.

Yours very truly,

WOODROW & PERRY

Donna Woodrow

DW/dc

FIGURE 8.4 Letter forwarding information to client

WOODROW & PERRY
Barristers & Solicitors

1605 Treetop Road
Peterborough, Ontario
K9K 1G2
Telephone: 705-743-5796
Facsimile: 705-749-3492

woodrow.perry@shaw.ca

April 27, 20--

Mr. Cameron Keates
2024 Denure Avenue
Peterborough, ON
K9K 1Z2

Dear Mr. Keates:

Re: Keates v. Baldwin, File #106/11/EW

I am enclosing a copy of Miss Hoggets's letter dated March 8, 20-- for your information.

Yours very truly,

WOODROW & PERRY

Elizabeth Woodrow

EW/dc

Enclosure: 1

FIGURE 8.5 Payment to third party re: client disbursement

WOODROW & PERRY
Barristers & Solicitors

1605 Treetop Road
Peterborough, Ontario
K9K 1G2

Telephone: 705-743-5796
Facsimile: 705-749-3492

woodrow.perry@shaw.ca

August 16, 20--

Christian and Rice Inc.
3069 – 10 Abernathy Drive
Toronto, ON
M3B 2R2

Dear Sir/Madam:

RE: Your File No.: 210/BR
       Our File No.: 386/05/DW

Please find enclosed our cheque in the amount of $691.65, in payment of your invoice dated June 7, 20--.

Thank you for your assistance.

Yours very truly,

WOODROW & PERRY

Renée Perry

RP:dc

Encl.: 1

Proper Titles

Proper titles and honorifics such as "Mr.," "Ms.," "Dr.," and Jr." should be considered part of a correspondent's name. Titles and honorifics are generally abbreviated and are used to indicate social position, family position, an advanced or professional degree, or an official position in government. It is important to use proper titles in order to present your correspondence in a professional and accurate manner. For example, the "Sr." in "Mr. William Carpenter Sr." indicates family position and the "QC" in "Cody Carpenter, QC" indicates a professional title (Queen's Counsel). Professional titles and degrees are preceded and followed by commas. Family positions can be preceded and followed by commas, or can omit commas entirely. Avoid using both a pre-title and post-title (for example, write either "Dr. Rosemary Gow" or "Rosemary Gow, MD," but not "Dr. Rosemary Gow, MD"). If family position and a title are used, always include the person's first name as well so that the family position makes sense (for example, write "Mr. David Smith Jr.," not "Mr. Smith Jr.").

Above all else, defer to the correspondent's preference. If you are unsure, contact the person's office and obtain the correct information.

Figure 8.6 covers the proper use of titles and honorifics, as well as their abbreviations.

FIGURE 8.6 Titles and honorifics

Type	Example	Explanation
Courtesy	**Mister (Mr.)** Mr. Jeffrey Collis (singular) Messrs. Forget, Wilson, and Dunn (plural)	Used to address a man. The plural of "Mr." is "Messrs." and is used to address two or more men. In a salutation, this courtesy title should always be accompanied by at least the recipient's last name. Dear Mr. Collis:
	Ms. Ms. Natasha Bruce (sing.) Mss. Kerr and Wilson (pl.)	Unless otherwise specified by the recipient, this should be the title used to address a woman, because it avoids any implication of marital (and other) status. Because this title is not an abbreviation, the period is optional. However, be consistent in spelling it with or without a period. Dear Ms Bruce:
	Miss Miss Jennifer Collis (sing.) Misses Carpenter and Collis (pl.)	Used only to address unmarried women. However, this use is increasingly considered condescending. Use "Ms." instead whenever possible.
	Mistress (Mrs.) Mrs. Smith (sing.) Mesdames Lamrock and Keates (pl.)	Used to address women who are married and who wish to be identified as such. The plural of "Mrs." is "Mesdames" and is used to address two or more women.

Type	Example	Explanation
Professional	**Professor (Prof.)** Professor Burgis Prof. Robert B. Burgis	"Professor" should be spelled in full when used only with a surname, but may be abbreviated when accompanying a full name. "Professor" should not stand alone in a salutation. Dear Professor Burgis:
Academic	**Doctor of Medicine (Dr., MD)** Doctor Sam Phillips Dr. Phillips Sam Phillips, MD **Other** LLB (bachelor of laws) BA (bachelor of arts) MA (master of arts) P.Eng. (professional engineer) Ph.D. (doctor of philosophy)	You can include periods in abbreviations of academic degrees and religious titles, but it is not mandatory—follow office protocol. No space is required between the letters. Do not use two different methods of identifying the same designation (e.g., do not use "Dr." and "MD" together).
Religious	**Reverend (Rev.)** Reverend Tanya Dunn	The title should be written in full in formal correspondence. Dear Reverend Dunn:
Honorary	**Supreme Court Chief Justice** The Right Honourable Beverley McLachlin, PC, Chief Justice of Canada **Supreme Court Justice** The Honourable Mr. Justice John C. Major **Federal Court Chief Justice** The Honourable John D. Richard Chief Justice **Federal Court Justice** The Honourable Madam Justice Karen Sharlow **Provincial High Court Justice** The Honourable Mr. Justice Cleaveland **Provincial or County Court Judge** Judge Davidson	Salutations: 　Dear Madam Justice McLachlin: 　Your Honour: 　Dear Mr. Justice Major: 　Your Honour: 　Dear Mr. Justice Richard: 　Your Honour: 　Dear Madam Justice Sharlow: 　Your Honour: 　Dear Mr. Justice Cleaveland: 　Your Honour: 　Dear Judge Davidson: 　Dear Mr. Justice Davidson: 　Your Honour:
	Justice of the Peace Her Worship Justice of the Peace Elizabeth Campbell His Worship Justice of the Peace William Carpenter	The abbreviation "JP" is a commonly used colloquialism, but is unacceptable in the courtroom and is considered disrespectful. 　Your Worship:

Type	Example	Explanation
Government officials	**Governor General** His Excellency the Right Honourable David Johnston **Prime Minister** The Right Honourable Stephen Harper **Lieutenant Governor** His Honour, the Honourable David C. Onley **Provincial Premier** The Honourable Dalton McGuinty **Mayor** Her Worship Mayor Hazel McCallion	Salutations: Your Excellency: Dear Mr. Prime Minister: Dear Prime Minister: Your Honour: Dear Mr. Premier: Dear Premier: Dear Mayor McCallion: Your Worship:
Family position	Nicolas P. Forget Jr. Nicolas P. Forget IV Nicolas P. Forget, Jr., MD Forget, Nicolas P., Sr.	Abbreviated designations end with a period. The comma preceding "Jr." and "Sr." is optional. No comma precedes "III," "IV," etc.

Business Letter Styles

There are three basic letter styles commonly used in office writing: block (or full block style), modified block, and semiblock. The most common of the three is the block style. In the block style, no paragraphs or lines are indented and a double line space separates paragraphs. In the modified block style, the date and closing are centred horizontally. All paragraphs begin at the left margin, with a double line space between them. The least commonly used format is the semiblock style, in which the date and closing are centred horizontally and the first line of every paragraph is indented.

Figures 8.7, 8.8, and 8.9 illustrate the three basic letter styles.

Some offices use a combination of the three main letter styles. Before you begin preparing any legal correspondence, ensure that you are following the accepted format of your office.

NOTES:

FIGURE 8.7 Full block letter style

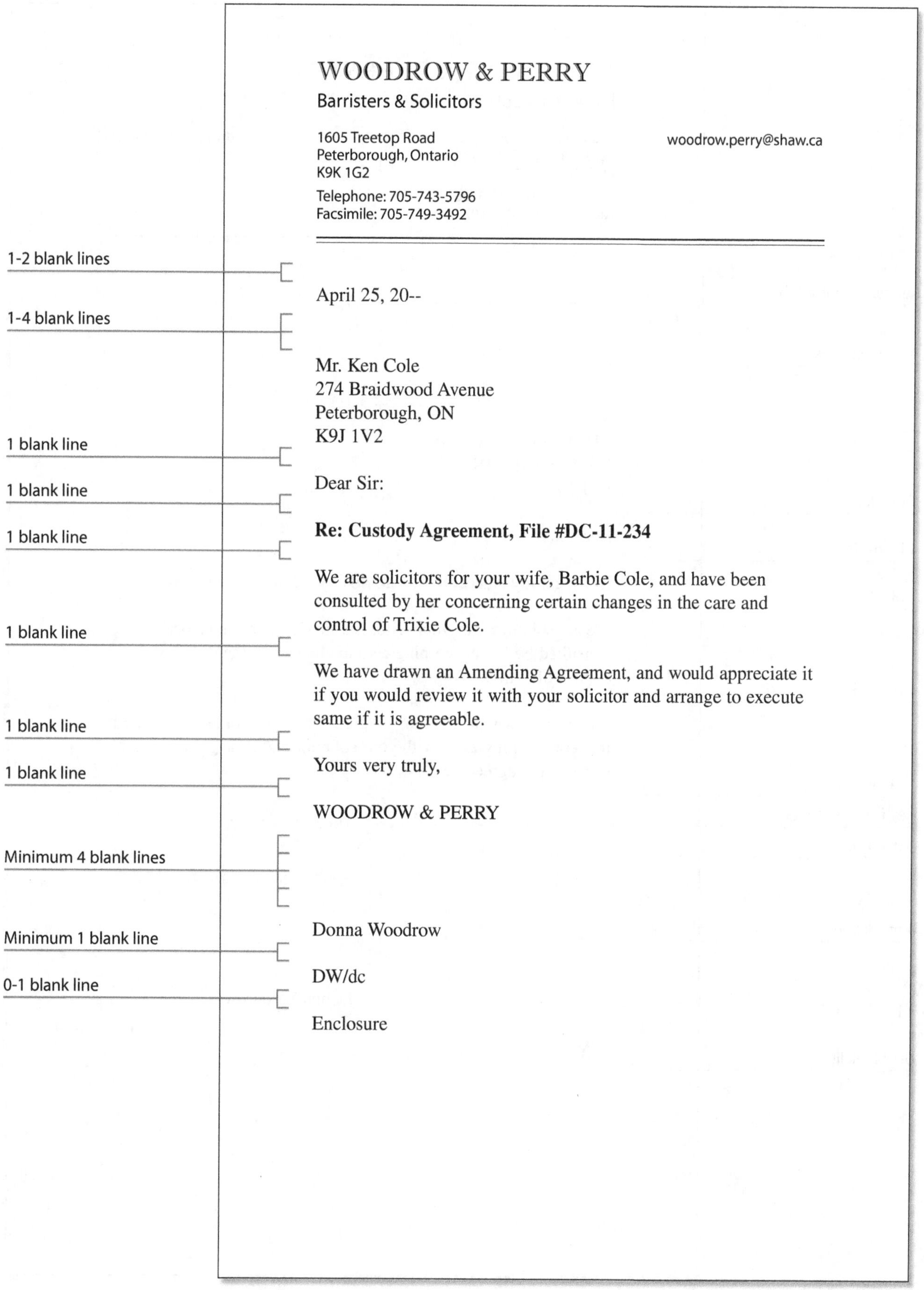

WOODROW & PERRY

Barristers & Solicitors

1605 Treetop Road
Peterborough, Ontario
K9K 1G2

woodrow.perry@shaw.ca

Telephone: 705-743-5796
Facsimile: 705-749-3492

1-2 blank lines

April 25, 20--

1-4 blank lines

Mr. Ken Cole
274 Braidwood Avenue
Peterborough, ON
K9J 1V2

1 blank line

Dear Sir:

1 blank line

Re: Custody Agreement, File #DC-11-234

1 blank line

We are solicitors for your wife, Barbie Cole, and have been consulted by her concerning certain changes in the care and control of Trixie Cole.

1 blank line

We have drawn an Amending Agreement, and would appreciate it if you would review it with your solicitor and arrange to execute same if it is agreeable.

1 blank line

Yours very truly,

1 blank line

WOODROW & PERRY

Minimum 4 blank lines

Donna Woodrow

Minimum 1 blank line

DW/dc

0-1 blank line

Enclosure

FIGURE 8.8 Modified block letter style

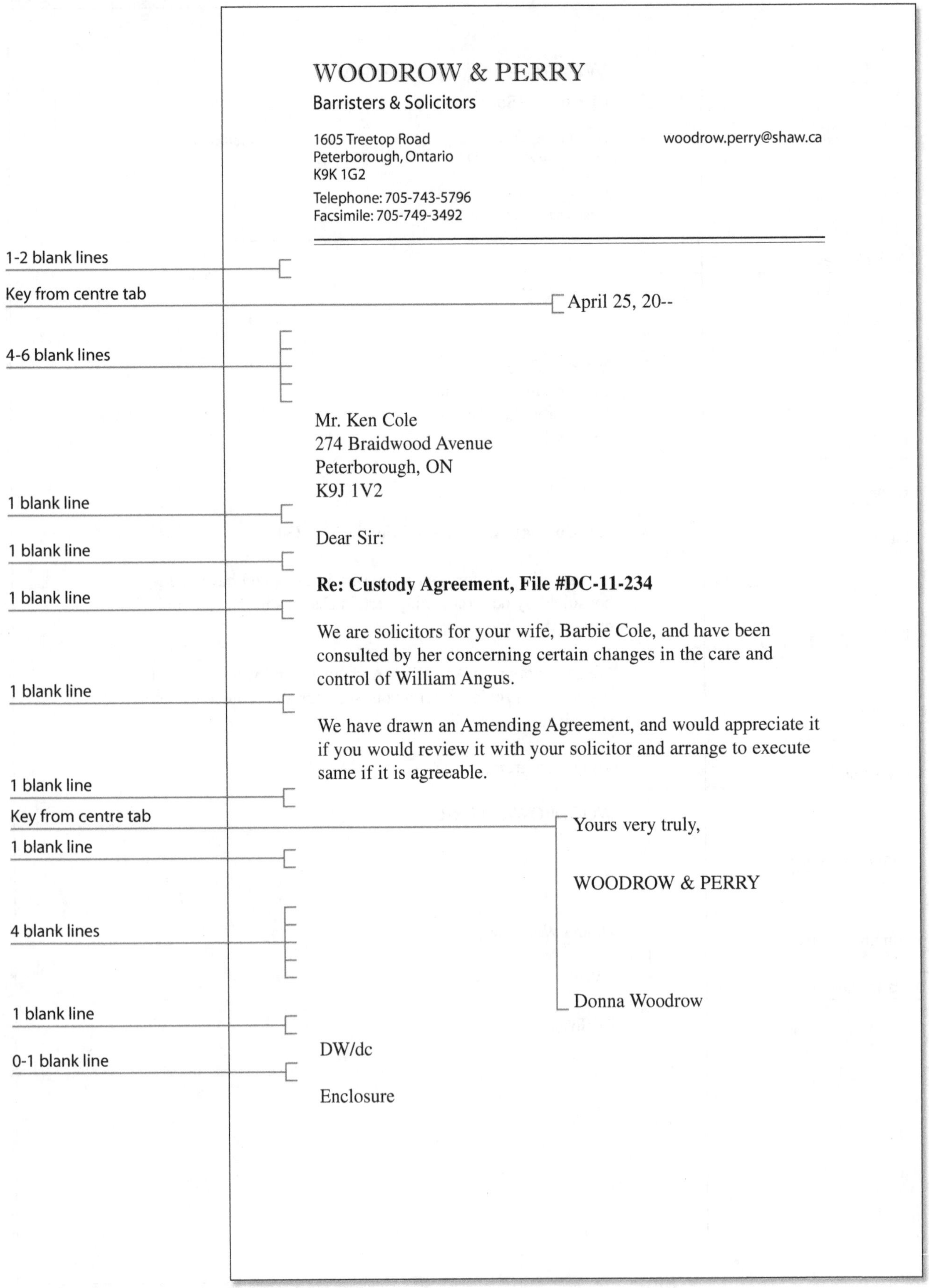

WOODROW & PERRY
Barristers & Solicitors

1605 Treetop Road
Peterborough, Ontario
K9K 1G2

Telephone: 705-743-5796
Facsimile: 705-749-3492

woodrow.perry@shaw.ca

1-2 blank lines

Key from centre tab — April 25, 20--

4-6 blank lines

Mr. Ken Cole
274 Braidwood Avenue
Peterborough, ON
K9J 1V2

1 blank line

Dear Sir:

1 blank line

Re: Custody Agreement, File #DC-11-234

1 blank line

We are solicitors for your wife, Barbie Cole, and have been
consulted by her concerning certain changes in the care and
control of William Angus.

1 blank line

We have drawn an Amending Agreement, and would appreciate it
if you would review it with your solicitor and arrange to execute
same if it is agreeable.

1 blank line

Key from centre tab — Yours very truly,

1 blank line

WOODROW & PERRY

4 blank lines

Donna Woodrow

1 blank line

DW/dc

0-1 blank line

Enclosure

FIGURE 8.9   Semiblock letter style

WOODROW & PERRY
Barristers & Solicitors

1605 Treetop Road
Peterborough, Ontario
K9K 1G2

woodrow.perry@shaw.ca

Telephone: 705-743-5796
Facsimile: 705-749-3492

1-2 blank lines

Key from centre tab

April 25, 20--

4-6 blank lines

Mr. Ken Cole
274 Braidwood Avenue
Peterborough, ON
K9J 1V2

1 blank line

Dear Sir:

1 blank line

Re: Custody Agreement, File #DC-11-234

1 blank line

Indented first line

We are solicitors for your wife, Barbie Cole, and have been consulted by her concerning certain changes in the care and control of William Angus.

1 blank line

Indented first line

We have drawn an Amending Agreement, and would appreciate it if you would review it with your solicitor and arrange to execute same if it is agreeable.

1 blank line

Key from centre tab

Yours very truly,

1 blank line

WOODROW & PERRY

4 blank lines

Donna Woodrow

1 blank line

DW/dc

0-1 blank line

Enclosure

Anatomy of a Letter

Regardless of which letter style you use, the following are the common elements of a business letter:

- letterhead
- special notations
- date line
- inside address
- attention line
- salutation
- subject line
- file number
- body
- complimentary closing
- signature
- reference initials
- enclosures
- copies/blind copies.

Some of these elements are always included in your correspondence, while others are included or omitted depending on the requirements of the document.

To ensure that your correspondence is professional and presentable, refer to the guidelines in figure 8.10 when preparing your correspondence. When formatting and presenting your correspondence, refer to the conventions listed in figure 8.11.

If your office has devised its own standard, you should follow it. Variations will likely be minor and should not compromise the quality of your correspondence. Remember, the primary objective of any formatting convention is to make a letter easy to read. Maintain consistency, make improvements only as permitted, and ensure that departures from convention do not result in any confusion in delivery or content.

Figures 8.12 to 8.27 illustrate the various elements and variations found in legal correspondence.

FIGURE 8.10 Anatomy of a letter

	Element	Details
1	Letterhead	The information in the letterhead includes: • the firm or company name and address • the sender's phone number, extension number (if any), and, optionally, fax number and email address. Sometimes the law firm's name is followed by the letters "LLP," which stand for "limited liability partnership." An LLP is a professional partnership that limits the amount by which partners may be liable for negligence and damages.
2	Notation	This notation appears either below the letterhead or below the date line. Key in full caps, bold-faced, and underlined. **<u>WITHOUT PREJUDICE</u>** The term is used only on the lawyer's instruction. It is used when a lawyer puts forward a certain position or offer in writing. The lawyer does not want the client to be prejudiced in any future proceedings with the content of the letter. The sending firm's file number may also be referenced here (see chapter 4, pages 75-80).
3	Special mailing notations and on-arrival notations	Special mailing notations are used when a method other than mail is used to deliver correspondence. If used, this notation appears between the letterhead and the date line. Key in all caps. BY HAND AND MAIL BY FAX AND MAIL BY COURIER On-arrival notations are used when confidential correspondence such as medical information is being sent. If used, this notation appears between the letterhead and the date line. Key in all caps. CONFIDENTIAL PERSONAL PERSONAL AND CONFIDENTIAL
4	Date line	The date line indicates the date the letter was written (finalized). Type it in month-day-year format (unless your office uses another style). July 22, 20-- Add 1-4 blank lines below the date line. Generally, use 2 blank lines. If the letter is long, use 1 blank line. If the letter is short, use 3-4 blank lines.

(Continued on the next page.)

	Element	Details
5	Inside address	Always enter a business or other entity name exactly as it appears on incoming correspondence (e.g., letterhead), including punctuation and abbreviations.
		Ms. Ashlyn Baldwin Barrister and Solicitor 1221 Empress Avenue Oshawa, ON L0V 1T5
		or
		Baldwin & Traynor Barristers and Solicitors 1221 Empress Avenue Oshawa, ON L0V 1T5
		If you are corresponding with another law office or a government office, you can use the *Canadian Law List* to gather the correct information. Address formatting is discussed in greater detail in chapter 9, Processing Correspondence.
6	Attention line	The attention line (and the letter itself) is directed to the lawyer dealing with the matter.
		Attention: Ashlyn Baldwin
		Omit the attention line if you have already included the recipient's name in the inside address.
7	Salutation	The recipient's name is generally preceded by "Dear" and an abbreviation or word that indicates the person's gender, marital status, or title. A generic salutation may also be used.
		Dear Mr. Baldwin: Dear Sir
		See figure 8.6 for an explanation of titles and their abbreviations. See figure 8.11 for an explanation of different styles for punctuating the salutation.
8	Subject line	The subject line relates to the legal matter being dealt with by the firm. The line may begin "Subject:," "Re.," or "RE:"; follow the style used in your office. Generally, the whole line is bold-faced; sometimes the last line is also underlined. The wording of the line depends on the subject of the letter. Sometimes it describes the topic being addressed.
		RE: Will and Power of Attorney
		If it is a civil matter, the name of the sender's client is placed first, followed by the recipient's client name.
		RE: Dunn v. Knowles
		The sending firm's file number may also be referenced here.
		RE: Dunn v. Knowles, Our File 203-06-DC
		Some offices may enter the recipient's file (reference) number here.
		RE: Dunn v. Knowles, Your File 19800PL

	Element	Details
9	Body	Most letters are single-spaced, with a double space (a blank line) between paragraphs. The commonly accepted length for a business letter is three paragraphs: Paragraph 1: Introduce yourself and the purpose of the correspondence. Paragraph 2: Offer information, answer questions, or make requests. Paragraph 3: Summarize the purpose of the letter, reiterate important dates, thank the recipient, offer further assistance, etc.
10	Complimentary closing	The complimentary closing can be worded in any number of ways. A comma is typically used at the end of the closing (except when open punctuation is used). Regards, Sincerely, Yours very truly, Respectfully yours,
11	Firm name	The firm name often appears (in all caps) between the complimentary closing and the lawyer's signature. This style is used to emphasize that the signing lawyer is acting as an agent or representative of the law firm.
12	Signature block	Allow four line spaces for the signature.
13	Sender's name	Type the sender's title (if used), first name, last name, and professional degrees (if used).
14	Reference initials	Type the initials of the author in all caps, followed by the typist's (i.e., your) initials in lower-case letters, and separate them with a slash or a colon. DC/cf DC:cf
15	Enclosures	When enclosing documents along with the letter, such as a statement of account, a draft contract, or a medical report, type "Enclosure" or "Encl." one or two lines below the reference initials. It is optional to specify the name or the number of enclosures. Encl. Encl. 1 Enclosure: Statement of Account
16	Copies	List the names of the people who are receiving a copy of the letter. This line appears on all copies of the letter. Common notations are: c (copy) cc (carbon copy) pc (photocopy) The notation may have no punctuation or may be followed by a colon, a dash, or a period.
17	Blind copies	The blind copy notation is used when a copy of the letter is sent to someone but the sender does not want the primary recipient to know that someone else is receiving it. The line appears only on the copy sent to the blind recipient. Common notations are: bc bcc bpc The notation may have no punctuation or may be followed by a colon, a dash, or a period.

FIGURE 8.11 Other business letter formatting considerations

Element	Details
Paper	Good quality, medium weight (20 lb.), white, 216 × 279 mm (8.5 × 11 inch) paper
Font	The most commonly used font is Times New Roman (or Times) 10 or 12 point. Other options include Calibri, Cambria, Courier (or New Courier) and Arial (or Helvetica).
Style	The three most commonly used business letter formats are block (or full block), modified block, and semiblock. The full block style is generally preferred simply because it is easiest to type on a computer. See figures 8.7, 8.8, and 8.9 for examples of these standard business letter styles.
Margins	Left and right: 2.54 cm (1 inch) Top: 1.27 cm (1/2 inch) Bottom: 2.54 cm (1 inch)
Punctuation	Like any other written document, letters are governed by general punctuation rules. However, additional rules apply to the introductory and closing elements of a letter. The two punctuation styles most often used are open and mixed. A third style, closed, is seldom used. **Open:** No punctuation after the salutation or the complimentary closing. Dear Mrs. Miller Yours truly **Mixed:** A colon after the salutation and a comma after the complimentary closing. Dear Mrs. Miller: Yours truly, **Closed:** Punctuation used at the end of each line throughout the introductory and closing elements of the letter, including the inside address, the attention line, the salutation, and the complimentary closing. David Keates and Julie McFadden, 763 Brown Street, Peterborough, ON K9J 4K9 Dear David Keates and Julie McFadden: Yours truly,

Alignment	Left-justified text is aligned on the left side with a ragged right edge. This setting is usually the default for new documents.
	        Right-justified text is aligned on the right side (with a ragged left edge). This setting is often used for court file numbers and page numbers.
	        Centred text is spaced evenly between the left and right margins and is used for court names, party names, or document titles. Letterhead and page numbers are also sometimes centred.
	        Justified text is aligned flush on both sides, and is usually reserved for the body of a letter.
	        In lists of numbers and dollar amounts, such as in a statement of account, it is important to align the numbers on the decimal. Decimal alignment makes it easy to read the numbers and to perform calculations.

Line spacing	Letters are generally typed in single-space format with a double space (a blank line) between various elements such as the letterhead, date line, inside address, and salutation. However, the line spacing may need to be adjusted so that the letter can fit on the page.

FIGURE 8.12 Full block letter style with mixed punctuation, special mailing notification, enclosures, and copies: Requesting execution of enclosed documents

1 Letterhead	**WOODROW & PERRY** Barristers & Solicitors 1605 Treetop Road Peterborough, Ontario K9K 1G2 Telephone: 705-743-5796 Facsimile: 705-749-3492 woodrow.perry@shaw.ca
3 Special mailing notation	BY HAND AND MAIL
4 Date line	April 25, 20--
5 Inside address	Collis and Forget Barristers & Solicitors 89 Lansdowne Street Peterborough, Ontario K9C 1V2
6 Attention line	Attention: Jennifer Collis
7 Salutation	Dear Ms. Collis:
8 Subject line	**Subject: Cole domestic** **File #DC-11-234**
9 Body	Further to your letter of April 1, 2011, I am returning herewith three copies of the Separation Agreement duly executed by Mrs. Cole. There are a number of Affidavits in the agreements that have not had either your signature or Mr. Cole's signature properly commissioned. I have identified the relevant pages by way of yellow tab. Would you kindly arrange for the proper execution of the enclosed agreements and return two copies to me as soon as possible. Should you have any questions, please do not hesitate to call.
10 Complimentary closing	Yours very truly,
11 Firm name	WOODROW & PERRY
12 Signature block	
13 Sender's name	Cameron Woodrow
14 Reference initials	CW:dc
15 Enclosures	Enclosures: 3
16 Copies	cc: client

FIGURE 8.13 Full block letter style with mixed punctuation, without prejudice notation, and copies: Demand letter detailed/interest incurred

1 Letterhead	**WOODROW & PERRY** Barristers & Solicitors 1605 Treetop Road · woodrow.perry@shaw.ca Peterborough, Ontario K9K 1G2 Telephone: 705-743-5796 Facsimile: 705-749-3492
2 Notation	**WITHOUT PREJUDICE**
4 Date line	August 24, 20--
5 Inside address	Brian Campbell 290 Aberdeen Avenue Peterborough, ON K9K 1G2
7 Salutation	Dear Mr. Campbell:
8 Subject line	**Re: Brownie's Truck Repair Outstanding Account**
9 Body	Please be advised that I have been retained by Mr. John Brown of Brownie's Truck Repair Ltd. to collect your long-overdue account. On May 5, 20--, you contracted with Brownie's Truck Repair to make several repairs to your TerraPro Mack Truck. You picked up your truck on May 20th and agreed to pay $45,000.00 for the repairs. You further agreed to make payment in full within 30 days of the date of receipt of the truck. To date, no payments have been made despite several attempts by Mr. Brown to collect the amount owing. At present your overdue account is in the amount of $45,000.00 plus accrued interest of $300.00. Interest accrues at the rate of 16% per annum. If the entire amount of $45,300.00 is not paid to this office by way of cash or certified cheque payable to Woodrow & Perry, in trust, within 7 (seven) days, all proper steps will be taken to collect this account. Such action will no doubt affect your credit rating. All costs, interest, and disbursements incurred in the resulting court action will be in addition to the amount of your overdue account. Kindly govern yourself accordingly and forward the requested sum to my office without delay.
10 Complimentary closing	Regards,
12 Signature block	
13 Sender's name	Tom Woodrow
16 Copies	Copy: Client

FIGURE 8.14 Full block letter style with open punctuation and without prejudice notation: Demand letter requesting costs

1 Letterhead

WOODROW & PERRY

Barristers & Solicitors

1605 Treetop Road
Peterborough, Ontario
K9K 1G2

woodrow.perry@shaw.ca

Telephone: 705-743-5796
Facsimile: 705-749-3492

2 Notation

WITHOUT PREJUDICE

4 Date line

October 1, 20--

5 Inside address

Mr. Batten
231 Circular Road
Oriface, Ontario
L6P 4F4

7 Salutation

Dear Mr. Batten

8 Subject line

Re: Ingram v. Batten, NSF Cheque

9 Body

Please be advised that I have been retained by Ms. Ingram to collect the moneys owed to her due to the return of your NSF cheque dated July 15th, 20-- in payment for her services rendered.

At present, your overdue account is in the amount of $15,000.00. Further to this amount Ms. Ingram is seeking legal costs to date for collection of this debt in the amount of $75.00.

If the entire amount of $15,075.00 is not paid to this office by way of cash or certified cheque by October 15, 20--, made payable to Woodrow & Perry in trust, all proper steps will be taken to collect this account.

Kindly govern yourself accordingly and forward the requested sum to my office without delay.

10 Complimentary closing

Yours truly

12 Signature block

13 Sender's name

Barbara Moyle
Paralegal

14 Reference initials

BM/cc

16 Copies

pc: Client

FIGURE 8.15 Full block letter style with mixed punctuation: Demand letter with request to contact firm

1 Letterhead

WOODROW & PERRY
Barristers & Solicitors

1605 Treetop Road
Peterborough, Ontario
K9K 1G2

Telephone: 705-743-5796
Facsimile: 705-749-3492

woodrow.perry@shaw.ca

4 Date line

October 7, 20--

5 Inside address

Russell Sampson
663 Aylmer St. N.
Peterborough, ON
K9H 6X6

7 Salutation

Dear Sir,

8 Subject line

Re: 5 STARS Building and Renovating

9 Body

We have been retained by 5 STARS Building and Renovating.

According to the records of 5 STARS Building and Renovating, you currently owe $6,722.63 for goods sold.

Demand is hereby made upon you to pay this amount in full.

You are instructed to contact me, before 5 p.m. on Wednesday, October 20, 20-- to discuss payment in full of your account, or face legal action. If we are not contacted by 5 p.m. on Wednesday, October 20, 20--, legal proceedings will be brought against you in the appropriate court.

Govern yourself accordingly.

10 Complimentary closing

Yours truly,

12 Signature block

13 Sender's name

Adam Baker

16 Copies

cc: Client

FIGURE 8.16   Full block letter style with open punctuation, special notation, enclosures, and copies: Requesting acceptance of enclosed agreement

1 Letterhead

WOODROW & PERRY

Barristers & Solicitors

1605 Treetop Road
Peterborough, Ontario
K9K 1G2

woodrow.perry@shaw.ca

Telephone: 705-743-5796
Facsimile: 705-749-3492

3 Special mailing notation

SPECIAL DELIVERY

4 Date line

August 24, 20--

5 Inside address

Forget and Keates
Barristers and Solicitors
2121 Grandview Avenue
Peterborough, ON
K9K 1V2

6 Attention line

Attention: Lawrence R. Keates

7 Salutation

Dear Sir

8 Subject line

Re: Our File No. 213/DW05
Agreement of Purchase and Sale
Ashvin purchase from John Smith Hardware Limited

9 Body

Thank you for your letter dated August 17, 20-- with the proposed agreement from your client, John Smith.

We have reviewed the proposed agreement with our client; we have made certain obvious changes as you will note; and our client has signed the agreement for presentation to your client.

Obviously, if your client accepts the enclosed agreement and submits to us a deposit in the amount of $500.00 as provided for under the provisions, then the agreement becomes effective at that point only.

10 Complimentary closing

Yours very truly

12 Signature block

13 Sender's name

Cody Woodrow

14 Reference initials

CW/dc

15 Enclosures

Encl.: 1

16 Copies

cc — John Smith Hardware Limited

FIGURE 8.17   Full block letter style with mixed punctuation and enclosures:
Request to review and make an appointment

1   Letterhead

WOODROW & PERRY
Barristers & Solicitors

1605 Treetop Road
Peterborough, Ontario
K9K 1G2

Telephone: 705-743-5796
Facsimile: 705-749-3492

woodrow.perry@shaw.ca

4   Date line

July 25, 20--

5   Inside address

Mrs. Lynn Sampson
12 Bangor Drive
Mississauga, ON
K9K 1Z2

7   Salutation

Dear Mrs. Sampson:

8   Subject line

Re: Will and Power of Attorney – File #2011-298-KL

9   Body

Enclosed are copies of your draft Will and Power of Attorney.
Please review them carefully and feel free to contact me with any
questions or corrections.

If you are satisfied with the Will and Power of Attorney as drafted,
please call my office and make an appointment to sign them.

10   Complimentary closing

Yours very truly,

11   Firm name

WOODROW & PERRY

12   Signature block

13   Sender's name

Kelsey Perry

14   Reference initials

KP/dc

15   Enclosures

Enclosures: 2

FIGURE 8.18   Full block letter style with closed punctuation and enclosures: Closing letter to client for criminal matter

1   Letterhead

WOODROW & PERRY
Barristers & Solicitors

1605 Treetop Road
Peterborough, Ontario
K9K 1G2

woodrow.perry@shaw.ca

Telephone: 705-743-5796
Facsimile: 705-749-3492

4   Date line

September 14, 20--

5   Inside address

John Jones,
1193 Braidwood Avenue,
Peterborough, ON,
K4J 1V0

7   Salutation

Dear Mr. Jones:

8   Subject line

**Re: Our file #2011/163
          Breach of Probation**

9   Body

I am writing to update you on the status of your case.

On August 30, 20-- at 10:00 a.m. I attended court on your behalf regarding your criminal matter. Justice Carpenter sentenced you to a conditional discharge and 10 months' probation. As discussed, you are to attend the probation office immediately. I think this is a very good outcome for your case.

Since all of the work relating to your case is now complete, please find enclosed my final statement of account for professional services rendered on your behalf to date. I would appreciate it if you would pay me the balance owing of $561.82 as soon as possible. If you have already sent your payment, please disregard this notice. If you have any questions regarding your statement, please do not hesitate to contact me.

I would confirm that once payment is received I will close your file. However, you are most welcome to call me if you have any questions regarding this letter or your case.

Once again, thank you for providing me with this opportunity to represent you. It was a pleasure meeting you. If you require legal services in the future, I would be pleased to assist you.

10   Complimentary closing

Yours very truly,

12   Signature block

13   Sender's name

Ayden Woodrow

14   Reference initials

AW:dc

15   Enclosures

Encl. Statement of Account

FIGURE 8.19 Full block letter style with open punctuation and enclosures: Copy of document sent to the client

1 Letterhead	**WOODROW & PERRY** Barristers & Solicitors 1605 Treetop Road woodrow.perry@shaw.ca Peterborough, Ontario K9K 1G2 Telephone: 705-743-5796 Facsimile: 705-749-3492
2 Notation	**Our file #DC-11-234**
4 Date line	April 15, 20--
5 Inside address	Barbie Cole 1193 Grandview Avenue Peterborough, ON K9J 5P7
7 Salutation	Dear Ms. Cole
8 Subject line	**Re: Domestic**
9 Body	As per our telephone conversation yesterday, I am enclosing a copy of your Divorce Order for your records. Please note that you are not free to remarry until 31 days from the date of the Divorce Order and until you obtain your Divorce Certificate. If you have any questions regarding the above, please do not hesitate to contact us.
10 Complimentary closing	Yours very truly
12 Signature block	
13 Sender's name	Ryder Woodrow
14 Reference initials	RW:dc
15 Enclosures	Encl. Divorce Order

FIGURE 8.20 Full block letter style, multipage, with mixed punctuation:
File opening letter for real estate transaction

1 Letterhead

WOODROW & PERRY
Barristers & Solicitors

1605 Treetop Road   woodrow.perry@shaw.ca
Peterborough, Ontario
K9K 1G2

Telephone: 705-743-5796
Facsimile: 705-749-3492

4 Date line

January 28, 20--

5 Inside address

David Baker and Julie Eve
763 Brown Street
Peterborough, Ontario
K9K 4K9

7 Salutation

Dear David Baker and Julie Eve:

8 Subject line

RE: Your purchase from Dunn/Slice
274 Braidwood Ave., Peterborough
Part Lot 110, Plan 30Q
Closing Date: April 26, 2006
My File No.: 26606

9 Body

I am pleased to act for you in the above transaction and
acknowledge receipt of your instructions.

The transaction is scheduled to close April 26, 20-- and shortly
before closing I will require you to provide me with funds to cover
the balance due on closing as adjusted, and the registration fees for
your Transfer/Deed of Land.

I would confirm that you wish to hold title to the subject property in
the following manner:

David Ross Baker, date of birth: March 20, 1946
Julie Lynn Eve, date of birth: September 25, 1957

as joint tenants and not as tenants in common.

In addition, I would ask that you have your mortgage institution
forward their instructions to me as soon as possible.

As there will be documents to complete, I will contact you at a later
date to arrange an appointment.

/2

(Continued on the next page.)

Heading

(see page 241)

Woodrow & Perry
Page 2
January 28, 20--

I am attempting to discover if there is an existing location survey of the property prepared by an Ontario Land Surveyor. I will advise you as to whether one is found and discuss either that survey or the lack of one at a later date. If, however, a survey does not exist, I will be recommending that you have a survey prepared as it is a general prerequisite of institutional lenders and a prerequisite for my delivering a full title opinion.

9 Body *(cont.)*

To avoid the possible interruption of public utility services during this transaction, you should contact all local utilities supplied to this property to arrange that the utility accounts be placed in your name on the day of closing.

It will be necessary for you to arrange fire insurance coverage as of the date of closing, which should show loss payable to the first mortgagee. Please have your insurance agent forward to us by fax a binder letter showing the particulars of the policy as soon as you have arranged same.

If you have any questions as to the foregoing, please call the writer.

10 Complimentary closing

Yours very truly,

12 Signature block

13 Sender's name

Jordan Woodrow

11 Firm name

WOODROW & PERRY

14 Reference initials

JW:dc

FIGURE 8.21   Full block letter style, closed punctuation, special notation, and enclosures: Request to amend Legal Aid certificate

1 Letterhead	**WOODROW & PERRY** Barristers & Solicitors 1605 Treetop Road woodrow.perry@shaw.ca Peterborough, Ontario K9K 1G2 Telephone: 705-743-5796 Facsimile: 705-749-3492
2 Notation	**REPLY TO: CURTIS INMAN**
3 Special mailing notation	SENT BY FAX
4 Date line	October 1, 20--
5 Inside address	Legal Aid Ontario, Water Street, Peterborough, ON K9K 1G2
7 Salutation	Dear Madam:
8 Subject line	**Re: Fellion – Section 365 CCC Cert. No. CE54485590**
9 Body	Would you please amend the above-noted certificate to include the charges set out on the attached charge screening forms.
10 Complimentary closing	Yours very truly,
12 Signature block	
13 Sender's name	Curtis Inman
14 Reference initials	CI/th
15 Enclosures	Enclosure: 1

FIGURE 8.22 Full block letter style, mixed punctuation, and special notation: Request for documentation in a criminal matter

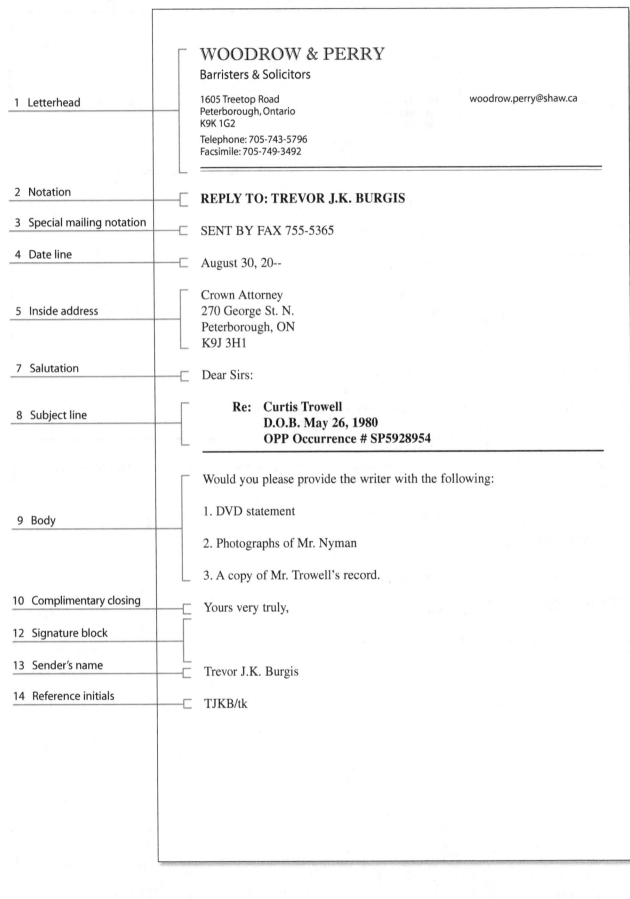

1 Letterhead

WOODROW & PERRY
Barristers & Solicitors

1605 Treetop Road
Peterborough, Ontario
K9K 1G2

Telephone: 705-743-5796
Facsimile: 705-749-3492

woodrow.perry@shaw.ca

2 Notation

REPLY TO: TREVOR J.K. BURGIS

3 Special mailing notation

SENT BY FAX 755-5365

4 Date line

August 30, 20--

5 Inside address

Crown Attorney
270 George St. N.
Peterborough, ON
K9J 3H1

7 Salutation

Dear Sirs:

8 Subject line

Re: Curtis Trowell
D.O.B. May 26, 1980
OPP Occurrence # SP5928954

9 Body

Would you please provide the writer with the following:

1. DVD statement

2. Photographs of Mr. Nyman

3. A copy of Mr. Trowell's record.

10 Complimentary closing

Yours very truly,

12 Signature block

13 Sender's name

Trevor J.K. Burgis

14 Reference initials

TJKB/tk

FIGURE 8.23   Full block letter style, open punctuation, special notation, and copies: Request by both parties to the trial coordinator

1 Letterhead	**WOODROW & PERRY** Barristers & Solicitors 1605 Treetop Road woodrow.perry@shaw.ca Peterborough, Ontario K9K 1G2 Telephone: 705-743-5796 Facsimile: 705-749-3492
2 Notation 3 Special mailing notation	**Please refer to: Shannon Smith File No. 12776-S07**
4 Date line	June 22, 20-- *By Facsimile Transmission: 705-745-3526* *1 Page*
5 Inside address	Trial Co-ordinator Tri-County Trial Office 470 Water Street Peterborough, Ontario K9H 3M3
7 Salutation	Dear Madam:
8 Subject line	**Re: ONTARIO SUPERIOR COURT OF JUSTICE, FAMILY COURT PETERBOROUGH — COURT FILE NO.: 299/009 SUSAN SMITH v. SHANE SMITH**
9 Body	I am the solicitor for the Respondent in the above-captioned matter and Mr. John McQuade is the solicitor for the Applicant. On consent, the parties are requesting that a Trial Management Conference be scheduled for Thursday August 19, 20-- and we would be obliged to receive written confirmation that this date and appropriate time is available. We thank you for your assistance in this matter.
10 Complimentary closing	Yours very truly,
12 Signature block 13 Sender's name	Shannon Smith
14 Reference initials	SS/pv
16 Copies	c.c. Mr. John McQuade Client

FIGURE 8.24 Full block letter style with mixed punctuation: Letter of thanks/agency representation

1 Letterhead	**WOODROW & PERRY** Barristers & Solicitors 1605 Treetop Road Peterborough, Ontario K9K 1G2 Telephone: 705-743-5796 Facsimile: 705-749-3492

woodrow.perry@shaw.ca

3 Special mailing notation

VIA FAX

4 Date line

September 8, 20--

5 Inside address

Donna Armstrong MacKay
Barrister & Solicitor
1212 Justice Avenue
Peterborough, Ontario K9H 3M7

7 Salutation

Dear Ms. Donna Armstrong MacKay:

8 Subject line

Re: Janet Barnes Breach of Trust
Criminal Court Lindsay – September 9, 20--

9 Body

Thank you for agreeing to speak to the above-noted matter in Lindsay on September 9, 20--. I can go on the record and Mr. Barnes will be in attendance. Would you please obtain disclosure and have the matter adjourned to October 7, 20-- in order that I may review same with him.

10 Complimentary closing

Yours very truly,

12 Signature block

13 Sender's name

Trevor J.K. Burgis

14 Reference initials

TJKB/lb

FIGURE 8.25 Full block letter style, mixed punctuation, special notation, enclosures, and copies: Consent letter, both parties

1 Letterhead	**WOODROW & PERRY** Barristers & Solicitors 1605 Treetop Road woodrow.perry@shaw.ca Peterborough, Ontario K9K 1G2 Telephone: 705-743-5796 Facsimile: 705-749-3492
2 Notation	Please refer to: Tom Woodrow
3 Special mailing notation	File No.: 12788-S07
4 Date line	*By Facsimile Transmission* August 21, 20--
5 Inside address	Townsend & Kavanagh Actuarial Consultants Box 20047 Taylor Kidd P.O. Kingston, Ontario K7P 2T6
6 Attention line	Attention: Mr. Douglas Townsend
7 Salutation	Dear Mr. Townsend:
8 Subject line	**Re: Smith Domestic**
9 Body	Please be advised that my client Susan Smith has separated from her husband Shane Smith, who is being represented by Mr. John McQuade. Mr. McQuade and I have agreed to jointly retain you to prepare two valuations, one being Mrs. Smith's OPSEU pension plan and the second being Mr. Smith's Teachers pension plan. For the purpose of your calculations, we have agreed to use a valuation date of <u>March 11, 20--</u>. I am enclosing the following documentation to facilitate your valuation: 1. Correspondence dated May 25, 20-- from OPSEU Pension Plan; and 2. Copies of Mr. and Mrs. Smith's 20-- annual statements. The date of marriage was February 14, 1989 and their dates of birth are on their pension statements. Your entire account should be remitted to my law firm for payment and Mr. McQuade will settle his client's share with me in due course. We thank you for your assistance in this matter.
10 Complimentary closing	Yours very truly,
12 Signature block	
13 Sender's name	Tom Woodrow
14 Reference initials	TW/tk
15 Enclosures	Encl.
16 Copies	c.c. Client, Mr. McQuade

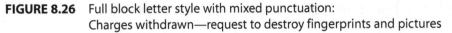

FIGURE 8.26   Full block letter style with mixed punctuation:
Charges withdrawn—request to destroy fingerprints and pictures

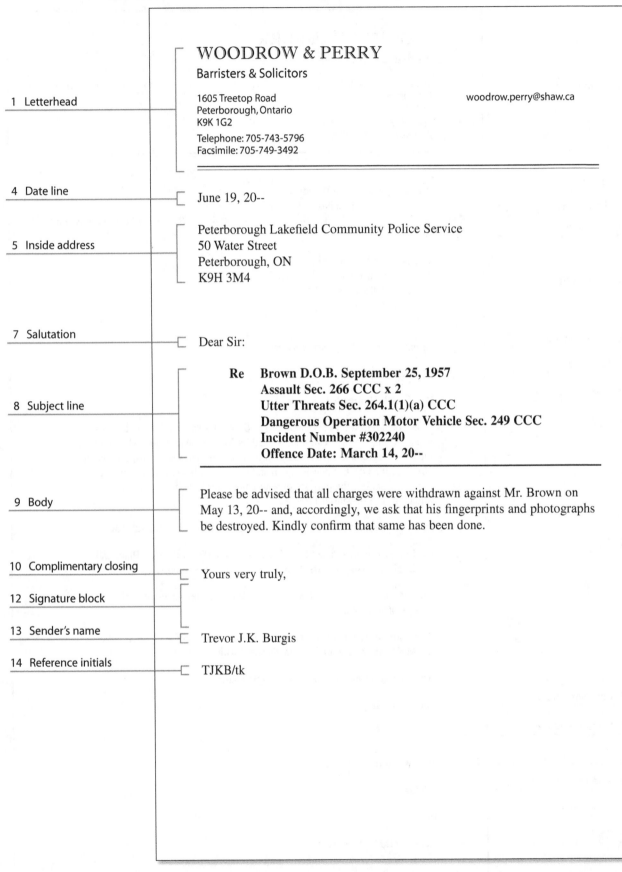

1 Letterhead

WOODROW & PERRY

Barristers & Solicitors

1605 Treetop Road
Peterborough, Ontario
K9K 1G2

woodrow.perry@shaw.ca

Telephone: 705-743-5796
Facsimile: 705-749-3492

4 Date line

June 19, 20--

5 Inside address

Peterborough Lakefield Community Police Service
50 Water Street
Peterborough, ON
K9H 3M4

7 Salutation

Dear Sir:

8 Subject line

Re   Brown D.O.B. September 25, 1957
Assault Sec. 266 CCC x 2
Utter Threats Sec. 264.1(1)(a) CCC
Dangerous Operation Motor Vehicle Sec. 249 CCC
Incident Number #302240
Offence Date: March 14, 20--

9 Body

Please be advised that all charges were withdrawn against Mr. Brown on
May 13, 20-- and, accordingly, we ask that his fingerprints and photographs
be destroyed. Kindly confirm that same has been done.

10 Complimentary closing

Yours very truly,

12 Signature block

13 Sender's name

Trevor J.K. Burgis

14 Reference initials

TJKB/tk

FIGURE 8.27 Full block letter style, multipage, open punctuation, special notation: Letter confirming instructions from client

1 Letterhead	**WOODROW & PERRY** Barristers & Solicitors 1605 Treetop Road woodrow.perry@shaw.ca Peterborough, Ontario K9K 1G2 Telephone: 705-743-5796 Facsimile: 705-749-3492
2 Notation	**REPLY TO: TREVOR J.K. BURGIS**
3 Special mailing notation	DELIVERED
4 Date line	January 10, 20--
5 Inside address	Mr. John Smith c/o Central East Correctional Centre 541 Hwy 35 Lindsay, ON K9V 4S6
7 Salutation	Dear Sir:
8 Subject line	**Re: Various Criminal Court Charges – File # TB-011-178** **Trial Date: February 1 & 2, 20--**
9 Body	I understand that you have instructed me to proceed with a trial on all matters before the Court, including multiple assaults, multiple utter threats, mischief, aggravated assault, and breach of court order. This trial is to be conducted on February 1 and 2, 20--. I point out that you have the following difficulties:

1. Sally Jones has a significant injury to her eye and alleges that you choked her and, as a result, endangered her life.

2. On the July 2, 20-- incident, the Crown has an independent witness, Trish Goodwin.

3. On the September 1, 20-- assault and utter threat charges, the Crown has an independent witness.

4. On the October 1, 20-- assault, utter threats, and cruelty to animals charges, they have an independent witness who has picked you out of a photo lineup.

5. On the November 15, 20-- aggravated assault and forcible confinement charges, there are multiple witnesses including police officers.

/2

(Continued on the next page.)

Heading

(see page 241)

Woodrow & Perry
Page 2
January 10, 20--

6. On the November 16, 20-- possession of property and break and enter charges and the November 18, 20-- disobey court order, they have two special constables who indicate that they witnessed you gesture to her.

On the positive side, Ms. Sally Jones is known to have lied to police on previous occasions. I note that you are not prepared to accept that you caused Ms. Jones her black eye or that you assaulted her or that at any point did you confine her or cause harm to the dog.

9 Body *(cont.)*

Notwithstanding the above, you have instructed me to proceed with the trial of these matters.

This letter is acknowledging your written instructions to conduct the trial on all matters.

10 Complimentary closing

Yours very truly

12 Signature block

13 Sender's name

Trevor J.K. Burgis

14 Reference initials

TJKB/ca

Multipage Letters

The examples of letters in this chapter (with the exception of figures 8.20 and 8.27) all fit onto a single page—as many letters do in a typical law office. But many letters also run longer than a page. The second and subsequent pages of a multipage letter differ from the first. They are typed or printed on blank paper, not letterhead, and therefore require heading information. This information can include the name of the addressee, the name of the sender, the date of the letter, its subject matter, and, last but almost never omitted, the page number.

The heading of the second and subsequent pages of multipage letters begins approximately 1.27 cm (one-half inch) from the top of the page. The body of the letter continues a double or triple space (one or two blank lines) below the heading. Most word-processing programs have a header/footer feature that, when set up, will automatically enter the desired information on each page. The format and content of multipage headers vary from office to office. Some offices bold-face certain information and/or insert a dividing line before continuing the body of the letter. Common heading formats for second and subsequent pages are illustrated in the following examples.

Sometimes the footer of a multipage document shows the next page number in a format such as "/2" or "... /2." Such a footer is helpful, but is not necessary.

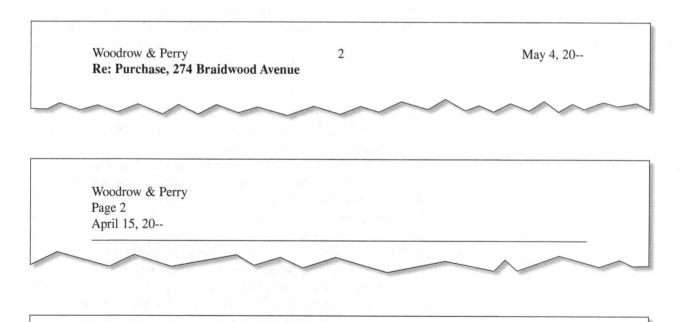

Woodrow & Perry   2   May 4, 20--
Re: Purchase, 274 Braidwood Avenue

Woodrow & Perry
Page 2
April 15, 20--

Woodrow & Perry
Re: Separation Agreement
Page 2
July 5, 20--

Using Templates

The number and kinds of letters and memos that are prepared in a law office are as diverse as the types of law practices that produce them. Examples include retainer letters, retainer agreements, demand letters, information letters, reporting letters, authorizations, and statements of account. The format and structure of these documents are often fixed. It is thus a great time saver to have on hand preformatted documents that are already partially completed. Sometimes, all you need to do is fill in specific file details such as client information and you're done.

In-House Templates

Many law offices maintain examples of often-used correspondence, known as templates. These templates consist of standard text that can be customized to fit specific situations. Templates are also referred to as precedents or boilerplates. The templates are typed and saved in a precedent folder on the central server. Sometimes a printed copy is produced and maintained in a precedent manual or file.

Word-Processing Templates

Most word-processing programs have a variety of preformatted templates that can be used to create different types of documents. Microsoft Word offers a number of downloadable templates that can be found by accessing Microsoft Online in the New Document dialogue box.

The easiest way to create a new template in Microsoft Word is to create the document you wish to use as a template and save it in the templates folder. To do so, follow these steps:

1. In the **Save As** dialog box, do one of the following:
   a. In Windows 7, scroll to the top of the folder list and under **Microsoft Word**, click **Templates**.
   b. In Windows Vista, under **Favorite Links**, click **Templates**.
   c. In Windows XP, under **Save in**, click **Trusted Templates**.
2. Give the new template a file name, select **Word Template** in the **Save as type** list, and then click **Save**.
3. Close the template.
4. The template can be accessed for editing by selecting as follows:
   a. Word 2000 and earlier: Select **New...** on the **File** menu. This opens the **New** dialog box.
   b. Word 2002 and 2003: Select **New...** on the **File** menu. This opens the **New Document** task pane, where you can either select a **Recently Used Template** or click on **General Templates**.
   c. Word 2007 and 2010: Click the **Office Button** and select **New**. This opens the **New Document** dialog box , where you can select a **Recently Used Template** or click on **My Templates**.

You can save the template as a Word Macro-Enabled Template (.dotm file) or a Word 97-2003 Template (.dot file).

Anatomy of an Internal Memorandum

There are two types of memos prepared in a law office. One, commonly known simply as a memo, is used for internal office communication on a client file or on a general office matter. The other, known as a legal memorandum, is used in conjunction with legal research. Legal memorandums have certain formatting rules that differ from those for internal memorandums. The formatting rules for legal memorandums are discussed in detail in chapter 11, Legal Terminology and Citation.

Purpose and Format

An internal memo, as its name suggests, is used for communication within the office; it is not used for communication with people outside the office. A typical memo is used for a variety of purposes. The overriding purpose, though, is to provide a record or paper trail of a matter, an event, an activity—anything—related to a client file. A typical memo might

- provide information to several staff members at once
- remind people about meetings and appointments
- request that something be done
- ask and answer questions
- give details about a telephone conversation or a meeting.

A memo is short, to the point, and very direct in style. It is generally divided into three sections:

1. the title
2. the heading, which includes the name(s) of the recipient(s), the name of the sender, the date it was written, and the subject matter
3. the body, which deals with the purpose of the memo.

There are no strict rules for the format of a memo. Many offices use a self-duplicating, "no carbon required" (NCR) memo form, while others create their own memo template.

Figures 8.28 to 8.30 illustrate the format and content of internal memorandums. Figure 8.31 offers detailed formatting guidelines.

PRACTICE TIP

In today's office, email is increasingly replacing the memo. If email is used instead of a memo, the email must be printed and placed in the relevant client file.

FIGURE 8.28   Sample internal memorandum

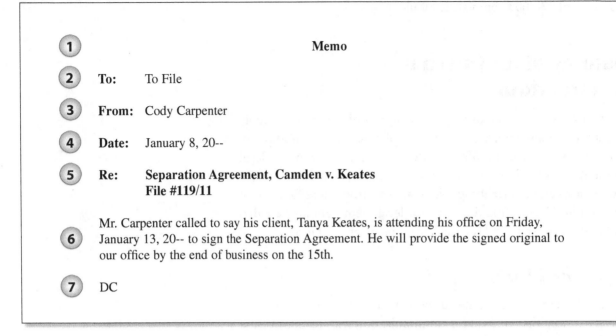

① **Memo**

② **To:**   To File

③ **From:**   Cody Carpenter

④ **Date:**   January 8, 20--

⑤ **Re:**   **Separation Agreement, Camden v. Keates**
             File #119/11

⑥ Mr. Carpenter called to say his client, Tanya Keates, is attending his office on Friday, January 13, 20-- to sign the Separation Agreement. He will provide the signed original to our office by the end of business on the 15th.

⑦ DC

FIGURE 8.29   Sample internal memorandum

① **Memorandum**

② **To:**   To File

③ **From:**   Allicia Perry

④ **Date:**   February 20, 20--

⑤ **Re:**   Anderson MVA
             File #221/11

⑥ Mrs. Anderson phoned. Wanted to know whether you were still going to court next Thursday, because her mother has passed away. I told her we are keeping the date for court, but I'm not sure what exactly we will be doing that day (March 2nd).

What do you want me to tell her?

FIGURE 8.30 Sample internal memorandum

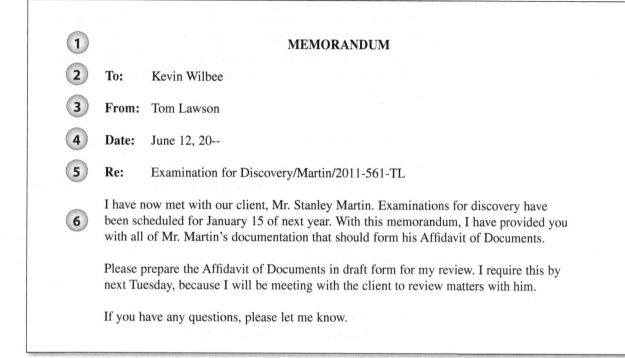

MEMORANDUM

To: Kevin Wilbee

From: Tom Lawson

Date: June 12, 20--

Re: Examination for Discovery/Martin/2011-561-TL

I have now met with our client, Mr. Stanley Martin. Examinations for discovery have been scheduled for January 15 of next year. With this memorandum, I have provided you with all of Mr. Martin's documentation that should form his Affidavit of Documents.

Please prepare the Affidavit of Documents in draft form for my review. I require this by next Tuesday, because I will be meeting with the client to review matters with him.

If you have any questions, please let me know.

FIGURE 8.31 Anatomy of an internal memorandum

	Element	Details
	Paper	A preprinted duplicate memo form or white 216 × 279 mm (8.5 × 11 inch) paper.
1	Letterhead	Letterhead is not used on memos. The memo is titled "Memo" or "Memorandum." The title may be in all caps or title case, may be in bold-face type, and is usually centred at the top of the page.
2	To:	The recipient's name. The recipient may be another lawyer in the firm, or simply "To File." There may be more than one recipient.
3	From:	The author's name.
4	Date:	The date the memo was prepared.
5	Re:	The subject matter. The "Re:" line should include the file or matter number, as well as a brief description of the subject covered in the memo.
6	Body	The body of the memo is single-spaced with a double line space (a blank line) between paragraphs.
7	Closing	A complimentary closing or signature line is not necessary in a memo. The author's hand-written initials can be included at the bottom of the memo or beside his or her name. The transcriber's initials can be keyed below the body of the memo.
	Format rules	All headings should start at the left margin. Use tabs to vertically align the recipient's name, the author's name, the date, and the subject information.

Email Use in Business

In recent years email has become an effective and widely used method of personal and professional communication. In many offices, it is increasingly replacing the business letter and memo altogether. The advantages and disadvantages of email, as well as tips on email etiquette, were discussed in chapter 7.

Email Guidelines

Before you start using email to communicate with colleagues, business associates, and others, you should be aware of the proper use of electronic communication. When writing and sending email:

- keep the message short and to the point

- make sure the subject line is informative

- start with the person's name and end with your name, in full

- if you want, include your phone number, fax number, or "snail mail" address in the email signature

- as discussed in chapter 7, be careful about what you say and how you say it

- avoid using special characters such as curly (typographer's) quotation marks and apostrophes, because they may not be readable by the recipient

- use proper grammar and check your spelling—although this is an email, it is still a professional communication

- proofread your message before you send it

- ensure that a confidentiality disclaimer is included (see chapter 9, figures 9.12 and 9.13).

Figure 8.32 shows the message window of an email program, and figure 8.33 offers detailed usage and formatting guidelines.

NOTES:

FIGURE 8.32 An email message window

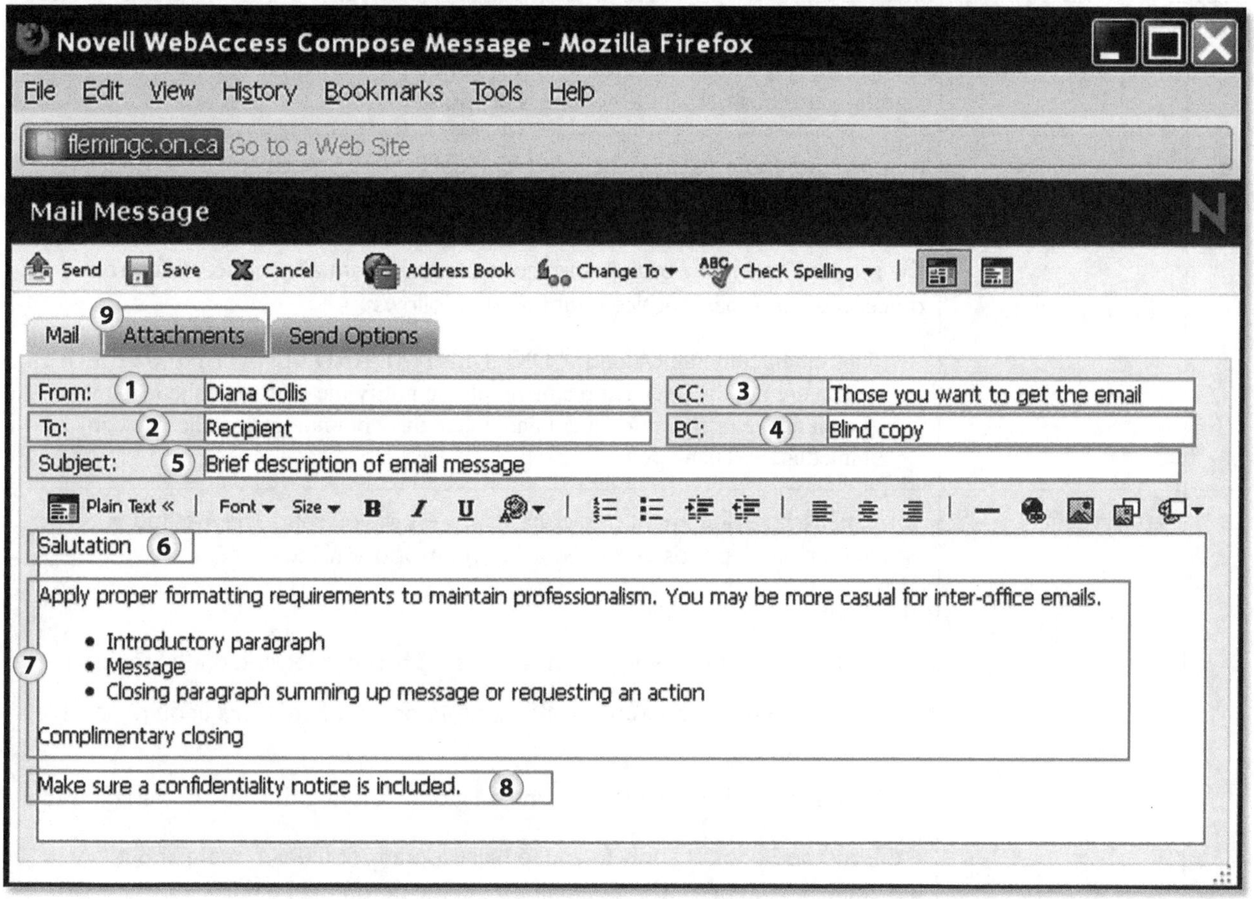

```
┌─────────────────────────────────────────────────────────────────────────────┐
│ 🌐 Novell WebAccess Compose Message - Mozilla Firefox          ▭ ☐ ✕         │
├─────────────────────────────────────────────────────────────────────────────┤
│ File  Edit  View  History  Bookmarks  Tools  Help                            │
│ ┌─────────────────────────────────────────────────────────────────────────┐ │
│ │ ▮ flemingc.on.ca  Go to a Web Site                                        │ │
│ └─────────────────────────────────────────────────────────────────────────┘ │
│ Mail Message                                                             N    │
│ 📤 Send  💾 Save  ✖ Cancel  |  📖 Address Book  🔄 Change To ▾  ᴬᴮᶜ Check Spelling ▾  |  ▦ ▦  │
└─────────────────────────────────────────────────────────────────────────────┘
```

Mail ⑨ Attachments	Send Options
From: ① Diana Collis	CC: ③ Those you want to get the email
To: ② Recipient	BC: ④ Blind copy
Subject: ⑤ Brief description of email message	

Plain Text « | Font ▾ Size ▾ **B** *I* U 🎨▾ | ☰ ☰ ☰ ☰ | ☰ ☰ ☰ | — ⊛ 🖼 📷 🎬▾

Salutation ⑥

Apply proper formatting requirements to maintain professionalism. You may be more casual for inter-office emails.

⑦
- Introductory paragraph
- Message
- Closing paragraph summing up message or requesting an action

Complimentary closing

Make sure a confidentiality notice is included. ⑧

FIGURE 8.33 Anatomy of an email

	Element	Details
1	From:	The sender's email address.
2	To:	The recipient's email address. There may be more than one recipient.
3	CC:	The email addresses of recipients of a copy.
4	BC:	The email addresses of recipients of a blind copy.
5	Subject:	A brief but informative description of the email contents.
6	Salutation	If the email is replacing a formal letter, ensure that a professional salutation is used.
		Always use the name of the individual if you know it.
		If you want to highlight the letter to someone in particular in the organization, use an attention line.
		Attention: Mr. B. Burgess, LLB, and Mr. M. Jackson, LLM
		If you are addressing government officials, be sure to use their proper titles. (See figure 8.6 for the correct forms of titles and honorifics.)

	Element	Details
7	Contents	People tend to write less formally when it comes to email. But remember that you are still writing a business letter—only the mode of delivery is different. The standards for business-letter writing still apply.
8	Confidentiality notice	A boilerplate footer is often included for legal liability purposes. It gives notice to the recipient that the email communication is confidential and legally privileged, and asks unintended recipients of an email to destroy the message and to inform the sender. The exact wording and scope of a confidentiality notice differ from office to office. A basic notice might read as follows: This email communication is CONFIDENTIAL AND LEGALLY PRIVILEGED. If you are not the intended recipient, please notify me at the telephone number shown above or by return email and delete this communication and any copy immediately. Thank you.
9	Attachments	You can attach a document or picture to any email you send. The method of attaching a file depends on the email program you're using. In general: • click on the attachment icon (such as a paper clip located on the toolbar) • locate the file you want to attach, either on your hard drive or on removable media • select the file by double-clicking on it or by clicking the "OK" or "ADD" button. If this method doesn't apply to your email program, or to learn more about attaching a document to your email, access the program's help file.

REVIEW QUESTIONS

1. Before preparing outgoing correspondence, what resources do you need?

2. What is the commonly accepted length for a business letter?

3. What are the three basic letter styles used in a law office?

4. True or false? When using open punctuation, punctuation marks are required at the end of the salutation and the complimentary closing.

_____

_____

_____

_____

_____

_____

_____

5. What is the name of the formatting style used when the date line and the complimentary closing begin at the left margin?

_____

_____

_____

_____

_____

_____

_____

6. The signature block appears directly above

   a. the copies notation

   b. the enclosures notation

   c. the reference initials

   d. the sender's name

7. What is the spacing between the inside address and the date line?

   a. single space

   b. double space

   c. triple space

   d. varies depending on the length of the letter

8. The subject line of a letter is located

   a. above the inside address

   b. between the salutation and the body

   c. between the attention line and the salutation

   d. above the date line

9. How do you determine which style of business letter to use?

   _____

   _____

   _____

   _____

   _____

   _____

   _____

10. Why would a memo, rather than a letter, be used within an office?

   _____

   _____

   _____

   _____

   _____

   _____

   _____

11. What is the advantage of using a template when preparing a letter, court document, or memo?

   _____

   _____

   _____

   _____

   _____

   _____

   _____

   _____

ACTIVITIES

Mr. Woodrow has asked you to prepare the following letters for his signature. The preferred formatting style is full block, left justified.

1. Send survey to David Keates and Julie McFadden, 763 Brown Street, Peterborough, ON K9J 4K9

   File #296/11/DW

   Re: Keates/McFadden purchase from Lodge, 756 Vernon Place, Ancaster, ON L96 3H3

   We have enclosed a copy of the location survey received for the above-noted property. [NP] Please review the survey and advise whether any additions or alterations have been made to the dwelling since the survey was prepared.

2. Request for employment records from J & J Manufacturing, 996 – 51 Sydenham Street, Peterborough, ON K9J 7V7

   File #386/11/PL

   Re: Lift Truck Accident, John Carpenter

   RE: Our Client:

       SIN:

       Accident:

       Our File No.:

   Please be advised that we represent the above-noted employee of your company for the purpose of recovering damages for personal injuries occasioned in the above-noted incident, and we are advised that because of the injuries sustained, our client has been absent from employment with your firm.

   Would you be kind enough to forward to us a letter containing the following information:

   (a) our client's position or occupation;

   (b) confirmation that our client was employed by you at the time of the incident;

   (c) our client's period of absence since the incident;

   (d) our client's hourly or weekly rate of pay, including vacation pay;

   (e) the amount of wages and benefits our client lost as a result of the incident, including vacation pay;

   (f) the amount of wages and benefits paid by you, the employer, or pursuant to a disability insurance plan during our client's absence from work;

(g) if benefits were paid to our client during our client's absence from work, the amount of wages and benefits, in percentage terms, our client received;

(h) if our client had a disability plan with you that paid all or a portion of our client's wages, the amount our client contributed in any way to the payment of the premiums for such a plan;

(i) if our client was paid all or a percentage of wages during his absence from work, the deduction from our client's sick bank for the days missed;

(j) lost overtime pay/shift premiums; and

(k) whether our client missed out on any promotions or opportunities to apply for promotions.

Would you also please provide us with a complete copy of our client's personnel file.

We are enclosing at this time a written authorization executed by our client authorizing you to release the requisite information to us.

3. Request for medical information from the Medical Records Department at Peterborough Regional Health Centre, 1 Hospital Drive, Peterborough, ON K3Y 2P9

> File #386/11/PL
>
> Re: Lift Truck Accident, John Carpenter
>
> RE: Our Client:
>
>> Date of Incident:
>>
>> Health Card No.:
>>
>> Date of Birth:
>>
>> Our File No.:
>
> Please be advised that we have been retained by the above-noted client to prosecute a claim for damages arising out of the above-noted incident. Our client advises that he was in attendance at your hospital for the incident in issue and perhaps for other unrelated incidents.
>
> Would you be kind enough to forward to us copies of all the records you have pertaining to our client, and we emphasize that we would like to receive all of your records. We ask that you not exercise your discretion and forward only selected documents to us because this could have a prejudicial effect on our client's claim. Specifically, would you be kind enough to forward to us copies of the following:
>
> (a) admission and discharge records;
>
> (b) reports of all X-rays taken;

(c) diagnostic studies;

(d) consultations;

(e) histories and operative reports;

(f) doctors' orders;

(g) nurses' notes;

(h) laboratory reports;

(i) medication schedules;

(j) all physiotherapy records including clinical notes, records, treatment charts, and consultation reports;

(k) all occupational therapy records including clinical notes, records, treatment charts, and consultation reports; and

(l) any and all other documentation you have on file.

We are enclosing a medical authorization executed by our client authorizing the release of the requested records along with our firm cheque payable to you in the sum of $150.00.

We thank you in advance for your anticipated cooperation.

Yours very truly,

4. Using the sample correspondence in this chapter, determine which precedent document is appropriate and prepare the following correspondence:

- Correspondence to Mr. Randall requesting that his outstanding balance of $668.96 be paid.

- Correspondence to Dr. Leslie Allan, along with a payment of $345.61, for her medical report related to the Wilkins file, invoice date May 26, file #206/11/AW.

- Correspondence to the Crown requesting disclosure with respect to Ms. Jennifer Applegate. (Confirm the charge with your professor.)

- Correspondence to the Crown requesting evidence with respect to Mr. Gerry Jones.

Processing Correspondence

I was working on the proof of one of my poems all the morning, and took out a comma. In the afternoon I put it back again.
—Oscar Wilde

Introduction

In previous chapters, you learned the rules and procedures for encoding a message in a professional manner (how to create and format various documents) as well as the rules and procedures for assembling the content of a message (what information to include, where to find it, and how to include it). Your job does not end there. A number of additional steps are necessary to ensure accuracy and efficient delivery of your correspondence and other documents.

Revisions: Editing and Proofreading

Your lawyer needs to send someone a letter and has asked you to write it. You know what needs to be written, you've done the necessary research and collected all the information, and you've written a first draft. You may think you're finished, but the important process of revising your work is just beginning.

Even the most careful writers overlook errors and weaknesses in their first drafts. Spelling mistakes, missing words, poor phrasing, and other problems make your document—and you, and your firm—look unprofessional. To avoid creating a bad impression, you need to revise your document.

To start, create some distance between you and your writing. If you try to revise your document immediately after finishing the first draft, you run the risk of missing errors and overlooking key details. This happens because you are too close to the document: you know what you wrote, you know what it should say. You will only repeat the same mistakes when you go to revise the document; your familiarity with it stands in the way of effective revision. Let the document sit for a while, and allow yourself to become more objective before taking another look.

There are two separate and distinguishable stages in the revision process: editing and proofreading.

Editing

Editing is the first stage. When editing a document, you review its content and structure for clarity and style. You may have to read through the document a number of times before you are satisfied with the final product. Try to develop your own system or process. For example, on your first read-through, you may be focusing strictly on content and clarity; on the next read-through, you may be concentrating on structure and style. Figure 9.1 highlights key areas you should focus on while editing your documents. Be patient: As you practise the process of editing and learn to identify your own weaknesses in writing, you will gradually become more skilled at the task.

You can edit either on paper or on screen. Always work on a *copy* of the original document. This way, if you change your mind about your edits, you can simply go back to the original document. If you're working on paper, you may want to increase the text size and line spacing before you print out a copy, so that you'll have enough room to mark your changes. But if you do, print out the original document so that you can refer to the original formatting if necessary.

Whether you edit on paper or on screen, keep reference resources handy. The basic resource is a dictionary. You may also want to have a thesaurus, a French–English dictionary, and a grammar/usage guide. The Writing Guide appendix to this text may serve as a useful reference. If your firm has a style guide that lists preferred spellings and rules regarding capitalization and punctuation, use it. The purpose of any reference resource is to ensure consistency and accuracy in all your documents.

When editing on paper, use a pencil to mark your revisions. Make the edits as close as possible to the text you want to change—above the line generally, or below it if you don't have room. If a change is too big to fit between the lines, write it in the margin and then draw a line from the new text to the old text, and make sure that the line does not cross through other text. Be clear in your markings: if you want to delete or replace a word, draw a definite line through it; do not just circle it lightly. But don't be too heavy-handed: your lawyer may want to review your edits, so the original text should still be readable underneath your markings.

Develop a system for indicating your progress through the revision process, so you don't have to question whether or not you've done something already. If you verify a fact (a name, a file number, a date, an address), put a check mark beside it to show that it doesn't need to be verified again. If you can't check a fact or if you have a question about something in the document that you can't answer, put a circled question mark or a circled capital Q beside it or in the margin to indicate that the text is in doubt.

Ensure that your markings are clear and legible: Once you've finished your edit on paper, your lawyer may want to review your work and may make further changes (or may override or "stet" some of your changes). As well, when the document is finally ready to be corrected, the person who inputs the changes (you or a colleague) will be grateful that your work is neatly written and clearly marked.

FIGURE 9.1   Editing guidelines

Reading	Action
1st reading	Read through the document quickly, as the reader would, focusing on the overall document, its key points, its general meaning, and its presentation. Use the following questions to help you assess the overall document and to guide your editing. Make note of problematic elements to address on subsequent readings, or, if a change is simple, make it now. • Is the message clear? Will the reader know immediately what the document is about and why it was written? • Is it clear what the reader should do in response to the document (e.g., send a document in return, pay an invoice)? • Is all the necessary information included? • Does the document appear professional and visually inviting? • Is the tone appropriate and consistent? • In a large document, are there headings and subheadings to guide the reader? • Are all reference details (file name/number, dollar tables, dates, etc.) correct?
2nd reading	Read the document more slowly. Focus on each paragraph. Use the following questions to help you assess each paragraph and to guide your editing. If you answer no to any question, change the document to eliminate the problem. • Are the key points of the document organized in a logical order? • Does each paragraph relate to only one main idea? • Is the main idea of each paragraph clearly stated in the opening sentence? • Does the closing sentence of one paragraph flow logically and naturally into the opening sentence of the next paragraph?
3rd reading	Read the document paragraph by paragraph, focusing on the sentences in each paragraph. Use the following questions to help you assess sentences and to guide your editing. If you answer no to any question, change the document to eliminate the problem. • Are all the sentences necessary? • Are the sentences well structured? • Do the sentences flow together logically and naturally? • Are the sentences varied: long, short, complex, simple?
4th reading	Read the document to evaluate the appropriateness of its language. Use the following questions to help you assess the document's language and to guide your editing. If you answer no to any specific question, change the document to eliminate the problem. • Are the language level and vocabulary appropriate for the reader? • Is the document free of all ambiguous words or phrases that might lead the reader to confusion or uncertainty? • Is the document free of any words that might offend the reader? • Is the document free of unnecessary words, clichés, and acronyms?
5th reading	Finally, read the document to confirm that all edits have improved the document.

If you are editing a document on screen, it is especially important to be sure that you're working on a copy of the original. As when editing on paper, you should keep track of the revisions you make, in case you change your mind about any of them. Word-processing programs have various features to help you do this: change tracking, blacklining (or redlining), annotations, and manual formatting. If your firm has a protocol for making and indicating changes to electronic documents, learn it and follow it. If the choice of method is up to you, experiment with different methods and choose the one that works best for you.

If you mark changes manually in a word-processing program, develop a system for showing different kinds of changes. For example, if you want to delete text, apply strikethrough formatting to it. If you want to add text, apply a different colour to the new text. If you want to show that you've checked something, apply a second colour to it. If you want to indicate that you have a question about something, apply underline formatting to it (or a third colour) and add a bold-face question mark in parentheses or brackets after it. Once you finish editing the document, all of these changes still have to be implemented—strikethrough text must be deleted, underlining must be removed, and coloured text must be changed back to black.

If you use Microsoft Word, you can use its Track Changes feature to automate the process of indicating revisions. Track Changes highlights deletions and insertions in a fashion similar to manual tracking. It can also keep track of changes by different people. Once you finish editing the document, Track Changes allows you to accept or reject the revisions, either all at once or on a change-by-change basis. Because Track Changes allows you, in effect, to implement edits as you make them, it can be a great time saver.

Proofreading

Proofreading is the second stage of revision and should only be done when the editing stage is complete. When proofreading, you are trying to identify surface errors, or errors in the appearance of the document. These include spelling mistakes, keystroke errors, and grammatical and punctuation errors. You may want to use a ruler or straightedge to proofread to make it easier to spot errors; place the ruler or straightedge just below the line of text you're reading to help you focus only on that line.

Technological assistants such as spell checkers, grammar checkers, and autocorrect features can be helpful, but you should not become dependent on them. You may have made a keystroke error, but if the typed word is contained in the word processor's dictionary, it will not be recognized as a mistake. For example:

The law clerk gave the file tot he lawyer.

The words "tot" and "he" are found in the dictionary, but clearly a keystroke error was made; the sentence should have read: "The law clerk gave the file to the lawyer."

PRACTICE TIP

When editing or proofreading, develop regular routines and habits:

- Refer to your resources when you are unsure (for example, use the Writing Guide in the appendix).
- Create a checklist of your most common errors to serve as a quick reference.
- Revise your work during the time of day that suits you best.
- Try proofreading aloud, if there is a place where this is appropriate.
- Trust yourself: If it doesn't make sense to you, it probably won't make sense to others.

During the proofreading stage, use specific marks and symbols to note your intended changes. These notations are a kind of shorthand—they allow you to express your intention with a few easily interpreted strokes of a pencil or pen, instead of with cumbersome words that might be misread or misinterpreted. Proofreading marks make the process more efficient, especially when it comes time to enter revisions. Figure 9.2 shows suggested proofreading marks.

When proofreading, write your changes in the margins, and, as much as possible, indicate where to make changes by means of insert marks and strikethroughs. If there are multiple corrections within one line, separate your marks in the margin with a vertical or diagonal line. For example, you might mark up the sentence above as follows:

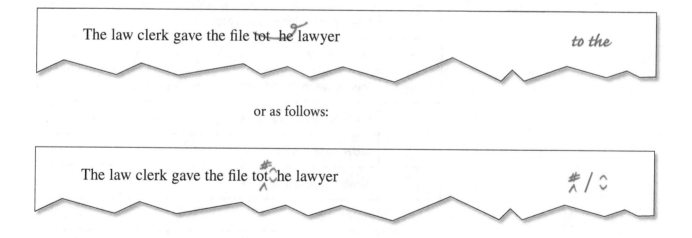

To see how the proofreading marks are applied in practice, look at the marked-up correspondence in Figure 9.3. Figure 9.4 shows the finalized document, once the errors have been corrected.

FIGURE 9.2   Proofreading marks and meanings

Mark	Meaning
¶	Begin new paragraph
no ¶	No new paragraph
⟊	Transpose letters
⟶	Move word
⌐	Delete letter
⟍ϱ	Delete word
⌣	Close up space (between letters, words, or paragraphs)
/	Make letter lower case
≡	Capitalize/make letter upper case
b̰f̰	Bold-face
Ital	Italicize
∧	Insert (e.g., letter, word, phrase, sentence)
#∧	Insert space
##∧	Insert two spaces
⊙∧ ⟨;⟩∧	Insert period, insert semicolon, etc.
⹀∧	Insert hyphen
stet	Stet (leave in the letter or word marked for deletion)
(SP)	Spell out an abbreviation
⌐	Move to the right
⌐	Move to the left
⌐⌐	Centre text
‖	Align vertically
⌐	Break line or word
ss	Single-space
ds	Double-space
ts	Triple-space

FIGURE 9.3 Marked-up correspondence

April 25, 20--

Ms Tanya Keates

10 Anywhere Street

Peterborugh, ON L0A 1GO

Dear Mrs. Keate:

Re: Yourself and Your husband

I have taken instruction of your husband, Larry Carpenter to act on his

behalf with respect to your family difficulties Mr. Carpenter instructed me

to explore the possibility of resolving all matter in issue between you

pursuant to the Family Law Act, 1986 through negotiations which would

lead to the singing of a separation Agreement containing terms exceptable

too both of you.

Mr. Carpenter advised me which you had consulted with Bob Collis of

Colis and Collis and I attempted to contact her by telephone on April 1,

20--, but was advised that he was one holidays. Upon his return I had a

conversation with him and he authorized my to remit this

correspondence directly to you with a copy to him as he indicated that

you had simply had a consultation with him and he was uncertain

weather you would retaining him with respect of further negotiations.

In any event my definate instructions from Mrs. Carpenter are

move to a speedy resolution of all of standard issues including property

and support issues and if possible to do so in an amicable fashion. I

(Continued on the next page.)

would appreciate it if you would immediatly upon reciept of this

correspondence retaine your solicitor and instruct to enter into

Negotiations with me; I will except contact from your counsel within

Days of the date this letter

Yours very Truly,

WOODROW & PERRY

Natasha Bruce

NB/dc

cc: Bob Collis

cc: Mr. Lary Carpenter

FIGURE 9.4 Revised correspondence

WOODROW & PERRY
Barristers & Solicitors

1605 Treetop Road
Peterborough, Ontario
K9K 1G2

woodrow.perry@shaw.ca

Telephone: 705-743-5796
Facsimile: 705-749-3492

April 25, 20--

Ms. Tanya Keates
10 Anywhere Street
Peterborough, ON L0A 1GO

Dear Ms. Keates:

Re: Yourself and Your Husband

I have taken instruction from your husband, Larry Carpenter, to act on his behalf with respect to your family difficulties. Mr. Carpenter instructed me to explore the possibility of resolving all matters in issue between you pursuant to the *Family Law Act, 1986* through negotiations, which would lead to the signing of a Separation Agreement containing terms acceptable to both of you.

Mr. Carpenter advised me that you had consulted with Bob Collis of Collis and Collis, and I attempted to contact him by telephone on April 1, 20--, but was advised that he was on holidays. Upon his return I had a conversation with him and he authorized me to remit this correspondence directly to you with a copy to him. He indicated that you had simply had a consultation with him and he was uncertain whether you would be retaining him with respect to further negotiations.

In any event, my definite instructions from Mr. Carpenter are to move to a speedy resolution of all standard issues including property and support issues, and if possible to do so in an amicable fashion. I would appreciate it if you would immediately upon receipt of this correspondence retain your solicitor and instruct him or her to enter into negotiations with me. I will expect contact from your counsel within seven days of the date of this letter.

Yours very truly,

WOODROW & PERRY

Natasha Bruce

NB/dc

cc: Bob Collis
cc: Mr. Larry Carpenter

Distributing Outgoing Correspondence

Once you've edited, proofread, and corrected your document, you're ready to distribute it. Documents are often sent to multiple recipients, in addition to the main addressee. Pay special attention to ensure that all intended parties will receive a copy of the document. First have the original signed, then make the necessary photocopies. At the end of the document should be a list of recipients; on the copy that is to be sent to, say, Mr. Jones, highlight Mr. Jones's name. It is helpful to stamp the duplicated documents as "copy" or "For your information only." Be careful not to cover over or obscure any of the contents of the correspondence.

Blind copies are sent when the writer wants someone to receive the correspondence, but does not want other recipients to know about it. To make a blind copy, print the original document and then amend it by adding a blind copy notation ("bcc" or "bc"), along with the recipient's name. This notation follows the other copy notations, and appears only on the confidential recipient's copy. Print the amended copy, highlight the blind copy recipient's name, and follow the usual procedure for distributing documents. Ensure that other parties do not receive a copy indicating the confidential recipient.

When you have made and distributed all necessary copies, forward the original to the addressee. If you send the original by fax and do not forward it by mail, keep the original document and fax confirmation sheet together in the file. If you send it by email, print the email and place in the file. (See the sections on faxes and emails later in this chapter.) Regardless of the method of delivery, always ensure that a copy is maintained for the file. The file copy should also indicate that all copies were distributed, including blind copies. This is usually done by placing a handwritten check mark beside each recipient's name. Initialling beside the check mark is also helpful, especially if the file is seen or worked on by more than one person.

Handling Incoming Correspondence

The process for handling incoming mail is important. Inefficiencies can lead to lost or misplaced documents, which can have serious consequences for your clients. Large firms usually have a specialized mail department with trained staff to deal with all correspondence. In smaller firms, one person is usually designated to process all mail. Although the specific procedures for handling incoming mail may differ among firms, their purposes will be similar for all.

The processing of incoming mail includes opening, date-stamping, and distributing the correspondence to the appropriate recipient.

Many documents that are received in a law office are time-sensitive. To help keep track of time, all incoming mail is marked to indicate the date of receipt, even if it is not opened on that particular date. The date is typically stamped on the front of the document; in some instances it is stamped on the back. If the date is stamped on the front, care should be taken not to cover or obscure any of the contents of the document. If the incoming mail is client-related, you may be instructed to pull the relevant client file. Be sure to find out the office practice for what should be date-stamped and where that information should be placed.

If an envelope is marked "Personal" or "Confidential," you should open it only at the direction of the recipient.

Law offices usually use a multi-tray or folder system for incoming mail. Separate the mail into appropriate categories, including miscellaneous mail (such as flyers for upcoming legal education classes), incoming client mail, and payable invoices.

Lawyers will review their mail, or may instruct you to read and highlight pertinent areas of concern. After the mail is read, the lawyer will then instruct you on how to proceed. Once letters have been received and reviewed, file them as soon as possible. This is especially important when, for example, a lawyer is in court on a client matter and the most up-to-date correspondence is required.

Methods of Delivery

There are many different methods of delivery used in law offices. They include Canada Post, courier services, hand-delivery or document exchange services, and faxing.

Xpresspost™ and Priority™ Next A.M. can be tracked, regardless of whether you request a signature upon delivery.

Canada Post

Canada Post offers a number of delivery services. The most familiar of these is Lettermail™ (regular mail), which is available to everyone and is the most convenient way in Canada to send

- personal correspondence

- business correspondence

- invoices

- billing statements

- receipts.

This method of delivery is very reliable and cost-effective. Typically, mail is delivered locally in two days, within the province in three days, and across Canada in four days (not including weekends and statutory holidays).

Canada Post offers other methods of delivery as well:

- Registered mail is an additional fee service to Lettermail, and provides proof of delivery with a signature; it can be tracked online. Delivery is locally in two days, regionally in three days, and nationally in four days, between and within major centres

DID YOU KNOW?
Canada Post delivers over 11 billion pieces of mail each year to 14 million destinations.

in Canada. The delivery information is archived for seven years. Mail will be redirected or returned to the sender if it is not delivered. A signature is mandatory before the mail will be released. If the addressee or their representative refuse to sign for the item, it will be returned to the sender.

- Priority™ Next A.M. is the best choice for time-sensitive documents. This service provides an on-time delivery guarantee locally and regionally the next morning, and nationally in one day. You can track your items online. Signature, redirection and return-to-sender services are provided at no extra charge.

- Xpresspost™ is faster than regular mail. This service provides delivery the next day locally, regionally the next day and in two days, and nationally in two days. You can track your items online. For an additional charge you can request a signature upon delivery and verify who signed for the delivery.

- Xpresspost™ Certified can be used for deliveries that are time sensitive. This service guarantees the same delivery times and tracking as Xpresspost, providing the signature feature at no extra charge. For a charge, you can receive a hard copy of the recipient's signature by Lettermail service or fax.

International Services
- Priority™ Worldwide provides Canada Post's fastest international shipping service. Delivery by noon the next business day to the United States, and to other world destinations in two to three days (between major urban centres, with some restrictions).

The primary advantages of Canada Post are that it is familiar, easily accessible, and trustworthy. The primary disadvantages of Canada Post are that it is at best a next-day service, and that it operates on an inflexible pickup schedule. If a document is not posted by a certain time, it will have to wait until the next scheduled pickup.

Courier Services

Courier services offer an alternative to Canada Post. Some couriers, such as FedEx and UPS, offer services that are comparable to Purolator's. Other couriers offer same-day pickup and delivery on a flexible schedule. They can be called for immediate pickup and will promise delivery within various time frames (from one hour to eight hours). Rates vary. Taxicabs and bike couriers can also be used for urgent pickup and delivery.

Document Exchange Services

Legal documents often need to be served or delivered in adherence to intricate rules of process. For these purposes, standard delivery services such as couriers and Canada Post may not suffice. In their stead, there are hand-delivery services that specialize in serving and submitting documents on behalf of law offices. Document exchange services are useful and often necessary because they are familiar with legal procedures and know how to navigate the network of law offices and government ministries to ensure that documents are delivered properly. Because these services deal with legal documents, they will usually require written authorization and instructions, signed and sent by fax.

Envelope Formatting

Proper preparation and correct addressing of envelopes ensures timely delivery of your correspondence. Canada Post recommends the following standards:

- All lines of the address (collectively referred to as "the address block") should be printed in upper case.

- Characters in the address block must not be underlined.

- All lines in the address block should be formatted with a uniform left margin.

- Punctuation should not be used unless it is part of a proper name (for example, "ST. JOHN'S").

- Accents are considered an integral part of language; they are not considered punctuation (for example, "TROIS-RIVIÈRES").

- The number symbol ("#") or the French equivalent ("n°") should not be used as part of the address.

- The municipality, province, and postal code should always appear on the same line.

- The postal code must be printed in upper case, with the first three characters separated from the last three by one space (not a hyphen).

- Address lines must be fewer than 40 characters, excluding spaces.

- The return address should be formatted in the same fashion as the destination address (upper case, left aligned). It should be located in the top-left corner of the mail piece, clearly separated from the destination address, or on the back of the mail piece at the top of the flap.

- Use a standard font such as Arial, Calibri, Cambria, Courier New, or Times New Roman.

- All characters in the address should be in a 10- to 12-point font. The return address may use smaller characters but must not be larger than the destination address.

- The space between lines of the address block must be at least 5 mm but no greater than one blank line.

PRACTICE TIP

Handwritten addresses on envelopes can look unprofessional. Instead, use word-processing software to print addresses directly onto envelopes or onto adhesive labels. In Microsoft Word, you will find this feature in the "Envelopes" and "Labels" menu items in the "Tools" dropdown menu.

Canada Post Abbreviations

Figures 9.5, 9.6, and 9.7 show the Canada Post abbreviations for envelope addressing.

FIGURE 9.5 Canada Post street address abbreviations

Street Type	Abbreviation
Avenue	AVE
Bay	BAY
Beach	BEACH
Boulevard	BLVD
Bypass	BYPASS
Byway	BYWAY
Centre	CTR
Circle	CIR
Concession	CONC
Corners	CRNRS
Court	CRT
Crescent	CRES
Crossing	CROSS

Street Type	Abbreviation
Drive	DR
Expressway	EXPY
Extension	EXTEN
Freeway	FWY
Grounds	GRNDS
Heights	HTS
Highlands	HGHLDS
Highway	HWY
Mountain	MTN
Orchard	ORCH
Park	PK
Parkway	PKY
Passage	PASS

Street Type	Abbreviation
Pathway	PTWAY
Place	PL
Point	PT
Private	PVT
Promenade	PROM
Range	RG
Road	RD
Route	RTE
Square	SQ
Street	ST
Subdivision	SUBDIV
Terrace	TERR

FIGURE 9.6 Canada Post street directions abbreviations

Street Direction	Abbreviation
East	E
North	N
Northeast	NE
Northwest	NW

Street Direction	Abbreviation
South	S
Southeast	SE
Southwest	SW
West	W

FIGURE 9.7 Canada Post province/territory abbreviations

Province/Territory	Abbreviation
Alberta	AB
British Columbia	BC
Manitoba	MB
New Brunswick	NB
Newfoundland and Labrador	NL
Northwest Territories	NT
Nova Scotia	NS

Province/Territory	Abbreviation
Nunavut	NU
Ontario	ON
Prince Edward Island	PE
Quebec	QC
Saskatchewan	SK
Yukon	YT

Envelope-Formatting Guidelines

Envelope-formatting guidelines are spelled out in figure 9.8, and examples are shown in figure 9.9.

FIGURE 9.8   Envelope-formatting guidelines

	Element	Details
	Envelope size	The envelope should be large enough to properly accommodate the contents. A business-sized (No. 10) envelope is typically used for all legal correspondence. A document (No. 40) envelope is used for correspondence longer than two pages.
1	Return address	Individual name, title Firm or company name Address, including street number and name, municipality, province, and postal code (see figures 9.5 to 9.7 for street address, street direction, and province/territory abbreviations)
2	Mailing notation	If a letter is being sent by a method other than mail, or in addition to mail, indicate this one line space below the return address. The notation is capitalized and bold-faced. For example: **BY HAND** **BY HAND AND BY MAIL** **CERTIFIED** **REGISTERED** **SPECIAL DELIVERY**
3	On arrival notations	If the notation "Personal" or "Confidential" appears on the correspondence, it must also appear on the envelope. Type the notation one line space below the return address, or one line space below the addressee's complete mailing information. The notation is capitalized, bold-faced, and underlined. For example: **PERSONAL** **CONFIDENTIAL** **PERSONAL AND CONFIDENTIAL**

4	Address block	The information for the addressee that appears on the envelope should be identical to the information on the correspondence. The addressee's information will be situated either
		
		   • in the horizontal and vertical centre of the envelope or
		
		   • in the horizontal centre and bottom third of the envelope.
		
		If the correspondence includes an attention line, add the line above the address block.

FIGURE 9.9   Illustrations of envelope formatting

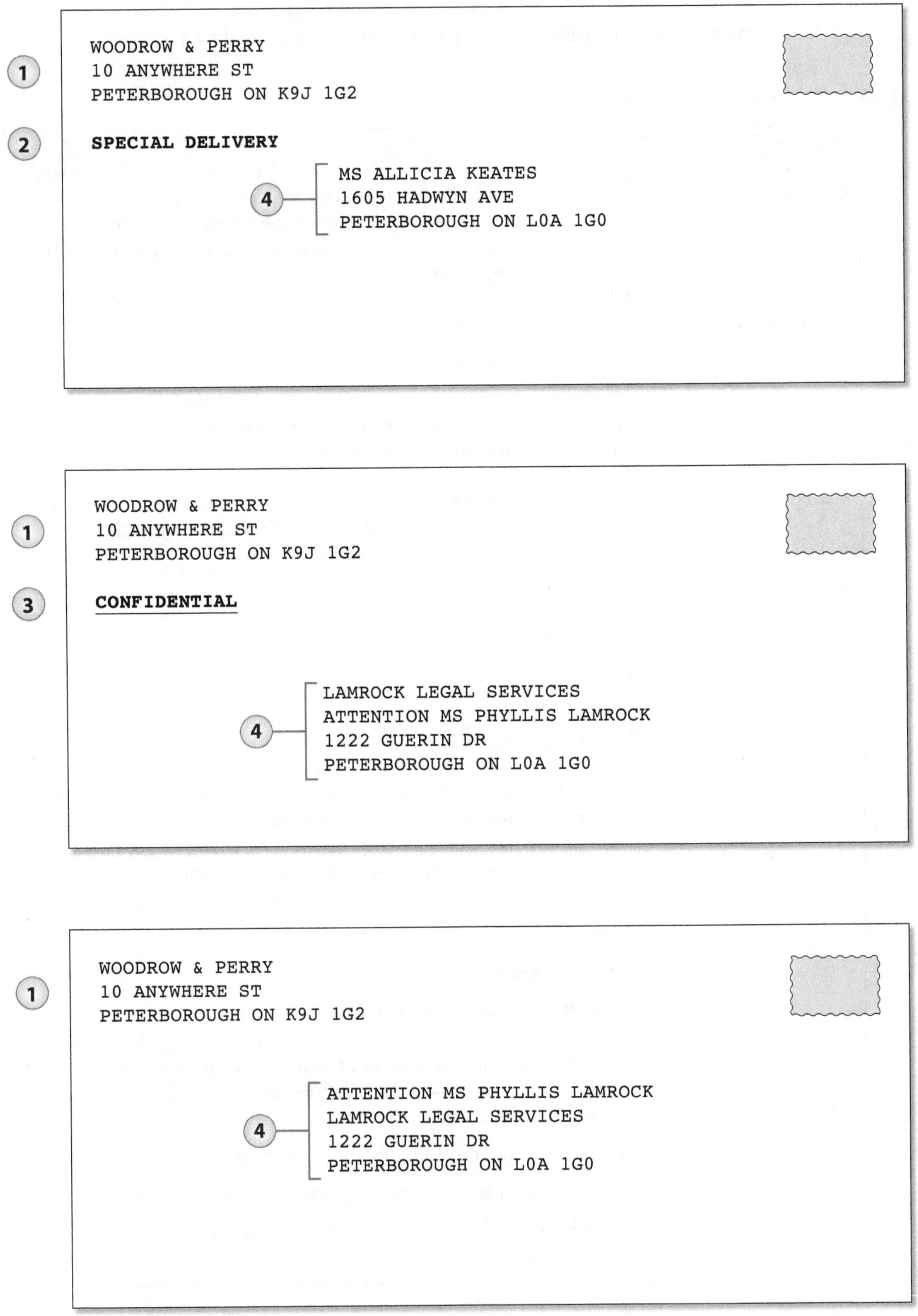

```
①  WOODROW & PERRY
    10 ANYWHERE ST
    PETERBOROUGH ON K9J 1G2

②  SPECIAL DELIVERY

             ┌  MS ALLICIA KEATES
         ④ ──┤  1605 HADWYN AVE
             └  PETERBOROUGH ON L0A 1G0
```

```
①  WOODROW & PERRY
    10 ANYWHERE ST
    PETERBOROUGH ON K9J 1G2

③  CONFIDENTIAL

             ┌  LAMROCK LEGAL SERVICES
             │  ATTENTION MS PHYLLIS LAMROCK
         ④ ──┤  1222 GUERIN DR
             └  PETERBOROUGH ON L0A 1G0
```

```
①  WOODROW & PERRY
    10 ANYWHERE ST
    PETERBOROUGH ON K9J 1G2


             ┌  ATTENTION MS PHYLLIS LAMROCK
             │  LAMROCK LEGAL SERVICES
         ④ ──┤  1222 GUERIN DR
             └  PETERBOROUGH ON L0A 1G0
```

Selecting the Proper Size of Envelope

Envelopes are an important but often overlooked part of business correspondence. Whenever a client or lawyer receives a letter from your office, the envelope is the first thing they see.

The standard No. 10 commercial envelope is commonly used for mailing one to two sheets of 216 × 279 mm (8.5 × 11 inch paper). If you are mailing more than two pages, you should use a No. 40 document envelope. A one- to two-page document, when folded in thirds, will fit securely into a No. 10 envelope. Documents of more than two pages cannot be folded as neatly, and the result can look unprofessional. Also, longer documents that have been folded and forced into a small envelope will not unfold neatly, and will often be difficult for the recipient to handle. No. 40 document envelopes come in various sizes and weights to accommodate most multipage mailing needs.

Figure 9.10 illustrates the standard folding technique for letters. Figure 9.11 illustrates a good folding technique for letters that need to have the address facing outward in an envelope window, or simply as an alternative to the standard technique.

Window envelopes are most often used for bills or for large-volume mailings. The envelope has a hole cut in the bottom left side of the front, which allows the letter within to be seen. The window is covered with translucent plastic so that when the letter is folded properly (as illustrated in figure 9.11) the inside address is visible. The sender does not have to duplicate address information on the envelope itself, thus saving valuable time and reducing the possibility of transcription error.

NOTES:

FIGURE 9.10 Standard letter-folding technique

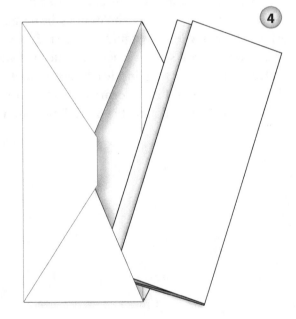

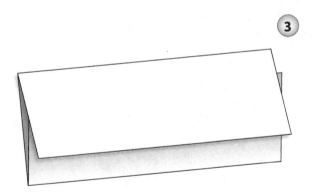

NOTES:

FIGURE 9.11   Letter-folding technique for displaying the recipient's address in the envelope window

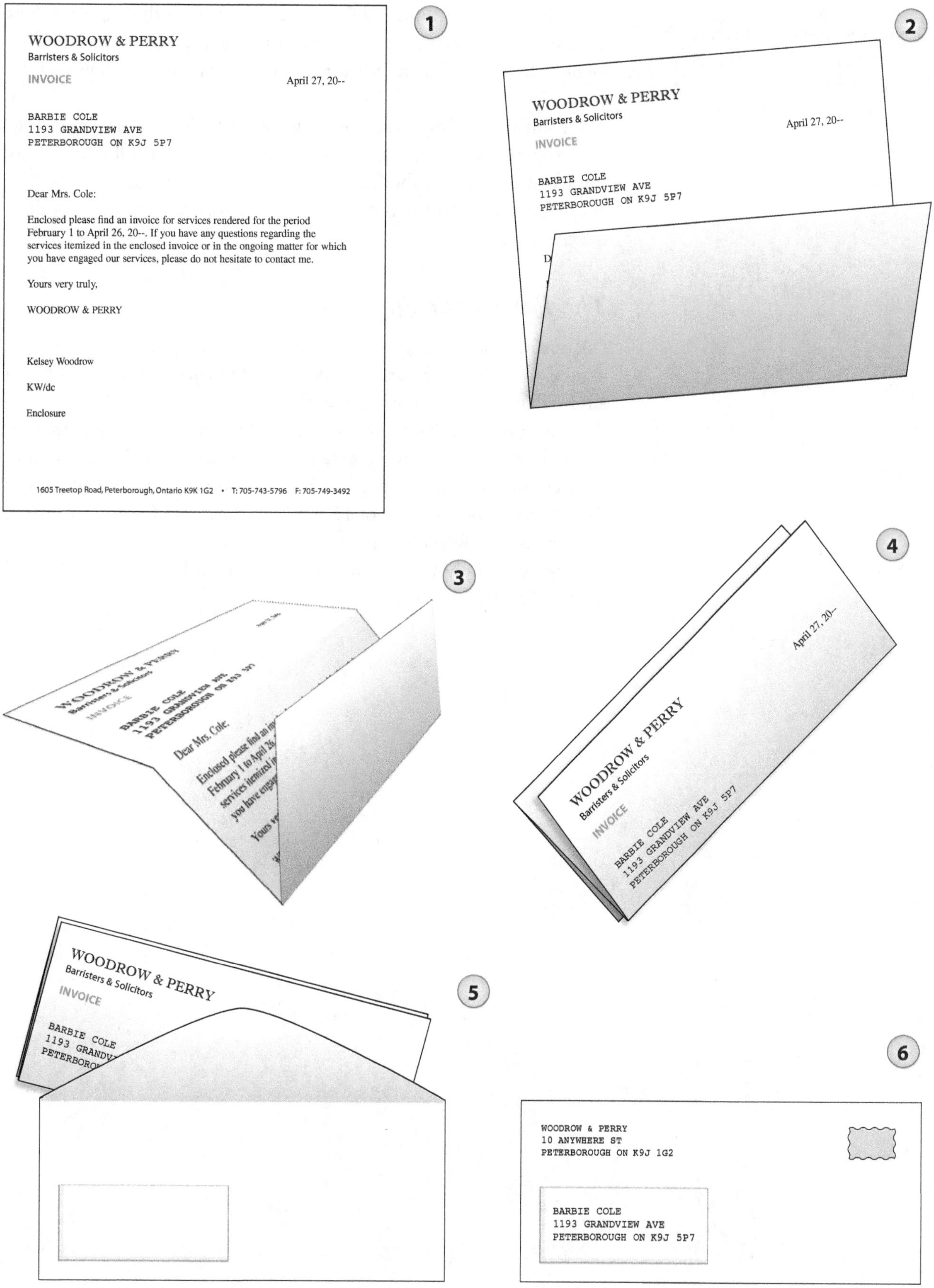

Facsimiles (Faxes)

Facsimile (fax) a machine that transmits and receives copies of documents

Faxes are sent when time is of the essence, or when the recipient does not have to receive originals. It is also common practice to send a document by fax first, with an indication that originals are to follow by mail or courier.

If you are sending a fax, especially if it is lengthy, call the recipient to request permission to send it. Once the fax is sent, you will receive a fax confirmation sheet (if the fax machine has been configured to produce one). Attach the confirmation sheet to the document and place both in the client file.

The Fax Cover Page

Documents that are sent by fax should have a cover page. The cover page is used to route your correspondence to the correct recipient and to ensure that all pages have been received.

It is important that your fax cover sheet have a professional format. A standard fax cover page generally includes the firm's letterhead and contact information, and is saved as a word-processing template. Use a simple and legible font; 11- or 12-point Arial, Calibri, Cambria, Courier, and Times New Roman transmit clearly.

Figure 9.12 shows an example of a standard fax cover page, and figure 9.13 spells out its elements.

NOTES:

FIGURE 9.12 Standard fax cover page

WOODROW & PERRY
Barristers & Solicitors

(2) FAX COVER PAGE

(1) 1605 Treetop Road
Peterborough, Ontario
K9K 1G2

Telephone: 705-743-5796
Facsimile: 705-749-3492

woodrow.perry@shaw.ca

(3) Date: _____

(4) From: _____

(5) To: _____

(6) Fax #: _____

(7) Phone #: _____

(8) RE: _____

_____

_____

_____

_____

_____

(9) Number of pages including cover page: _____

(10) ***IMPORTANT WARNING:*** *THIS FAX IS DIRECTED IN CONFIDENCE SOLELY TO THE PERSON NAMED ABOVE AND MAY NOT OTHERWISE BE DISTRIBUTED, COPIED, OR DISCLOSED. THE CONTENTS OF THIS FAX MAY ALSO BE SUBJECT TO SOLICITOR–CLIENT PRIVILEGE AND ALL RIGHTS TO THAT PRIVILEGE ARE EXPRESSLY CLAIMED AND NOT WAIVED. IF YOU RECEIVE THIS FAX IN ERROR, PLEASE DESTROY IT IMMEDIATELY. THANK YOU.*

FIGURE 9.13 Elements of a standard fax cover page

	Element	Details
	Paper	Good-quality, medium weight (20 lb.), white 216 × 279 mm (8.5 × 11 inch) paper
1	Letterhead	Sender's information Firm or company name Address, phone number, extension number (if any), fax number, email address (if desired). Letterhead information should be in the same format as the correspondence used by the office.
2	Title	"Fax Cover Sheet," "Fax," or similar description of the cover sheet.
3	Date:	The date the fax is sent.
4	From:	Sender's name
5	To:	Recipient's name
6	Fax #:	Recipient's fax number
7	Phone #:	Recipient's phone number
8	RE:	The file name and number, if applicable; subject matter of the fax; and any other short message.
9	Number of pages including cover page:	The number of fax pages being sent, including the cover page.
10	Confidentiality statement	Lawyers have an obligation to keep all information arising from the lawyer–client relationship in strict confidence. This obligation continues even after the lawyer ceases to represent the client. The use of the confidentiality disclaimer protects the lawyer in the event that a document is inadvertently sent to or received by someone other than the intended recipient.

A young law clerk was leaving the office late one evening when she found a lawyer standing in front of the paper shredder with a document in his hand.

"Listen," said the lawyer, "this is a very sensitive and important document here, and my secretary has gone for the night. Can you make this thing work?"

"Certainly," said the young law clerk. She turned on the machine, inserted the paper, and pressed the start button.

"Excellent, excellent!" said the lawyer as his paper disappeared. "I just need one copy."

Email

As discussed in chapter 8, Legal Correspondence, email is a widely used and accepted method of communication. Despite the many benefits of email, there are risks as well. Information sent and received by email that is not encrypted may not be treated as privileged or confidential if received by someone other than the intended recipient. Using email as a means of communication with a client or others should only be done with consent.

It is becoming more common to send legal correspondence and other documents as attachments via emails. Before you send an attachment, you need to make sure that the recipient can open the particular file format. Attachments are often converted to Portable Document Format (PDF), which is viewable by virtually anyone.

If you are sending correspondence or other documents by email, follow the guidelines set out in chapter 7, Communication. Once you have written your email, use the appropriate tool to locate and attach the appropriate document(s). Make sure your firm's privacy disclaimer is in the body of the email, if required. For example:

> This email, including attachments, is confidential and may be subject to solicitor–client privilege. If you received it in error, please reply to notify me, and then delete this message, your reply and any attachments from your computer and server. Any unauthorized use or disclosure is strictly prohibited. Thank you.

You may want to request a "read receipt" when you send the email, asking the recipient to notify you when they have read it. After sending an attachment, attach a printed copy of the email to the hard copy of the attachment and put it in the client file.

PRACTICE TIP

To avoid sending emails without the proper attachments, get in the habit of checking to see that all the necessary attachments are in fact attached before you press "Send." You can check for this at the same time as you verify the recipients and addresses.

NOTES:

REVIEW QUESTIONS

1. What are the two steps in the revision process?

2. What are you checking for when editing?

3. List four aids to help you in the revision process. Explain the relevance of each.

4. What are you checking for when proofreading?

_____

_____

_____

_____

_____

_____

_____

5. How are proofreading marks useful?

_____

_____

_____

_____

_____

_____

_____

6. How do you ensure that all intended parties receive a copy of the correspondence?

_____

_____

_____

_____

_____

7. What is the difference between a "copy" and a "blind copy" notation?

_____

_____

_____

_____

_____

8. What are the basic steps related to dealing with incoming mail?

_____

_____

_____

_____

_____

_____

_____

_____

_____

9. What is the importance of a mail-processing system?

_____

_____

_____

_____

_____

_____

_____

_____

_____

_____

10. Name and briefly describe three methods of delivering correspondence.

_____

_____

_____

_____

_____

_____

_____

_____

_____

_____

11. List five important practices or procedures that you should apply while editing. Consider editing on hard copy as well in electronic form.

_____

_____

_____

_____

_____

_____

_____

12. Why would a document be sent by fax or email rather than mail?

_____

_____

_____

_____

_____

_____

_____

_____

_____

_____

ACTIVITIES

1. Refer to the document that you edited and proofread in this chapter. Create an envelope for the document using a word-processing program.

2. Research how to operate a fax machine. Prepare a memo outlining the steps to sending a fax. Create and complete a fax cover page. Send the memo to your instructor by fax. Keep the fax confirmation sheet. Submit the entire package to your instructor for evaluation.

3. Carefully review the correspondence on the following page. Mark all errors using the proofreading symbols in figure 9.2 on page 260. Make your markings as neat and as clear as possible. Follow your instructor's directions for submission of the correspondence in final format.

4. Review your work in question 3. Based on the errors you found, create a checklist of errors to watch for when creating and processing correspondence (for example, checking margins, spacing, etc.). Use this checklist as a starting point for one you can use and add to throughout your career.

RElpY TO: TREVOR J. K. BURGIS

January 10, 20--

Mr. John Smith
c/o Central East Correctional Centre
541 Hwy 35
Lindsay, ON K9V 4S6

Dear ms Smith:

> **Re: Various Criminal Court Charges – File # TB-011-178**
> **Trial Date: February 1 & 2, 20--**

_____

I understand that have instructed me of proceed with a trial of all matters before the Court, including multiple assaults, multiple utter threats, Mischief, aggravated assault breach of court Order. This trial is to be condcuted on February 1 and 2, 2011. I point out you have the following difficulties:

1. Sally Jones has a significants injury to her eye and alleges that you choked him and as a result endangered her life.

2.   On the July 2, 20-- incident, the crown has an independent witnes,   Trish Goodwin;

2. On the September 1, 20-- assault and utter threat charges, the Crown has an independent
3. witness;

4.   On the October 1, 20-- Assault, utter threat and cruelty of animals, you have an indepentent witness who has picked you out of a photo up line up.

5.   On the November 15, 20-- aggravated assault and forcible refinement they're are multiple witnesses including police officers;

6.   On the November 16, 20--, possession of property and break and enter charges and the November 18, 2010 disobey court order, they have 2 Special constables who indicate
they   witnessed you gesture to her.

On the positive side, Ms. Sally Jones its known too have lied to police on previous occasions as I

note that you are not prepared ot accept you caused Mr. Jones his black eye or that you assaulted her or that at any point did you corfine her or cause harm to the dog at any time.

Notwithstanding the above have instructed me to proceed with the trial of these matters.

This letter is acknowledgeing your written instructions conduct to the trial of all mattiers.

Yours very Truly

Trevor J. K. Burgis

Legal Documents

The lawyer's greatest weapon is clarity, and its whetstone is succinctness.

—Judge Prettyman

10

Introduction

As discussed, the lawyer (and in Ontario, the paralegal) is responsible for the content of all client-related documents. Legal documents are binding on the parties who sign them, and it is essential that they be drafted efficiently, neatly, and—above all—accurately. That responsibility typically falls to the law clerk, the legal assistant, or legal secretary.

What Is a Legal Document?

In general, every legal document is either a client document or a court document. Client documents, commonly known as *contracts* or *agreements*, are what clients use in their everyday personal or business transactions.

Contracts, whether oral or written, are legally binding. Broadly defined, a written contract is a signed agreement between two or more capable parties in which the parties promise something of value to each other. Most commonly, in what is known as an exchange of goods or services for "valuable consideration," one person trades money for the other person's promise to provide goods or services. This exchange is put in writing to ensure that all parties agree on and clearly understand the terms of the deal and their respective rights and obligations. If properly drafted, the written contract will then be enforceable in court.

Court documents form part of legal proceedings. Many follow standard formats that are dictated by court administrations in each province. Chapter 12, Legal Forms, includes many examples of court and other procedural documents used in Ontario. This chapter will focus on client documents.

CHAPTER OBJECTIVES

After reading this chapter you will understand:

- the differences between a court document and a client document

- the statutory and technical requirements of contracts and other legal documents

- the stages of initiating, preparing, and formatting a legal document

- the importance of proofreading

- how to collate, copy, and properly store a legal document

- the benefits of creating, and how to use, precedent documents

Statutory Requirements

Most provinces have adopted statutes that require the following legal documents to be in writing:

- contracts for the transfer or encumbrance of real property

- contracts related to marriage

- contracts to guarantee the debt of another

- business agreements

- wills.

The appendixes to this chapter show a complete separation agreement, partnership agreement, and will.

Technical Requirements

Every written contract should include the following information in order to be legally enforceable:

- the identities (names or descriptions) of the parties to the contract

- the terms of the contract, including the offer that has been accepted and the consideration to be given

- the parties' signatures, either written or stamped. An actual signature is preferable in case there is a concern about whether a party actually signed an agreement.

Some contracts, such as deeds, debt guarantees, or agreements concerning gifts must also be "under seal." The seal is meant to indicate the seriousness of the contract and to confirm the parties' willingness to be bound by it. At the end of such a contract, next to their signatures, one of the parties affixes a gummed seal (readily available at any office supply store) or a wax paper impression. An alternative to the gummed seal is to have one party's lawyer draw a circle and label it "L.S." ("*locus sigilli*") or "legal seal" or simply "seal." The seal is especially important if the contract involves a gift; in this case, the seal shows an intent to be bound to contribute the gift without the need to get anything in return.

Another type of seal is the corporate seal. Where a corporation is involved in a contract, the corporate seal signifies the contract's authority to bind the corporation. Some jurisdictions no longer mandate corporate seals, but others still require that such a seal appear next to the signature of the corporate officer. When a corporation purchases land, both the corporate seal and the gummed seal are required. This ensures that there has been compliance with all legal formalities.

In theory, contracts need not be witnessed unless there is a statutory requirement to this effect, but having a third party witness a contract is always a good idea. You never know when a court will require proof that the signature on the contract is legitimate. Some contracts, such as wills, do require a witness, along with a corresponding affidavit of execution in which the witness swears that they watched the party sign the document. The affidavit of execution authenticates the parties' signatures.

Initiation and Preparation

When a client calls and asks for a legal document, you need to be prepared. You'll collect some preliminary information, schedule an appointment, and ask the client to bring in further information. Depending on the document requested, you may ask the client to bring financial records, or information about spouses and dependants. Many offices nowadays automatically mail a preformatted client questionnaire that the client is expected to complete and bring to the first appointment. The questionnaire is designed to elicit the following important information:

- purpose of the contract

- names of the parties

- roles of the parties

- responsibilities of the parties

- relevant financial information.

During the first visit, the lawyer interviews the client to gather information before offering advice about the relevant area of law. To structure the questioning, lawyers often use a checklist that outlines basic statutory rights or obligations the client should consider, as well as clauses that the lawyer wants to include in the contract. Review the partial checklists shown in figures 10.1 and 10.2, which were adapted from those prepared by the Law Society of British Columbia.

In contracts, parties are free to agree to whatever they want, provided that the terms are legal and do not offend public policy. Your most important concern is making sure that in the event of a dispute, a court will uphold the document as valid.

Because legal documents are often long and complex, and require several revisions, you must always carefully draft and proofread them. Before you begin, ensure that you are following your office's accepted format and style. During drafting and revision, be consistent and never make changes that could compromise the intent of the contract.

As when preparing correspondence, you should do background work before starting to type a legal document. Make sure you have everything you need to begin, including the client file, client questionnaire, lawyer's notes, checklist, precedent, and any other relevant material.

FIGURE 10.1 Checklist for drafting a separation agreement

Contents
1. Date of agreement
2. Names and addresses of parties
3. Recitals
4. Introductory clauses
5. Guardianship
6. Custody of child or children
7. Access
8. Child support
9. Spousal support
10. Responsibility for debts
11. Division of property
12. Provision for death
13. General clauses
14. Schedules
15. Appendices

2. Names and Addresses of Parties
2.1 First party (e.g., wife).
2.2 Second party (e.g., husband).
2.3 Others (e.g., a company, trustee, or escrow holder).

3. Recitals
3.1 Particulars of marriage (date and place of marriage) or marriage-like relationship (cohabitation date and place of relationship), birthdates of parties.
3.2 Dates of separation and reconciliation, if necessary.
3.3 Children
.1 Names, ages, and birth dates of dependent children.
.2 List independent children, if necessary. ...

Source: Adapted from the Law Society of British Columbia, http://www.lawsociety.bc.ca/page.cfm?cid=359&t =Checklist-Manual.

FIGURE 10.2 Checklist for drafting a partnership agreement

Contents
1. Effective date of agreement
2. Identification of parties
3. Recitals
4. Interpretation
5. Partnership
6. Conduct of the affairs of the partnership
7. Financing
8. Partnership property
9. Transfer and encumbrance of interest in partnership
10. Effect on the partnership of various events
11. Dissolution
12. Miscellaneous and general provisions

1. Effective Date of Agreement

2. Identification of Parties
2.1 Distinguish general and limited partners.
2.2 Provide for the addition of partners (usually limited partners).

3. Recitals
3.1 General statement of the legal relationship between the parties and the reasons for entering into the agreement.
3.2 Statement relating the recitals to the rest of the agreement. ...

Source: Adapted from the Law Society of British Columbia, http://www.lawsociety.bc.ca/page.cfm?cid=359&t =Checklist-Manual

NOTES:

Formatting a Legal Document

To ensure that your document is professional, attractive, and presentable, refer to the formatting guidelines shown in figure 10.3.

FIGURE 10.3 General formatting guidelines for a legal document

Element	Guidelines
Paper	Good quality medium-weight (20 lb), white, 216 × 279 mm (8.5 × 11 inch) paper.
	The paper may be plain, ruled right margin, or ruled left and right margin. Rulings are red, vertical, preprinted lines that form the boundaries of the document.
	The rulings are illustrated in figure 10.6.
	(NOTE: Some lawyers may still use legal-size (216 × 356 mm (8.5 × 14 inch)) paper for some documents.)
Font	While not required, the most commonly used font is Times New Roman, 10 to 12 point. Calibri, Cambria, Courier New, and Arial fonts are also acceptable.
Margins	Left: 3.81 cm (1.5 inches)
	Right: 1.27 cm (0.5 inch) to 2.54 cm (1 inch)
	Top: 1.27 cm (0.5 inch)
	Bottom: 2.54 cm (1 inch), no less than 1.27 cm (0.5 inch)
	When using ruled paper, keep your text within 1 to 2 keyed spaces of the ruling.
Page numbering	Numbering begins on page 2.
	Centre the page number between the left and right margins at the top of the page.
	Typical formats are as follows:
	–2– page 2 of 10 page two of ten
Numbers	Standard rules for numbering apply.
	Sums of money, measurements, and other numerical data are often typed as words and then included as figures, in brackets.
	For example:
	One hundred and twenty and 29/100 dollars ($120.29) Eighteen (18)
	Dates may be written in words or in both words and numbers.
	For example:
	Seventh of July 7th of July July 7

(Continued on the next page.)

Element	Guidelines
Capitalization	Rules for capitalization are standard as outlined in the Writing Guide appenix to this text. Words and phrases that are typically capitalized are the following: • The title of the document • The names of the parties Certain important expressions or directive words are also capitalized: WHEREAS AND WHEREAS THEREFORE NOW THEREFORE SIGNED, SEALED AND DELIVERED I HEREBY I GIVE I DIRECT
Quotations	Rules for quotations are standard as outlined in the Writing Guide appendix and chapter 11, Legal Terminology and Citation. Indent the entire quotation 5 to 10 spaces from the left margin. Leave the right margin of the quotation as is or indent it 5 spaces. If the quotation includes more than one paragraph, indent the first line of subsequent paragraphs a further 5 spaces.

Anatomy of a Contract

No two contracts are identical. However, the anatomy of a contract, though not prescribed by statute, does follow a widely accepted format. Generally, it contains the following components:

- Commencement
- Parties
- Recitals
- Consideration
- Body
- Testimonium
- Attestation.

NOTES:

Commencement

The contract begins with the commencement, which is composed of the document's title and, in many cases, the date. The title identifies the type of agreement, such as "THIS Separation Agreement dated" or "THIS Partnership Agreement dated," and the date beside it indicates when the contract takes effect. When drafting the document, you should leave this date blank; it will be inserted by hand when the contract is signed. However, some lawyers prefer to include the date only in the testimonium clause at the contract's end. Figure 10.4 outlines the commencement format typically found in legal documents.

Parties

Any legal agreement must identify its parties: the promisor and the promisee. The promisor undertakes to do something (for example, an author who contracts to write a book for a publisher) and the promisee (the publisher who will end up with the manuscript) receives the benefit of that promise. Or, to take another example, each partner in a partnership promises the other to do certain things, and each partner will benefit from those promises. In the case of a domestic contract such as a separation agreement, both parties make promises that will be mutually beneficial.

FIGURE 10.4   Commencement format

	Element	Details
1	Title and date	Start at least half an inch (1.27 cm) from the top of the page.
		Capitalize the title of the document.
		Either centre or left-justify the title.
		The following are examples of the title and date component for different kinds of agreements:
		THIS SEPARATION AGREEMENT made the _____ day of July 20--
		THIS PARTNERSHIP AGREEMENT made the _____ day of July 20--
		THIS AGREEMENT made the _____ day of July 20-- Diana Lynn Collis

NOTES:

Depending on office preference, the parties' addresses (municipality, city, or province) may be included after their names. You might also describe, in one or two words, the parties' roles or occupations, and then use these designations in the rest of the document. For example, if one party is "David Keates, Landlord," you would refer to him as "Landlord" for the rest of the document. Some law offices use the phrase "hereinafter [or herein] referred to as" in introducing this designation. However, many offices now simply include the party's designation in parentheses or quotation marks following the party's name. Your law office may also use the traditional party designation "OF THE FIRST PART" and "OF THE SECOND PART" as a convenient way to identify and separate the parties.

Figure 10.5 is a general guide to the formatting of a contract heading, which is typically composed of the commencement, the parties, and the designation.

Figures 10.6, 10.7, 10.8, 10.9, and 10.10 show examples of headings for different legal situations.

FIGURE 10.5 Formatting guidelines for a contract heading

	Element	Guidelines
2	"BETWEEN:"	Leave one to two line spaces between the title/date line and the line on which the word "BETWEEN" appears, keyed in at the left margin. This word is usually bold-faced and capitalized.
3	Parties	Leave one to two more line spaces before entering the party information.
		The parties' names are typed in full and capitalized.
		The parties' names and addresses, and in some cases their roles or occupations, are single-spaced, centred, and typed in block format.
		(Note: Underlining may also be used for emphasis.)
4	Designation	The party designation is • located one to two line spaces below the party information • either keyed in full caps and set at the right margin or • keyed in lower case and centred.
5	"AND" or "–and–"	Party information is separated by the party designation and the word "AND" or "–and–." The word "AND" is • placed two or three line spaces below the party designation • keyed either in full caps or lower case • sometimes followed by a colon • centred below the party names.

FIGURE 10.6   Heading for a partnership agreement between two individuals

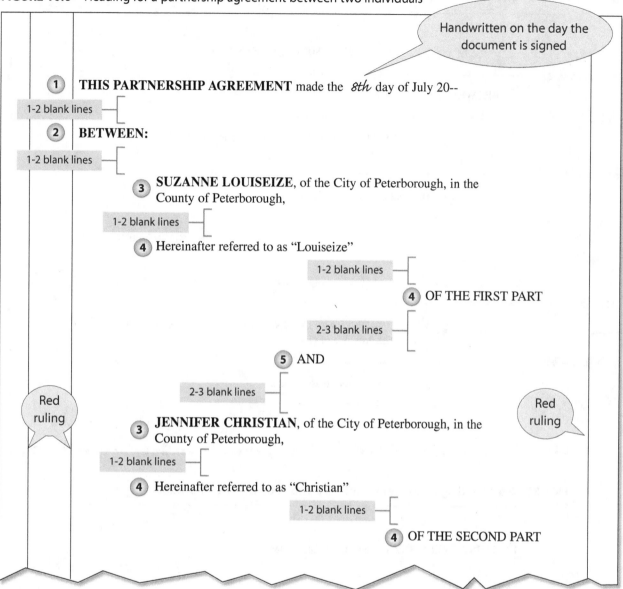

NOTES:

FIGURE 10.7 Heading for a partnership agreement between an individual and a corporation

1 EMPLOYMENT AGREEMENT

1-2 blank lines

2 BETWEEN:

1-2 blank lines

3 PAUL LEGACY, of the City of Peterborough, in the County of Peterborough,

1-2 blank lines

4 Hereinafter referred to as "Legacy"

1-2 blank lines

4 OF THE FIRST PART

2-3 blank lines

5 AND

2-3 blank lines

3 KEATZE KONTRACTING INC., a corporation incorporated under the laws of the Province of Ontario,

1-2 blank lines

4 Hereinafter referred to as "Keatze"

1-2 blank lines

4 OF THE SECOND PART

FIGURE 10.8 Heading for a contract between two people and an individual

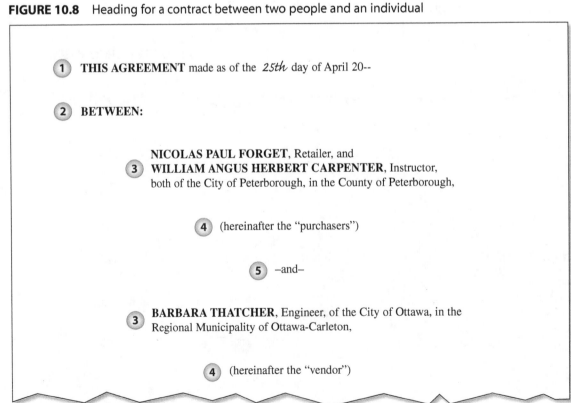

1 THIS AGREEMENT made as of the *25th* day of April 20--

2 BETWEEN:

3 NICOLAS PAUL FORGET, Retailer, and
WILLIAM ANGUS HERBERT CARPENTER, Instructor,
both of the City of Peterborough, in the County of Peterborough,

4 (hereinafter the "purchasers")

5 –and–

3 BARBARA THATCHER, Engineer, of the City of Ottawa, in the Regional Municipality of Ottawa-Carleton,

4 (hereinafter the "vendor")

FIGURE 10.9   Heading for a separation agreement between husband and wife

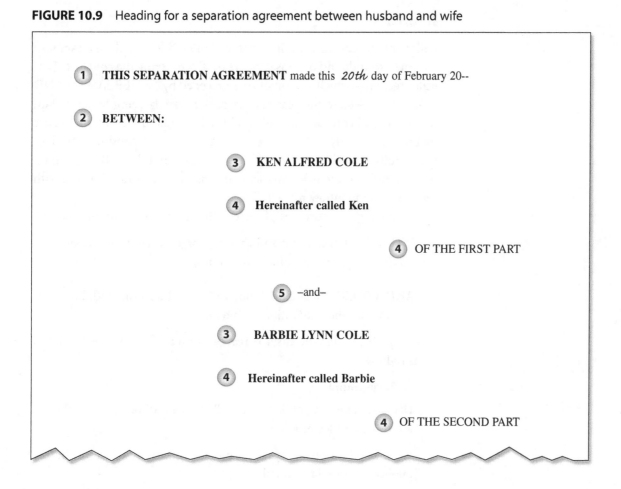

FIGURE 10.10   Heading for an agreement between three parties

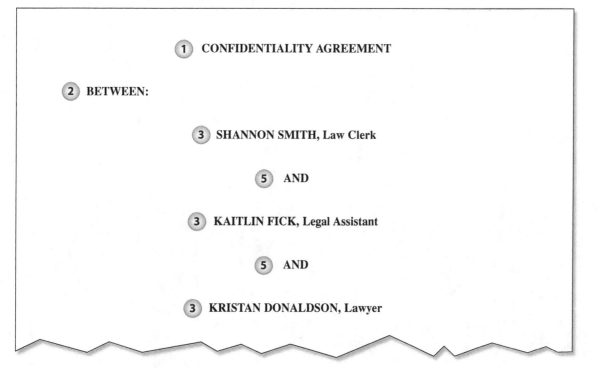

Recitals

Following the contract heading, you will often find recitals that establish the backgrounds and purposes of the parties entering the contract. Typically, recitals—which are sometimes preceded by "WHEREAS" or "AND WHEREAS"—state the reasons the parties are agreeing to do certain things. Not all contracts include recitals. If you do use them, make sure that they are clearly and accurately stated. To this end, consider introducing recitals with titles such as "Recitals," "Preamble," or "Background," or with an introductory statement such as "This contract is made with reference to the following facts."

Following are examples of recitals that follow a traditional format:

WHEREAS Diana Collis and Cynthia Forget will write a textbook on the subject of legal office procedures;

AND WHEREAS Emond Montgomery Publications Ltd. has a contract for the publication of said book;

A much simpler and easy-to-read version of the same recital would be as follows:

1. Background

Diana Collis and Cynthia Forget will write a textbook on the subject of legal office procedures.

Emond Montgomery Publications Ltd. has a contract for the publication of said textbook.

Formatting guidelines for sample recitals are shown in figure 10.11. Sample recitals for a variety of contracts are shown in figures 10.12, 10.13, and 10.14.

NOTES:

FIGURE 10.11   Format for recitals

6	Recitals	Begin the recitals one or two line spaces below the party information.
		Single-space the recitals with a double line space between each recital.
		Traditional introductory terms in recitals are
		WHEREAS **AND WHEREAS**
		These terms are bold-faced and capitalized.
		In the absence of these traditional introductory terms, identify each recital by numerical/alphabetical or alternate designation.

FIGURE 10.12   Sample recital for confidentiality agreement

⑥
WHEREAS the undersigned agree that they may be in receipt of certain confidential information pertaining to any and all aspects of the Parties' business operations and finances;

AND WHEREAS both Parties agree that the dissemination of such information to any other person or the use by either Party of such information in competition with each other will cause significant harm to either Party;

FIGURE 10.13   Sample recital for separation agreement

⑥
Background

A. The parties were married to each other at Peterborough, in the County of Peterborough, in the Province of Ontario, on the 21st day of July 1979. Throughout this Agreement they are called respectively the "husband" and the "wife." In the event that the marriage is dissolved, the terms shall be construed to mean "former husband" and "former wife."

B. The husband and wife further acknowledge that there are two children of the marriage who are dependent upon the parties, namely DAVID ALLAN, born July 15, 1980, and ANGELA BARBARA, born January 24, 1982, hereinafter called the "children."

FIGURE 10.14   Sample recital for partnership agreement

⑥
The Partners wish to set forth, in writing, the terms and conditions by which they will conduct themselves in business.

Consideration

As discussed earlier, the consideration clause identifies what one party is giving in exchange for something promised by the other party. Promises to exchange money for goods or services are common forms of consideration. Keep in mind that consideration can be a promise either to do or not to do something.

The consideration clause generally follows the recitals, and either precedes or is part of the body of the contract. Following are examples of consideration that follow a traditional format:

> **NOW, THEREFORE,** in consideration of the premises and the mutual covenants set forth herein and for other good and valuable consideration, the receipt and sufficiency of which are hereby acknowledged, the parties hereto covenant and agree as follows: …

or

> **NOW, THEREFORE,** for good and valuable consideration, the receipt of which is hereby acknowledged by each party, the parties to this Agreement, intending to be legally bound, pledge, covenant, and agree as follows: …

Another option is to simplify the wording in the consideration clause. Consider these more readable and equally effective examples:

> The parties therefore agree as follows: …

or

> The parties agree to the following: …

Another way to introduce the clause is to enter it as one of the numbered paragraphs in the body of the contract, as in the following example:

> 3. Agreement: The husband and wife each agree to be bound by the provisions of this Agreement.

Figure 10.15 provides formatting guidelines for the consideration clause. Figures 10.16 and 10.17 illustrate, respectively, consideration clauses typically found in a separation agreement and a partnership agreement. Figure 10.18 shows some other sample consideration clauses.

NOTES:

FIGURE 10.15 Format for the consideration clause

7	Consideration	The consideration clause begins two line spaces below the recitals.
		The traditional introductory terms for considerations are
		NOW, THEREFORE
		THEREFORE
		NOW AND THEREFORE
		These terms are bold-faced and capitalized.

FIGURE 10.16 Sample consideration clause of a separation agreement

7 In consideration of the several promises and the undertakings the one to the other herein contained, the parties mutually promise and agree as follows:

FIGURE 10.17 Sample consideration clause of a partnership agreement

7 **NOW AND THEREFORE THIS AGREEMENT WITNESSES THAT**, in consideration of the mutual covenants and agreements herein and subject to the terms and conditions in this Agreement, the parties agree as follows:

FIGURE 10.18 Alternative formats of the consideration clause

7 In consideration of the matters referred to, the parties agree as follows:

7 **NOW THEREFORE THIS AGREEMENT WITNESSES THAT**, in Consideration of the sum of one thousand dollars ($1,000.00) paid by Michelle Goodison to Melanie Chambers, the receipt of which is acknowledged, and of other good and valuable consideration, the parties agree as follows:

7 **NOW THEREFORE** THIS AGREEMENT WITNESSES THAT, **in Consideration of** the sum of one dollar ($1.00) paid by each of the parties to the other of them, the receipt of which is acknowledged by each of them, the parties agree as follows:

Body

The body sets out the terms, also called the covenants, of a contract. Because the body's text addresses the parties' obligations to each other, it must be clear, concise, and unambiguous. Accordingly, it's a good idea to use headings to divide the information into a logical format, and to keep your terms consistent throughout. Figure 10.19 provides formatting guidelines for terms in the body of the contract.

Keep in mind that terms in the body will vary, depending on the type of document that you are drafting. For example, figure 10.20 shows the terms common to separation agreements, while figure 10.21 illustrates the terms and conditions found in a typical partnership agreement.

FIGURE 10.19 Format for terms in the body of the contract

	Element	Details
8	Body	The terms or covenants in the body • begin one or two line spaces below the consideration clause • are set out in numbered paragraphs • are indented 5 or 10 spaces from the paragraph number • are confined to one issue • are one sentence in length and occupy no more than 10 lines • make use of commas to ensure clarity • are generally 1.5× spaced to double spaced, with one line space between paragraphs • can be single-spaced if they are lengthy, with one line space between paragraphs • are consistently spaced throughout. Note: At least two lines of the body must appear on the last page of the document, before the testimonium. Blank space that is created on the second-last page is usually filled with a Z-ruling (see the end of figure 10.20).

NOTES:

FIGURE 10.20   Body terms common to a separation agreement

-10-

(8)

Five spaces

1 to 2×
spacing

13.   CHOICE OF LAWS: The parties hereto agree that this Agreement shall be

interpreted in accordance with the laws of Ontario.

14.   RELEASE: Without limiting in any way the benefits and obligations given to the

parties in this Separation Agreement, it is agreed that neither party has any further claim

against the other for any matter whatsoever and

(a)   all their property has been divided between them to their mutual

satisfaction;

(b)   each releases all rights to and interests in property owned by the other

which he or she has or may acquire under the laws of any jurisdiction, and in particular

the *Family Law Act*, 1990 including all rights to and interests in:

(i)   ownership in property, and

Note the spacing
between the clauses

(ii)   division of property.

15.   SEPARATION AGREEMENT TO SURVIVE DIVORCE: If either the husband or

the wife obtains a Decree of Divorce, all the terms of this Agreement shall survive and

continue in force.

16.   EXECUTION OF OTHER DOCUMENTS: The husband and wife shall, at any time

and from time to time, execute and deliver to the other any documents or documents that

the other reasonably requires to give effect to the terms of this Agreement.

17.   RECONCILIATION: If at any future time the husband and the wife, with their

mutual consent, cohabit as husband and wife for a continuous period of not less than

four months, all the covenants, provisions, and terms herein contained shall become

void, provided that nothing herein contained shall alter, affect, set aside, revoke, or

(Continued on the next page.)

-11-

invalidate any payment, conveyance, act, matter, or thing aforesaid made or done under and pursuant to the terms of this Agreement. In the event that the parties cohabit at any time or times for a period or periods in the aggregate totalling less than four months, then, upon a subsequent separation of the parties, this Agreement shall (unless the parties in writing agree) be deemed to be reinstated and of full force and effect notwithstanding the periods of cohabitation.

Z-ruling.
Some lawyers prefer to fill the space with a series of Xs. Others leave it blank.

FIGURE 10.21   Body terms and conditions found in a typical partnership agreement

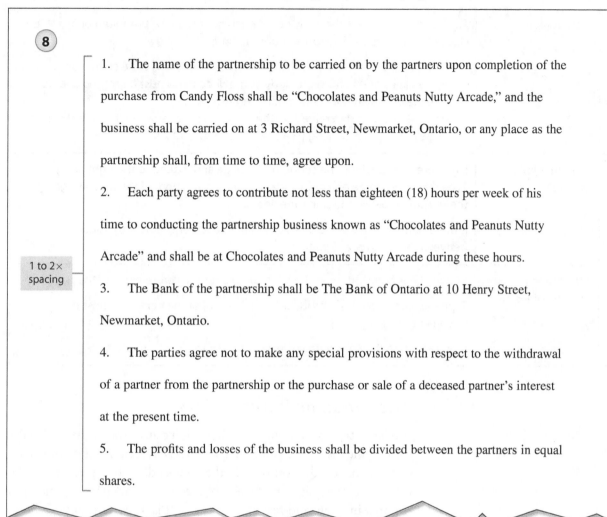

Testimonium

The testimonium clause is found at the end of the document. It is a declaration by the parties to the agreement that it has been signed and, if necessary, sealed, and that both sides are in possession of an original copy. The format of the testimonium varies depending on how many signatures are required, whether all parties are signing the document at the same time and place, and whether the parties are individuals, corporations, or otherwise. But its effect is always the same. Some common introductory expressions in the testimonium clause are as follows:

AS WITNESS to my hand and seal …

IN WITNESS WHEREOF I hereunto have affixed my hand and seal …

IN WITNESS WHEREOF the parties have …

IN EVIDENCE WHEREOF …

The formatting and conventions of the testimonium clause are discussed in figure 10.22.

FIGURE 10.22   Format for the testimonium clause, signature lines, and attestation

9	Testimonium	The clause that follows the body of the document is the testimonium or attestation clause. Keep the following conventions in mind: • Leave one to three blank lines between the body and the testimonium clause. • Two lines of text from the body of the document must be carried over to the page on which the testimonium begins. • Blank space that's created on the second-last page of the document should be filled with a Z-ruling (see the end of figure 10.20).
10	Signature lines (parties)	Signature lines begin at the centre of the page and extend to the right margin. Type the name (some offices include title and occupation) of the person signing the document below the signature line. If there is more than one person signing the document, leave 3 to 4 spaces between the lines for a signature.
11	Attestation (witness) lines	Witness lines begin either at the left margin or at the centre point of the page. Type the name (some offices include occupation) of the person witnessing the document. If there is more than one witness, leave 3 to 4 spaces for a signature.

Attestation or Witness Lines

Similar to the testimonium, the attestation clause, sometimes called the witness lines, is a declaration that a witness has seen the party or parties sign and/or seal the contract. To the same end, as discussed earlier, the witness may also sign an affidavit of execution, a document sometimes required in estate and real estate matters. It is important to note, however, that a witness is swearing only to having watched the party sign, not to the accuracy or truthfulness of the document itself.

You should be aware that the signing and witnessing of a contract may not always occur at one time or in one place. For example, one party may sign on one date in one office, while another may sign later, in another office or another province.

To familiarize yourself with possible variations of the testimonium, signature lines, and attestation, review the samples shown in figures 10.23 to 10.30.

NOTES:

FIGURE 10.23   Signing and witnessing format for a contract signed by two people at different times in different locations

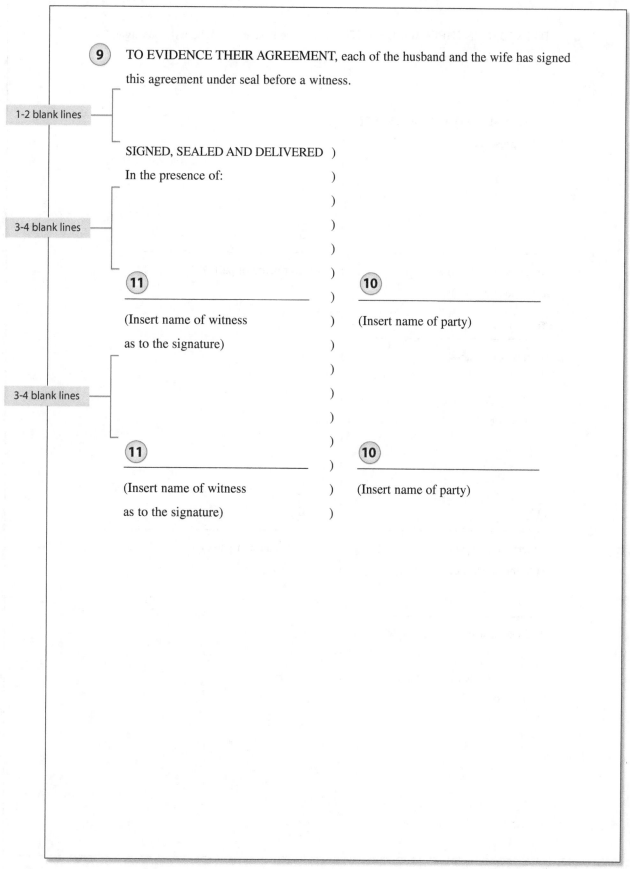

FIGURE 10.24 Alternative signing and witnessing format for two people signing together

(9) TO EVIDENCE THEIR AGREEMENT, each of the husband and the wife has signed this Agreement under seal before a witness.

SIGNED, SEALED AND DELIVERED)
In the presence of:)
)
)
)
(11) _____) (10) _____
)
(Insert name of witness) (Insert name of party)
as to the signature))
)
_____)
)
Address of witness)
)
_____)
)
Occupation)
)
)
)
(11) _____) (10) _____
)
(Insert name of witness) (Insert name of party)
as to the signature))
)
_____)
)
Address of witness)
)
_____)
)
Occupation)

FIGURE 10.25 Signing and witnessing format for a contract signed by two people at the same time in the same location

⑨ IN WITNESS WHEREOF the parties have hereunto set their hands and seals.

SIGNED, SEALED AND DELIVERED)

In the presence of:)

)

)

)

)

⑪ _____) ⑩ _____

(Insert name of witness) (Insert name of party)

as to the signatures))

)

)

) ⑩ _____

) (Insert name of party)

FIGURE 10.26   Alternative signing and witnessing format for two people signing together

⑨   IN WITNESS WHEREOF the parties have set their hands and seals this *26th* day of
May 20--

> Handwritten on the day the document is signed

SIGNED, SEALED AND DELIVERED   )
In the presence of:)
)
)
)
)
⑪ _____   )   ⑩ _____
)
(Insert name of witness   )   (Insert name of party)
as to the signature)   )
)
)
_____   )
)
Address of witness   )
)
_____   )
)
Occupation   )
)
)
)
)
⑪ _____   )   ⑩ _____
)
(Insert name of witness   )   (Insert name of party)
as to the signature)   )
)
_____   )
)
Address of witness   )
)
_____   )
)
Occupation   )

FIGURE 10.27   Signing and witnessing format for one person

⑨   IN WITNESS WHEREOF I have set my hand and seal this *10th* day of April 20--

SIGNED, SEALED AND DELIVERED)

In the presence of:)

)

)

)

⑪ _____   )   ⑩ _____

(Insert name of witness   )   (Insert name of party)

as to the signature)   )

)

_____   )

Address of witness   )

)

_____   )

Occupation   )

FIGURE 10.28   Alternative signing format for one person

⑨   IN WITNESS WHEREOF I have set my hand and seal.

SIGNED, SEALED AND DELIVERED)

In the presence of:)

)

)

)

)

⑪ _____   )   ⑩ _____

(Insert name of witness   )   (Insert name of party)

as to the signature)   )

)

_____   )

Address of witness   )

)

_____   )

Occupation   )

FIGURE 10.29   Alternative signing format for one person

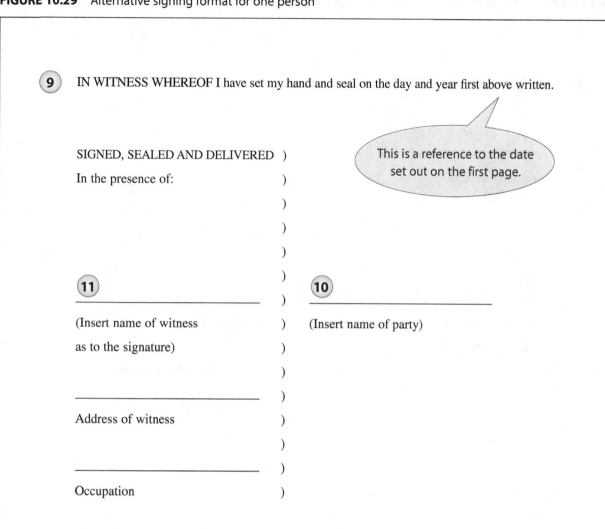

FIGURE 10.30 Alternative signing format for a corporation

⑨ IN WITNESS WHEREOF I have set my hand and seal.

SIGNED, SEALED AND DELIVERED)

In the presence of:)

)

)

)

)

⑪ _____) ⑩ _____

(Insert name of witness) (Insert name of party)

as to the signature))

) I have authority to bind the corporation

)

_____)

Address of witness)

)

_____)

Occupation)

Endorsements

An endorsement page—commonly referred to as a "backpage"—is a separate page found at the end of a contract that identifies the contract that has been created. It contains the following information:

- the date of the document

- the parties to the document

- the name of the document

- the name and address of the lawyer who prepared the document.

To prepare an endorsement ensure that the page layout is in landscape format. Simply key the information in the middle panel (second third) of the page on good quality 216 × 279 mm (8.5 × 11 inch) paper.

Figure 10.31 illustrates the most common format of an endorsement page.

> **PRACTICE TIP**
>
> **Review, Review, Review**
> Once you've drafted your legal documents, you should review them, following the procedures described in chapter 9, Processing Correspondence. Proofreading and editing are always important, but nowhere more so than with legal documents, where errors can have serious ramifications.
>
> Note that if you revise a legal document, you *must* ensure that both parties initial, in the margin, each and every handwritten change. Even one missed change may result in a court's setting aside the contract.

FIGURE 10.31 Format of an endorsement page

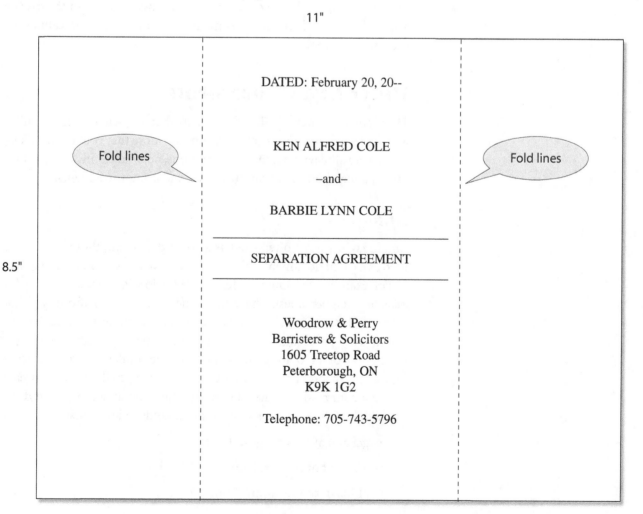

Collating and Copying

Once you have prepared, checked, and revised the document, it's time to collate the document. To do this, assemble the pages in the proper numerical order. Once the original document has been signed and witnessed and the endorsement page prepared, you must make one copy for each party and an extra copy for your file. If other lawyers are involved in the case, it's a good idea to make an additional copy for each of them as well. Then put the endorsement page, face out, at the end of the document. Finally, neatly staple the top left corner of the document. Some lawyers favour a blue cardboard corner, available at any office supply store. To use a corner, slide the top left corner of the document into it and staple the pages together, as illustrated in figure 10.32.

Once signed, collated, and stapled, the document should be folded lengthwise in thirds (a legal-size document should be folded lengthwise in quarters) and placed in a document envelope as illustrated in figures 10.33 and 10.34.

Storage

Depending on the nature of the document, the client may either take the signed original home or leave it for the lawyer to file. In the case of a will, the lawyer is required to maintain a fireproof filing cabinet or vault for safekeeping.

Other Legal Documents

There are a number of other documents that you will become familiar with while working in a legal office. Among those that you're most likely to draft are affidavits, statutory declarations, notarial certificates, releases, undertakings, authorization/directions, and acknowledgments.

Affidavits

An affidavit is most often used as a court document, though it can be used as a client document if the administrative body concerned requires it. For example, the Ontario Teachers' Pension Plan requires that if a pension member doesn't have his or her marriage certificate and got married outside Ontario, an affidavit of marital status must be sworn.

In legal proceedings, parties give their evidence either orally (as testimony) or in writing (by affidavit). The affidavit is the witness's signed first-hand account of an event. On signing, the witness swears before a commissioner that the information contained in the affidavit is true. The following are some common kinds of affidavits:

- general affidavit, figure 10.36
- affidavit of service, figure 10.37
- affidavit of execution, figure 10.38.

FIGURE 10.32 Stapled and collated document with corner: front and back view

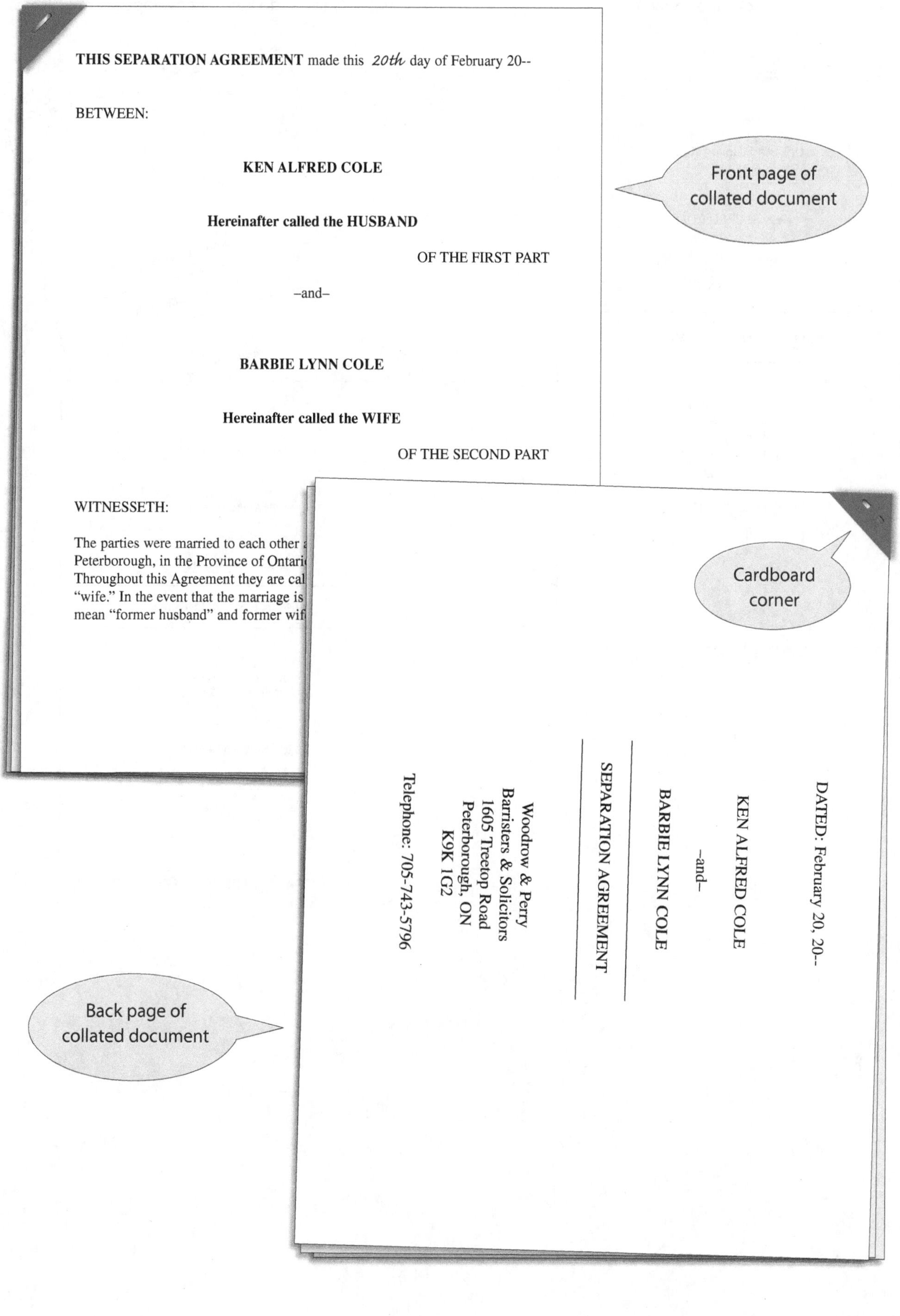

THIS SEPARATION AGREEMENT made this *20th* day of February 20--

BETWEEN:

KEN ALFRED COLE

Hereinafter called the HUSBAND

OF THE FIRST PART

–and–

BARBIE LYNN COLE

Hereinafter called the WIFE

OF THE SECOND PART

WITNESSETH:

The parties were married to each other a
Peterborough, in the Province of Ontari
Throughout this Agreement they are cal
"wife." In the event that the marriage is
mean "former husband" and former wif

Front page of collated document

Cardboard corner

Back page of collated document

DATED: February 20, 20--

KEN ALFRED COLE

–and–

BARBIE LYNN COLE

SEPARATION AGREEMENT

Woodrow & Perry
Barristers & Solicitors
1605 Treetop Road
Peterborough, ON
K9K 1G2

Telephone: 705-743-5796

FIGURE 10.33 Folded document, with backpage showing

FIGURE 10.34 Folded document put into document envelope

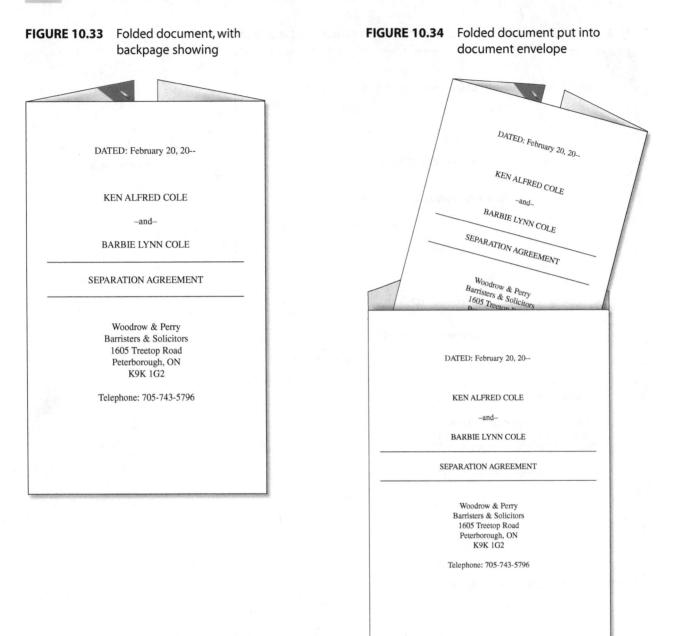

NOTES:

An affidavit is

- a written statement

- written in the first person

- used to prove a fact or facts

- primarily used in court actions

- submitted by a deponent

- sworn before a commissioner.

Because affidavits are typically used in court, and court requirements vary from province to province, each province has its own rules detailing the format requirements for the preparation of affidavits. You should be alert to these variations in required format and information. In Ontario, for example, you'll follow rule 4 of the *Rules of Civil Procedure*, which sets out the general rules related to formatting court documents in a civil procedure. Then you'll consult rule 4.6, which sets out the specific rule for drafting an affidavit. In British Columbia, on the other hand, it's the *Superior Court Civil Rules* that govern these areas. In Nova Scotia, it's the *Civil Procedure Rules* that apply if you're drafting an affidavit. If it's a family law affidavit you're creating, the rules will likewise be different depending on where you are.

The best way to stay on top of the myriad rules governing the particular affidavit you're drafting is to check the relevant ones in your province. To get started, refer to figure 2.4 in chapter 2, Canada's Justice System, for a list of the different provincial websites that will link you to the relevant rules of court.

Once you find the particular rule applicable to your affidavit, simply follow the format outlined there and use the guidelines found earlier in this chapter. Although formats for affidavits vary slightly, you'll find that the content is relatively consistent. Essentially, an affidavit is composed of the heading, and/or the title, the body, and the ending.

Heading

An affidavit's heading format may call for a court-assigned file number and the name of the applicable court level. If the affidavit will be used in a court proceeding, the heading should include a title of proceedings, identifying the names of the parties, as well as their status as plaintiff or defendant, and the title of the document. If the affidavit is not for use in a court proceeding, the document begins with the title of the document.

Title

The title of an affidavit appears between the heading and the body if the affidavit will be used in a court proceeding, or at the beginning of the document otherwise. The title identifies the content of document—for example, a general affidavit may be titled, "Affidavit of Kyle Guerin," while an affidavit prescribed by a court rule may be titled "Affidavit of Service," or "Affidavit of Execution."

Body

The body of an affidavit includes a statement setting out the name and address of the person swearing the affidavit (for example, "I, Karen Mitchell, of the City of Warkworth, in the Province of Ontario, make oath and say/affirm:"). In some cases, the heading may also set out the employment or role of the person swearing the affidavit, and a statement of the relevant facts.

The statement of facts is confined to a first-hand, factual account by the person swearing the affidavit; it should never refer to the person's opinion. Organize the facts into consecutively numbered paragraphs that describe a chronological sequence of events, and be sure to limit each paragraph to a succinct one-sentence statement of fact. Consider the sample shown in figure 10.36.

If the affidavit is more than one page, number each page, beginning on page 2.

Ending

At the end of the body, you'll find the jurat, which is a clause stating when, where, and by whom the document was sworn or affirmed. It refers to a commissioner, who is the person authorized by provincial or territorial law to take the deponent's oath or affirmation that the affidavit is true. As a member of a law firm, you may be appointed by application to commission documents.

In commissioning the affidavit, the commissioner must follow certain guidelines. After he or she is satisfied that the person signing is in fact the person named in the affidavit, the commissioner must ensure that the person has read and understood the document's contents. Only then will he or she administer a verbal oath or affirmation such as the following: "Do you swear that the information herein is true?" The deponent then swears or affirms the contents of the affidavit to be true. The commissioner must watch the person sign, and then the commissioner signs the jurat.

In drafting the affidavit ending, you should key the jurat at the left margin of the page as illustrated in figure 10.35. If the affidavit runs

NOTES:

FIGURE 10.35 Affidavit ending/jurat

SWORN BEFORE ME at the   )

City of ....   )

in the County of ....   )

in the Province of ....   )   _____

on the .... day of   )   *[Key in name of deponent.]*

.............................., 20--   )

)

....   )

Commissioner for taking Affidavits

longer than one page, however, make sure that at least two lines of the body of the affidavit are on the same page as the jurat. Otherwise, the document is null and void because there is no way to prove that the commissioner administered the oath in this particular document. Finally, be sure to use the jurat required by your province or territory.

Exhibits

Sometimes you will need to attach other documents, known as exhibits, to your affidavit. The exhibits are referred to in the affidavit. Again, there is a specific formula to follow for this.

Start by ordering your exhibits alphabetically (for example, "Exhibit A," "Exhibit B," "Exhibit C"). Then number all exhibit pages consecutively. For example, if Exhibit A contains six pages, Exhibit B three, and Exhibit C four, Exhibit A is numbered from 1 to 6, Exhibit B from 7 to 9, and Exhibit C from 10 to 13. On the first page of each new exhibit, use an exhibit stamp, as shown in figure 10.39.

NOTES:

FIGURE 10.36 Format of a general affidavit

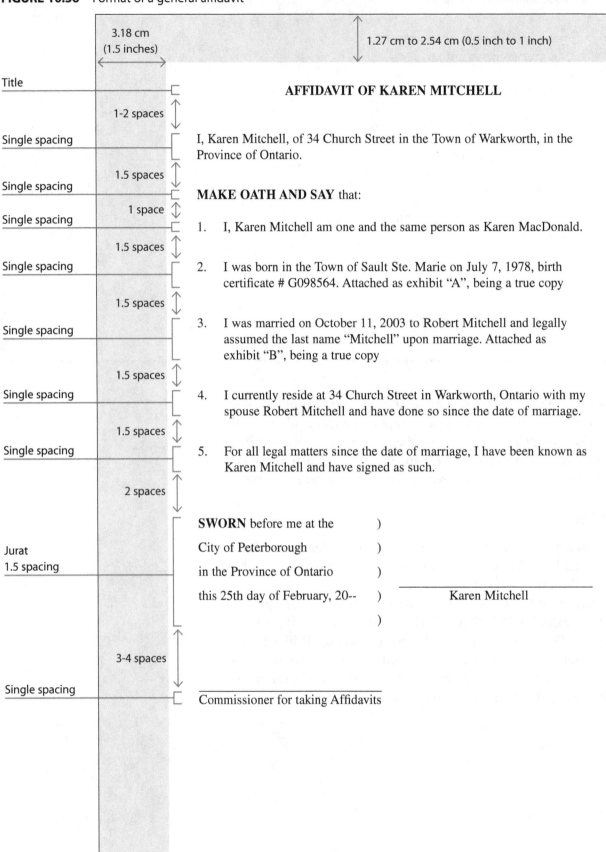

3.18 cm (1.5 inches)	1.27 cm to 2.54 cm (0.5 inch to 1 inch)

Title

1-2 spaces

Single spacing

AFFIDAVIT OF KAREN MITCHELL

I, Karen Mitchell, of 34 Church Street in the Town of Warkworth, in the Province of Ontario.

1.5 spaces

Single spacing

MAKE OATH AND SAY that:

1 space

Single spacing

1.   I, Karen Mitchell am one and the same person as Karen MacDonald.

1.5 spaces

Single spacing

2.   I was born in the Town of Sault Ste. Marie on July 7, 1978, birth certificate # G098564. Attached as exhibit "A", being a true copy

1.5 spaces

Single spacing

3.   I was married on October 11, 2003 to Robert Mitchell and legally assumed the last name "Mitchell" upon marriage. Attached as exhibit "B", being a true copy

1.5 spaces

Single spacing

4.   I currently reside at 34 Church Street in Warkworth, Ontario with my spouse Robert Mitchell and have done so since the date of marriage.

1.5 spaces

Single spacing

5.   For all legal matters since the date of marriage, I have been known as Karen Mitchell and have signed as such.

2 spaces

Jurat
1.5 spacing

SWORN before me at the   )

City of Peterborough   )

in the Province of Ontario   )

this 25th day of February, 20--   )   _____
)   Karen Mitchell
)

3-4 spaces

Single spacing

_____
Commissioner for taking Affidavits

FIGURE 10.37   Format and anatomy of an affidavit of service—personal service

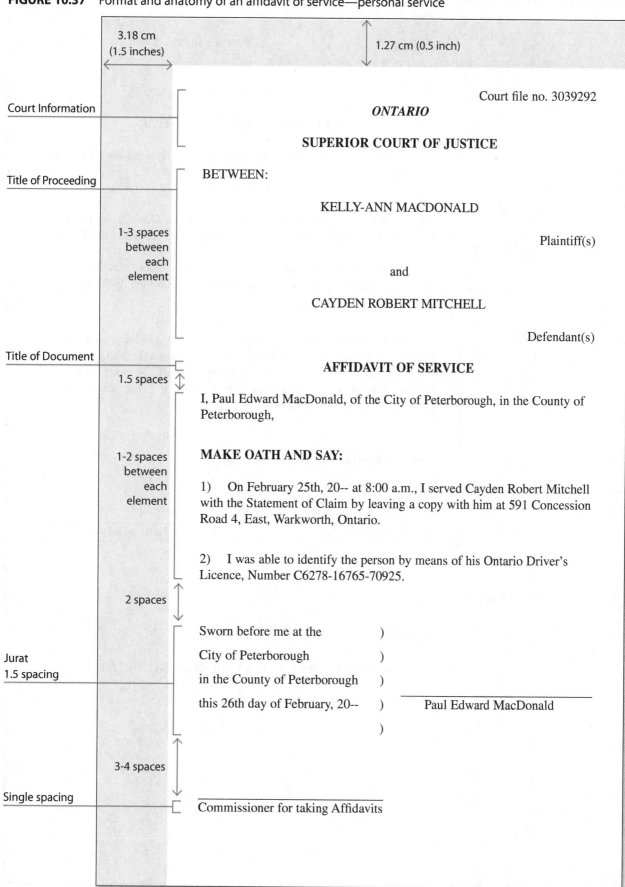

3.18 cm
(1.5 inches)

1.27 cm (0.5 inch)

Court Information

Title of Proceeding

1-3 spaces
between
each
element

Title of Document

1.5 spaces

1-2 spaces
between
each
element

2 spaces

Jurat
1.5 spacing

3-4 spaces

Single spacing

Court file no. 3039292

ONTARIO

SUPERIOR COURT OF JUSTICE

BETWEEN:

KELLY-ANN MACDONALD

Plaintiff(s)

and

CAYDEN ROBERT MITCHELL

Defendant(s)

AFFIDAVIT OF SERVICE

I, Paul Edward MacDonald, of the City of Peterborough, in the County of Peterborough,

MAKE OATH AND SAY:

1)   On February 25th, 20-- at 8:00 a.m., I served Cayden Robert Mitchell with the Statement of Claim by leaving a copy with him at 591 Concession Road 4, East, Warkworth, Ontario.

2)   I was able to identify the person by means of his Ontario Driver's Licence, Number C6278-16765-70925.

Sworn before me at the   )

City of Peterborough   )

in the County of Peterborough   )

this 26th day of February, 20--   )   _____

)   Paul Edward MacDonald

)

_____
Commissioner for taking Affidavits

FIGURE 10.38 Format and anatomy of an affidavit of execution

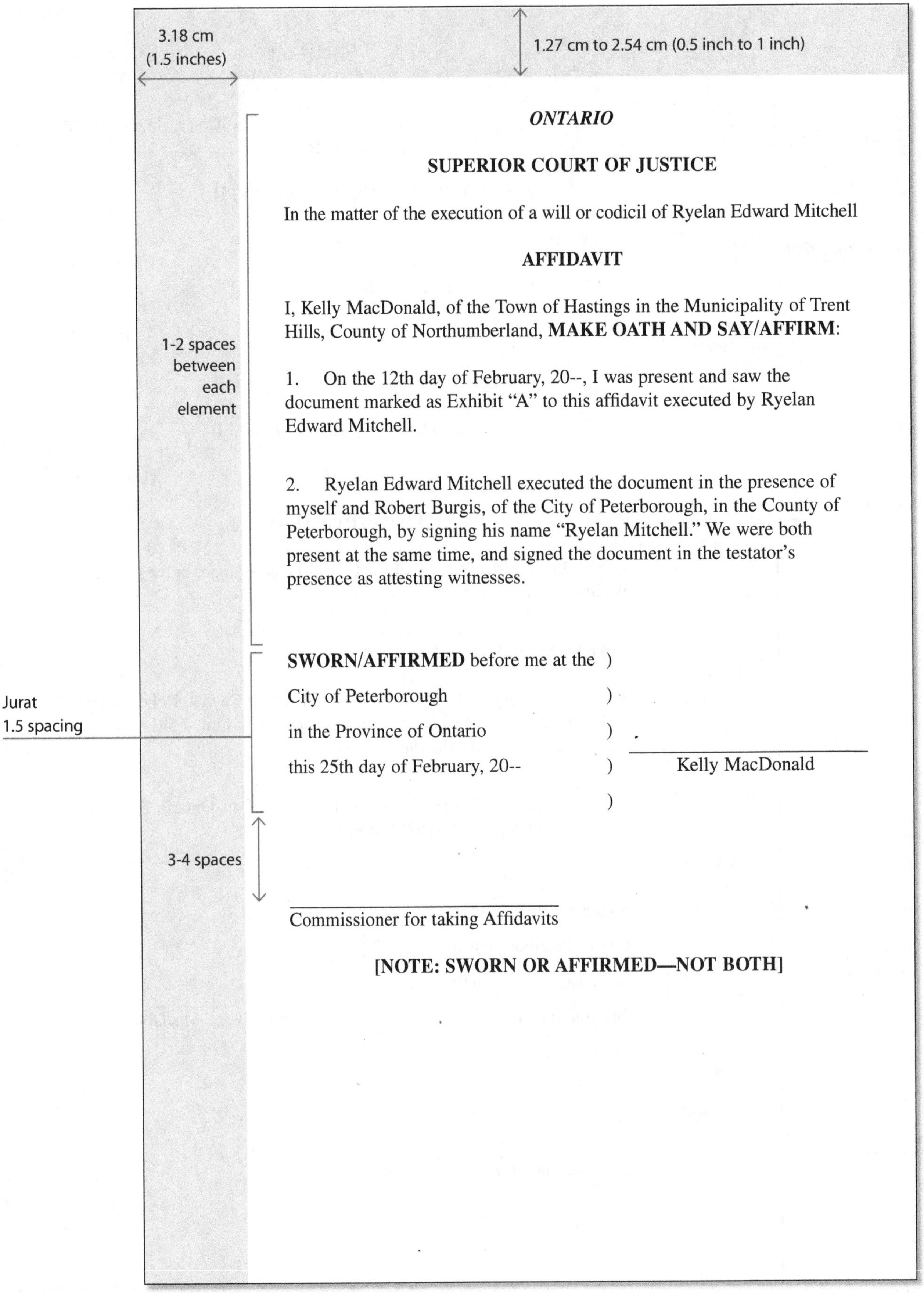

3.18 cm
(1.5 inches)

1.27 cm to 2.54 cm (0.5 inch to 1 inch)

1-2 spaces
between
each
element

Jurat
1.5 spacing

3-4 spaces

ONTARIO

SUPERIOR COURT OF JUSTICE

In the matter of the execution of a will or codicil of Ryelan Edward Mitchell

AFFIDAVIT

I, Kelly MacDonald, of the Town of Hastings in the Municipality of Trent Hills, County of Northumberland, **MAKE OATH AND SAY/AFFIRM**:

1.   On the 12th day of February, 20--, I was present and saw the document marked as Exhibit "A" to this affidavit executed by Ryelan Edward Mitchell.

2.   Ryelan Edward Mitchell executed the document in the presence of myself and Robert Burgis, of the City of Peterborough, in the County of Peterborough, by signing his name "Ryelan Mitchell." We were both present at the same time, and signed the document in the testator's presence as attesting witnesses.

SWORN/AFFIRMED before me at the)

City of Peterborough   )

in the Province of Ontario   )   _____

this 25th day of February, 20--   )   Kelly MacDonald

)

_____

Commissioner for taking Affidavits

[NOTE: SWORN OR AFFIRMED—NOT BOTH]

FIGURE 10.39 Exhibit stamp

This is Exhibit "   " referred to in the affidavit of ....

Sworn before me at .... this ...... day of ...., 20--

....

Commissioner for taking Affidavits

Statutory Declarations

If there is no court proceeding but you still need someone to provide a sworn statement of facts, you would use a statutory declaration. Like an affidavit, a statutory declaration is a person's first-hand, factual account of an event, sworn or affirmed before a commissioner. Also like an affidavit, it is composed of the heading, the body, and the ending. The only tangible difference between the two documents is the fact that the declaration will not be used in court and so is not subject to any official prescriptions about format and content.

A statutory declaration is

- a written statement of facts
- used to prove a fact or facts
- not used in a court action
- submitted by a declarant
- sworn before a commissioner.

With the exception of the heading information, the requirements for formatting a statutory declaration are the same as those for an affidavit. The heading of a statutory declaration identifies the place where the declaration was prepared and the topic of the declaration. In some areas of law, statutes prescribe specific declarations for use in their proceedings. In other situations, administrative practice recommends the use of declarations in order to simplify the collection of information. For example, the Ontario Teachers' Pension Plan requires plan contributors who are in a common-law relationship to provide certain information in order to be eligible for survivor benefits from the plan. To simplify things for contributors, the plan administrators provide a standard form declaration that contributors can use (see figure 10.40).

For the standard statutory declaration, though, the format and anatomy should not vary. Just follow the format shown in figure 10.41.

FIGURE 10.40 Ontario Teachers' Pension Plan statutory declaration of common-law relationship

TEACHERS' PENSION PLAN
ONTARIO

Statutory Declaration of Common-law Relationship

1. The member completes Part A of this form then signs it before a Commissioner of Oaths.
2. A Commissioner of Oaths witnesses the member's signing of the declaration then completes Part B.
3. The member's common-law spouse completes Part C.

What is common-law?

Common-law means that you are living with a person of the same or opposite sex in a conjugal relationship for:

- at least three continuous years; or
- a shorter period if both of you are the biological or adoptive parents of a child.

Part A –
to be completed
by member

SIN or Teachers' pension account number

Name *last*　　　　*first*

Address *street*　　　　*city*

province　　　　*postal code*

(　)　　　　(　)

Telephone *home*　　　　*work*

If you have lived at two or more addresses during your common-law relationship, include all other addresses of the past three years on a separate sheet of paper.

If you have lived at separate addresses at any point during the last three years, please attach an explanation.

I, _____ , solemnly declare that I have lived together with
　　name of member

_____ in a continuous conjugal relationship from
　name of common-law spouse

yyyy　mm　dd

_____ to the present time.

1. Both my common-law spouse and I are the biological or adoptive parents of a child:

　__Yes __No ▸ If yes, provide the following information for a child:

　First name　　　　Last name

　Date of birth　　　　　　　　　　　Date of adoption
　yyyy　mm　dd ▸ If child was adopted, also　*yyyy　mm　dd*
　　　　　　　provide the date of adoption

2. My common-law spouse and I:

　a) have jointly signed a residential lease, mortgage or purchase agreement relating to a residence in which we both live(d) __Yes __No

　b) jointly own(ed) property other than our residence __Yes __No

　c) have joint bank, trust, credit union or charge card accounts __Yes __No

　d) have declared each other as spouses on federal income tax returns __Yes __No

5650 Yonge Street, Toronto, Ontario M2M 4H5　Website: www.otpp.com　0425 (04/10)
416.226.2700 or 1.800.668.0105　Fax: 416.730.7807 or 1.800.949.8208

**Part A –
to be completed
by member (continued)**

No children or joint finances?

If you checked "No" in all of the boxes on the previous page, provide other documentary evidence that would show your continuous cohabitation as common-law spouses. For example, copies of household bills, insurance information or other items that include dates, addresses and your names.

By signing below I hereby declare that, to the best of my knowledge, the information on this declaration is true and complete. I also undertake to notify the Ontario Teachers' Pension Plan in the event my marital status changes. (Providing false information may be considered fraudulent and/or may change your pension entitlement.)

Important!
*Please do not sign until
a Commissioner of
Oaths is present to wit-
ness your signature.*

Please remember to sign this form before faxing or mailing.

| yyyy | mm | dd |

Member's signature

**Part B –
to be completed by
Commissioner of Oaths**

Signed and declared before me at _____ , _____
                                    city, town or village   *province or territory*

| yyyy | mm | dd |

on _____ .

_____   *Please remember to sign this form before faxing or mailing.*
Name of Commissioner   *Commissioner's signature*

*A Commissioner of
Oaths is any lawyer in
Ontario, a notary out-
side of Ontario, or an
individual who has been
named a Commissioner
by the Ontario Ministry
of the Attorney General.*

Please choose your source of authority to commission this document:

☐ Lawyer or Judge – Please provide your law society number: | | | | | |
☐ Commissioner of Oaths or Notary Public

Please provide your stamp or seal ⇨

**Part C –
to be completed by
common-law spouse**

| yyyy | mm | dd |

I, _____ , born on _____ , solemnly declare
   name of common-law spouse

that I have lived together with _____ in a continuous
                                 name of member

| yyyy | mm | dd |

conjugal relationship from _____ to the present time.

Please remember to sign this form before faxing or mailing.

| yyyy | mm | dd |

Common-law spouse's signature

Source: Ontario Teachers' Pension Plan, http://docs.www.otpp.com/StatDeclCommonLaw.pdf.

FIGURE 10.41   Format and anatomy of a statutory declaration

3.18 cm
(1.5 inches)

1.27 cm to 2.54 cm (0.5 inch to 1 inch)

Heading
1.5 spaces

)   **IN THE MATTER OF**
)
Province of Ontario   )   **Exclusion in Support of**
)   **Last Will and Testament**
)

I, Carole E. MacDonald, of 52 New Street in the Town of Hastings, in the Province of Ontario

Do Solemnly Declare that:

1)   I was born on March 18, 1949, now being sixty-two years of age and of sound mind and body.

2)   This declaration is made in support of my Last Will and Testament, which was made with independent counsel on February 21, 20--.

3)   I have four children, Kelly-Ann MacDonald born September 12, 1974, Karen Mitchell born April 10, 1976, Zoey MacDonald born March 16, 1978 and Mark MacDonald born October 19, 1980.

1-2 spaces
between
each
element

4)   I make this declaration in support of my Last Will and Testament in which I am excluding two of my four children, named Kelly-Ann MacDonald born September 12, 1974 and Zoey MacDonald born March 16, 1978.

5)   I fully understand the implications of exclusion as provided by independent counsel.

6)   I have excluded Kelly-Ann MacDonald born September 12, 1974 and Zoey MacDonald born March 16, 1978 for reasons of independent wealth already acquired.

And I make this solemn declaration conscientiously believing it to be true, and knowing that it is of the same force and effect as if made under oath.

Jurat
1.5 spacing

DECLARED before me at   )

City of Peterborough   )

in the Province of Ontario   )

this 25th day of February, 20--   )

)   _____
Carole E. MacDonald

3-4 spaces

_____
Commissioner for taking Affidavits

Notarial Certificates

Clients often ask lawyers to notarize copies of documents for authenticity. All lawyers in Ontario are automatically notaries public. The job of notarizing a document begins with the notary comparing the copy of the document with its contents to affirm that it is an exact replica. Your job is to prepare the notarial certificate.

As you can see in figure 10.42, the certificate is composed of three elements:

1. the heading, identifying the province where the document is prepared;

2. the body, detailing the original document by name and date; and

3. the ending, where the notary swears the certificate.

A notarial certificate:

- is a written statement

- certifies the authenticity of the document to which it is attached

- is signed by a notary public.

When preparing a notarial certificate, it is essential that you proofread it carefully to ensure that you have accurately referred to the original.

Once satisfied that the copy is identical to the original, the notary signs the bottom of the notarial certificate and affixes the "notarial seal." Some notaries also affix the seal to the copy. The copy of the document, now sworn as an exact replica, is titled the "notarial copy" and is attached to the notarial certificate.

Release

A release is a document where the party or parties give up their rights or claim in a legal matter. See figure 10.43 for an example of a release used in a civil matter.

NOTES:

FIGURE 10.42   Format and anatomy of a notarial certificate

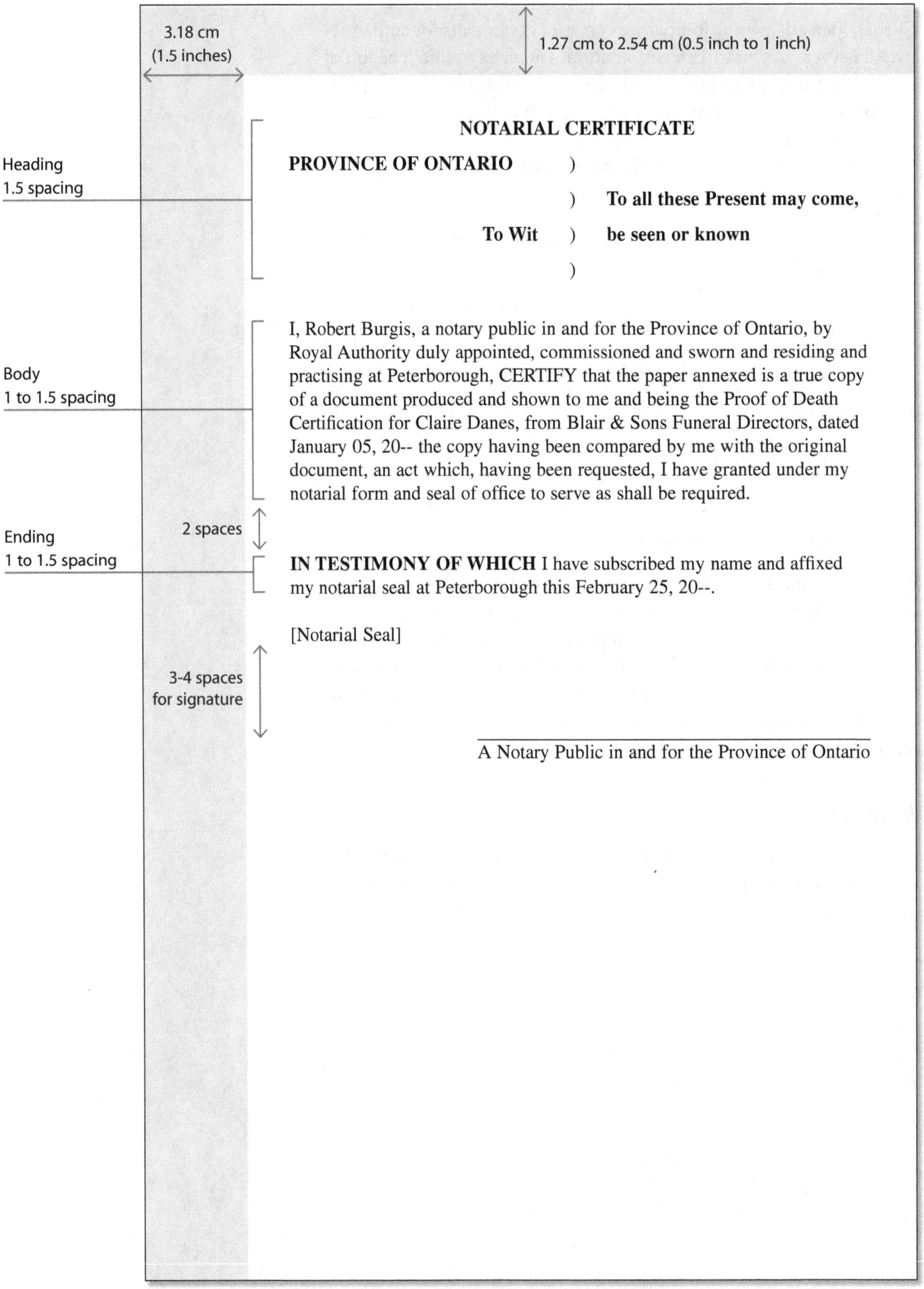

3.18 cm (1.5 inches)	1.27 cm to 2.54 cm (0.5 inch to 1 inch)

NOTARIAL CERTIFICATE

PROVINCE OF ONTARIO)

) **To all these Present may come,**

To Wit) **be seen or known**

)

Heading
1.5 spacing

Body
1 to 1.5 spacing

I, Robert Burgis, a notary public in and for the Province of Ontario, by Royal Authority duly appointed, commissioned and sworn and residing and practising at Peterborough, CERTIFY that the paper annexed is a true copy of a document produced and shown to me and being the Proof of Death Certification for Claire Danes, from Blair & Sons Funeral Directors, dated January 05, 20-- the copy having been compared by me with the original document, an act which, having been requested, I have granted under my notarial form and seal of office to serve as shall be required.

2 spaces

Ending
1 to 1.5 spacing

IN TESTIMONY OF WHICH I have subscribed my name and affixed my notarial seal at Peterborough this February 25, 20--.

[Notarial Seal]

3-4 spaces
for signature

_____

A Notary Public in and for the Province of Ontario

FIGURE 10.43   Release used in a civil matter

Heading
1 to 2 spaces
between each
element

R E L E A S E

B E T W E E N

SHANTEL INGRAM

RELEASOR

A N D

BILL BATTEN

RELEASEE

Body
1.5 to 2 spaces
between each
element

The Releasor hereby releases, acquits, remises and forever discharges, from any and all actions, causes of action, suits, debts, dues, accounts, covenants, contracts, demands, proceedings, tribunals, and claims for injuries, losses or damages of any kind whatsoever which the Releasor has had, now has or may hereafter have against the Releasee, for or by reason of any cause, matter or thing whatsoever existing up to the present time and without loss of generality, all matters raised in the pleadings filed in **PE512/11A**, as commenced in Peterborough, Ontario.

IT IS AGREED AND UNDERSTOOD that the Releasor undertakes and agrees not to take any steps or initiate any proceedings against any person, partnership, corporation or other such entity which might be entitled to claim contribution, indemnity or other relief over against the Releasee, under the provisions of any statute or otherwise, with respect to any of the matters which the Releasor releases by this release or with respect to which the Releasor agrees herein not to make any claim or take any proceedings.

AND IT IS AGREED AND UNDERSTOOD that the Releasor represents and warrants that the Releasor has not assigned to any person, partnership, corporation or other such entity any of the matters which the Releasor releases by this Release or with respect to which the Releasor agrees herein not to make any claim or take any proceedings.

AND IT IS FURTHER AGREED AND UNDERSTOOD that the Releasee does not admit any liabilities or obligations whatsoever to the Releasor and such liabilities and obligations are, in fact, denied.

THIS RELEASE SHALL BE BINDING upon and shall inure to the benefit of the respective successors, assigns, executors, administrators and representatives of the Releasor and the Releasee.

IT IS DECLARED that the terms of this release are fully understood and that the said release is given voluntarily for the purpose of making a full and final compromise, adjustment and settlement of all claims as aforesaid.

IN WITNESS WHEREOF, the releasor has hereunto set her hand and seal.

DATED at Peterborough, in the County of Peterborough this 28th day of June, 20--.

Testimonium
3 to 4 spaces
for signatures

_____   _____
Witness   Party

_____   _____
Witness   Party

Undertakings

An undertaking is a personal promise to perform a task or provide a document. An undertaking must not be given if it cannot be fulfilled. Undertakings must be in writing or, if given orally, confirmed in writing. They must be clear and unambiguous. An undertaking that is not fulfilled is considered a breach of law society rules. See figure 10.44 for an example of an undertaking used in a real property transaction.

> **Law Society of Upper Canada Rules Regarding Undertakings**
>
> According to the LSUC, "A lawyer shall not give an undertaking that cannot be fulfilled and shall fulfill every undertaking given" (rule 6.03(10)). Unless an undertaking clearly states otherwise, a lawyer or paralegal's undertaking is a "personal promise" and the lawyer's or paralegal's "personal responsibility" (rule 4.01(7) for lawyers, rule 2.02 for paralegals).

Authorization and Direction

An authorization and direction is a statement giving someone else the authority to fulfill an obligation on the behalf of the person giving the direction. For example, permission to release all file-related documents. See figure 10.45 for an example of an authorization and direction used for the release of documentation in a legal matter.

Acknowledgments

An acknowledgment is a statement confirming or certifying an act or an action or the receipt of a document. See figure 10.46 for an example of an acknowledgment used in a criminal matter.

Promissory Note

A promissory note is a promise to pay a debt to a person or company, either on a fixed date or on demand. See figure 10.47 for an example of a promissory note used in relation to debt repayment.

NOTES:

FIGURE 10.44 Undertaking used in a real estate transaction

<u>**UNDERTAKING**</u>

TO: PETER VANCE, the purchaser herein

AND TO: The solicitor for the purchaser, STEPHEN MILLER

RE: VANCE purchase from KUIAK/BROWN

                274 Inbar Avenue, Peterborough, Ontario, Part Lot 110, Plan 30Q

                Monaghan, City of Peterborough, County of Peterborough

In consideration of the closing of this transaction, each of the undersigned vendors undertakes as follows:

1.   To deliver all keys and vacant possession of the property on closing;

2.   To pay any hydro-electric, water, gas, and any other utility accounts, including charges for snow-clearing and grass-cutting, and realty taxes to the date of closing for which the vendor is responsible in accordance with the statement of adjustments;

3.   To readjust upon demand any item in the statement of adjustments resulting from error or omission;

4.   To leave on the premises, free and clear of all liens or encumbrances, the chattels and additional items that were agreed to be included in the transaction;

5.   To pay off and register a proper discharge for any mortgage, lien, execution, or encumbrance against the property not, by the agreement, assumed by the purchasers.

DATED AT PETERBOROUGH, this 14th day of August, 20--.

_____   _____

TASHA KUIAK   LISA BROWN

1.5 to 2× spacing

3 to 4 spaces for signatures

FIGURE 10.45 Authorization and direction used in a legal matter

AUTHORIZATION & DIRECTION

TO: **Noah Keates**
              Woodrow & Perry

FROM: **Ted Rathwell**
RE: **Rathwell – Unlawful Assembly Sec. 66 CCC (File # NH/11/101)**

I THE UNDERSIGNED, hereby authorize and direct you to release to my lawyer:

Tyren Hadwyn
Barrister & Solicitor
5 Sherbrooke Street
Peterborough, Ontario K9J 6K5
Tel: 705-332-9080
Fax: 705-332-9081
Email: t.hadwyn@shaw.ca

any and all information or documentation that he requests in relation to my file.

This authorization is in accordance with any consent required under the *Personal Information and Protection of Electronic Documents Act* to release this information.

THIS IS AN IRREVOCABLE DIRECTION.

Dated this 10th day of April, 20--

_____   _____
Witness   Ted Rathwell

[NOTE: FORMATTING—FOLLOW OFFICE PREFERENCE]

FIGURE 10.46   Acknowledgment used in a criminal matter

PLEA ACKNOWLEDGMENT

TO: PAUL ATKINSON _____

FROM: JOHN WELLS _____

CHARGES: VAGRANCY 179 CCC _____

I confirm my instructions to you that I will plead **guilty** to the *Criminal Code* of Canada charges and I acknowledge that:

1) We fully discussed all aspects of this case on numerous occasions;
2) I am making this plea voluntarily;
3) I am responsible for the essential elements of the offence(s);
4) I admit that I committed the offence(s);
5) I acknowledge that you, my counsel, explained the nature and consequences of the plea and that I understand the consequences of pleading guilty;
6) I understand the Judge is not bound by any agreement made between the defence and the Crown Attorney and will make the final decision about sentencing;
7) I understand that by making this plea, I am waiving and giving up my right to proceed to trial; and
8) I do not require the Crown to prove its case against me.

Dated: _____

Signed: _____

[NOTE: FORMATTING—FOLLOW OFFICE PREFERENCE]

FIGURE 10.47   Promissory note

PROMISSORY NOTE

   I, STEPHEN BUCKLE of 32 Downer Avenue, in the City of Peterborough, in the Province of Ontario, DO PROMISE TO PAY, to the order of TANYA GUERIN AND WILLIAM CARPENTER of 970806 Coones Road in the City of Peterborough, in the Province of Ontario, the sum of THREE THOUSAND ($3000.00) DOLLARS payable at the rate of THREE HUNDRED ($300.00) DOLLARS per month commencing June 15, 20--.

Signed at the City of Peterborough on the 26th day of May, 20--

_____   _____
STEPHEN BUCKLE   WITNESS

[NOTE: FORMATTING—FOLLOW OFFICE PREFERENCE]

Creating Precedent Documents

There are times when it seems that law offices are all paper. Each area of law has its own authoritative documents, and you may be referring to and accessing the same pages again and again. As discussed in chapter 8, Legal Correspondence, because of the repetitive nature of this work, you're better off creating the needed documents according to a pre-set form, often referred to as a "precedent," "template," or "boilerplate."

Each province and area of law subscribes to certain precedents. If you find yourself in need of a precedent, there are useful reference materials, such as *O'Brien's Encyclopedia of Forms* and *Preparation of Wills and Powers of Attorney* (both published by Canada Law Book), that contain a wide range of time-saving pre-set forms. Familiarize yourself with their particular formatting, and always use their precedents with care.

There are also a variety of software packages to help you with this: for example, DivorceMate for family matters, Estate-a-base for estate matters, and Conveyancer for real estate matters. All you have to do with these packages is key your client's specific information—names, addresses, and dates—into the blank spaces provided. Boilerplates work particularly well for most routine documents, but they can be used to develop less routine ones as well. Keep in mind, however, that although drafting new documents by boilerplate is time-efficient, it also entails a risk of costly legal error if you forget to omit a clause that doesn't apply to the case at hand.

You can also save time by using your word-processing package, such as Microsoft Word or Corel WordPerfect, to create your own precedent document rather than purchasing a document package. Whatever method you use, remember that every client's situation is unique, and, this being the case, that clauses within the precedent document must be adapted to fit the client's particular needs.

NOTES:

Appendix 10.A: Separation Agreement

THIS IS A SEPARATION AGREEMENT DATED JUNE 10, 20--

Between

Barbie Cole
Hereinafter called Barbie

Of the first Part

–and–

Ken Cole
Hereinafter called Ken

Of the second Part

1.   Background

1.1   Barbie and Ken were married on August 21, 1991.

1.2   They separated on May 1, 2005. The parties will continue living separate and apart.

1.3   They have one child, Trixie Cole, born April 22, 2004 ("Trixie").

1.4   They agree to be bound by this Agreement, which settles all issues between them.

2.   Definitions

2.1   In this Agreement:

(a)   "child" means Trixie,

(b)   "cohabit" means to live with another person in a relationship resembling marriage,

(c)   "equalization payment" means the payment referred to in s. 5(1) of the *Family Law Act*,

(d)   "CRA" means Canada Revenue Agency,

(e)   "Family Responsibility Office" (FRO) means the Family Responsibility Office described in the *Family Responsibility and Support Arrears Enforcement Act*, or any successor support enforcement agency,

-2-

(f) "Guidelines" means the Child Support Guidelines, as defined in s. 2(1) of the *Divorce Act*,

(g) "indexing factor" means the percentage change for a given month in the Consumer Price Index for Canada for prices of All-Items (as published by Statistics Canada) from the same month of the previous year,

(h) "matrimonial home" means the property at 12 Label Street, in Peterborough, ON K9K 1G2,

(i) "net family property" means net family property as defined in the *Family Law Act*, and

(j) "property" means property as defined in the *Family Law Act*.

3. Freedom From The Other

3.1 Barbie and Ken will not harass or speak ill of each other.

4. Parenting

4.1 Barbie and Ken will prefer Trixie's interests to their own. Barbie and Ken will:

(a) exchange information about Trixie,

(b) encourage Trixie to have a good relationship with each parent,

(c) refrain from making disparaging remarks to Trixie about the other parent, and

(d) consult each other regularly about important issues such as Trixie's education, health care, and religious upbringing.

4.2 Barbie will have custody of Trixie.

4.3 Ken will have access on:

(a) Tuesday and Thursday evenings from 4:30 p.m. until 10:00 p.m.,

(b) on alternating weekends from 4:30 p.m. on Fridays until 6:30 p.m. on Sundays.

4.4 This holiday schedule overrides the regular schedule.

School Spring Break

(a) Trixie will reside with Ken in odd-numbered years and with Barbie in even-numbered years, from her leaving school as the school spring break starts until her return to school following the break.

-3-

Easter Weekend

(b)   Trixie will reside with Barbie in odd-numbered years and with Ken in even-numbered years, from her leaving school on the Thursday before the Easter weekend until her return to school on the following Tuesday.

Summer Vacation

(c)   Trixie will reside with each parent for 8 consecutive or non-consecutive weeks during Trixie's summer school vacation. Barbie and Ken will advise each other by April 1st of their chosen weeks, with Ken to have first choice in odd-numbered years and Barbie to have first choice in even-numbered years. In making plans, each parent will take into account Trixie's camp and other scheduled activities.

Christmas

(d)   The parties will share equally Trixie's Christmas school break. Trixie will reside with Ken for the first half of the break in odd-numbered years and with Barbie for the first half in even-numbered years. The first half will start at 3:30 p.m. on Trixie's last day of school in December. The second half will end on the morning Trixie returns to school in January.

Child's Birthday

(e)   Trixie will spend her birthday in accordance with the regular schedule.

4.5   Barbie and Ken may make inquiries and be given information by Trixie's teachers, school officials, doctors, dentists, health-care providers, summer-camp counsellors, or others involved with Trixie.

4.6   Both parents may attend all school functions. The parents may/will attend parent–teacher meetings together or separately.

4.7   Each parent may/will obtain his or her own school calendar and school notices.

5.   Dispute Resolution

5.1   If Barbie and Ken disagree about a reviewable aspect of this Agreement, they will try to resolve the dispute through negotiation.

5.2   If the parties cannot come to a negotiated settlement between themselves, the parties are to consult a mediator, which shall be funded jointly by the parties. If no settlement arises from their attempted negotiations outside of litigation, either party is permitted to retain legal counsel, which will be funded separately by each party, and no costs shall be awarded in this regard.

-4-

6. Child Support

6.1 In this section,

(a) "Table" and "income" mean "Table" and "income" as those terms are defined in s. 2(1) of the Guidelines,

(b) "special or extraordinary expenses" means "special or extraordinary expenses" as this phrase is defined in s. 7(1) of the Guidelines,

(c) "child support" refers to the monthly amount upon which the parties have agreed and may include both Table support and special or extraordinary expenses.

6.2 Starting July 1, 2011 and on the first day of each month, Ken will pay to Barbie as child support for Trixie:

(a) the Table amount of $785.00 until one or more of the following occurs:

(i) Trixie ceases to be a "child" as defined in the *Divorce Act,*

(ii) Trixie no longer resides with the custodial parent ("resides" includes Trixie living away from home for school, summer employment, or vacation),

(iii) Trixie turns 18, unless Trixie is unable to become self-supporting due to illness, disability, education, or other cause,

(iv) Trixie becomes self-supporting,

(v) Trixie obtains one postsecondary degree or diploma,

(vi) Trixie turns 25 years of age,

(vii) Trixie marries,

(viii) Trixie dies, or

(ix) a party dies, provided that the security in the section of this Agreement entitled "Life Insurance" is in place at the time of death.

6.3 When Trixie begins to live away from home for educational purposes, the parties will review the amount of support payable by Ken in order to take into account the reduced costs to Barbie and the fact that Ken is contributing to tuition and residency costs.

6.4 If Trixie ceases to be a "child" as defined in the Guidelines because she has interrupted her schooling for any purpose, but she later returns to school full time and is still under the age of 25, then she will be deemed once again to be a "child" as defined in the Guidelines and support will resume until a terminating event under section 6.2.

6.5 Starting July 1, 2012 and on every July thereafter, child support will increase by the indexing factor for May of the previous year.

-5-

7. Spousal Support

7.1 Barbie and Ken are each financially independent of each other and will release his or her right to spousal support from the other forever. Barbie and Ken intend this Agreement to inoculate them from any judicial review.

7.2 Barbie and Ken know that their financial circumstances, health, employment, or the cost of living may all change. They may be unable to work for various reasons, or earn less than they expect. These changes may be catastrophic, unanticipated, or beyond imagining. Nevertheless, no change will ever entitle Ken or Barbie to spousal support from the other.

7.3 Barbie and Ken do not want any court to order a change that deviates from or overrides the terms of this Agreement, especially this release. Barbie and Ken want the court to uphold this Agreement in its entirety because they are basing their future lives upon this release.

7.4 This Agreement recognizes all economic advantages or disadvantages to the parties arising from the marriage and its breakdown, has apportioned between them all financial consequences arising from the care of the child in addition to any obligation for the support of the child, relieves any economic hardship arising from the marriage breakdown, and, insofar as is practicable, promotes the economic self-sufficiency of Barbie and Ken within a reasonable period of time.

8. Medical and Dental Benefits

8.1 Barbie and Ken are each responsible for his or her own medical, extended health, and dental expenses.

9. Life Insurance

9.1 The parties will jointly apply for two life insurance policies ("the policies") on Ken's life, each in the amount of $500,000.00 to secure child support. Ken will take any medical examinations or tests required to obtain the policies.

10. Matrimonial Home

10.1 Barbie and Ken jointly own the matrimonial home located at 12 Label Street, Peterborough.

10.2 On signing this Agreement, Ken will transfer his interest in the matrimonial home to Barbie, free of all encumbrances. Barbie will pay the cost of the preparation and registration of the transfer.

10.3 Barbie will obtain a release of Ken's mortgage obligations from TD Canada Trust. If Barbie cannot obtain Ken's release, she will refinance the home and discharge the current mortgage. Barbie will pay all penalties, interest, and costs resulting from this mortgage.

10.4 Barbie and Ken have divided their household contents.

-6-

11. Debts

11.1 Neither Barbie nor Ken will pledge the credit of the other or bind the other for any debts he or she may incur after the signing of this Agreement. Barbie and Ken acknowledge that they have not pledged the credit of the other since separation.

12. Releases

12.1 This Agreement is a full and final settlement of all issues between Barbie and Ken and all rights and obligations arising out of their relationship.

12.2 Except as otherwise provided in this Agreement, Barbie and Ken release each other from all claims at common law, in equity, or by statute against each other, including claims under the *Divorce Act*, the *Family Law Act*, and the *Succession Law Reform Act*.

13. General Terms

13.1 If Barbie and Ken agree to try and reconcile their relationship but they cohabit for no longer than 90 days, this Agreement will not be affected. If they cohabit for more than 90 days, this Agreement will become void, except that any transfers or payments made to that time will not be affected or invalidated.

13.2 If a divorce judgment or order issues, all of the terms of this Agreement will continue.

13.3 Barbie and Ken have each had independent legal advice, Ken from Jennifer Eve and Barbie from Nick Miller.

13.4 The effective date of this Agreement is the date on which the last party signs it.

TO EVIDENCE THEIR AGREEMENT, BARBIE COLE AND KEN COLE HAVE SIGNED THIS AGREEMENT BEFORE A WITNESS.

DATE:

_____   _____
Witness   Barbie Cole

DATE:

_____   _____
Witness   Ken Cole

Appendix 10.B: Partnership Agreement

THIS AGREEMENT made this 20th day of February 20--

BETWEEN:

<u>DONALD JOSEPH TRUMP</u> of the Township of
Cavan, in the County of Peterborough

Hereinafter called "Trump"

OF THE FIRST PART

and

<u>LAWRENCE ROSS KEATES</u> of the Village
of Millbrook, in the County of Peterborough

Hereinafter called "Keates"

OF THE SECOND PART

Witnesses:

That in consideration of the mutual covenants and agreements hereinafter
contained, the said parties hereto each covenant and agree with the other, as follows:

1.   The said parties agree to purchase the business and business premises known as
     "Millbrook Bowling Lanes" from Linda Skilton.

2.   The name of the partnership to be carried on by the partners upon completion of
     the purchase from Linda Skilton shall be "Millbrook Bowling Lanes", and the
     business shall be carried on at 12 Malt Street, Millbrook, Ontario, or any other
     place as the partnership shall, from time to time, agree upon.

3.   The Bank of the partnership shall be TD Canada Trust, at 15 King Street,
     Millbrook, Ontario.

4.   The capital of the partnership shall be the funds necessary to purchase the business
     known as "Millbrook Bowling Lanes", in accordance with the Agreement of
     Purchase and Sale executed by the parties hereto as purchasers and dated the 20th
     day of February 20--, together with all costs for legal fees and disbursements and
     other costs, and it is agreed that the funds will be contributed equally by the
     parties.

5.   The profits and losses of the business shall be divided between the partners in
     equal shares.

-2-

6.   Proper accounts shall be kept of all partnership transactions and on the day established by the accountant of the partnership in every year, or as soon afterward as possible, balance sheets shall be made out showing the assets and liabilities of the partnership and what belongs and is due to each partner for capital and share of profits, and the said balance sheets shall be signed by both partners, and when so signed shall be conclusive, except that if a manifest error shall be discovered therein within thirty (30) days after the signing thereof, such error shall be rectified.

7.   The accountant for the partnership shall be Mrs. Janice Miller, MILLER ACCOUNTING SERVICES, 710 Dough Avenue, Peterborough, Ontario.

8.   The capital of the partnership shall also consist of the property credits and stock in trade of the said partnership which are from time to time extant.

9.   Each party agrees to contribute not less than eighteen (18) hours per week of his time to conducting the partnership business known as "Millbrook Bowling Lanes", and shall be at "Millbrook Bowling Lanes" during these hours.

10. Neither partner shall sign any promissory note or bill in the name of the firm nor shall give credit after warning from his co partner, nor shall without his written consent borrow money or compound debts or become surety for bail, or enter into a contract for more than ONE HUNDRED DOLLARS ($100.00) or hire any employee, or engage in any other business similar to the type of business carried on by "Millbrook Bowling Lanes".

   All cheques and bills of exchange of the partnership shall be signed by both partners.

11. Any contract or liability entered into or incurred by either partner in contravention of the preceding two paragraphs shall be at his exclusive risk and the partnership shall be indemnified out of his separate property.

12. Accounts shall be kept and books of all partnership transactions and such books together with all other documents connected with the partnership business shall be kept at, and not removed from, the principal place of business and be accessible to each partner.

13. On the determination of the partnership, a full written account shall be taken of all the partnership property, stock, credits, and liabilities, and a written valuation shall be made of all that is capable of valuation, and such accounts and valuation shall be settled and provisions shall be made for the payment of the liabilities of the partnership, and the balance of such property, stock, and credit shall be divided equally between the partners, and each shall execute to the other proper releases and proper instruments for vesting in the other and enabling him to get in such property, stock, and credits.

14. All matters in difference in relation to the partnership affairs shall be referred to the arbitration of a single arbitrator, if the parties agree upon one, otherwise to three arbitrators, one to be appointed by each party and a third to be chosen by the

-3-

two first named before they enter upon the business of arbitration, and the award and determination of such arbitrator or arbitrators, or any two of such three arbitrators, shall be binding upon the parties hereto and their respective executors, administrators, and assigns.

15. Upon the determination of the partnership, the assets of the partnership shall be realized and shall be applied first in the payment of debts and liabilities of the partnership, and second in paying to each partner the amount of his capital in the business, and the surplus, if any, shall be divided between the partners.

16. The parties agree not to make any special provisions with respect to the withdrawal of a partner from the partnership or the purchase or sale of a deceased partner's interest at the present time.

17. This agreement shall be to the benefit of and be binding upon the heirs, executors, administrators, and assigns of the parties.

IN WITNESS WHEREOF the said parties have set their hands and seals.

SIGNED, SEALED & DELIVERED   )

　　　　　　　　　　　　　　　　　)

In the presence of:　　　　　　)

　　　　　　　　　　　　　　　　　)

　　　　　　　　　　　　　　　　　)

　　　　　　　　　　　　　　　　　)

_____   )   _____

Witness　　　　　　　　　　　　)   Donald Joseph Trump

　　　　　　　　　　　　　　　　　)

　　　　　　　　　　　　　　　　　)

　　　　　　　　　　　　　　　　　)

_____   )   _____

Witness　　　　　　　　　　　　)   Lawrence Ross Keates

Appendix 10.C: Will

THIS IS THE WILL of me, GLENN JONES, of the City of Peterborough in the County of Peterborough, and Province of Ontario, made this 29th day of May, 20--.

I.   REVOCATION

I revoke all Wills and Codicils previously made by me.

II.   EXECUTOR AND TRUSTEE

I appoint my wife Sharon Jones to be the Executor and Trustee of my Will. If my spouse does not survive me or is or becomes unwilling or unable to act as my Executor and Trustee before all the trusts set out in my Will have been fully performed, I appoint Cheri Douglas and Brenda Yu to be the Executors and Trustees of my Will.

In my Will, I refer to the Executor and Trustee or Executors and Trustees, original or substituted or surviving, as my "Estate Trustee".

III.   TRANSFERS TO ESTATE TRUSTEE

I give all my property to my Estate Trustee upon the following trusts:

1.   Personal Property

My Estate Trustee shall deliver to my spouse, Sharon Jones, if she is living on the 30th day following the date of my death, all remaining articles of personal and household use or ornament, and all automobiles and their accessories.

If my spouse is not then living, my Estate Trustee shall divide all such articles among my children then living in such manner as they may agree or, failing agreement, in such manner as my Estate Trustee in the exercise of an absolute discretion considers appropriate. Any articles not distributed shall fall into the residue of my estate.

If my Estate Trustee is of the opinion that a child of mine is not old enough to make use of such articles, my Estate Trustee may either dispose of such articles or any of them and add the proceeds of sale if any to the residue of my estate, or hold such articles or any of them until my child is old enough to make use of them.

I authorize my Estate Trustee to deliver any articles to my children at such times as my Estate Trustee considers appropriate, whether or not a child may be under the age of majority. The delivery of any articles to such child shall be a complete release to my Estate Trustee.

Any articles not distributed or retained shall become part of the residue of my estate.

2.   Debts and Death Taxes

My Estate Trustee shall pay out of the capital of my estate all my just debts, including any income taxes payable for the year(s) prior to my death and in the year of my death to the date of my death, funeral and testamentary expenses, and

-2-

all succession duties, estate, gift, inheritance, and death taxes, whether imposed pursuant to the law of this or any other jurisdiction, otherwise payable by any beneficiary under my Will or any Codicil or of any settlement made by me, by any beneficiary named by me in any insurance policy, plan or contract owned by me, or by any donee of any gift made by me.

3. Conversion of My Assets

My Estate Trustee shall call in the assets of my estate and may sell the assets at such times, for such price, in such manner and upon such terms as my Estate Trustee in the exercise of an absolute discretion considers appropriate.

I authorize my Estate Trustee to hold any asset of my estate without liability for loss or depreciation for as long as my Estate Trustee in the exercise of an absolute discretion considers appropriate, whether or not it may not be an investment in which a trustee may by law invest trust funds.

4. Residue

If my spouse, Sharon Jones is living on the 30th day following the date of my death, my Estate Trustee shall pay and transfer the residue of my estate to my spouse for her own use absolutely.

5. Alternate Residue

If my spouse is not living on the 30th day following the date of my death, my Estate Trustee shall divide the residue of my estate equally among David Lawrence Jones, Kevin Scott Jones, William Angus Jones, and Sarah Elizabeth Jones then living in equal shares *per stirpes*.

IV. PAYMENTS FOR MINORS

If any person becomes entitled to receive any share of my estate while under the age of majority, I direct my Estate Trustee to keep that share invested until such person attains the age of majority. In the meantime, my Estate Trustee shall pay or apply such amounts out of the income and capital as my Estate Trustee in the exercise of an absolute discretion considers advisable for the benefit of such person.

I authorize my Estate Trustee to make any payments for any person under the age of majority which my Estate Trustee is entitled to make under the terms of my Will to a parent or guardian or other person standing *in loco parentis* to such person, or to make any such payment directly to such person or to any other person for such person, all as my Estate Trustee in the exercise of an absolute discretion considers appropriate. Any evidence that my Estate Trustee has made any payment shall be a sufficient discharge to my Estate Trustee.

V. POWERS OF ESTATE TRUSTEE

In order to carry out the trusts of my Will, I give my Estate Trustee the following powers to be used in the exercise of an absolute discretion at any time:

-3-

1. Investments

My Estate Trustee shall make any investments for my estate that my Estate Trustee considers appropriate, including units or other interests of any mutual funds, common trust funds, unit trusts, or similar investments, without being limited to those investments authorized by law for trustees. My Estate Trustee shall not be liable for any loss that may happen to my estate as a result of any investment made by my Estate Trustee in good faith.

2. Selling and Disposing

My Estate Trustee shall realize or dispose of the assets of my estate, subject to the trusts of my Will, in any manner and on any terms.

3. Retention of Assets

My Estate Trustee shall hold any of my assets in the form in which they may be at the time of my death for any length of time, whether or not they might not be assets in which trustees would otherwise be entitled to invest trust monies. Those assets so retained shall be deemed to be authorized investments.

4. Distribution in Specie

My Estate Trustee shall make any division, distribution, or allocation of the assets of my estate in kind and at such valuations as my Estate Trustee in the exercise of an absolute discretion considers appropriate. In determining such valuations, my Estate Trustee may consider such future expectations for such assets as my Estate Trustee in the exercise of an absolute discretion considers appropriate, including any tax liability or credit. Any decision of my Estate Trustee in this regard shall be binding on all persons concerned.

5. Employment of Agents

If my Estate Trustee considers it necessary to engage any corporation or person to carry out some or all of the directions in my Will, my Estate Trustee may employ such corporation or person and may pay compensation out of my estate, all as my Estate Trustee considers appropriate.

6. Real Property

If any real or leasehold property forms part of my estate, my Estate Trustee may lease such property for any term and subject to such conditions as my Estate Trustee considers appropriate. My Estate Trustee may accept surrenders of leases and tenancies, may pay money out of the income or capital of my estate for repairs and improvements, and may generally manage the property. My Estate Trustee may give any options that my Estate Trustee may consider advisable. My Estate Trustee may renew any mortgage, may borrow money on any real estate upon any mortgage, and may pay off any mortgage that may exist at my death or at any renewal.

-4-

7. Loans to Beneficiaries

My Estate Trustee may lend money or other assets of my estate to any beneficiary, or guarantee any loans for any beneficiary or for any company owned or controlled by my estate or by a beneficiary, or in which my estate or a beneficiary may have an interest, upon such terms, with or without interest, and with or without security, all as my Estate Trustee in the exercise of an absolute discretion considers appropriate.

8. Borrowing

My Estate Trustee may borrow on behalf of my estate such amounts as my Estate Trustee considers appropriate, and may mortgage or otherwise charge any of the assets of my estate.

9. Settlement of Claims

Without the consent of any person interested under my Will, my Estate Trustee may compromise, settle, or waive any claim at any time due to or by my estate and may make any agreement with any person, government, or corporation which shall be binding upon all persons interested in my estate.

10. Securities

My Estate Trustee may deal with any securities, shares, or other interests of any corporation that is held by my estate, to the same extent as if I were alive. My Estate Trustee may take up new or further shares or other interests, may join in any reorganization, may exchange shares or other interests, and may give or accept and exercise options. My Estate Trustee may pay out of my estate any monies that may be necessary for any of these purposes.

11. Elections

My Estate Trustee may at any time make, or choose not to make, any election or designation, or may do, or choose not to do, any other act or exercise any discretion or authority referred to in the *Income Tax Act*, R.S.C. 1985, c. 1 (5th Supp.), that my Estate Trustee considers in the best interests of my estate and my beneficiaries or any of them.

12. Transactions with Estate Trustee

In my Estate Trustee's personal capacity, my Estate Trustee may purchase assets from my estate if the purchase price and other terms are unanimously approved by my Estate Trustee and by the adult beneficiaries of my estate. My Estate Trustee shall not be required to obtain the approval of any court for such purchase.

VI. EXCLUSIONS FROM NET FAMILY PROPERTY

I declare that the income, including capital gains, arising from any interest passing to a beneficiary under my Will shall be excluded from such beneficiary's net family property or from the value of the beneficiary's assets on the death, divorce, or separation of such beneficiary, pursuant to the *Family Law Act*, R.S.O. 1990, c. F.3.

-5-

All gifts made to a beneficiary shall be the separate property of my beneficiaries and shall not fall into any Community of Property or be subject to any other matrimonial rights of the spouses of my beneficiaries and shall not be liable for the obligations of any such spouses or Community. All such gifts shall not be subject to seizure for the payment of any debts of beneficiaries or their representatives while in the possession and control of my Estate Trustee.

VII. GOVERNING LAW

My Will shall be governed by and construed in accordance with the laws of the Province of Ontario.

IN TESTIMONY WHEREOF I have to my Will which is written upon this and the _____ preceding pages of paper, subscribed my name on the day and year first written above.

Signed by _____
as his will, in the presence
of us both, present at the same
time, who at his request, in
his presence and in the   _____
presence of each other, have subscribed   Signature of testator
our names as witnesses:

1. _____   )
SIGNATURE OF WITNESS   )
)
)
_____   )
NAME   )
)
)
_____   )
OCCUPATION   )
)
)
2. _____   )
SIGNATURE OF WITNESS   )
)
)
_____   )
NAME   )
)
)
_____   )
OCCUPATION   )

REVIEW QUESTIONS

1. What is the difference between a court document and a client document?

_____

_____

_____

_____

_____

_____

_____

_____

2. What types of contracts are required by law to be in writing?

_____

_____

_____

_____

_____

_____

_____

_____

_____

3. List the tools you need in front of you before starting to type a contract.

_____

_____

_____

_____

_____

_____

_____

_____

4. What are the main components of a legal document?

_____

_____

_____

_____

_____

_____

_____

_____

5. State the purpose of each of the following:

   a. recital clause

_____

_____

_____

_____

   b. consideration clause

_____

_____

_____

_____

   c. attestation clause

_____

_____

_____

_____

6. What is a covenant?

_____

_____

_____

_____

_____

_____

_____

7. What is the role of the witness?

8. Does a legal document need to be witnessed? Why or why not?

9. The _____ is the person in a firm who is
    authorized to witness the signing of an affidavit.

10. Briefly distinguish between an affidavit and a statutory declaration.

11. The legal instrument that certifies the authenticity of the copy of
     a document is a(n) _____.

12. A sworn replica of a document is referred to as a(n)
     _____.

ACTIVITIES

1. Using the samples shown in this chapter, prepare a heading for each of the following:

    a. A separation agreement for Fred and Wilma Flintstone.

    b. A lease agreement for Cody Carpenter and Camden Carpenter leasing from Devils' Realty Incorporated.

    c. An employment agreement for Raymond Meadus, a typesetter who is being employed by Tanya Carpenter, owner of Roscoe Publishing.

2. Prepare endings for each of the agreements described in the previous question. Assume that Fred and Wilma are signing their agreement at separate locations.

3. When you arrive at your desk this morning there is a memo outlining a few tasks that need to be completed.

    To: Student

    From: Lawyer

    Date: Today's Date

    Re: Today's Activities

    a. Prepare an affidavit for Sarah Carpenter and Shane Hadwyn. Sarah Carpenter will drop by the office this morning for commissioning. Sarah and Shane live at 274 Braidwood Avenue, Peterborough, Ontario.

    Note the following about the two parties:

    - They are common-law spouses who have been living together since July 29, 2001.
    - There are three children of the relationship: Ayden Hadwyn, born May 26, 2002; Ryder Hadwyn, born April 5, 2004; and Tyren Hadwyn, born August 31, 2008.

    b. Amy Hogget requires a statutory declaration for division of pension benefits. Amy lives at 1092 Eldson Street, Oshawa, Ontario.

    Following are the relevant facts about Amy:

    - She was married to Robert Hogget on September 25, 1976.
    - They separated on February 12, 2003 and were divorced on April 10, 2005.
    - There were no periods where they lived separate and apart.

c.   Prepare notarial certificates as needed for each of the following:

- Nicolas Forget requires a true copy of his birth certificate (provided by instructor) in order to obtain a Canadian passport.

- Allicia Keates is applying to the Pharmacy Examining Board of Canada. She requires a true copy of her marriage licence (provided by instructor) to support her identity on her application.

Legal Terminology and Citation

Research is creating new knowledge.

—Neil Armstrong

Introduction

Of central importance to the efficient production of legal writings are a knowledge of the terminology used within particular areas of law and the way in which legal sources are cited. For this reason, a good grounding in legal terminology, as well as a knowledge of where to find legal sources and how to cite them properly, are essential for all who work in the legal field. As part of your duties in a law office, you may be asked to research a specific topic and then prepare a case brief or legal memorandum. This chapter will help prepare you to undertake these important tasks with confidence.

> Abstract words are ancient coins whose concrete images in the busy give-and-take of talk have worn away with use.
>
> —Julian Jaynes, *The Origin of Consciousness in the Breakdown of the Bicameral Mind* (1976)

The Tradition of Legal Terminology

Like any specialty, the field of law has its own "insider" language. To lawyers, the words and phrases found in statutes, court decisions, contracts, and other documents read like plain English, but the rest of us—at least initially—are sure to throw up our hands and exclaim, "It's all Greek to me!" And in a sense we're right, because a lot of Canadian legal jargon has Greek as well as Latin (Roman) roots.

Legal principles in the Western world evolved from the Roman Empire, which borrowed its concepts from the traditions of the ancient Greeks. The Romans left their mark on virtually every aspect of European civilization, including governments, universities, churches, and courts. The legal language that we use today—sometimes called "legalese"—is rife with Latin expressions such as *caveat emptor* and *habeas corpus*.

CHAPTER OBJECTIVES

After reading this chapter, you will understand:

- the tradition and definitions of legal terminology and Latin terms

- common words, phrases, and terms used in specific areas of law

- how to use primary and secondary sources to conduct legal research

- how to use electronic resources to conduct legal research

- how to correctly cite primary, secondary, and electronic sources

- the purpose, format, and content of case briefs and legal memoranda

Although such expressions can be mystifying to outsiders, they neatly express legal principles that have guided civil society for millennia.

The law relies a great deal on *precedents*—forms of expression that have been used many times before. These days, when lawyers draft documents, they often use compound words, redundant phrases, and archaic forms of expression. They do so because they learned the law from precedents, as did their teachers, and so on. The language in a run-of-the-mill contract may, in fact, be hundreds of years old. However, when these precedents were originally created, the drafters were concerned not only with, say, putting a contract between two people into writing, but also with ensuring that they alone could do the writing. In a time when few people were educated and literate, it paid to be verbose. But much of the redundant wording in today's legal documents can and should be simplified.

Consider this portion of an introductory paragraph from a precedent for a lease:

> In consideration of the rents, covenants, and agreements hereinafter reserved and contained on the part of the tenant, the landlord demises and LEASES unto the tenant, her executors, administrators, successors, and assigns, those premises situated, lying and being in the …

A plain-language version of the same paragraph might read:

> Ms. Rice agrees to rent apartment 3 at 47 Green St., Cobourg, to Ms. Thain on the following terms: …

Of course, you can't properly revise a legal document without first understanding legalese. You'll need to be able to differentiate the necessary legal terminology from the phrases that do little or no work. Words like "certify" and "attest," for example, are helpful, but no one is likely to miss "hereinafter" or "whatsoever." To get a handle on legalese, you should buy a comprehensive Canadian legal dictionary such as the *Canadian Law Dictionary* by John A. Yogis, and use it often. For most legal professionals, such a resource quickly becomes an essential tool of the trade.

NOTES:

Latin Terms

The following Latin terms are commonly found in cases and legal documents. Although many of them might be replaced with English equivalents, they are well accepted and, again, are compact expressions of legal principles with long histories. It's in your interest to learn them.

actio in personam	action against a person
actus reus	as an element of criminal responsibility, the wrongful act or omission that comprises the physical components of a crime
ad hoc	for this purpose
ad hominem	to the man (appealing to a person's interests or prejudices rather than to reason)
ad infinitum	forever; without limit; indefinitely
ad litem	for the suit; a person appointed only for the purposes of prosecuting or defending an action on behalf of another, such as a child or mentally challenged person; also called a guardian *ad litem*
bona fide	in good faith
caveat emptor	let the buyer beware
corpus delicti	body of the crime; material evidence that a crime has occurred
de facto	according to the fact or deed
de jure	according to law; by right
ex curia	out of court
ex lege	arising from the law; as a matter of law
ex officio	by virtue of the office held
ex post facto	from the deed afterward (acting retroactively)
habeas corpus	you may have the body; a writ requiring that a party be brought to court promptly
ignorantia legis neminem excusat	ignorance of the law excuses no one
in camera	in chamber; in secret; closed session
in facie curiae	in the face or presence of the court
in flagrante delicto	in the act
intra vires	within the powers; within the authority of a legislative body
ipso facto	by the fact itself; by that very fact; by the very deed
lex scripta	written law

mala fide	in or with bad faith; treacherously
mala in se	bad or evil in itself
mens rea	Latin for "guilty mind"; guilty knowledge or intention to commit a prohibited act (criminal law generally requires proof of both *actus reus* and *mens rea* on the part of a defendant in order to establish criminal liability)
modus operandi	manner of working or operating
nolle prosequi	I do not wish to pursue; I do not wish to prosecute (said by a prosecutor who is dropping all or part of an indictment)
nolo contendere	I do not wish to contend (a guilty plea, leaving open the option of denying alleged facts in later proceedings)
non compos mentis	not having control of the mind; not of sane mind (not legally responsible)
nunc pro tunc	now for then (indicating an action in the present that should have been taken before)
obiter dictum, obiter dicta	thing(s) said by the way; a judge's incidental remark, observation, or opinion that is not binding
per se	in or by itself
prima facie	at first sight; on first appearance
pro forma	as a matter of form only; according to form
pro tempore	for the time being; temporarily
quid pro quo	something in exchange for something; a fair exchange
res gestae	things done; deeds; facts of a case that are admissible as evidence
sine die	without a day (set for reconvening); indefinitely
sine qua non	without which not; an essential element or condition
stare decisis	to abide by decided cases (a principle of common law that lower courts must follow the decisions of higher courts where the legal issues are the same)
status quo	manner in which; condition; legal condition of a person or thing; the existing state of affairs
sub judice	before the judge or court; under judicial consideration
subpoena	under penalty
sui juris	of one's own right (capable of managing one's own affairs)
ultra vires	beyond the powers (an action that is invalid because it exceeds the authority of the person or organization that performs it; a company cannot normally be bound by an act it is not empowered to do by its memorandum of association)

Common Words and Phrases

The following words and phrases are commonly found in statutes, cases, and other legal documents. Some are redundant ("each and every"), some archaic ("witnesseth"), some useful ("waive"). Familiarity with all of them will make legalese less intimidating.

above-described
above-entitled
above-mentioned
above-named
affix
aforesaid
annexed
attests
certify
comes now
commonly known
constitute and appoint
deposes and says
do hereby agree
duly sworn
each and every
execute
foregoing
forthwith
from time to time
good and valuable consideration
govern yourself accordingly
heirs and assigns
hereafter
hereby

herein
hereinabove
hereinafter
hereinbefore
hereof
hereto
hereunto
in consideration of
in the matter of
in witness whereof
inasmuch as
insofar as
it is hereby ordered, adjudged, and decreed
it is hereby stipulated
jointly and severally
just and proper
know all men by these presents
mutual covenants
nominal consideration
on or about
ordered
parties hereto
resolved
subscribed and sworn to

their hand and seal
thenceforth
thereafter
therefore
therein
thereof
thereon
thereto
thereupon
therewith
to wit
together with
undersigned
upon reasonable notice
waive
whatsoever
whereas
whereat
wherefore
whereof
wheresoever
whomsoever
whosoever
witness
witnesseth

NOTES:

Common Terms of Particular Legal Disciplines

The practice of law is divided into a number of legal disciplines—real estate law, family law, and so on—and within each discipline are words, phrases, and concepts that are unique to the discipline. The following sections define the terms most commonly encountered in a number of legal disciplines.

Common Real Estate Law Terms

assessment roll number	a 19-digit numerical identifier given to property for municipal tax purposes
abstract of title	a condensed history of the title to a parcel of land, consisting of a synopsis of every recorded instrument affecting the title to that land, arranged in chronological order of recording
agreement of purchase and sale	a written contract signed by the buyer and the seller of a property, stating the terms and conditions under which the property will be sold
amortization	the gradual repayment of a debt by means of partial payment of the principal and interest at regular intervals over an established period of time
charge/mortgage of land	the instrument representing a loan that has been obtained and secured against a particular party
chattel	a movable article of property; any article of tangible property other than land, buildings, and other things annexed to land
closing	the time at which a transaction is consummated, as when the seller conveys title and the buyer pays the purchase price
condominium	the fee ownership of a specified amount of space in a multiple dwelling or other multi-occupancy building with tenancy-in-common ownership of portions used jointly with other owners
condominium estoppel certificate	a written statement of a condominium unit's current financial and legal status
conveyance	a written document that transfers the title to land from one person to another
declaration of possession	a sworn document, signed by a vendor, confirming the vendor's ownership of the property; given to the purchaser on closing
deed	a document that transfers ownership of land
disbursements	a lawyer's out-of-pocket expenses, or money actually spent on behalf of a client
discharge of charge/mortgage	a document given by a chargee/mortgagee to a chargor/mortgagor, confirming that a loan has been paid in full and extinguishing the chargee's interest in property
electronic registration	a system of registering an instrument electronically by creating and signing the instrument on a computer in the lawyer's office using Teraview software, and then submitting it to the Registry Office for registration over the Internet
in escrow	the holding of funds or documents by a third party to be released only on certain specified conditions

execution	the signing of a document; also a short name for a writ of execution or a writ of seizure and sale
fee simple	the right to exclusive possession of land and the right to dispose of the land at will
foreclosure	a court action whereby a chargee obtains legal title to a property after default by a chargor
joint tenants	two or more people who own property where, on the death of one tenant, the deceased's share is inherited by the survivors
Land Titles System	the land registration system in Ontario governed by the *Land Titles Act*
land transfer tax	a provincial or municipal tax on the transfer of land
lease	a contract, either written or oral, whereby, for a consideration usually termed rent, the lawful owner of real property transfers the rights of use, possession, and enjoyment to another for life, for a specified period of time, or at will
letter of requisition	a letter, prepared by a purchaser's lawyer and delivered to a vendor, that sets out all of the problems with title to the subject property that the vendor must correct before closing, and that sets out all other items that the vendor must deliver to the purchaser
lien	a charge for payment of a debt that allows the land to be sold to satisfy the debt
metes and bounds	the boundaries and dimensions of a parcel of land in relation to lot lines
per diem	per day; for each day; daily
real estate agent commission	a percentage paid to a real estate agent on the sale of a property
real property	land, including everything that is attached to it
recital	a statement in a document that sets out the facts on which the document is based
Registry System	the land registration system in Ontario governed by the *Registry Act*
requisition on title	a query of directives made by a purchaser that asks a vendor to remedy problems with title to the subject property
right of survivorship	the automatic vesting of an interest in the surviving joint tenant or tenants when one joint tenant dies
statement of adjustments	a statement that outlines the various credits and debits against the purchase price of a property and that specifies the exact amount to be paid on closing
tenants in common	two or more people who own property where, on the death of one tenant, the deceased person's share passes to his or her heirs rather than the other owners, with no right of survivorship
title search	an examination of the title records for a property to determine whether anyone other than the presumed owner of the property has a claim to the property
transfer	a document that transfers ownership of land
undertaking	a written promise to do something

Common Family Law Terms

certificate of divorce	a document that indicates that a divorce is final
Children's Lawyer	a public official whose legal staff looks after the financial and other interests of children who are involved in or have an interest in civil proceedings
cohabitation agreement	an agreement between two persons who are cohabiting or who intend to cohabit and who are not married to each other, in which they agree on their respective rights and obligations during cohabitation, on ceasing to cohabit, or on death
divorce	the legal ending of a marriage by court order
Divorce Act	the federal law that gives the superior court of a province the authority to grant divorces and, as part of the divorce, to deal with child and spousal support, child custody, and access
divorce order	a court document that sets out the terms of a divorce and indicates the date on which the divorce becomes final
domestic contract	a marriage contract, separation agreement, or cohabitation agreement
Family Law Rules	rules governing family law proceedings
grounds for divorce	the reasons for the breakdown of a marriage: the parties have lived separate and apart for one year, the respondent (the person being divorced) has committed adultery since entering the marriage, or the respondent has treated his or her spouse with physical or mental cruelty
joint petition for divorce	a joint application by spouses to begin divorce proceedings
marriage contract	an agreement between two persons who are married or who intend to marry, in which they agree on their respective rights and obligations under the marriage or separation, annulment, divorce, or death
matrimonial home	the home and real property in which the family usually resided during the marriage; regardless of which spouse is the registered owner of the home, each spouse has one-half interest in the home and has the same right to use and reside in the home
separation agreement	a contract between spouses to live apart on certain terms and conditions; it may address custody and access, support, and division of matrimonial property
summons	a court order that requires a person to appear in court at a specific time
trial management conference	a conference held between parties, prior to trial, to explore ways to make more efficient use of trial time

Common Estate Law Terms

administration bond	a fiduciary bond that guarantees the faithful performance and fidelity of an executor or administrator of a will, trust, or estate
beneficiary	a person for whom trust property is held
bequest	the act of leaving an estate or piece of property to someone by will
certificate of appointment of estate trustee with a will	a document issued by a court that proves the authority of an estate trustee to administer the provisions of a deceased's will
certificate of appointment of estate trustee without a will	a document issued by a court that gives authority to an estate trustee to manage and distribute the estate of a deceased who died without having made a will
codicil	a formal document that amends a will
estate	all of a person's assets and liabilities, especially at death
estate trustee	the person or party named in the last will and testament of a deceased who has the primary responsibility for the administration of the deceased's estate
estate trustee during litigation	a grant made under a court order that appoints someone to act for an estate when there is a dispute about the validity of the will or about who should administer the estate; during litigation the estate trustee has control of estate assets but has no authority to make payouts until the court has dealt with the validity of the will or decided who should administer the estate
executor	a person appointed by a testator to carry out the terms of the testator's will
executrix	a woman appointed by a testator to carry out the terms of the testator's will; "executor" is often preferred
guardian	a person with legal custody of another person and their property when that person is incapable of managing their own affairs
holograph will	a handwritten will
legacy	a gift left in a will
last will and testament	a documentary instrument by which a person (the testator) regulates the rights of others over the testator's property or family after their death
per stirpes	a distribution to surviving descendants of a predeceased beneficiary whereby the original gift flows downward by representation
power of attorney	a person's authority to act for another person in legal or financial matters
probate	the official proving of a will; a verified copy of a will with a certificate as handed to the executors
revocation clause	a clause in a will that provides that all previous wills are no longer valid and that this will is the legally binding will
testate	to die having left a will
testator	a person who makes a will
testatrix	a woman who makes a will; "testator" is often preferred
testament	a will
will	directions in legal form for the disposition of one's property after death

Common Civil Litigation Terms

affidavit	a written statement that sets out the evidence of the person who swears or affirms its contents are true
affidavit of documents	an affidavit in which a party identifies documents that are relevant to the issues in the proceeding and that the party has in their possession, power, and control and can produce; the party must also identify those documents they once had in their power, possession, and control but no longer have, and those that they object to producing
affidavit of service	a written statement that tells when, where, and how documents have been served on a person, and how that person was found and identified; it is sworn or affirmed to and signed by the person who served the documents
application	one of two procedures by which a civil matter is commenced in Superior Court; the other is an action
assessment of costs	a tally made by an assessment officer of a specific amount of costs payable; a court then determines which party is entitled to costs
bill of costs	a list of allowable fees and disbursements that is used by an assessment officer to assess a litigant's costs after the litigant is successful in obtaining judgment; does not include all fees charged to a client
civil case	a court proceeding that involves legal issues between individuals, organizations, and/or governments; court proceedings other than criminal matters; may or may not refer to cases involving family law disputes
common law	law that is made by judges following precedents set by higher courts; often called "case law"
counterclaim	a claim made by a defendant against a plaintiff or against a plaintiff and other persons
cross-claim	a claim brought by one defendant whom a plaintiff is suing against another defendant whom the plaintiff is suing
default judgment	a judgment entered in favour of a plaintiff when a defendant takes no action and files no defence on being sued
defendant	a person being sued or accused in a court of law
deponent	a person who makes an affidavit
discovery	the process that occurs after the close of pleadings in which the parties obtain more information about each other's cases before trial
dismissal	a judgment that disposes of the matter without a trial
docket	the list or schedule of court cases to be heard on a particular day; a brief record of the proceedings in the court for a particular day
examination-in-chief	questioning of a witness by the lawyer for the party who called the witness
factum	a document that sets out the facts, statutes, and cases relied upon by a party in seeking a favourable decision
general damages	monetary damages for pain and suffering that cannot be determined on the basis of a formula

judgment	a court ruling that resolves the key questions in a lawsuit and determines the rights and obligations of the opposing parties
limitation period	a specified time within which court proceedings must be commenced
litigation guardian	a competent adult who directs and takes responsibility for the litigation of a legally disabled party, such as a minor, an absentee, or a mentally disabled person
minor	a person who does not have the legal rights of an adult; a person who has not yet reached the age of majority (18 in Ontario)
notice of action	a document that informs defendants that they have been sued
notice of motion	a document that states what remedy is sought and the reasons for it
order	a generic term used in the *Rules of Civil Procedure* to describe commands issued by courts on motions and at trials
originating process	the first document in a lawsuit that tells parties that they are being sued
party-and-party costs	the costs that may be awarded by a court to a party in accordance with the tariff or schedule of costs set by the court for that particular proceeding (e.g., costs set by the court for the hearing of a motion); does not include the parties' lawyers' fees
plaintiff	the person who initiates a claim
pleading	written statement of a party's position in a civil case
precedent	an essential doctrine of common law that requires judges to follow the rule in previously decided cases where those cases dealt with facts or issues similar to those in the present case
pre-trial conference	a meeting between the parties and/or their lawyers and a judge to settle procedural questions and define or narrow the issues to be tried; trial issues may be settled at the conference
record	a written account of all the acts and proceedings in a lawsuit
rules of court	the procedures that govern the proceedings in the court and that parties are to follow
sheriff	the official appointed by the provincial government to assist in various court-related functions, such as the enforcement of orders and judgments
solicitor-and-client costs	costs awarded by a court to a party, including the legal fees (or a portion thereof) of the party who has been awarded costs; costs are paid to the party by the other party; also called "lawyer-and-client costs"
solicitor of record	the lawyer recognized by a court as the legal representative of a party in a proceeding
special damages	monetary damages that are specific, ascertainable, and measured on an objective basis; also called "out-of-pocket expenses"
statement of claim	a pleading in a civil law proceeding in which the plaintiff alleges the facts relied upon in support of the relief or remedy claimed; the document that commences an action or "lawsuit"
statement of defence	a pleading in response or defence to a statement of claim in a civil law proceeding in which the defendant alleges the facts relied upon in defence of the claim made in the action or "lawsuit"
summary judgment	a decision by a judge that resolves a lawsuit in favour of one party

summons	an order of the court that commands the person named on the summons to attend trial and give evidence
tariff of fees	a list or schedule of the costs of particular court processes and filings with the court; costs that are awarded to a party are usually based on the tariff established by the court
third-party claim	a claim brought by a defendant against a person who is not already a party to the action
title of proceedings	the formal name of a court case; the "case name" (sometimes called "style of cause"); the heading in a court document that names the parties to the proceeding; in civil proceedings the parties are the plaintiff and the defendant (e.g., "*John Smith v. John Jones*"); in criminal proceedings the parties are the Crown and the defendant (e.g., "*The Queen v. John Smith*")
transcript	the official paper record of a court proceeding that is produced by the transcribing of a recording of the proceedings taken in court (e.g., from an audio cassette or digital disc recording)
trial record	a document that assembles and organizes documents pertaining to a trial; used by the trial judge
unliquidated damages	damages that cannot be fixed by a mathematical or measured calculation but that require information from a source outside the contract
writ of seizure and sale	a court order to the sheriff to seize and sell a defendant's property and hold the proceeds to satisfy the judgment debt owing to the plaintiff; also called "writ of execution"

Common Debtor–Creditor Law Terms

assignment in bankruptcy	a process by which a debtor without sufficient income to pay debts assigns to a trustee in bankruptcy all of the debtor's assets for distribution to creditors, after which the debtor may emerge from bankruptcy with most debts wiped out; also called "voluntary bankruptcy"
bankruptcy court	an informal branch of the Ontario Superior Court of Justice that hears bankruptcy cases in Toronto, Ottawa, and London
examination for discovery	a pre-trial process in which the lawyer for each party questions the opposite party about allegations in the statement of claim or statement of defence
execution	an act of the sheriff in enforcing a writ of seizure and sale (also called "writ of execution"), writ of delivery, or writ of sequestration; term used to describe individual writs of execution on file; when "searching executions" a lawyer searches the sheriff's records for any writs of seizure and sale against the lawyer's client
execution creditor	a creditor who has obtained a judgment against a debtor and is in the process of executing or enforcing the judgment
execution debtor	a debtor who is the subject of enforcement proceedings at the hands of an execution creditor
exigible assets	assets that may be seized by a sheriff when executing a writ of seizure and sale; non-eligible assets are those that are exempt from seizure

guarantor	a person who is obliged to pay a creditor when the principal debtor defaults
issued and entered	a judgment or order is issued when it is signed by a judge or registrar and the court's seal is affixed to it; it is entered when it is recorded by the registrar
judgment creditor	a creditor who has obtained a judgment for debt against a debtor
judgment debtor	a debtor against whom a judgment has been obtained
judgment-proof debtor	a debtor against whom a judgment cannot be enforced because the debtor has no assets or has hidden or encumbered assets that cannot be easily seized
lien	a claim to a right to sell or seize property
Mareva injunction	an injunction that allows a creditor to secure a debtor's assets where the debtor is likely to dispose of or remove all assets from the jurisdiction, before judgment, leaving no assets to satisfy the judgment debt
official receiver	a government official in the Office of the Superintendent of Bankruptcy who receives proposals, examines bankrupts under oath, and chairs meetings of creditors
owner's equity	the amount of a property's value that actually belongs to the property owner
privity of contract	the rule that only parties to a contract can enforce contract rights
receivable	money that is owing to a creditor (also called "account receivable")
relief from forfeiture	a remedy granted to a debtor whose property has been seized by a creditor who has acted in an oppressive or capricious manner
secured credit transaction	a loan or extension of credit in which a debtor gives a creditor the right to seize property of the debtor if the debt is not repaid
specific performance	a remedy in which a court orders a defendant to fulfill the precise terms of a contract, where breach of the contract cannot be properly compensated by monetary damages
Superintendent of Bankruptcy	the federal government official who supervises and oversees the administration of the *Bankruptcy and Insolvency Act*
trustee in bankruptcy	an individual, usually an accountant, who is licensed to act as a trustee under the *Bankruptcy and Insolvency Act*
unsecured credit transaction	a loan or extension of credit in which a debtor does not give a creditor the right to seize property of the debtor if the debt is not repaid

NOTES:

Common Corporate Law Terms

articles of incorporation	a document that creates a corporation
bylaws	a corporation's own rules regarding the management of the corporation
capital	all money and other property of a corporation
common shares	the simplest type of shares; typically include the right to vote at shareholders' meetings and the right to receive the remaining property of the corporation on its dissolution
corporate seal	an impression on paper that bears the corporation's name and the name of the statute under which it was incorporated; the impression, which is produced by a simple hand-operated device, denotes the corporation's assent to the document on which it appears
corporation	an entity, created under the authority of a statute, with the legal rights and responsibilities of a natural person
director	a person elected by a corporation's shareholders (or, in the case of a first director, appointed by the incorporators) to oversee its affairs
minute book	the book in which minutes of shareholders' and directors' meetings and other corporate documents are kept
Newly Upgraded Automated Name Search (NUANS)	a computerized search of Industry Canada's database of corporate and other business names and trademarks
non-offering corporation	a corporation that does not offer its shares to the public; also called "private corporation"
notarial certificate	a document that certifies the authenticity of the document to which it is attached
offering corporation	a corporation that offers its shares for sale to the public; also called "public corporation"
officers	individuals appointed by the directors of a corporation to manage the day-to-day affairs of the corporation
preferred shares	shares that confer a right or rights on their holders superior to a right or rights conferred by common shares (e.g., in the payment of dividends); also called "preference shares" or "special shares"
quorum	the minimum number of members of a group who must be present for its transactions to be valid
resolutions	formal decisions of a corporation's directors or shareholders
share	a unit of ownership in a corporation
share certificates	documents that evidence share ownership
shareholders	the holders of a corporation's shares

Common Criminal Law Terms

accused	a person against whom a criminal or quasi-criminal charge has been laid
acquit	to find an accused not guilty of an offence
adjournment	postponement of a matter to a future date
aggravating factor	a fact or condition regarding either the offence itself or the offender that increases the punishment; used in sentencing for crimes
appeal	a review or challenge of a legal decision in a court of higher jurisdiction
appearance notice	a document given to a person who is to be charged with committing a minor offence that requires that person to be in court on a certain date and time to answer to the charge
argument	verbal or written pleadings presented to the court summarizing an accused's position; submitted to obtain a favourable outcome; also called "submissions"
arraign	to formally read the charges of an information or indictment to a person in open court
assignment court	a hearing in the superior court to set a date for trial
bail	the release of a person accused of a crime before trial, with or without conditions; also called judicial interim release
bench warrant	authorization/order for a person to be arrested, placed in custody, and brought before the court; issued when an accused person fails to appear in court
burden of proof	the requirement that a party prove a particular fact at trial; onus
Canadian Charter of Rights and Freedoms	the constitutional document that sets out the rights and freedoms enjoyed by all people of Canada; commonly referred to as "the Charter"
case brief	a summary of a legal judgment prepared for research purposes
case law	previously decided court cases, specifically represented by the written reasons for judgment
certificate of readiness	a document completed by the defence lawyer and the Crown attorney, presented to the court, to indicate that a matter is ready to proceed to trial
Charter motion	a motion to the court claiming that the rights of the accused under the Charter were breached
conditional sentence	a sentence that allows a convicted person to serve their sentence in the community (usually their home) with a number of conditions, rather than in a correctional facility
conviction	a guilty verdict; a finding by a judge or jury that an accused committed an offence
counsel	a formal term for lawyer
count	a single charge on a charging document

discharge	the release of an accused after a finding of guilt, either with or without conditions
disclosure	the requirement that the prosecution and police provide to the defence any and all evidence relevant to the charges against an accused
disposition	the outcome of a matter on a given day (e.g., adjourned, sentenced)
exhibit	an item or document presented to and accepted by the court as evidence in a case; maintained by the court clerk
hybrid offence	a crime that allows the prosecution to elect to proceed by way of summary conviction or by way of indictment
indictment	a form of charging document used for serious (indictable) offences
information	a form of charging document used in provincial courts; a sworn affidavit that serves as an application for a search warrant
issue resolution meeting	a meeting between the defence lawyer and the Crown attorney to discuss a resolution, issues, witnesses, time for trial, etc.; also called a "Crown pre-trial"
judge's order for production of prisoner	an order signed by a judge directing a correctional facility to bring an accused before the court on a specified date and time; commonly referred to as a "judge's order"
judicial pre-trial	a meeting between the judge, the defence lawyer, and the Crown attorney to settle procedural questions, define or narrow trial issues, and set an amount of time required for trial
mitigating factor	a fact or condition regarding either the offence itself or the offender that decreases the punishment; used in sentencing for crimes
onus	burden of proof; the requirement that a party prove a particular fact at trial
plea	a statement of a legal position (guilty or not guilty); a legal argument or basis for a claim
preliminary discovery hearing	similar to a preliminary hearing, but where the defence lawyer has stipulated that committal for trial is not in argument; the hearing proceeds as a discovery without a presiding judge
preliminary inquiry/ hearing	a judicial hearing where the prosecution must prove that it has enough evidence to prove at trial that an accused is guilty of the charges against them
pre-sentence report	a document prepared by a probation officer at the request of a judge that provides background on an offender for use in deciding on a sentence for the offender
probation	a type of sentence that does not involve imprisonment but allows the accused to remain free, subject to conditions
probation order	the list of conditions that apply to an accused released on bail or a convicted person released on parole
prohibition order	authorization/order forbidding a person to do something (e.g., prohibited from possessing weapons); part of a sentence

prosecution	the Crown attorney or attorneys who are given the task of proving an accused guilty of an offence
quash	to overthrow or void
recognizance	a promise by an accused—e.g., to appear at trial if released on bail, or to abide by certain terms and conditions
remand	an authorization to hold an accused person in custody until a future court date; adjournment
restraining order	an authorization directing a person to remain away from a person and/or place
Rules of Criminal Procedure	rules outlining the protocols and procedures for criminal matters before the court
search warrant	a written authorization to conduct a search
sentence	the punishment imposed on a person convicted of an offence
show cause	another name for a bail hearing, where the prosecution must "show cause" as to why the accused should not be released before trial
status hearing/readiness hearing	a hearing before the judge of a provincial court to determine the readiness of a matter to proceed to trial
stay	a decision by a judge to drop the charges against an accused, usually as a result of improper actions on the part of the police or the prosecution
surety	monetary guarantee that a person will appear in court to answer the charges against them; a person who guarantees to the court that the accused person shall abide by the terms and conditions of release
telewarrant	a search warrant that is issued by telephone or other telecommunication method, such as a fax
video remand	a method whereby an accused person in custody appears before the court by way of video from the correctional facility, rather than in person
victim impact statement	a written statement (sometimes presented to the court in writing or verbally) that relays the effects and impact that the accused and their actions had on the victim; considered during the sentencing phase
voir dire	a hearing within a hearing (e.g., within a trial, a hearing to determine the admissibility of evidence)
waive	to give up a legal right, such as the right to counsel or the right to silence
warrant of committal	the document of authorization outlining the sentence of an accused after conviction; a holding document for correctional facilities
Youth Criminal Justice Act (YCJA)	the act that is applicable to persons between the ages of 12 and 17

Sources of Research

Primary Sources

As part of your duties, you may need to research a specific legal issue and then prepare a case brief or legal memorandum (discussed later in this chapter under "Case Briefs and Legal Memorandums") that shows how the law applies to a particular problem. A legal memorandum can also be called a memo of law. In researching your legal question, you will need to consult both case law and legislation. These documents are known as primary sources.

Primary sources can have legal force and effect, and therefore affect a party's rights and obligations. In your memo, you will use them to support your legal argument. Primary sources are statutes, case law, and regulations. For example, the *Residential Tenancies Act, 2006*, S.O. 2006, c. 17 is a primary authority on residential tenancies in Ontario. Some primary sources are *binding* because they must be strictly applied, and others are simply *persuasive* and may be used to support your argument. To determine whether a primary source is binding or persuasive, you should assess whether or not the rule must be applied. For example, Supreme Court of Canada decisions must be followed in cases that deal with the same legal issues at a lower court. This is known as the principle of *stare decisis*. However, higher levels of court are not bound to follow the decisions of lower levels, though they may be persuaded to take the same approach if that approach seems reasonable. Decisions from other jurisdictions (other provinces or common-law countries) may also be persuasive but not considered binding.

Statutes

Statutes (or acts) are laws that are passed by federal or provincial/territorial lawmakers and then published. Traditionally, Canadian federal statutes are consolidated every 20 years or so in the *Revised Statutes of Canada*. Federal statutes were last consolidated in 1985 (in R.S.C. 1985). Traditionally, Ontario statutes are consolidated every 10 years or so in the *Revised Statutes of Ontario*. Ontario statutes were last consolidated in 1990 (in R.S.O. 1990). (With the advent of electronic publishing, consolidation has become somewhat less important than it used to be, because consolidation and revision can, in effect, occur continuously, without the labour and expense of paper publication.)

In addition, the *Canadian Statute Citator* (federal) and the *Ontario Statute Citator* (provincial) provide monthly annotated updates that detail recent changes in laws that have occurred, such as amendments and repeals. Be sure to consult these summaries as part of your research, but be aware that these citators are not published by the government, so in the event of error or omission, any factual inaccuracies on a point of law will be your responsibility.

Figure 11.1 lists federal and provincial/territorial statute volumes and their abbreviations.

FIGURE 11.1   Statute volumes and abbreviations

Statutes

Abbreviation	Volume
S.C.	Statutes of Canada
S.A.	Statutes of Alberta
S.B.C.	Statutes of British Columbia
S.S.	Statutes of Saskatchewan
S.M.	Statutes of Manitoba
S.O.	Statutes of Ontario
S.Q.	Statutes of Quebec
S.N.B.	Statutes of New Brunswick
S.N.S.	Statutes of Nova Scotia
S.P.E.I.	Statutes of Prince Edward Island
S.N.L.	Statutes of Newfoundland and Labrador
S.Y.	Statutes of Yukon
S.N.W.T.	Statutes of the Northwest Territories
S.Nu.	Statutes of Nunavut

Revised Statutes

Abbreviation	Volume
R.S.C.	Revised Statutes of Canada
R.S.A.	Revised Statutes of Alberta
R.S.B.C.	Revised Statutes of British Columbia
R.S.S.	Revised Statutes of Saskatchewan
R.S.M.	Re-enacted Statutes of Manitoba
R.S.O.	Revised Statutes of Ontario
R.S.Q.	Revised Statutes of Quebec
R.S.N.B.	Revised Statutes of New Brunswick
R.S.N.S.	Revised Statutes of Nova Scotia
R.S.P.E.I.	Revised Statutes of Prince Edward Island
R.S.N.L.	Revised Statutes of Newfoundland and Labrador
R.S.Y.	Revised Statutes of Yukon
R.S.N.W.T.	Revised Statutes of the Northwest Territories
R.S.N.W.T. (Nu.)	Revised Statutes of Nunavut

Case Law

Case law consists of the decisions or judgments of courts and administrative tribunals. These judgments interpret, explain, and apply the law (both statutory and case law) to real-life situations and can be used as precedents in subsequent court cases. These decisions are regularly published in books called law reports. There are generally three kinds of law reports: (1) those that publish cases from one court (such as the *Supreme Court Reports*) or one jurisdiction (such as the *Ontario Reports*); (2) those that publish cases on numerous topics from numerous jurisdictions (such as the *Dominion Law Reports*); and (3) those that publish cases on a single topic of law (such as the *Family Law Reports*). Most law reports annotate cases with several key topic identifiers, and provide helpful indexes by which to search for cases according to topic. Because there are many law reporting services, you'll often find the same case reported in different series. For example, you'll find Supreme Court of Canada decisions in the *Supreme Court Reports*, the *Dominion Law Reports*, the *National Reporter*, and the appropriate topical reporter. Figures 11.2 and 11.3 list commonly encountered jurisdictions and courts and their abbreviations. (Note that the format of these jurisdiction abbreviations differs from Canada Post jurisdiction abbreviations, given in figure 9.7.) Figure 11.4 lists Canada's law reports and their abbreviations.

Canada's legal system is based on the *common-law* approach to precedents that was developed in the United Kingdom. When Canadian lawyers and legal researchers look for precedent-setting cases, they check for Canadian precedents first, but they will then expand their search to other common-law jurisdictions, such as Australia, Ireland, and, of course, the United Kingdom. Figure 11.5 lists the major U.K. law reports and their abbreviations.

FIGURE 11.2 Jurisdictions and abbreviations

Abbreviation	Province/Territory
Alta.	Alberta
B.C.	British Columbia
Man.	Manitoba
N.B.	New Brunswick
N.L.	Newfoundland and Labrador
N.W.T.	Northwest Territories
N.S.	Nova Scotia
Nu.	Nunavut
Ont.	Ontario
P.E.I.	Prince Edward Island
Q.	Quebec
Sask.	Saskatchewan
Y.	Yukon

FIGURE 11.3 Courts and abbreviations

Abbreviation	Court
C.A.	Court of Appeal
Ch. D.	Chancery, Chancery Division
Ct. Sess.	Court of Session (Scotland)
E.A.B.	Environmental Appeal Board
Ex. Ct.	Exchequer Court
F.C.	Federal Court
F.C.A.	Federal Court of Appeal
H.L.	House of Lords
Gen. Div.	General Division
H.C.J.	High Court of Justice (Ontario)
K.B.	Court of King's Bench
O.L.R.B.	Ontario Labour Relations Board
P.C.	Privy Council
Prov. Div.	Provincial Division
Q.B.	Court of Queen's Bench
S.C.	Supreme Court
S.C.C.	Supreme Court of Canada
Sup. Ct.	Superior Court (British Columbia and Quebec)
T.C.C.	Tax Court of Canada
T.D.	Trial Division
Terr. Ct.	Territorial Court (Yukon and Northwest Territories)

FIGURE 11.4   Canadian law reports

Abbreviation	Title	Abbreviation	Title
A.C.W.S.	All Canada Weekly Summaries	E.T.R.	Estates and Trusts Reports
Admin. L.R.	Administrative Law Reports	Ex. C.R.	Canada Law Reports—Exchequer Court
Alta. L.R.	Alberta Law Reports		
A.P.R.	Atlantic Provinces Reports	F.C.	Canada Federal Court Reports
A.R.	Alberta Reports	F.T.R.	Federal Trial Reports
B.C.L.R.	British Columbia Law Reports	I.L.R.	Canadian Insurance Law Reporter
B.L.R.	Business Law Reports	Imm. L.R.	Immigration Law Reporter; Immigration Law Reporter, First Series
B.R.	Rapports judiciares de Québec, Cour du Banc de la Reine		
C.A.	Recueils de jurisprudence du Quebec, Cour d'appel	L.A.C.	Labour Arbitration Cases
		L.C.R.	Land Compensation Reports
C.B.R.	Canadian Bankruptcy Reports	Man. R.	Manitoba Reports
C.C.C.	Canadian Criminal Cases	M.P.L.R.	Municipal and Planning Law Reports
C.C.E.L.	Canadian Cases on Employment Law	M.V.R.	Motor Vehicle Reports
C.C.L.I.	Canadian Cases on the Law of Insurance	N.B.R.	New Brunswick Reports
		Nfld. & P.E.I.R.	Newfoundland and Prince Edward Island Reports
C.C.L.T.	Canadian Cases on the Law of Torts		
C.C.P.B.	Canadian Cases on Pensions and Benefits	N.R.	National Reporter
		N.S.R.	Nova Scotia Reports
C.E.L.R.	Canadian Environmental Law Reports	N.W.T.R.	Northwest Territories Reports
C.H.R.R.	Canadian Human Rights Reporter	O.A.C.	Ontario Appeal Cases
C.I.P.R.	Canadian Intellectual Property Reports	O.L.R.	Ontario Law Reports
C.L.L.C.	Canadian Labour Law Cases	O.L.R.B. Rep.	Ontario Labour Relations Board Reports
C.L.R.	Construction Law Reports		
C.L.R.B.R.	Canadian Labour Relations Board Reports	O.M.B.R.	Ontario Municipal Board Reports
		O.R.	Ontario Reports
C.N.L.R.	Canadian Native Law Reporter	O.W.N.	Ontario Weekly Notes
C.P.C.	Carswell's Practice Cases	P.P.S.A.C.	Personal Property Security Act Cases
C.P.R.	Canadian Patent Reporter	Q.A.C.	Quebec Appeal Cases
C.R., C.R.N.S.	Criminal Reports; Criminal Reports, New Series	R.F.L.	Reports of Family Law
		R.J.Q.	Recueils de Jurisprudence du Québec
C.R.R.	Canadian Rights Reporter	R.P.R.	Real Property Reports
C.S.	Recueils de jurisprudence du Québec, Cour supérieure	Sask. R.	Saskatchewan Reports
		S.C.R.	Supreme Court Reports
C.T.C.	Canada Tax Cases	W.C.B.	Weekly Criminal Bulletin
D.L.R.	Dominion Law Reports	W.W.R.	Western Weekly Reports
D.T.C.	Dominion Tax Cases	Y.R.	Yukon Reports

FIGURE 11.5 U.K. law reports

Abbreviation	Title
A.C.	*Appeal Cases*
All E.R.	*All England Reports*
Ch.	*Chancery*
Cr. App. R.	*Criminal Appeal Reports*
E.R.	*English Reports*
Ex. D.	*Exchequer Division*
Fam.	*Family Division*
H.L.	*English and Irish Appeals* (House of Lords)
K.B.	*King's Bench* (Queen's Bench)
L.R. … A.C.	*Law Reports, Appeal Cases*
L.R. … Ch.	*Law Reports, Chancery*
L.R. … H.L.	*Law Reports, House of Lords*
L.R. … P.C.	*Law Reports, Privy Council*
L.T.	*Law Times Reports*
P.	*Probate*
Q.B.	*Queen's Bench* (King's Bench)
R.R.	*Revised Reports*
T.L.R.	*Times Law Reports*
W.L.R.	*Weekly Law Reports*

Secondary Sources

Secondary sources include academic commentary and critique, such as textbooks, newspaper reports, journal articles, case comments, and encyclopedia summaries of law or publications of opinion. These sources are not legally binding, but they can help to clarify and interpret the law. The information in these sources offers valuable insight into potential legal arguments, questions, and issues. Furthermore, because secondary sources usually provide a synopsis of the law and often list the most relevant primary sources, they are an excellent starting point for your research.

These sources are not necessarily cited in a case brief or memorandum. However, a noted citation allows you or the reader to locate the research used.

Electronic Resources

Electronic resources are fast becoming one of the most widely used tools for legal research. Available sources include the Internet, online databases (such as Quicklaw and Westlaw), and CD-ROMs. These digital libraries offer fast, convenient access with extensive search capabilities available anytime.

Electronic resources are a good source of primary-source materials related to the issue at hand. (Secondary-source materials are also available in electronic format, but their availability varies by legal discipline.)

Research methods using electronic sources are discussed in detail in *The Law Workbook: Developing Skills for Legal Research and Writing*, 2d ed., as well as in *Legal Research: Step by Step*, 3d ed., both published by Emond Montgomery. The discussion that follows is intended to introduce and clarify the use of citations in relation to electronic research.

The Internet

As with any information obtained from the Internet, you should exercise care and judgment in relying on the authority of the sources you consult. That said, many major and reputable institutions are making great efforts to publish and maintain accurate, up-to-date collections that are reliable and easily accessible through their websites.

The first and most obvious Internet sources to consult in your legal research are the websites of the Canadian federal and provincial/territorial governments. Statutes and regulations obtained from government websites are considered official and can be relied on. Figure 11.6 lists the websites where the laws of Canadian federal and provincial/territorial governments can be found.

Specific law societies' websites will also be useful to your research. (The websites of provincial and territorial law societies are listed in figure 1.1 in chapter 1.)

The Canadian Department of Justice website (http://laws.justice.gc.ca) has an extensive collection of federal statutes and regulations that can be accessed in a number of ways, including by key word, by title, by subject, and by point in time. It also contains links to federal and provincial case

FIGURE 11.6   Federal and provincial/territorial statutes and regulations online

Jurisdiction	Website
Canada	http://laws.justice.gc.ca/en/index.html
Alberta	http://www.qp.gov.ab.ca
British Columbia	http://www.qp.gov.bc.ca/statreg/default.htm
Manitoba	http://web2.gov.mb.ca/laws/statutes/index.php
New Brunswick	http://www.gnb.ca/0062/acts/index-e.asp
Newfoundland and Labrador	http://www.assembly.nl.ca
Northwest Territories	http://www.canlii.org/en/nt
Nova Scotia	http://nslegislature.ca/legc/index.htm (statutes)
	http://www.gov.ns.ca/just/regulations/consregs.htm (regulations)
Nunavut	http://www.canlii.org/en/nu
Ontario	http://www.e-laws.gov.on.ca
Prince Edward Island	http://www.gov.pe.ca/law/index.php3
Quebec	http://www.publicationsduquebec.gouv.qc.ca/accueil.en.html
Saskatchewan	http://www.qp.gov.sk.ca
Yukon	http://www.canlii.org/en/yk

law, the *Canada Gazette,* and other Canadian Internet legal sources. Figure 11.7 shows the results of a statute by letter search in the Table of Public Statutes and Responsible Ministers for statutes that begin with "D."

Provincial legislation is accessible through provincial government websites. In Ontario, for example, statutes and regulations are collected on e-Laws (http://www.e-laws.gov.on.ca). This site also has links to the *Ontario Gazette* and federal legislation. A search for statutes and regulations can be done in a number of ways. To find the text of a statute, select "Current Consolidated Law." Enter the name of the statute or regulation you are looking for, or click the letter of the statute you are looking for to browse. Figure 11.8 illustrates a search for the *Law Society Act* after clicking on the letter "L." Note that there are five regulations found under the Act. The statute and the regulations can be opened in html or Word format. You also have the option of looking at the historical information associated with the statute.

The website of the Canadian Legal Information Institute (CanLII) (http://www.canlii.org) (see figure 11.9) provides access to primary-source materials—statutes, regulations, court and tribunal decisions, and materials in other jurisdictions. Some secondary-source material is also available on the website. Searches can be done within CanLII by alphabetical listing, key words, statue name, case name, citation or docket number, and point in time. The World Legal Information Institute (WorldLII) (http://www.worldlii.org) contains links to over one thousand databases of legislation, case law, and materials from over one hundred jurisdictions.

CanLII Search Tips Using Operators

Find	Operator (case sensitive)	Example
This exact *phrase*	" "	"R. v. Draper"
All these words	*AND* or no operator (just a space)	radio *AND* licensing radio licensing
Any of these words	*OR*	town *OR* city
None of these unwanted words	*NOT*	knife *NOT* blade
Words within the same *paragraph*	*/p*	levy */p* poison
Words within the same *sentence*	*/s*	dog */s* biting
Words within a specified number of words of another	*/n*	spousal */5* support
Exclude *plurals* and *derivatives*	*EXACT()*	*EXACT*(education)

FIGURE 11.7 Search results using the Table of Public Statutes and Responsible Ministers function for finding statutes

Department of Justice Canada — Ministère de la Justice Canada

Canada

Department of Justice
www.justice.gc.ca

Français | Home | Contact Us | Help | Search | canada.gc.ca

Home > Table of Public Statutes > Statutes beginning with D

Laws
- Main Page
- Consolidated Acts
- Consolidated Regulations
- Constitutional Documents
- Annual Statutes

Search
- Basic Search
- Advanced Search

Resources
- Table of Public Statutes and Responsible Ministers
- Table of Private Acts
- Consolidated Index of Statutory Instruments
- Related Resources

Help
- Accessibility
- FAQ
- General
- Search Help
- PDF Help
- How to Create Stable Links
- Printing
- Glossary
- Important Note
- Contact Us

Proactive Disclosure

Table of Public Statutes and Responsible Ministers

Updated up to 2011, c. 19 and Canada Gazette, Part II, Vol. 145, No. 15 (2011-07-20)

Access to individual Statutes beginning with:

A B C D E F G H I J K L M N O P Q R S T U V W X Y Z (HTML Format)

PDF Version of this page [177 KB]

Highlight on page

Daylight Saving Act — 1918, c. 2

(Utilisation de la lumière du jour, Loi concernant l')

ACT REPEALED 1988, c. 2, s. 68 (Sch. IV, item 60)
CIF, 1988, c. 2, s. 68 in force 04.02.88

Debt Servicing and Reduction Account Act — 1992, c. 18

(Compte de service et de réduction de la dette, Loi sur le)

Minister of Finance

ACT REPEALED 2003, c. 15, s. 43
s. 5, 1997, c. 10, s. 270
CIF, 1992, c. 18 in force on assent 18.06.92
CIF, 1997, c. 10, s. 270 in force on assent 20.03.97
CIF, 2003, c. 15, s. 43 in force on assent 19.06.2003

Defence Appropriation Act, 1950 — 1950-51, c. 5

(Crédits de défense, 1950)

Defence Production Act — R.S., 1985, c. D-1

(Production de défense, Loi sur la)

NOTES:

FIGURE 11.8 Listing results with regulations for the Law Society Act

Browse Current Consolidated Law 🛈		? Help

Letter A | B | C | D | E | F | G | H | I | J | K | L | M | N | O | P | Q | R | S | T | U | V | W | X | Y | Z

Select a **letter** to get all Current Consolidated Statutes beginning with that letter and their associated Regulations.

Note: If you are looking for a Statute that has been enacted or a Regulation that has been filed in the past week, check **Source Law**.

Click on the plus sign (⊕) beside the Statute Title to get all the Regulations under that Statute.

Found 28 items   ⊙ Page 1 ⬍ of 1 ⊕   Items 1 - 28 of 28

Current Consolidated Law (HTML)		Download	Legislative History
⊕ Laboratory and Specimen Collection Centre Licensing Act, R.S.O. 1990, c. L.1		📄	H
⊕ Labour Relations Act, 1995, S.O. 1995, c. 1, Sched. A		📄	H
⊕ Lake Simcoe Protection Act, 2008, S.O. 2008, c. 23		📄	H
⊕ Lakes and Rivers Improvement Act, R.S.O. 1990, c. L.3		📄	H
⊕ Land Registration Reform Act, R.S.O. 1990, c. L.4		📄	H
⊕ Land Titles Act, R.S.O. 1990, c. L.5		📄	H
⊕ Land Transfer Tax Act, R.S.O. 1990, c. L.6		📄	H
⊖ Law Society Act, R.S.O. 1990, c. L.8		📄	H
O. Reg. 771/92	CLASS PROCEEDINGS	📄	H
O. Reg. 31/99	COMPLAINTS RESOLUTION COMMISSIONER	📄	H
R.R.O. 1990, Reg. 708	COUNTY AND DISTRICT LAW ASSOCIATIONS	📄	H
O. Reg. 167/07	HEARINGS BEFORE THE HEARING AND APPEAL PANELS	📄	H
R.R.O. 1990, Reg. 709	LAW FOUNDATION	📄	H

▸ Glossary
▸ FAQs
▸ Order
▸ Contact Us
Frequently Accessed Law ❯
Other Resources ⌄
▸ Current Bills
▸ Ontario Gazette
▸ Canada (federal) Legislation
▸ More Links
Survey ⌄
▸ Would You Like to Rate Our Service?

FIGURE 11.9 CanLII's "Statutes and Regulations of Ontario" page

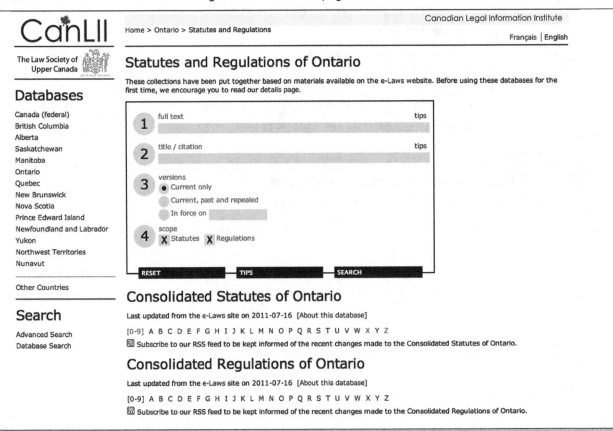

Figure 11.10 illustrates the results of a search for a case using the case name *Cain v. Peterson*, 2005. Figure 11.11 shows the history of the cases that were cited within the *Cain v. Peterson* case.

Canadian databases such as Quicklaw and Westlaw are subscription services that maintain a large electronic collection of statutes, regulations, cases, periodicals, and other materials. One of the advantages of using such services is the ability to search by keyword. This is especially useful when you do not know the title of a statute or a case but only, for example, the name of a party or a general issue or topic. Figure 11.12 shows an example of the same case as above on LexisNexis/Quicklaw.

General search engines, such as Google and Yahoo, may also be used. The Advanced Search tool on Google allows you to search in more precise ways—for example, to search only within a specific domain, such as ".gc.ca" or ".edu," or to exclude certain terms from search results.

Finally, university law library websites, such as those of the University of Toronto (http://www.law-lib.utoronto.ca) and Queen's University (http://library.queensu.ca/law/), can be helpful for their diverse array of information, both primary and secondary, which is often international in scope. Many university law library websites also provide useful guides to performing legal research and citing legal resources.

FIGURE 11.10   CanLII Cain v. Peterson, 2005

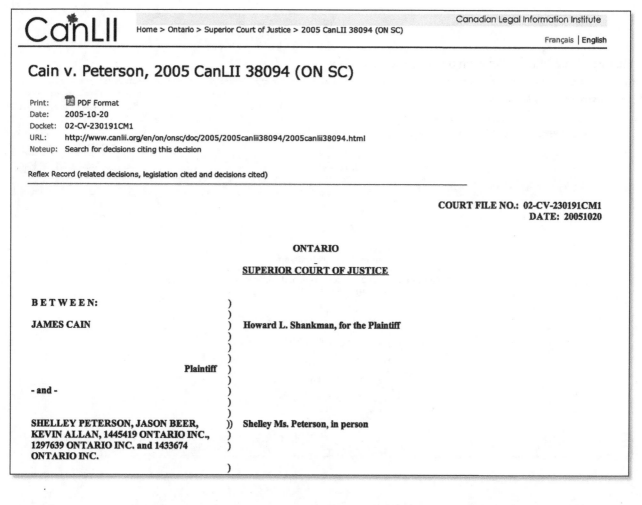

FIGURE 11.11 History of the cases that were cited within the Cain v. Peterson case

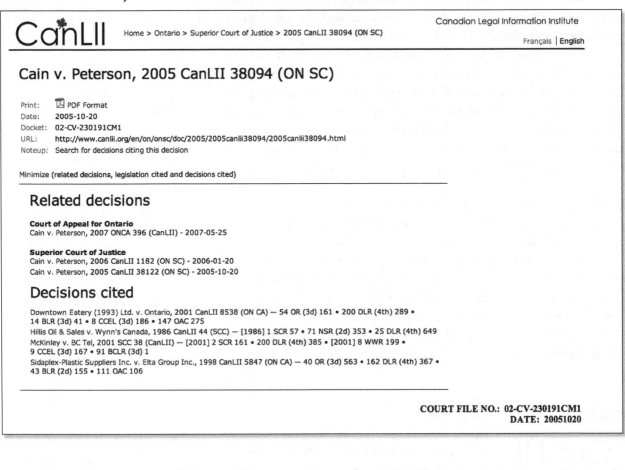

FIGURE 11.12 Cain v. Peterson on LexisNexis/Quicklaw

Legal Citations

When you've finished your research, you must properly cite all statutes, case law, and other sources in a case brief or legal citation. It is especially helpful and convenient for your readers if, before starting your discussion, you list all the primary and secondary sources you will cite. Citations allow your readers to identify the documents that you refer to, supply them with extra information about the statute or case, and make your argument easier to follow.

For a complete discussion of proper Canadian citation style, including a list of the abbreviations of periodicals, refer to the *Canadian Guide to Uniform Legal Citation*, 6th ed. (Toronto: Carswell, 2006), known informally as the *McGill Guide*.

> The 7th edition of the *McGill Guide* removes periods from citations. The removal of periods has not been widely accepted as of the date of publication of this book. Ensure that you follow your employer's preferred method of citation.

Primary-Source Citations

Statutes

A complete statute citation includes the full title of the statute, the abbreviation of the statute reporter, the year of publication or consolidation, the chapter number or alphanumeric identifier, and the section number (if you have referred to a particular provision of the statute).

Anatomy of a Statute Citation

	Element	Details
1	Title	The short title of the statute, found at the beginning of the statute (e.g., *Income Tax Act*), underlined or italicized, followed by a comma.
2	Name of the statute volume and the year of publication or consolidation	Refer to figure 11.1 for the abbreviations of federal and provincial/territorial statutes. No comma separates the statute volume and the year of publication or consolidation. A comma follows the year.
3	Chapter number or alphanumeric identifier	Cite the specific chapter number assigned to the statute as found in the volume. Abbreviate "chapter" as "c." and add a space. Follow the style of the statute reporter's number or alphanumeric identifier (e.g., federal revised statutes are identified by a capital letter, a hyphen, and a number; Ontario revised statutes in R.S.O. 1990 are identified by a capital letter, a period, and a number).
4	Section number	If you have referred to a specific provision of the statute, include the section number. Abbreviate "section" as "s." ("sections" as "ss.") and add a space. Follow the style of the statute reporter's section number, but remove spaces that separate different elements of the number (e.g., "s. 7(1)(a)," not "s. 7 (1) (a)").

Examples

1	2	3	4
Holidays Act,	R.S.C. 1985,	c. H-5,	s. 4

1	2	3	4
Legal Aid Services Act, 1998,	S.O. 1998,	c. 26,	s. 67(2)

Cases (Citations)

A complete case citation includes the style of cause, the date, the volume number (if any), the abbreviation of the law reporter, the law reporter series (if any), the page number, and the abbreviation of the court or the court jurisdiction.

Anatomy of a Case Citation

	Element	Details
1	Style of cause	Identifies the parties to the case. The last names of parties are typically used, with the plaintiff's name listed first.
		Party names are separated by "v." (an abbreviation for "versus").
		Underline or italicize the names of the parties as well as the "v."
		Where there is more than one plaintiff or defendant, often only one name is listed, followed by "et al." (*et alii*, "and others").
		Law reporters usually indicate, near the beginning of a case, how the case is indexed. If a case includes an "Indexed as" notation, use that style of cause.
2	Date of the decision or publication	Some law reports identify cases by the year of decision; others identify cases by the year of publication of the law report. Follow the style used by the law report.
		Enclose the year the case was decided in parenthesis (round brackets). When using parentheses, add a comma after the closing parenthesis.
		Enclose the year of the case report in square brackets. When using square brackets, add a comma after the style of cause.
3	Volume number of the law report (if any)	Found on the spine of the law report and on most pages.
		Not all law reports have a volume number.
4	Abbreviation of the law report	Refer to figures 11.4 and 11.5 for the abbreviations of Canadian and major U.K. law reports.
5	Series number of the law report (if any)	If there is more than one series, cite the series number.
		The series number is abbreviated and placed in parentheses following the report title.
		Note: Legal ordinal abbreviations differ slightly from the typical abbreviations. "Second" is abbreviated "2d" and "third" is abbreviated "3d."

	Element	Details
6	Page number	Cite the first page of the text of the case.
7	Court	Refer to figures 11.2 and 11.3 for the abbreviations of Canadian jurisdictions and courts.
		Enclose the abbreviations in parentheses.
		If the title of the law report implies the court, do not include the abbreviation of the court (e.g., "S.C.R." implies the Supreme Court of Canada, so do not include "(S.C.C.)").
		If the title of the law report implies the jurisdiction of the court, do not include the abbreviation of jurisdiction with the court's abbreviation (e.g., "O.R." implies Ontario, so cite the Ontario Court of Appeal as "C.A.," not as "Ont. C.A.").

Examples

1	2	3	4	5	6	7
Barret v. Glynn	(2002),	209	D.L.R.	(4th)	735	(Nfld. C.A.)

1	2	3	4	5	6	7
Regina v. Terry	(1994),	91	C.C.C.	(3d)	209	(B.C.C.A.)

Secondary-Source Citations

Books (Texts)

A complete book citation includes the author's name, the title, the edition number (if any), the place of publication, the publisher, the year of publication, and the page number (if any).

Anatomy of a Book Citation

	Element	Details
1	Author's name	The author's first name and/or initials and then the last name, followed by a comma.
		If there are more than three authors, cite only the first author (without a comma) and indicate the other authors by "et al." (followed by a comma).
2	Book title	The title of the book is italicized or underlined (followed by a comma if there is an edition number).
		Capitalize nouns, pronouns, verbs, adverbs, and adjectives. Capitalize the first and last words. Capitalize the first word following a colon or dash (em dash). Do not capitalize articles ("a," "an," "the"), prepositions (e.g., "in," "of," "on"), or coordinating conjunctions (e.g., "and," "but," "or").

	Element	Details
3	Edition number (if any)	If there has been more than one edition, include the edition number.
		Use legal ordinal abbreviation style ("2d," "3d").
		Abbreviate "edition" as "ed."
4	Place of publication	The city of publication, followed by a colon.
		If the city is not well known, include the abbreviation of the province or state. (See figure 9.7 for abbreviations of provinces/territories.)
5	Publisher	The name of the publishing company, followed by a comma.
		Use short forms of publisher names (e.g., "Emond Montgomery," not "Emond Montgomery Publications Limited").
6	Year of publication	Enclose the place of publication, the publisher, and the year of publication in parentheses.
7	Page number	The first page where the information is found.
		Precede the page number with "at."
		Add a period at the end of the citation (after the page number or after the closing parenthesis).

Examples

1	2	3	4	5	6	7
Lynn Fournier-Ruggles	<u>Canadian Immigration and Refugee Law for Legal Professionals</u>		(Toronto:	Emond Montgomery,	2009)	at 189.

1	2	3	4	5	6	7
Margaret Kerr et al.,	*Legal Research: Step by Step,*	3d ed.	(Toronto:	Emond Montgomery,	2009)	at 20.

NOTES:

Periodicals (Journals)

A complete periodical or journal citation includes the author's name, the article title, the year of publication, the volume number, the name of the periodical, and the page number.

Anatomy of a Periodical (Journal) Citation

	Element	Details
1	Author's name	The author's first name and/or initials and then the last name, followed by a comma.
		If there are more than three authors, cite only the first author (without a comma) and indicate the other authors by "et al." (followed by a comma).
2	Article title	The title of the article, enclosed in quotation marks.
		Capitalize nouns, pronouns, verbs, adverbs, and adjectives. Capitalize the first and last words. Capitalize the first word following a colon or dash (em dash). Do not capitalize articles ("a," "an," "the"), prepositions (e.g., "in," "of," "on"), or coordinating conjunctions (e.g., "and," "but," "or").
3	Year of publication	Enclose the year of publication in parentheses.
4	Volume number	Found on the cover of the periodical and on most pages.
5	Name of the periodical (journal)	Abbreviate the name according to a standard list of abbreviations, such as the one at http://www.westlawecarswell.com/icll/periodicals.asp. If you cannot find an abbreviation, write the name out in full.
6	Page number	The first page of the article.
		Add a period at the end of the citation.

Example

1	2	3	4	5	6
Derek Lindy,	"Mini Firm, Mega Practice"	(2005)	29	Can. Law.	26.

NOTES:

Encyclopedias

A complete encyclopedia citation includes the title, the edition, the volume, the place of publication, the publisher, the year of publication, and the page number and/or paragraph number.

Anatomy of an Encyclopedia Citation

	Element	Details
1	Title	The title of the encyclopedia, italicized or underlined, followed by a comma.
2	Edition number	If there has been more than one edition, include the edition number. Use legal ordinal abbreviation style ("2d," "3d"). Abbreviate "edition" as "ed." followed by a comma.
3	Volume number	Abbreviate "volume" as "vol."
4	Place of publication	The city of publication, followed by a colon. If the city is not well known, include the abbreviation of the province or state. (See figure 9.7 for abbreviations of provinces/territories.)
5	Publisher	The name of the publishing company, followed by a comma. Use short forms of publisher names (e.g., "Emond Montgomery," not "Emond Montgomery Publications Limited").
6	Year of publication	Enclose the place of publication, the publisher, and the year of publication in parentheses.
7	Page number (if any)	The first page where the information is found. Precede the page number with "at." Omit the page number if the reference is general.
8	Paragraph number (if any)	If the encyclopedia uses paragraph numbers, include the paragraph where the information is found. Add a period at the end of the citation.

Example

1	2	3	4	5	6	7	8
O'Brien's Encyclopedia of Forms,	11th ed.,	vol. 4	(Aurora, ON:	Canada Law Book,	1996)	at 40-1.	

Electronic Resource Citations

Internet Resource Citations

When you research and consult legal documents online, you are, in essence, viewing an electronic copy of a printed document. When you cite a law, therefore, you should still refer to the original source when possible. If a document is only available electronically, it will likely have a file number. You may include a web address (URL) for convenience, but URLs may change, rendering your citation useless. Remember: your research should be focused on the law, not on a website. To include an electronic source in your citation, add a comma to the end of the official citation (as described earlier in this chapter) and then the word "online," a colon, and the web address within angle brackets ("<" less than and greater than ">" signs), followed by a period. For example:

1	2	3	4	5
Holidays Act,	R.S.C. 1985,	c. H-5,	s. 4,	online: .

1	2	3	4	5
Family Law Act,	R.S.O. 1990,	c. F.3,		online: .

It sometimes happens that cases are available online while they are still unavailable in print. Figure 11.11 shows an example of a case found on CanLII (http://www.canlii.org). The case is a decision rendered by the Ontario Superior Court of Justice that has not been published by a law reporter. To cite this case, you have to refer directly to CanLII. As you can see, even CanLII has named and organized the file numerically, so you do not have to rely solely on a web address. The citation in this case is exactly as shown at the top left of the web page:

Style of cause	Year of decision	Electronic source	Numerical identifier	Court name
Cain v. Peterson,	2005	CanLII	38094	(ON S.C.)

The page also shows an alternative method of citing this case: by date of decision, court-assigned number, court name, and electronic source. When all the elements are combined, the citation reads as follows:

Style of cause	Date of decision	Case identifier	Court name	Electronic source
Cain v. Peterson	(2005-10-20),	02-CV-230191CM1	(ON S.C.)	(CanLII)

CD-ROM and Online Database Citations

As when citing from an Internet resource, citing from an electronic database—whether accessed online or on CD-ROM—usually remains a simple matter of citing the case law or legislation from its source. There is no need to include the database reference, unless the case is unavailable in print. If the print version is unavailable, include the database abbreviation in parentheses at the end of the citation. For example:

Style of cause	Year of decision	Numerical identifier	Court name	Electronic source
Cain v. Peterson,	[2005]	O.J. No. 4459	(ON S.C.)	(QL)

Case Briefs and Legal Memorandums

Case briefs and legal memorandums (memos) differ from the types of memorandum discussed in chapter 8, Legal Correspondence—namely, internal memos used to create a paper trail noting instructions (perhaps from a lawyer or office associate) and events (such as telephone conversations with a client). A case brief provides a summary of a court decision, while a legal memo provides a summary of legal research that has been completed on a legal issue (or issues) of importance to a client.

This section outlines the basics of a case brief and legal memo and includes a sample of each. If your research and writing skills need honing, detailed reference guides such as *The Law Workbook: Developing Skills for Legal Research and Writing*, 2d ed. (2011) and *Legal Research: Step by Step*, 3d ed. (2009), both published by Emond Montgomery, are invaluable resources.

In preparing and writing a case brief and a legal memo, your goal is to distill your research findings into the most succinct summary possible. The style and format of each of these documents is as varied as the preference of the person asking you to do the research, and the type of law being researched. Paragraphs are usually short and numbered for easy reference, grouped together by topic, and identified by subheadings.

Many of the same elements are found in both a case brief and a legal memorandum. Figure 11.13 presents an overview of elements that can be found in both case briefs and legal memos. Figure 11.14 presents a sample case brief and figure 11.15 presents a sample legal memorandum. Note the elements that are similar. If your employer has devised their own standard, you should follow it.

PRACTICE TIP

Briefs and memos should be succinct and easy to read. Don't retell what has already been said. Instead, set out, in your own words, the events and people that are central to the issues being researched.

FIGURE 11.13 Overview of the elements found in case briefs and legal memorandums

	Element	Details
1	Introduction	Identify the following: To: From: Date: Re: You may also reference a client file number so that the time you spend on the memo can be docketed appropriately.
2	Citation (case brief), date heard, and date judgment rendered	As discussed on pages 384-85.
3	Procedural history of the case	Outline of a case's history.
4	Judge's name	The judge who wrote the decision. If it is a Supreme Court decision, include the names of concurring judges.
5	Representatives	Name of counsel and who they appeared for.
6	Who (appeal cases only)	Set out who is appealing—Crown or defence. What number of appeal is this? Is this an appeal of a previously appealed decision or is it a straight appeal?
7	Facts	Set out the relevant facts in the case or legal matter in chronological order. Provide only those facts the court found important. Be brief. Write in your own words.
8	Position/reasoning	The position of the court in its determination. If it's an appeal case, include the position of each level.
9	Holding/ruling/ disposition	The court's decision.
10	Issues (case brief)	The legal question the court must resolve. Write as a question. There may be one question or several. That is, "Do animal owners have a common law or statutory law duty to leash their animals? Did the defendant breach his responsibility?"
11	Issues (legal memo)	Identify the legal issues within the context of the legal matter that you are dealing with. Your writing can be narrow and descriptive. That is: a. Discuss any possible criminal charges that might be laid. b. Discuss any possible defences to the charges. c. Discuss any legal justification of suing in these cases. If so, what would the cause of action be? d. Can damages be collected from parents in either of these cases?

	Element	Details
11	Issues (legal memo) *(continued)*	Or your writing can cover a broader area: With regard to assisted suicide, and in light of the cases of Sue Rodriguez (*Rodriguez v. Attorney General of Canada*, [1993] 3 S.C.R. 519) and Nancy B. (*N.B. v. Hôtel-Dieu de Quebec* (1992), 86 D.L.R. (4th) 385 (Que. Sup. Ct.)), what are the circumstances in which a physician's criminal liability may be found?
12	Discussion/answer/ conclusion (legal memo)	Provide an objective discussion/answer to the issue set out above. Include the statutory, regulatory, and case law as it applies to the fact situation. Your discussion should set out the relative law being relied on.
13	Law (legal memo)	Set out the relevant statutory, regulatory, and case law with a full citation of each. (Proper citation style was described earlier in the chapter.)
14	Attachment (legal memo)	Attach the statutory, regulatory, and case law that you have cited in your memo.

FIGURE 11.14   Case brief example

1	**To: Lawyer/Paralegal** **From: Law Clerk/Legal Assistant/Researcher** **Date: March 14, 20--** **Re: Matter Name/Number**
2	*R. v. Harris*, 225 C.C.C. (3d) 193 Heard: May 22, 2007 Judgment rendered: August 24, 2007
3	**Trial level:** Ontario Court of Justice; accused acquitted of possession of cocaine for the purpose of trafficking **Appeal level:** Court of Appeal for Ontario; Crown Appeal Allowed, new trial ordered
4	*Ontario Court of Justice*: Caldwell J. *Court of Appeal for Ontario*: Doherty J.A. was the judge writing the majority decision McMurtry C.J.O., O'Connor A.C.J.O. concurring
5	Rick Visca and Amber Pashuk, for the Crown, appellant Jonathon Dawe, for accused, respondent
6	The appellant is the Crown, represented by Rick Visca and Amber Pashuk. This is an appeal to the Court of Appeal for Ontario; it is a straight appeal.
7	The case began in the Ontario Court of Justice where the accused was acquitted of possession of cocaine for the purpose of trafficking. The Crown appealed to the Ontario Court of Appeal where the judges decided to allow the appeal and ordered a new trial. The accused was a passenger in a vehicle that had been stopped for a minor traffic

violation. The officer, Lipkus, noticed the accused was not wearing a seatbelt. Lipkus then saw the accused lean forward with his hand down the small of his back. Lipkus ordered all people in the car to keep their hands in view. He then requested and received identification from all passengers in the vehicle. While checking the IDs, Lipkus discovered the accused was in breach of a bail condition. Lipkus then arrested the accused and, while searching him, found a quantity of cocaine hidden within the accused's waistband. The accused was charged with possession of cocaine for the purpose of trafficking and was advised of his right to counsel.

The trial judge excluded the cocaine from evidence, stating that the accused's rights were violated under ss. 8, 9, and 10(b) of the *Canadian Charter of Rights and Freedoms*. She found that the accused was arbitrarily detained, subjected to an unconstitutional search when he was asked to identify himself while detained in the vehicle, and denied his right to counsel while under arbitrary detention. The trial judge concluded that the cocaine seized from the accused was obtained as the result of these constitutional violations and should be excluded as evidence at trial. Without the cocaine, the Crown had no case and the accused was acquitted.

s. 8 Search or seizure
The lawful detention in itself did not warrant the officer requesting identification from the accused. At the time of the request, the officer had no reason to suspect the accused of anything; therefore, the seizure was unreasonable and violates the accused's rights under s. 8. However, the accused would have assumed providing identification would have afforded the officer information on the CPIC. Furthermore, had the officer requested identification in order to issue a ticket for the seatbelt violation, the accused's record would have come to light.

s. 9 Arbitrary detention or imprisonment
The appellant judges found the trial judge erred in her interpretation of the *Charter of Rights and Freedoms*. Regarding the detention of the accused, the appellant judges determined that while the accused was a passenger in the vehicle, it was not unreasonable to assume he would understand he was also detained along with the driver.

s. 10(b) Right to retain counsel
Because the accused was lawfully detained as part of a *Highway Traffic Act* stop, the appellant judges determined this detention did not trigger the rights set out in s. 10(b). Thus, the accused's rights were not violated.

24(2) Exclusion of evidence
After finding no violations to the accused's rights under the *Charter of Rights and Freedoms*, the appellant judges determined that the cocaine was seized under lawful conditions, and disallowed the exclusion of evidence.

8	The trial judge felt that the accused should be acquitted of possession of cocaine for the purpose of trafficking because she felt it was obtained illegally after violating the accused's Charter rights. The majority of the appellant judges felt that no violations had occurred regarding his Charter rights and that the discovery of cocaine was valid. They allowed the appeal and ordered a new trial.
9	The trial judge acquitted the accused of possession of cocaine for the purpose of trafficking. The Ontario Court of Appeal allowed the appeal and ordered a new trial.

FIGURE 11.15 Legal memorandum example

Legal Memorandum

To: Diana Collis
From: Kelly MacDonald
Date: August 10, 20--
Re: Duty of Care/Social Liability

Facts

Our clients allowed their 18-year-old son to host a birthday party for his girlfriend (who was turning 19) at their home. Unfortunately, two of the guests at the party (both 18 years old) were in a single-vehicle accident shortly after leaving the party. The female driver of the vehicle suffered a broken pelvis and serious scarring to her face, while her male passenger was rendered quadriplegic as a result of the accident.

Apparently, the car failed to negotiate a sharp turn that was a short distance from our clients' home and slammed into an oak tree after leaving the road. There was evidence that both occupants of the vehicle had consumed alcohol at the party.

Our clients are being sued by both injured teens.

Issues

a. Whether there are any possible criminal charges that may be laid.

b. What would possible defences to the charges be?

c. Is there any legal justification for suing? If so, what would the cause of action be?

d. Can damages be collected from the parents?

Conclusion

The relevant research has shown that our clients would not be charged with a criminal offence because there is no evidence to support. The only possible contention would be that a provincial offence charge could be pending under the *Liquor Licence Act* for serving a minor, if the evidence to support has been established. Whether our clients, as "social hosts," could be held liable for any civil negligence with respect to "a duty of care" is a determination for a court of law. Case precedence, as shown in this research, serves only as a guideline for determining negligence. The facts as they stand in our case cannot be absolute in determining whether it is likely or unlikely it will go to trial and to determine such action is premature.

Discussion

In researching for this case it was determined that there were no criminal charges that could be brought or enforced against our clients. However, under the *Liquor Licence Act*, s. 30, which states that no person shall knowingly sell or supply liquor to a person under 19 years of age, a summary charge could be laid. This Act also sets out the penalty to this offence, which entails a fine of not more than $200,000.00 or imprisonment for a term of not more than one year or both.

In response to the summary charge our clients could defend by denying any knowledge of the presence of alcohol. Although it was with consent that our clients allowed a party to be hosted by their 18-year-old son, they did not consent to the presence of alcohol and

(Continued on the next page.)

therefore there was not a foreseeable risk to guests at the party. Case law that applies is as follows:

In the case of *Kim v. Thammavong*, a Halloween party was thrown by Tracey Cheung while her parents Thomas and Rosaline Cheung were on vacation and an altercation between two guests, Daniel Kim and Phoungern Thammavong, occurred resulting in injuries to Mr. Kim. Mr. Kim as a result sued Mr. Thammavong for damages and Mr. and Mrs. Cheung for negligence and for occupier's liability. It was the court's decision, of Justice P. Perell, that they were not liable for negligence under the *Occupier's Liability Act* and the case was dismissed.

With respect to the legal justification of suing as it applies to this case, the defendants could raise a breach of "duty of care." The cause of action would be the negligence on the part of our clients. The law governing tort liability is clear that in order to establish a "duty of care" there is a two-part generalized test for determination that is applied due to the complexities of tort law (Margaret Kerr, JoAnn Kurtz, and Laurence M. Olivo, *Canadian Tort Law in a Nutshell*).

The primary case law governing the two-step process is in *Anns v. Merton London Borough Council*, where Lord Wilberforce proposed a two-part test for determining whether a duty of care arises. The first step focuses on the relationship between the plaintiff and the defendant, and asks whether it is close or "proximate" enough to give rise to a duty of care (at 742). The second step asks whether there are countervailing policy considerations that negate the duty of care. This test has become known as the "*Anns*" test and has been adopted by many negligence-based cases as precedent.

In the case of *Childs v. Desormeaux*, the Supreme Court applied these tests. Desmond Desormeaux was the driver of a motor vehicle that collided with another vehicle in which Zoe Childs was an occupant. As a result of the accident, Zoe Childs was rendered paraplegic. Childs sued Desmond Desormeaux, Julie Zimmerman and Dwight Courrier for negligence in the breach of a duty of care, claiming they fell below the standard of care. The proximate or close relationship had been found to be established between the defendants Julie Zimmerman, Dwight Courrier, and Desmond Desormeaux. However, the second test that they refer to as a duty negated by other policy considerations was not found to be established. For this, the courts focused on a comparison between commercial hosts and social hosts, but quickly concluded that the commercial host has too many benefits over a social host whereby granting a larger control over a situation where alcohol is being served. This of course takes into account the reasonable forseeability of risks of injuries to others. There was simply no evidence to support whether Julie Zimmerman or Dwight Courrier knew or ought to have known that Desmond Desormeaux was too intoxicated to drive, nor was there a reliance to monitor their guests. Therefore it is the Supreme Court of Canada's finding that a social host, where alcohol is served, is not deemed to owe a duty of care to "public users of highways." It further states that the consumption of alcohol is a personal choice and with this choice comes the assumed risk of impaired judgment. It is not up to the host to be liable for the personal choices of other adults.

Although this was a Supreme Court ruling for a third party claim in negligence that has been dismissed, what about the determinations of "a duty of care" for direct claimants who are hurt, as in our case? In the case of *Hamilton v. Kember*, Chelsie Free was a 17-year-old who held a party with the consent of her parents under certain conditions such as no serving of alcohol. The plaintiff Kyle Hamilton, an attendee of the party who was asked to leave, was standing on the sidewalk when he was injured in a motor vehicle accident. Jamie Kember swerved to avoid hitting several bystanders from Chelsie

(Continued on the next page.)

Free's party but ended up colliding with Kyle Hamilton. Hamilton has sued both parties but the primary focus has been on whether there was a duty of care owed by Chelsie Free and her parents as he was directly connected to the party. The defendants Robert and Joanne Free moved for summary judgment dismissing the action against them on the ground that there were no issues for trial. They relied heavily on the *Anns* test and the case of *Childs v. Desormeaux*. It is the court's finding of Justice J.F. Garry that it is not enough that alcohol was not served by Chelsie Free to "negate potential liability by the parents" to say no duty of care existed. Justice J.F. Garry found genuine issues for a trial judge to decide and the motion was dismissed.

Based on the issues raised in both these cases, each case is unique when determining "a duty of care." The facts of our case as they stand cannot be absolute when asking if they would or would not be held liable for negligence; therefore, damages may or may not be found.

Law

Anns v. Merton London Borough Council, [1978] A.C. 728 (H.L.)
Online: http://bailii.org/uk/cases/UKHL/4.html

Childs v. Desormeaux, 2006 SCC 18, [2006] 1 S.C.R. 643
Online: http://www.canlii.org/en/ca/scc/doc/2006/2006scc18/2006scc18.html

Hamilton v. Kember, 2008 CanLII 6988 (ON S.C.)
Online: http://www.canlii.org/en/on/onsc/doc/2008/2008canlii6988/2008canlii6988.html

Kerr et al., Margaret, *Canadian Tort Law in a Nutshell*, 2d ed. (Toronto: Thomson Carswell, 2005) at 38, 39

Kim v. Thammavong, 2007 CanLII 52791 (ON S.C.)
Online: http://www.canlii.org/en/on/onsc/doc/2007/2007canlii52791/2007canlii52791.html

Liquor Licence Act, R.S.O. 1990, c. L.19, s. 30 and s. 61(3.0.1)
Online: http://www.canlii.org/en/on/laws/stat/rso-1990-c-l19/latest

Occupiers' Liability Act, R.S.O. 1990, c. O.2, s. 5
Online: http://www.canlii.org/en/on/laws/stat/rso-1990-c-o2/latest

Quoting Sources

To add support to your memo, you should always aim to quote specific applicable passages from primary sources. Quote only from secondary sources when doing so helps further the reader's understanding of law.

In your memo discussion, short quotations may be embedded within paragraphs, contained in quotation marks. However, lengthier quotations—those exceeding three printed lines—should be set off in their own paragraphs, indented from the left and right margins and/or in a smaller type size. Do not enclose offset quotations in quotation marks.

Subsequent References

If you outline in detail all your sources at the outset of your memo, you can refer to your sources in the body of your discussion in abbreviated fashion. You can refer to statutes by their short title or abbreviation (for example, "the *Income Tax Act*" or "ITA"); cases by the first name in the style of cause (for example, "*Barret*" instead of "*Barret v. Glynn*"); and secondary sources by the author's last name (for example, "Kerr et al.") or, as with encyclopedias, by the name of the book (for example, "*O'Brien's*").

NOTES:

REVIEW QUESTIONS

1. What is a legal memorandum?

   _____

   _____

   _____

   _____

   _____

   _____

   _____

2. What is the difference between primary and secondary sources of research?

   _____

   _____

   _____

   _____

   _____

   _____

   _____

   _____

   _____

   _____

3. Explain the difference between primary sources that are binding and those that are persuasive.

   _____

   _____

   _____

   _____

   _____

   _____

   _____

   _____

   _____

4. Law reporters are primary sources for research. True or false? Explain your answer.

_____

_____

_____

_____

_____

_____

5. Why are secondary sources useful? Explain.

_____

_____

_____

_____

_____

_____

_____

_____

6. Ontario statutes were last consolidated and published in

   a. 1985

   b. 1990

   c. 1995

   d. 2000

   e. 2005

7. List three elements that can be found in both a case brief and a legal memo.

_____

_____

_____

_____

_____

_____

_____

8. How are cases published?

_____

_____

_____

_____

_____

_____

_____

_____

_____

9. Provide the names of three reporting series found in your library.

_____

_____

_____

_____

_____

_____

_____

_____

_____

10. What is the purpose of citation?

_____

_____

_____

_____

_____

_____

_____

_____

_____

_____

11. Which of the following citations is incorrect? (You do not need to know the citation, but you do need to know proper citation methods.)

    a. *Canada Evidence Act*, R.S.C. 1990, c. C-5

    b. *Workplace Safety and Insurance Act, 1997*, R.S.O. 1997, c. 26, Sch. A

    c. *Ontario Evidence Act*, R.S.O. 1995, C.E-14

    d. all of the above are incorrect

    e. a and b only

12. When is it appropriate to provide a citation for an electronic source of legal research?

    _____

    _____

    _____

    _____

    _____

    _____

    _____

    _____

    _____

    _____

ACTIVITIES

1. During some recent research you found the 1992 case *Varcoe v. Sterling* on page 574 in volume 10 of the third edition of the *Ontario Reports*. The case was heard in the Ontario Superior Court of Justice. Provide a proper citation for the case.

_____

_____

_____

_____

_____

_____

_____

_____

_____

_____

2. Ontario's *Legal Aid Services Act, 1998* is found at chapter 26 of the 1998 *Statutes of Ontario*. You are particularly interested in the following section:

> 67(2) The money required for the purposes of this Act shall be paid out of such money as is appropriated therefor by the Legislature.

Provide a proper citation for this section.

_____

_____

_____

_____

_____

_____

_____

_____

_____

_____

3. Provide a proper citation for each of the following cases.

    a. The case of *Hague v. Billings* was decided in the Ontario Court of Appeal on April 23, 1993. It is found on page 298 of the *Ontario Reports*, third edition, volume 13.

_____

_____

_____

_____

_____

_____

_____

    b. The case of *Soutzo v. Soutzo* was decided in the Alberta Court of Appeal on June 5, 1991. It is found on page 180 of the *Reports of Family Law*, third edition, volume 33.

_____

_____

_____

_____

_____

_____

_____

_____

4. Using Quicklaw or Westlaw, find and cite correctly:

    a. one federal and one provincial statute that tries to control actions that may harm the environment

_____

_____

_____

_____

_____

_____

_____

b. a provincial statute that controls lawyers and the practice of law in Ontario

_____

_____

_____

_____

_____

_____

_____

c. provincial legislation that allows you to change your name

_____

_____

_____

_____

_____

_____

_____

_____

5. Using the legal materials available in your college library, find the following and provide a proper citation for each:

a. a legal research and/or writing text

_____

_____

_____

_____

b. a book that provides names, addresses, and phone numbers for law offices and courts throughout Ontario

_____

_____

_____

_____

_____

c. a civil case, published in the *Ontario Reports*

_____

_____

_____

_____

_____

d. a criminal case, published in *Canadian Criminal Cases*

_____

_____

_____

_____

_____

6. Use CanLII to locate *R. v. McNeil*, 2009 SCC 3, [2009] 1 S.C.R. 66. Prepare a case brief. Review figures 11.13 and 11.14. Your professor will provide you with the elements that he or she would like included in the brief.

7. The purpose of a legal memorandum is to provide a summary of legal research you have completed on a legal issue (or issues) of importance to a client.

   The firm that you work for has been retained by a doctor whose practice includes many terminally ill patients, including some who are suffering in the advanced stages of ALS. Some of these patients have asked her about their options and her role, should they wish at some point to end their lives. You may make up additional facts as needed to fill out this case scenario to apply your findings on the legal question posed below.

   Your task is to write a legal memorandum on the questions that follow.

   With regard to assisted suicide, and in light of the cases of Sue Rodriguez (*Rodriguez v. Attorney General of Canada*, [1993] 3 S.C.R. 519) and Nancy B. (*N.B. v. Hotel-Dieu de Quebec* (1992), 86 D.L.R. (4th) 385 (Que. Sup. Ct.)), what are:

   (1) the circumstances in which physician criminal liability may be found?

   (2) the circumstances in which physician criminal liability might not be found?

Your memorandum should be written in a 12-point font, double spaced, with 1-inch margins all around. It should not be longer than 4 to 5 pages. If you can write it more succinctly, while providing a clear summary of the relevant law, that is acceptable. Make sure you provide complete citations and page references so the source material can be found if needed. Any relevant quotes should be placed in indented block format in a 10-point font. Begin page numbering on page 2 bottom centre. Marks for spelling and typos will be deducted to a maximum of 5 marks. Ensure that you include a cover page.

Write the memorandum in memo format broken up with appropriate headings.

To: Professor
From: Student Name
Date: Due date of assignment
Re: Subject heading of your memorandum

Facts

For the purposes of this assignment you do need to restate the facts found in your scenario. Otherwise, if you were working in a law office, a detailed statement of facts would be required, generally one paragraph in length.

Issues (Questions)

Under this heading, state the legal issues or issues (questions) raised by the scenario. Use appropriate numbering; e.g., 1a, 1b, etc. Phrase each question generically; in other words, do not use client names or terms such as "the plaintiff"; instead, use terms such as "a person" or "an agent." Quite often, legal issues begin with the word "whether" or "does."

Conclusion (Answers)

Under this heading, state your conclusions on the legal issues using the same headings or numbering used in the issues section.

Discussion

The discussion is simply that. Provide a non-biased discussion of the law as it applies to the facts. Organize your answer by discussing one issue at a time. Use analogies to other cases where appropriate.

Authorities/Law (this section may be found here or between the facts and issues sections)

Under this heading, properly cite primary sources relied on. Make sure you also include any secondary sources used. Typically, you should include a list of the relevant statutes and cases relied on.

Legal Forms

The devil is in the details.

—Gustave Flaubert

Introduction

Provincial and federal governments design standardized legal forms to ensure that law firms and the public submit the data necessary to process and complete various types of legal transactions in a consistent way. At first, the sheer number of forms may feel overwhelming. However, as you progress in your career and gain more experience, knowing which forms are used to commence, respond to, or complete a specific legal process will save you time.

Each area of law—and each province/territory—has different requirements for completing forms, making copies, filing within time limitations, etc. Ensure that you follow the proper rules and requirements set out by the governing body.

Familiarization

Be sure to familiarize yourself with the most commonly used forms in your office. Know when and how they are used, and maintain an efficient forms management system for quick access. Whether your forms management system is electronic or paper-based, it should organize and catalogue forms to allow you to identify and retrieve them quickly. Update your system as new forms are issued and others are revised. You may find it useful to keep examples of completed forms for quick reference.

Preparation and Accuracy

In the preparation of any legal form, accuracy and completeness are essential. Approach this aspect of your job with as much diligence as you apply to document production, business writing, or communication. When completing forms, refer to the client file, any relevant resources, and the instructions you received from your lawyer. Follow all guidelines set out on the form. Proofread all completed material, checking for accuracy, spelling, grammar, and word usage. Pay particular attention to names, dates, and other figures. Errors or omissions can have consequences for the client (in terms of time, outcome, or money) and can embarrass the firm. If you neglect to supply the correct information in the appropriate way, the legal transaction you are carrying out may not be binding.

Legal forms are available from the appropriate federal or provincial government ministry website or from a private sector source, such as *O'Brien's Encyclopedia of Forms*, 11th ed. (Aurora, ON: Canada Law Book) (looseleaf).

In the following sections, commonly used forms are presented and illustrated in the context of scenarios that are often encountered in civil law practices. Note that the forms in this chapter are current as of the time of writing.

Family Law

Law in Practice: Divorce

Barbie and Ken Cole have been married since August 21, 1991. They have one child, Trixie, who was born on April 22, 2004. On May 1, 2005 Barbie and Ken Cole separated. They subsequently entered into a separation agreement on May 1, 2005, resolving all issues between them. Barbie wishes to begin divorce proceedings against Ken.

Divorce procedures in Ontario are governed by the *Family Law Rules*. According to rule 36, the following forms must be completed, served, and filed to obtain a simple (uncontested) divorce in Ontario. The forms are available at http://www.ontariocourtforms.on.ca or from document-production software packages such as DivorceMate.

- Figure 12.1   Form 8A: Application (Divorce)
- Figure 12.2   Form 6B: Affidavit of Service
- Figure 12.3   Form 36: Affidavit for Divorce
- Figure 12.4   Form 25A: Divorce Order
- Figure 12.5   Form 36B: Certificate of Divorce

FIGURE 12.1 Form 8A: Application (Divorce)

		Court File Number
SEAL	*ONTARIO* Superior Court of Justice Family Court Branch *(Name of Court)* at 470 Water Street, Peterborough, ON K9H 3M3 *(Court office address)*	**Form 8A: Application (Divorce)** [x] Simple (divorce only) [ ] Joint

Applicant(s)

Full legal name & address for service — street & number, municipality, postal code, telephone & fax numbers and e-mail address (if any).	Lawyer's name & address — street & number, municipality, postal code, telephone & fax numbers and e-mail address (if any).
Barbie Cole 10 Brackley Avenue Peterborough, ON K9K 1G2 Tel: 705-745-9876	Nick Miller, Barrister and Solicitor 28 Jordan Street Peterborough, ON K9J 1P3 Tel: 705-821-8846

Respondent(s)

Full legal name & address for service — street & number, municipality, postal code, telephone & fax numbers and e-mail address (if any).	Lawyer's name & address — street & number, municipality, postal code, telephone & fax numbers and e-mail address (if any).
Ken Cole 621 Brumwell Street Peterborough, ON K9J 2Y3 Tel: 705-745-2121	

---

[x] **IN THIS CASE, THE APPLICANT IS CLAIMING DIVORCE ONLY.**

TO THE RESPONDENT(S): A COURT CASE FOR DIVORCE HAS BEEN STARTED AGAINST YOU IN THIS COURT. THE DETAILS ARE SET OUT ON THE ATTACHED PAGES.

THIS CASE IS ON THE STANDARD TRACK OF THE CASE MANAGEMENT SYSTEM. No court date has been set for this case but, if you have been served with a notice of motion, it has a court date and you or your lawyer should come to court for the motion. A case management judge will not be assigned until one of the parties asks the clerk of the court to schedule a case conference or until a motion is scheduled, whichever comes first.

IF, AFTER 365 DAYS, THE CASE HAS NOT BEEN SCHEDULED FOR TRIAL, the clerk of the court will send out a warning that the case will be dismissed within 60 days unless the parties file proof that the case has been settled or one of the parties asks for a case or a settlement conference.

IF YOU WANT TO OPPOSE ANY CLAIM IN THIS CASE, you or your lawyer must prepare an *Answer* (Form 10 — a blank copy should be attached), serve a copy on the applicant and file a copy in the court office with an *Affidavit of Service* (Form 6B).
YOU HAVE ONLY 30 DAYS AFTER THIS APPLICATION IS SERVED ON YOU (60 DAYS IF THIS APPLICATION IS SERVED ON YOU OUTSIDE CANADA OR THE UNITED STATES) TO SERVE AND FILE AN ANSWER. IF YOU DO NOT, THE CASE WILL GO AHEAD WITHOUT YOU AND THE COURT MAY MAKE AN ORDER AND ENFORCE IT AGAINST YOU.

IF YOU WANT TO MAKE A CLAIM OF YOUR OWN, you or your lawyer must fill out the claim portion in the Answer, serve a copy on the applicant(s) and file a copy in the court office with an Affidavit of Service.
- If you want to make a claim for support but do not want to make a claim for property or exclusive possession of the matrimonial home and its contents, you **MUST** fill out a Financial Statement (Form 13), serve a copy on the applicant(s) and file a copy in the court office.
- However, if your only claim for support is for child support in the table amount specified under the Child Support Guidelines, you do not need to fill out, serve or file a Financial Statement.
- If you want to make a claim for property or exclusive possession of the matrimonial home and its contents, whether or not it includes a claim for support, you **MUST** fill out a Financial Statement (Form 13.1, not Form 13), serve a copy on the applicant(s), and file a copy in the court office.

YOU SHOULD GET LEGAL ADVICE ABOUT THIS CASE RIGHT AWAY. If you cannot afford a lawyer, you may be able to get help from your local Legal Aid office. *(See your telephone directory under LEGAL AID.)*

[ ] **THIS CASE IS A JOINT APPLICATION FOR DIVORCE. THE DETAILS ARE SET OUT ON THE ATTACHED PAGES.** The application and affidavits in support of the application will be presented to a judge when the materials have been checked for completeness.

If you are requesting anything other than a simple divorce, such as support or property or exclusive possession of the matrimonial home and its contents, then refer to page 1 for instructions regarding the Financial Statement you should file.

January 28, 20—	*Kelsey Keates*
Date of issue	**Clerk of Court**

FLR 8A (June 15, 2007)   www.DIVORCEmate.com

FIGURE 12.1 Continued

Form 8A: Application (Divorce) (page 2)	Court File Number

FAMILY HISTORY

APPLICANT: Age: 34   Birthdate: *(d, m, y)* 10 April 1976

Resident in *(municipality & province)* Peterborough, Province of Ontario

since *(date)* 10 April 1976

Surname at birth: Tomms

Surname just before marriage: Tomms

Divorced before? [x] No   [ ] Yes *(Place and date of previous divorce)*

RESPONDENT/JOINT APPLICANT:

Age: 33   Birthdate: *(d, m, y)* 4 May 1977

Resident in *(municipality & province)* Peterborough, Province of Ontario

since *(date)* 4 May 1977

Surname at birth: Cole

Surname just before marriage: Cole

Divorced before? [x] No   [ ] Yes *(Place and date of previous divorce)*

RELATIONSHIP DATES

[x] Married on *(date)* August 21, 1991   [x] Started living together on *(date)* August 21, 1991

[x] Separated on *(date)* May 1, 2005   [ ] Never lived together

THE CHILD(REN)
List all children involved in this case, even if no claim is made for these children.

Full legal name	Age	Birthday *(d, m, y)*	Resident in *(municipality & province)*	Now Living with *(name of person and relationship to child)*
Trixie Cole	7	April 22, 2004	Peterborough, ON	Barbie Cole, Mother

PREVIOUS CASES OR AGREEMENTS

Have the parties or the children been in a court case before?
[x] No   [ ] Yes

Have the parties made a written agreement dealing with any matter involved in this case?
[ ] No   [x] Yes *(Give date of agreement. Indicate which of its items are in dispute.)*
Separation Agreement dated June 15, 2005. No terms in dispute.

FIGURE 12.1   Continued

Form 8A: Application (Divorce) (page 3)   Court File Number

CLAIMS

USE THIS FRAME ONLY IF THIS CASE IS A JOINT APPLICATION FOR DIVORCE.

WE JOINTLY ASK THE COURT FOR THE FOLLOWING:

Claims under the *Divorce Act*	Claims under the *Family Law Act* or *Children's Law Reform Act*	Claims relating to property
00 ☐ a divorce	10 ☐ spousal support	20 ☐ equalization of net family properties
01 ☐ spousal support	11 ☐ support for child(ren) – table amount	21 ☐ exclusive possession of matrimonial home
02 ☐ support for child(ren) – table amount	12 ☐ support for child(ren) - other than table amount	22 ☐ exclusive possession of contents of matrimonial home
03 ☐ support for child(ren) - other than table amount	13 ☐ custody of child(ren)	23 ☐ freezing assets
04 ☐ custody of child(ren)	14 ☐ access to child(ren)	24 ☐ sale of family property
05 ☐ access to child(ren)	15 ☐ restraining/non-harassment order	**Other Claims**
	16 ☐ indexing spousal support	
	17 ☐ declaration of parentage	30 ☐ costs
	18 ☐ guardianship over child's property	31 ☐ annulment of marriage
		32 ☐ prejudgment interest
		50 ☐ other (*Specify.*)

USE THIS FRAME ONLY IF THE APPLICANT'S ONLY CLAIM IN THIS CASE IS FOR DIVORCE.

I ASK THE COURT FOR:
(*Check if applicable.*)

00 ☒ a divorce   30 ☐ costs

IMPORTANT FACTS SUPPORTING THE CLAIM FOR DIVORCE

☒ **Separation:** The spouses have lived separate and apart since (*date*) May 1, 2005 and

  ☒ have not lived together again since that date in an unsuccessful attempt to reconcile.

  ☐ have lived together again during the following period(s) in an unsuccessful attempt to reconcile:
  (*Give dates.*)

☐ **Adultery:** (*Name of spouse*) ....
has committed adultery. (*Give details. It is not necessary to name any other person involved but if you do name the other person, then you must serve this application on the other person.*)

☐ **Cruelty:** (*Name of spouse*) ....
has treated (*name of spouse*) ....
with physical or mental cruelty of such a kind as to make continued cohabitation intolerable. (*Give details.*)

FIGURE 12.1 Continued

Form 8A: Application (Divorce) (page 4)   Court File Number

USE THIS FRAME ONLY IF THIS CASE IS A JOINT APPLICATION FOR DIVORCE.

The details of the other order(s) that we jointly ask the court to make are as follows: *(Include any amounts of support and the names of the children for whom support, custody or access is to be ordered.)*

IMPORTANT FACTS SUPPORTING OUR CLAIM(S)

(Set out the facts that form the legal basis for your claim(s)).

Put a line through any blank space left on this page.

Complete this section if your claim is for a divorce. Your lawyer, if you are represented, must complete the Lawyer's Certificate below.

January 27ᵗʰ, 20—	*Barbie Cole*
Date of signature	Signature of applicant

Complete this section if you are making a joint application for divorce. Your lawyer, if you are represented, must complete the Lawyer's Certificate below.

Date of signature	Signature of joint applicant

Date of signature	Signature of joint applicant

LAWYER'S CERTIFICATE

My name is: Nick Miller

and I am the lawyer for *(name)*   Barbie Cole

in this divorce case. I certify that I have complied with the requirements of section 9 of the *Divorce Act.*

January 28, 20—	*Nick Miller*
Date of signature	Signature of Lawyer

FIGURE 12.2   Form 6B: Affidavit of Service

ONTARIO	Court File Number
Superior Court of Justice Family Court Branch	123/11
(Name of court)	
at 470 Water Street, Peterborough, ON K9H 3M3	**Form 6B: Affidavit of Service**
(Court office address)	**sworn/affirmed**
	January 28, 20--

Applicant(s)

Full legal name & address for service — street & number, municipality, postal code, telephone & fax numbers and e-mail address (if any).	*Lawyer's name & address — street & number, municipality, postal code, telephone & fax numbers and e-mail address (if any).*
Barbie Cole	**Nick Miller, Barrister and Solicitor**
10 Brackley Avenue	**28 Jordan Street**
Peterborough, ON K9K 1G2	**Peterborough, ON K9J 1P3**
Tel: 705-745-9876	**Tel: 705-821-8846**

Respondent(s)

Full legal name & address for service — street & number, municipality, postal code, telephone & fax numbers and e-mail address (if any).	*Lawyer's name & address — street & number, municipality, postal code, telephone & fax numbers and e-mail address (if any).*
Ken Cole	
621 Brumwell Street	
Peterborough, ON K9J 2Y3	
Tel: 705-745-2121	

My name is
(full legal name)   Scott Knowles

I live in
(municipality and province)   Peterborough, ON

and I swear/affirm that the following is true:

1.   On   January 28, 20--   , I served *(name of person to be served)*
   Ken Cole

   with the following document(s) in this case: *(List the documents served.)*

Name of document	Author (if applicable)	Date when document signed, issued, sworn, etc.
Form 8A - Application	Barbie Cole	January 28, 20--

NOTE: *You can leave out any part of this form that is not applicable.*

2.   I served the document(s) mentioned in paragraph 1 by:

   [x]   special service. *(Go to paragraph 3 below if you used special service.)*

   [ ]   mail. *(Go to paragraph 4 if you used mailed service.)*

Check one box only and go to indicated paragraph.

   [ ]   courier. *(Go to paragraph 5 if you used courier.)*

   [ ]   deposit at a document exchange. *(Go to paragraph 6 if you used a document exchange.)*

   [ ]   fax. *(Go to paragraph 7 if you used fax.)*

   [ ]   substituted service or advertisement. *(Go to paragraph 8 if you used substituted service or*

FIGURE 12.2   Continued

Form 6B: Affidavit of Service (page 2)	Court File Number	123/11

3.   I carried out special service of the document(s) on the person named in paragraph 1 at *(place or address)*
621 Brumwell Street, Peterborough, ON K9J 2Y3

by:

[x]   leaving a copy with the person.

[ ]   leaving a copy with *(name)* ....

*Check one
box only.
Strike out
paragraphs 4
to 8 and go to
paragraph 9.*

[ ]   who is a lawyer who accepted service in writing on a copy of the document.

[ ]   who is the person's lawyer of record.

[ ]   who is the *(office or position)* ....
of the corporation named in paragraph 1.

[ ]   mailing a copy to the person together with a prepaid return postcard in Form 6 in an envelope
bearing the sender's return address. This postcard, in which receipt of the document(s) is
acknowledged, was returned and is attached to this affidavit.

[ ]   leaving a copy in a sealed envelope addressed to the person at the person's place of residence
with *(name)* ....
who provided me with identification to show that he/she was an adult person residing at the same
address and by mailing another copy of the same document(s) on the same or following day to the
person named in paragraph 1 at that place of residence.

[ ]   other *(Specify. See rule 6 for details.)*

4.   ~~I mailed the document(s) to be served by addressing the covering envelope to the person named in paragraph 1
at: *(set out
address.)*~~

~~which is the address~~   [ ]   ~~of the person's place of business.~~

[ ]   ~~of a lawyer who accepted service on the person's behalf.~~

*~~Check appropriate paragraph
and~~*   [ ]   ~~of the person's lawyer of record.~~

*~~strike out paragraphs 3, 5, 6, 7,
8~~*   [ ]   ~~of the person's home.~~

~~and 11.~~   [ ]   ~~on the document most recently filed in court by the person.~~

[ ]   ~~other *(Specify.)*~~

5.   ~~The document(s) to be served was/were placed in an envelope that was picked up at~~ .... ~~a.m./p.m.~~
~~on *(date)*~~ .... ~~by *(name of courier
service)*~~
~~a private courier service, a copy of whose receipt is attached to this affidavit.~~
~~The envelope was addressed to the person named in paragraph 1 at: *(Set out address.)*~~

FIGURE 12.2 Continued

Form 6B: Affidavit of Service (page 3)   **Court File Number**   123/11

---

which is the address   ☐ ~~of the person's place of business.~~

                        ☐ ~~of a lawyer who accepted service on the person's behalf.~~

Check appropriate paragraph   ☐ ~~of the person's lawyer of record.~~
and
strike out paragraphs 3, 4, 6, 7,   ☐ ~~of the person's home.~~
8
and 11.   ☐ ~~on the document most recently filed in court by the person.~~

                        ☐ ~~other (Specify.)~~

6. ~~The document(s) was/were deposited at a document exchange. The exchange's date stamp on the attached copy shows the date of the deposit. (Strike out paragraphs 3, 4, 5, 7, 8 and 11.)~~

7. ~~The document(s) to be served was/were faxed. The fax confirmation is attached to this affidavit. (Strike out paragraphs 3, 4, 5, 6, 8 and 11.)~~

8. ~~An order of this court made on (date) .... allowed~~

   ☐ ~~substituted service.~~

   ☐ ~~service by advertisement. (Attach advertisement.)~~

   ~~The order was carried out as follows: (Give details. Then go to paragraph 11 if you had to travel to serve substitutionally or by advertisement.)~~

9. My relationship to, or affiliation with, any party in this case is as follows:
   N/A

10. I am at least 18 years of age.

11. To serve the document(s), I had to travel   16   kilometres. My fee for service of the document(s) is
    $ ....88.00 , including travel.

Sworn/Affirmed before me at:
City of Peterborough
....
                              (municipality)
in   Province of Ontario
....
                    (province, state or country)
on   January 28, 20--
....
                    (date)

                                    _____
                                    Commissioner for taking affidavits
                                    *(Type or print name below if signature is
                                    illegible.)*

                                    Signature
                                    *(This form is to be signed in front of a
                                    lawyer,
                                    justice of the peace, notary public or
                                    commissioner for taking affidavits.)*

FIGURE 12.3 Form 36: Affidavit for Divorce

	ONTARIO	Court File Number
Superior Court of Justice Family Court Branch		123/11
(Name of Court)		

at   **470 Water Street, Peterborough, ON K9H 3M3**
(Court office address)

Form 36: Affidavit for Divorce

Applicant(s)

Full legal name & address for service — street & number, municipality, postal code, telephone & fax numbers and e-mail address (if any).	*Lawyer's name & address — street & number, municipality, postal code, telephone & fax numbers and e-mail address (if any).*
Barbie Cole	**Nick Miller, Barrister and Solicitor**
10 Brackley Avenue	**28 Jordan Street**
Peterborough, ON K9K 1G2	**Peterborough, ON K9J 1P3**
Tel: 705-745-9876	**Tel: 705-821-8846**

Respondent(s)

Full legal name & address for service — street & number, municipality, postal code, telephone & fax numbers and e-mail address (if any).	*Lawyer's name & address — street & number, municipality, postal code, telephone & fax numbers and e-mail address (if any).*
Ken Cole	
621 Brumwell Street	
Peterborough, ON K9J 2Y3	
Tel: 705-745-2121	

My name is *(full legal name)*   Barbie Cole

I live in *(municipality & province)*   Peterborough, Province of Ontario

And I swear/affirm that the following is true:

1. I am the applicant in this divorce case.

2. There is no chance of reconciliation between the respondent and me.

3. All information in the application in this case is correct, except: *(State any corrections or changes to the information in the application. Write "NONE" if there are no corrections or changes.)*

NONE

4. [X] The certificate or registration of my marriage to the respondent has been signed and sealed by the Registrar of Ontario and

    [X] has been filed with the application.

    [ ] is attached to this affidavit.

[ ] The certificate of my marriage to the respondent was issued outside Ontario. It is called *(title of certificate)*

....

It was issued at *(place of issue)*

....

on *(date)* .... by *(name and title of person who issued the certificate)*

....

and the information in it about my marriage is correct.

[ ] I have not been able to get a certificate or registration of my marriage. I was married to the respondent

on *(date)* ....

at *(place of marriage)* ....

The marriage was performed by *(name and title)*

who had the authority to perform marriages in that place.

FIGURE 12.3   Continued

Form 36: Affidavit for Divorce (page 2)   **Court File Number**   123/11

5.   The legal basis for the divorce is:

    ☒   that the respondent and I have been separated for at least one year.

          We separated on *(date)*   May 1, 2005

    ☐   *(Other. Specify.)*

6.   I do not know about and I am not involved in any arrangement to make up or to hide evidence or to deceive the court in this divorce case.

Strike out the following paragraphs if they do not apply.

7.   I do not want to make a claim for a division of property in this divorce case, even though I know that it may be legally impossible to make such a claim after the divorce.

8.   ~~I want the divorce order to include the following paragraph numbers of the attached consent, settlement, separation agreement or previous court order:~~ *(List the numbers of the paragraphs that you want included in the divorce order.)*

9.   There are *(number)*   1   children of the marriage. They are:

Full legal name of child	Birthdate *(d, m, y)*
Trixie Cole	April 22, 2004

10.   The custody and access arrangements for the child(ren) are as follows: *(Give summary.)*

I have custody of the child and the respondent has access every Wednesday evening from 3:30 p.m. until 8:30 p.m. and every other Friday evening from 6:00 p.m. until Sunday at 6:00 p.m.

11.   These are the arrangements that have been made for the support of the child(ren) of the marriage:

    (a)   The income of the party paying child support is ($)   92,000.00   per year.

    (b)   The number of children for whom support is supposed to be paid is *(number)*   1   .

    (c)   The amount of support that should be paid according to the applicable table in the child support guidelines is ($)   814.00   per month.

    (d)   The amount of child support actually being paid is ($)   814.00   per month.

        *(**NOTE:** - Where the dollar amounts in clauses [c] and [d] are different, you must fill out the frame on the next page. If the amounts in clauses [c] and [d] are the same, skip the frame and go directly to paragraph 12.)*

Fill out the information in this frame only if amounts in 11(c) & 11(d) are different. If they are the same, go to paragraph 12.

(a)   Child support is already covered by:

    (i)   ☐   a court order dated *(date)*   that was made before the child support guidelines came into effect *(before May 1st, 1997)*. I attach a copy of the order.

    (ii)   ☐   a domestic contract order dated *(date)*   that was made before the guidelines came into effect *(before May 1st, 1997)*. I attach a copy of the contract.

    (iii)   ☐   a court order or written agreement dated *(date)*   made after the guidelines came into effect that has some direct or indirect benefits for the child(ren). I attach a copy.

    (iv)   ☐   a written consent between the parties dated *(date)*   agreeing to the payment of an amount different from that set out in the guidelines.

FIGURE 12.3 Continued

Form 36: Affidavit for Divorce (page 3) **Court File Number** 123/11

(b) The child support clauses of this order or agreement require payment of ($) .... per month
in child support.

(c) These child support clauses

☐ are not indexed for any automatic cost-of-living increases.

☐ are indexed according to *(Give indexing formula)*

(d) These child support clauses

☐ have not been changed since the day the order or agreement was made.

☐ have been changed on *(Give dates and details of changes)*

Date(s)	Detail(s)

(e) *(If you ticked off box (i), you can go to paragraph 12. If you ticked off boxes (ii), (iii) or (iv) above, then fill out the information after box of the corresponding number below. For example, if you ticked off box (iii) above, you would fill out the information alongside box (iii) below.)*

(ii) ☐ The amount being paid under this agreement is a fair and reasonable arrangement for the support of the child(ren) because: *(Give reasons.)*

(iii) ☐ The order or agreement directly or indirectly benefits the child(ren) because: *(Give details of benefits.)*

(iv) ☐ The amount to which the parties have consented is reasonable for the support of the child(ren) because: *(Give reasons.)*

---

12. I am claiming costs in this case. The details of this claim are as follows: *(Give details.)*
N/A

13. The respondent's address last known to me is: *(Give address.)*
Ken Cole, 621 Brumwell Street, Peterborough, ON K9J 2Y3

Put a line through any blank space on this page.

Sworn/Affirmed before me at:	
City of Peterborough	
(municipality)	
in Province of Ontario	
(province, state or country)	
on March 1, 20--	Signature
(date)	*(This form is to be signed in front of a lawyer,*
	justice of the peace, notary public or commissioner
Commissioner for taking affidavits	*for taking affidavits.)*
(Type or print name below if signature is illegible)	

FIGURE 12.4   Form 25A: Divorce Order

	ONTARIO	Court File Number
	Superior Court of Justice Family Court Branch	**123/11**
	(Name of Court)	
SEAL	**at** 470 Water Street, Peterborough, ON K9H 3M3	**Form 25A: Divorce**
	(Court office address)	**Order**

Applicant(s)

Full legal name & address for service – street & number, municipality, postal code, telephone & fax numbers & email address *(if any)*.	Lawyer's name & address - street & number, municipality, postal code, telephone & fax numbers & e-mail address *(if any)*.
Barbie Cole	**Nick Miller, Barrister and Solicitor**
10 Brackley Avenue	**28 Jordan Street**
Peterborough, ON K9K 1G2	**Peterborough, ON K9J 1P3**
Tel: 705-745-9876	**Tel: 705-821-8846**

The Honourable

Robert Burgis

Judge (print or type name)

March 14, 20--

Date of order

Respondent(s)

Full legal name & address for service – street & number, municipality, postal code, telephone & fax numbers & email address *(if any)*.	Lawyer's name & address - street & number, municipality, postal code, telephone & fax numbers & e-mail address *(if any)*.
Ken Cole	
621 Brumwell Street	
Peterborough, ON K9J 2Y3	
Tel: 705-745-2121	

The court heard an application of *(name)* Barbie Cole

on *(date)* N/A

~~The following persons were in court~~ *~~(Give name of parties and lawyers in court. This paragraph may be struck out if the divorce is~~* ~~uncontested.)~~

This court received evidence and considered submissions on behalf of *(name or names)*

Barbie Cole

THIS COURT ORDERS THAT:

1.   *If the court decides that the divorce shall take effect earlier, replace "31" with the smaller number.*

(full legal names of spouses) Barbie Cole and Ken Cole

who were married at *(place)* Peterborough

on *(date)* August 21, 1991

be divorced and that the divorce take effect   31   days after the date of this order.

(Add further paragraphs where the court orders other relief.)

March 14, 20--	*Allicia Keates*
Date of signature	Signature of judge or clerk of the court

NOTE: *Neither spouse is free to remarry until this order takes effect, at which time you can get a* **Certificate of Divorce** *from the court office.*

FIGURE 12.5   Form 36B: Certificate of Divorce

SEAL

ONTARIO
Superior Court of Justice Family Court Branch
(Name of Court)
at **470 Water Street, Peterborough, ON K9H 3M3**
(Court office address)

Court File Number
123/11

Form 36B: Certificate of Divorce

Applicant

Full legal name & address for service — street & number, municipality, postal code, telephone & fax numbers and e-mail address (if any).	Lawyer's name & address — street & number, municipality, postal code, telephone & fax numbers and e-mail address (if any).
Barbie Cole **10 Brackley Avenue** **Peterborough, ON K9K 1G2** **Tel: 705-745-9876**	**Nick Miller, Barrister and Solicitor** **28 Jordan Street** **Peterborough, ON K9J 1P3** **Tel: 705-821-8846**

Respondent(s)

Full legal name & address for service — street & number, municipality, postal code, telephone & fax numbers and e-mail address (if any).	Lawyer's name & address — street & number, municipality, postal code, telephone & fax numbers and e-mail address (if any).
Ken Cole **621 Brumwell Street** **Peterborough, ON K9J 2Y3** **Tel: 705-745-2121**	

I CERTIFY THAT the marriage of *(full legal name of spouses)*

Barbie Cole

and

Ken Cole

which was solemnized at *(place of marriage)*

Peterborough

on *(date of marriage)*   August 21, 1991

was dissolved by an order of this court made on *(date of divorce order)* March 14, 20--

The divorce took effect on *(date when order took effect)*   April 14, 20--

---

Cody Carpenter

Signature of clerk of the court

April 15, 20—

Date of signature

NOTE: *This certificate can only be issued on or after the date on which the divorce takes effect.*

www.DIVORCEmate.com

Estates

Law in Practice: Estate trustee appointment

Katherine Jones died on March 31, 2006. She is survived by her husband, Todd Jones, her adult son, Scott Jones, and her infant daughter, Lily Jones. She died testate (with a will that was made in contemplation of her marriage to Todd).

Her husband is applying to be appointed estate trustee in the administration of her will. Todd also wants to ensure that, if he is not able to make decisions for himself concerning his finances or his health, his son will be able to do so on his behalf. Todd needs a Continuing Power of Attorney for Property and a Power of Attorney for Personal Care to give Scott this legal authority. The powers of attorney do not need to be filed with the court.

In Ontario, in order for an executor to deal with a will, the executor needs to be appointed trustee. According to the *Rules of Civil Procedure*, the following forms must be completed and filed with the court. The forms are available at http://www.ontariocourtforms.on.ca.

- Figure 12.6   Form 74.7: Notice of an Application for a Certificate of Appointment of Estate Trustee with a Will

- Figure 12.7   Form 74.4: Application for Certificate of Appointment of Estate Trustee with a Will (Individual Applicant)

- Figure 12.8   Form 74.6: Affidavit of Service of Notice

- Figure 12.9   Form 74.13: Certificate of Appointment of Estate Trustee with a Will

- Figure 12.10   Continuing Power of Attorney for Property

- Figure 12.11   Power of Attorney for Personal Care

FIGURE 12.6 Form 74.7: Notice of an Application for a Certificate of Appointment of Estate Trustee with a Will

FORM 74.7

Courts of Justice Act

NOTICE OF AN APPLICATION FOR A CERTIFICATE OF APPOINTMENT OF ESTATE TRUSTEE WITH A WILL

ONTARIO

SUPERIOR COURT OF JUSTICE

IN THE ESTATE OF   **KATHERINE JONES**   , deceased.

NOTICE OF AN APPLICATION FOR A
CERTIFICATE OF APPOINTMENT OF ESTATE
TRUSTEE WITH A WILL

1. The deceased died on   (*insert date*)   .

2. Attached to this notice are:

    (A) If the notice is sent to or in respect of a person entitled only to a specified item of property or stated amount of money, an extract of the part or parts of the will or codicil relating to the gift, or a copy of the will (and codicil(s), if any).

    (B) If the notice is sent to or in respect of any other beneficiary, a copy of the will (and codicil(s), if any).

    (C) If the notice is sent to the Children's Lawyer or the Public Guardian and Trustee, a copy of the will (and codicil(s), if any), and if it is not included in the notice, a statement of the estimated value of the interest of the person represented.

3. The applicant named in this notice is applying for a certificate of appointment of estate trustee with a will.

APPLICANT
Address
2121 Thatcher Blvd.
Name   Peterborough, ON K9J 7P4
Todd Andrew Jones

4. The following persons who are less than 18 years of age are entitled, whether their interest is contingent or vested, to share in the distribution of the estate:

Name	**Date of Birth** *(day, month, year)*	**Name and Address of Parent or Guardian**	**Estimated Value of** **Interest in Estate ***
Lily Jones	20/02/2006	Todd Jones 2121 Thatcher Blvd. Peterborough, ON K9J 7P4	

* Note: *The Estimated Value of Interest in Estate may be omitted in the form if it is included in a separate schedule attached to the notice sent to the Children's Lawyer.*

5. The following persons who are mentally incapable within the meaning of section 6 of the *Substitute Decisions Act, 1992* in respect of an issue in the proceeding, and who have guardians or attorneys acting under powers of attorney with authority to act in the proceeding, are entitled, whether their interest is contingent or vested, to share in the distribution of the estate:

Name and Address of Person   **Name and Address of Guardian or Attorney ***

* *Specify whether guardian or attorney*

6. The following persons who are mentally incapable within the meaning of section 6 of the *Substitute Decisions Act, 1992* in respect of an issue in the proceeding, and who do not have guardians or attorneys acting under powers of attorney with authority to act in the proceeding, are entitled, whether their interest is contingent or vested, to share in the distribution of the estate:

Name and Address of Person   **Estimated Value of**
                                                                 Interest in Estate *

* Note: *The Estimated Value of Interest in Estate may be omitted in the form if it is included in a separate schedule attached to the notice sent to the Public Guardian and Trustee.*

FIGURE 12.6   Continued

7.   ~~Unborn or unascertained persons may be entitled to share in the distribution of the estate.   *(Delete if not applicable)*~~

8.   All other persons and charities entitled, whether their interest is contingent or vested, to share in the distribution of the estate are as follows:

Name   **Address**

9.   This notice is being sent, by regular lettermail, to all adult persons and charities named above in this notice (except to an applicant who is entitled to share in the distribution of the estate), to the Public Guardian and Trustee if paragraph 6 applies, to a parent or guardian of the minor and to the Children's Lawyer if paragraph 4 applies, to the guardian or attorney if paragraph 5 applies, and to the Children's Lawyer if paragraph 7 applies.

10.   The following persons named in the Will or being a member of a class of beneficiaries under the Will may be entitled to be served but have not been served for the reasons shown below:

Name of person (as it appears in will, if applicable)   **Reason not served**

If paragraph 10 does not apply insert "Not Applicable."

DATE: May 26, 2006

RCP-E 74.7 (November 1, 2005)

FIGURE 12.7 Form 74.4: Application for Certificate of Appointment of Estate Trustee with a Will (Individual Applicant)

FORM 74.4

Courts of Justice Act

APPLICATION FOR CERTIFICATE OF APPOINTMENT OF ESTATE TRUSTEE
WITH A WILL (INDIVIDUAL APPLICANT)

ONTARIO

SUPERIOR COURT OF JUSTICE

at Peterborough

**APPLICATION FOR CERTIFICATE OF
APPOINTMENT OF ESTATE TRUSTEE WITH A
WILL (INDIVIDUAL APPLICANT)**

(Form 74.4 Under the Rules)

This application is filed by (*insert name and address*)
Nick Miller, Barrister and Solicitor, 28 Jordan Avenue, Peterborough, ON K9J 1P3
Tel: 705-821-8846 Fax: 705-821-8846

DETAILS ABOUT THE DECEASED PERSON

Complete in full as applicable

First given name KATHERINE	Second given name	Third given name	Surname JONES

And if the deceased was known by any other name(s), state below the full name(s) used including surname.

First given name	Second given name	Third given name	Surname

Address of fixed place of abode (*street or postal address*) (*city or town*) 2121 Thatcher Blvd., Peterborough, ON K9J 7P4	(*county or district*) Municipality of Peterborough

If the deceased person had no fixed place of abode in Ontario, did he or she have property in Ontario? ☐ No ☐ Yes N/A	**Last occupation of deceased person** Pharmacist

Place of death (*city or town; county or district*)	**Date of death** (*day, month, year*)	**Date of last will** (marked as Exhibit "A") (*day, month, year*)
Peterborough, ON	31/03/2006	13/01/2001

Was the deceased person 18 years of age or older at the date of the will (or 21 years of age or older if the will is dated earlier than September 1, 1971)? If not, explain why certificate is being sought. Give details in an attached schedule.	☐ No	X Yes

Date of codicil (marked as Exhibit "B") (*day, month, year*)	**Date of codicil** (marked as Exhibit "C") (*day, month, year*)

Marital Status ☐ Unmarried X Married ☐ Widowed ☐ Divorced

Did the deceased person marry after the date of the will? If yes, explain why certificate is being sought. Give details in an attached schedule.	X No	☐ Yes
Was a marriage of the deceased person terminated by a judgment absolute of divorce, or declared a nullity, after the date of the will? If yes, give details in an attached schedule.	X No	☐ Yes
Is any person who signed the will or a codicil as witness or for the testator, or the spouse of such person, a beneficiary under the will? If yes, give details in an attached schedule.	X No	☐ Yes

RCP-E 74.4 (November 1, 2005)

FIGURE 12.7   Continued

VALUE OF ASSETS OF ESTATE

Do not include in the total amount: insurance payable to a named beneficiary or assigned for value, property held jointly and passing by survivorship, or real estate outside Ontario.

Personal Property	Real estate, net of encumbrances	Total		
$ 268,000.00	$ 0.00	$ 268,000.00		
Is there any person entitled to an interest in the estate who is not an applicant?		☐ No	☐ Yes	N/A
If a person named in the will or a codicil as estate trustee is not an applicant, explain.				N/A
If a person not named in the will or a codicil as estate trustee is an applicant, explain why that person is entitled to apply.				N/A

If the spouse of the deceased is an applicant, has the spouse elected to receive the entitlement under section 5 of the *Family Law Act?*
If yes, explain why the spouse is entitled to apply.

X   No   ☐   Yes

AFFIDAVIT(S) OF APPLICANT(S)
(Attach a separate sheet for additional affidavits, if necessary)

I, an applicant named in this application, make oath and say/affirm:

1. I am 18 years of age or older.
2. The exhibit(s) referred to in this application are the last will and each codicil (where applicable) of the deceased person and I do not know of any later will or codicil.
3. I will faithfully administer the deceased person's property according to law and render a complete and true account of my administration when lawfully required.
4. If I am not named as estate trustee in the will or codicil, consents of persons who together have a majority interest in the value of the assets of the estate at the date of death are attached.
5. The information contained in this application and in any attached schedules is true, to the best of my knowledge and belief.

Name *(surname and forename(s))* Jones, Todd Andrew	**Occupation** Teacher		
Address *(street or postal address)* 2121 Thatcher Blvd.	*(city or town)* Peterborough	*(province)* ON	*(postal code)* K9J 7P4

Sworn/Affirmed before me at the City

of Peterborough

in the Municipality

of Peterborough

this 29th day of May, 2006

_____
Signature of applicant

_____
A Commissioner for taking Affidavits (*or as may be*)

RCP-E 74.4 (November 1, 2005)

FIGURE 12.8   Form 74.6: Affidavit of Service of Notice

FORM 74.6

Courts of Justice Act

AFFIDAVIT OF SERVICE OF NOTICE

ONTARIO

SUPERIOR COURT OF JUSTICE

IN THE ESTATE OF   KATHERINE JONES   , deceased.

AFFIDAVIT OF SERVICE OF NOTICE

I, Todd Andrew Jones, of the City of Peterborough, in the County of Peterborough, make oath and say/affirm:

1.   I am an applicant for a certificate of appointment of estate trustee with a will in the estate.

2.   I have sent or caused to be sent a notice in Form 74.7, a copy of which is marked as Exhibit "A" to this affidavit, to all adult persons and charities named in the notice (except to an applicant who is entitled to share in the distribution of the estate), to the Public Guardian and Trustee if paragraph 6 of the notice applies, to a parent or guardian of the minor and to the Children's Lawyer if paragraph 4 applies, to the guardian or attorney if paragraph 5 applies, and to the Children's Lawyer if paragraph 7 applies, all by regular lettermail sent to the person's last known address.

3.   I have attached or caused to be attached to each notice the following:

   (A)   In the case of a notice sent to or in respect of a person entitled only to a specified item of property or stated amount of money, an extract of the part or parts of the will or codicil relating to the gift, or a copy of the will (and codicil(s), if any).

   (B)   In the case of a notice sent to or in respect of any other beneficiary, a copy of the will (and codicil(s), if any).

   (C)   In the case of a notice sent to the Children's Lawyer or the Public Guardian and Trustee, a copy of the will (and codicil(s), if any) and a statement of the estimated value of the interest of the person represented.

4.   The following persons and charities specifically named in the Will are not entitled to be served for the reasons shown:

   Name of person (as it appears in will, if applicable)   **Reason not served**

   Not Applicable

   If paragraph 4 does not apply insert "Not Applicable."

5.   The following persons named in the Will or being a member of a class of beneficiaries under the Will may be entitled to be served but have not been served for the reasons shown below:

   Name of person (as it appears in will, if applicable)   **Reason not served**

   Not Applicable

   If paragraph 5 does not apply insert "Not Applicable."

6.   To the best of my knowledge and belief, subject to paragraph 5 (if applicable), the persons named in the notice are all the persons who are entitled to share in the distribution of the estate.

Sworn/Affirmed before me at the City	)
	)
of Peterborough	)
	)
in the Province	)
	)
of Ontario	) _____
	) Signature of applicant
this 29th day of May, 2006	)
	) Todd Andrew Jones
	)

_____

A Commissioner for taking Affidavits *(or as may be)*

RCP-E 74.6 (November 1, 2005)

FIGURE 12.9   Form 74.13: Certificate of Appointment of Estate Trustee with a Will

FORM 74.13

Courts of Justice Act

CERTIFICATE OF APPOINTMENT OF ESTATE TRUSTEE WITH A WILL

ONTARIO

SUPERIOR COURT OF JUSTICE

IN THE ESTATE OF   KATHERINE JONES   , deceased,

late of 2121 Thatcher Blvd., Peterborough, ON

occupation Pharmacist

who died on March 31, 2006

CERTIFICATE OF APPOINTMENT
OF ESTATE TRUSTEE WITH A WILL

Applicant	Address	Occupation
Todd Andrew Jones	2121 Thatcher Blvd. Peterborough, ON K9J 7P4	Teacher

This CERTIFICATE OF APPOINTMENT OF ESTATE TRUSTEE WITH A WILL is hereby issued under the seal of the court to the applicant named above. A copy of the deceased's last will (and codicil(s), if any) is attached.

DATE May 29, 2006

....
Registrar
Melody Campbell

Address of court office

470 Water Street
Peterborough, ON K9H 3M3

RCP-E 74.13 (November 1, 2005)

FIGURE 12.10 Continuing Power of Attorney for Property

CONTINUING POWER OF ATTORNEY FOR PROPERTY

THIS CONTINUING POWER OF ATTORNEY FOR PROPERTY is made by **TODD JONES**, of the City of Peterborough, in the County of Peterborough in the Province of Ontario.

APPOINTMENT

1. I APPOINT SCOTT JONES to be my attorney for property. I authorize my attorney to do, on my behalf, any acts which I can do by an attorney and specifically anything in respect of property that I could do if capable of managing property, subject to any conditions or restrictions contained in this Continuing Power of Attorney for Property.

POWER TO MANAGE PROPERTY

2. This document is a continuing power of attorney for property under the *Substitute Decisions Act, 1992*, S.O. 1992, c. 30, as amended, and may be used during my incapacity to manage property.

EFFECTIVE DATE

3. This Continuing Power of Attorney comes into effect on the date it is signed and witnessed.

CONDITIONS AND RESTRICTIONS

4. NONE

REVOCATION

5. I revoke any prior Continuing Power of Attorney for Property given by me.

MULTIPLE POWERS OF ATTORNEY

6. I retain the right to make multiple Continuing Powers of Attorney for Property.

DELEGATION

7. I authorize my attorney to delegate my attorney's authority to some other person and to revoke or suspend such delegation.

FAMILY LAW ACT CONSENT

8. I authorize my attorney named to exercise all of my rights with respect to the disposition, encumbrance or possession of a matrimonial home under the *Family Law Act*, R.S.O. 1990, c. F.3, whether or not my name appears on the title, including consenting to any disposition or encumbrance by my spouse of any interest in our matrimonial home.

FIGURE 12.10   Continued

OBLIGATIONS TO OTHERS

9. My attorney for property may manage my estate for my benefit, for the benefit of any other person, including my attorney, to fulfil any legal obligation I may have.

LITIGATION GUARDIAN

10. My attorney shall have the authority to act as my litigation guardian if one is required to commence, defend or represent me in any court proceedings.

COMPENSATION

11. I authorize my attorney for property to take annual compensation from my property in accordance with the fee scale prescribed by regulation for the compensation of guardians of property made pursuant to ss. 40(1) and 90 of the *Substitute Decisions Act, 1992*, as amended.

CANADA REVENUE AGENCY

12. My attorney for property is my "legal representative" for all purposes of the *Income Tax Act*, R.S.C. 1985, c. 1 (5th Supp.), with respect to any dealings with the Government of Canada or any institution controlled by the Government of Canada.

SIGNED BY: _____   **DATED:** _____

WITNESSES: We have signed this Power of Attorney in the presence of **TODD JONES** and in the presence of each other. Neither of us is an attorney named herein, a spouse or partner of the maker of the power of attorney, a child of the maker of the power of attorney to whom the maker has demonstrated a settled intention to treat as a child, nor a person whose property is under guardianship or who has a Guardian of the person, or who is a person less than 18 years old.

FIRST WITNESS: **SECOND WITNESS:**

_____   _____
Signature   Signature

_____   _____
Print name and address   Print name and address

FIGURE 12.11   Power of Attorney for Personal Care

POWER OF ATTORNEY FOR PERSONAL CARE

THIS POWER OF ATTORNEY FOR PERSONAL CARE is made by **TODD JONES**, of the City of Peterborough, in the Province of Ontario, on the 22nd day of June 20--.

APPOINTMENT

1. I appoint SCOTT JONES to be my attorney for personal care pursuant to the *Substitute Decisions Act, 1992*, S.O. 1992, c. 30.

AUTHORITY OF ATTORNEY

2. In accordance with the said Act, and in the full knowledge that my attorney for personal care will act in accordance with the wishes I have expressed, I authorize my attorney for personal care to make on my behalf any decisions concerning my personal care and to give or refuse consent on my behalf to any treatment to which the *Health Care Consent Act, 1996*, S.O. 1996, c. 2, Sch. A, applies, as my attorney in his or her discretion shall determine.

SUBSTITUTION

3. If SCOTT JONES refuses to act, or is unable to act by reason of death, court removal, becoming incapacitated or resignation, or is not available to act at the time the necessity for a decision by an attorney for personal care arises concerning my personal care or treatment to which the *Health Care Consent Act, 1996*, applies (the question of necessity to be determined conclusively by a qualified medical person in attendance upon me), I substitute and appoint WILLIAM CARPENTER AND TANYA GUERIN to act as my attorney for personal care, in the place of and with all of the powers conferred upon SCOTT JONES.

REIMBURSEMENT FOR EXPENSES

4. All expenses incurred by my attorney for personal care in carrying out his/her duties (including obtaining an assessment of my capacity, if required), shall be payable by me or my attorney for property out of my assets.

NO RESTRICTIONS

5. This Power of Attorney for Personal Care is not subject to any conditions or restrictions and is given by me with the understanding that my attorney for personal care has a genuine concern for my welfare and in full appreciation that he/she may be required to make decisions to which this power of attorney relates.

FIGURE 12.11   Continued

REVOCATION

6.   Any prior Power of Attorney for Personal Care or any prior power of attorney which affects my personal care given by me is revoked.

SIGNED BY: _____   **DATED:** _____

WITNESSES: We have signed this Power of Attorney in the presence of **TODD JONES** and in the presence of each other. Neither of us is an attorney named herein, a spouse or partner of the maker of the power of attorney, a child of the maker of the power of attorney to whom the maker has demonstrated a settled intention to treat as a child, nor a person whose property is under guardianship or who has a Guardian of the person, or who is a person less than 18 years old.

FIRST WITNESS: **SECOND WITNESS:**

_____   _____
Signature   Signature

_____   _____
Print name and address   Print name and address

Litigation (Small Claims)

> ## Law in Practice: Plaintiff's claim in Small Claims Court
>
> Brownie's Truck Repair, owned and operated by John Brown, repaired Fred Jones's truck on February 6, 20--. The cost of the repair was $4,121.28. John Brown has made several attempts to collect the moneys owed, including sending numerous late-payment notices. A demand letter was sent to Fred Jones requesting full payment of the debt owing. To date, the payment has not been made. Fred Jones has decided to proceed in Small Claims Court.

In Ontario, the Small Claims Court handles cases where the amount of money owed or value of the goods involved is $25,000 or less. Under the *Rules of the Small Claims Court*, a person making the claim (plaintiff) must complete, file, and serve on the other party (respondent) a "Plaintiff's Claim," Form 7A. The required forms and instructions can be found at http://www.ontariocourtforms.on.ca.

- Figure 12.12   Form 7A: Plaintiff's Claim in Small Claims Court and Schedules A, B, and C.

FIGURE 12.12   Form 7A: Plaintiff's Claim in Small Claims Court

---

ONTARIO

Superior Court of Justice
Cour supérieure de justice

Plaintiff's Claim
Demande du demandeur

Form / *Formule* 7A Ont. Reg. No. / *Règl. de l'Ont.* : 258/98

Seal / *Sceau*

Peterborough Small Claims Court

Small Claims Court / *Cour des petites créances de*

Claim No. / *N° de la demande*

70 Simcoe Street

Peterborough, Ontario K9H 7G9

Address / *Adresse*

705 876 3816

Phone number / *Numéro de téléphone*

Plaintiff No. 1 / *Demandeur n° 1*   ☐ Additional plaintiff(s) listed on attached Form 1A. / *Le ou les demandeurs additionnels sont mentionnés sur la formule 1A ci-jointe.*   ☐ Under 18 years of age. / *Moins de 18 ans.*

Last name, or name of company / *Nom de famille ou nom de la compagnie* Brown		
First name / *Premier prénom* John	Second name / *Deuxième prénom*	Also known as / *Également connu(e) sous le nom de*
Address (street number, apt., unit) / *Adresse (numéro et rue, app., unité)* 100 Front Street		
City/Town / *Cité/ville* Peterborough	Province Ontario	Phone no. / *N° de telephone* 705-741-2822
Postal code / *Code postal* K9J 5C7		Fax no. / *N° de télécopieur*
Representative / *Représentant(e)* Donna Woodrow		LSUC # / *N° du BHC* L054096
Address (street number, apt., unit) / *Adresse (numéro et rue, app., unité)* 1605 Treetop Road		
City/Town / *Cité/ville* Peterborough	Province ON	Phone no. / *N° de telephone* 705-876-7391
Postal code / *Code postal* K9K 1G2		Fax no. / *N° de télécopieur*

Defendant No. 1 / *Défendeur n° 1*   ☐ Additional defendant(s) listed on attached Form 1A. / *Le ou les défendeurs additionnels sont mentionnés sur la formule 1A ci-jointe.*   ☐ Under 18 years of age. / *Moins de 18 ans.*

Last name, or name of company / *Nom de famille ou nom de la compagnie* Jones		
First name / *Premier prénom* Fred	Second name / *Deuxième prénom*	Also known as / *Également connu(e) sous le nom de*
Address (street number, apt., unit) / *Adresse (numéro et rue, app., unité)* 45 Cleveland Avenue		
City/Town / *Cité/ville* Peterborough	Province ON	Phone no. / *N° de telephone* 705-745-9236
Postal code / *Code postal* K9K 1T7		Fax no. / *N° de télécopieur*
Representative / *Représentant(e)*		LSUC # / *N° du BHC*
Address (street number, apt., unit) / *Adresse (numéro et rue, app., unité)*		
City/Town / *Cité/ville*	Province	Phone no. / *N° de téléphone*
Postal code / *Code postal*		Fax no. / *N° de télécopieur*

FIGURE 12.12   Continued

FORM/FORMULA   **PAGE 2**

_____
Claim No. / N' de la Demande

REASONS FOR CLAIM AND DETAILS / _MOTIFS DE LA DEMANDE ET PRÉCISIONS_

Explain what happened, including where and when. Then explain how much money you are claiming or what goods you want returned.
Expliquez ce qui s'est passé, en précisant où et quand. Ensuite indiquez la somme d'argent que vous demandez ou les biens dont vous demandez la restitution, explication à l'appui.

If you are relying on any documents, you **MUST** attach copies to the claim. If evidence is lost or unavailable, you **MUST** explain why it is not attached.
Si vous vous appuyez sur des documents, vous **DEVEZ** en annexer des copies à la demande. Si une preuve est perdue ou n'est pas disponible, vous **DEVEZ** expliquer pourquoi elle n'est pas annexée.

What happened?   **SEE SCHEDULES A, B and C**
When?   _____

Que s'est-il
passé?
_ù?_
Quand?

SCR 7.01-7A (September 1, 2010 / _1er septembre 2010_) CSD   **Continued on next page /** _Suite à la page suivante_

FIGURE 12.12   Continued

FORM/FORMULA	PAGE 2	
		Claim No. / N' de la Demande

_____

_____

_____

_____

_____

_____

_____

_____

_____

_____

_____

_____

_____

How much? $ _____**$4,121.28**_____
Combien?   (Principal amount claimed / _Somme demandée_)

☐   ADDITIONAL PAGES ARE ATTACHED BECAUSE MORE ROOM WAS NEEDED.
    DES FEUILLES SUPPLÉMENTAIRES SONT ANNEXÉES EN RAISON DU MANQUE D'ESPACE.

The plaintiff also claims pre-judgment interest from   <u>February 6, 20--</u>   under:
Le demandeur demande aussi des intérêts   (Date)   _conformément à :_
antérieurs au jugement de

(Check only   ◉   the _Courts of Justice Act_
one box /   **Loi sur les tribunaux judiciaires**
Cochez une
seule case)

           ◻   an agreement at the rate of _____ % per year
                   _un accord au taux de_____   % par an_

and post-judgment interest, and court costs.
et des intérêts postérieurs au jugement, ainsi que les dépens.

Prepared on: _____ , 20 _____   _____
Fait le :   (Signature of plaintiff or representative / _Signature du_
                                                           demandeur/de la demanderesse ou du/de la représentant(e))

Issued on: _____ , 20 _____   _____
Délivré le :   (Signature of clerk / _Signature du greffier_)

CAUTION TO DEFENDANT:	**IF YOU DO NOT FILE A DEFENCE** (Form 9A) with the court within twenty (20) calendar days after you have been served with this Plaintiff's Claim, judgment may be obtained without notice and enforced against you. Forms and self-help materials are available at the Small Claims Court and on the following website: www.ontariocourtforms.on.ca.
AVERTISSEMENT AU DÉFENDEUR :	_**SI VOUS NE DÉPOSEZ PAS DE DÉFENSE** (formule 9A) auprès du tribunal au plus tard vingt (20) jours civils après avoir reçu signification de la présente demande du demandeur, un jugement peut être obtenu sans préavis et être exécuté contre vous. Vous pouvez obtenir les formules et la documentation à l'usage du client à la Cour des petites créances et sur le site Web suivant : www.ontariocourtforms.on.ca._

FIGURE 12.12 Continued

<hr>

SCHEDULE A

CLAIM

1. The plaintiff claims:

    a) Unpaid invoice in the amount of $4,121.28;

    b) Pre-judgment and post-judgment interest pursuant to the *Courts of Justice Act*, R.S.O. 1990, c. C.43;

    c) Costs of this action; and

    d) Such further and other relief as this Honourable Court deems just.

2. The plaintiff, John Brown, at all material times was the owner and operator of Brownie's Truck Repair located at 100 Front Street, Peterborough, Ontario.

3. The defendant, Fred Jones, is an individual residing at 45 Cleveland Avenue, Peterborough, Ontario, who at all material times was a customer of the plaintiff.

4. On February 6, 20--, the defendant brought his 1987 Peterbilt transport truck, VIN# HG773737, to the plaintiff's premises and instructed the plaintiff to repair and install a new brake system.

5. The plaintiff completed the repair the same day, and the defendant took delivery of his vehicle, along with the invoice for the repairs, totalling $4,121.28. This invoice was marked Net 30.

6. The defendant failed to pay the invoice within 30 days.

7. The plaintiff attempted to collect payment by sending additional copies of the invoice to the defendant, marked "Due Immediately," by attempting to contact the defendant by telephone, and by sending a demand letter. (See copies attached as Schedules B and C.)

8. To date, the defendant's account continues in arrears.

9. The plaintiff submits that the defendant is in breach of contract, and requests judgment in the amount of $4,121.28, plus costs and interest.

FIGURE 12.12   Continued

SCHEDULE B

INVOICE

BROWNIE'S TRUCK REPAIR LTD.
100 Front Street
Peterborough, Ontario K9H 8Y4

DATE: February 6, 20--

Customer: Fred Jones
Address: 45 Cleveland Avenue, Peterborough, Ontario K9K 1T7

Vehicle Identification: 1987 Peterbilt Transport Truck, VIN #HG773737

Inspect and repair: brake system
Labour and materials $3,583.72

PST $250.86
GST $286.70
                                         _____

Net payable due within 30 days $4,121.28

Due Immediately

FIGURE 12.12 Continued

SCHEDULE C

WOODROW & PERRY
Barristers & Solicitors

1605 Treetop Road
Peterborough, Ontario
K9K 1G2
Telephone: 705-743-5796
Facsimile: 705-749-3492

woodrow.perry@shaw.ca

WITHOUT PREJUDICE

April 10, 20--

Fred Jones
45 Cleveland Avenue
Peterborough, ON
K9K 1T7

Dear Mr. Jones:

Re: Brownie's Truck Repair Ltd.
Outstanding Account

Please be advised that I have been retained by Mr. John Brown of Brownie's Truck Repair Ltd. to collect your long overdue account. At present your overdue account is in the amount of $4,121.28.

If the entire amount of $4,121.28 is not paid to this office by way of certified cheque within seven days, all proper steps will be taken to collect this account. Such action will no doubt impact your credit rating. In addition, all additional costs, interest, and disbursements incurred in the resulting court action will be in addition to the amount of your overdue account.

Kindly govern yourself accordingly and forward the requested sum to my office without delay.

Yours truly,

Nicolas Perry
Barrister and Solicitor

NP/rc

c: John Brown

Business Name Registration

Law in Practice: Registering a business name

Larry Keates owns and operates a bowling alley as a sole proprietor in the village of Millbrook, Ontario. Under the *Business Names Act*, he is required to register his business name of "Millbrook Bowling Centre." Once the name is registered, Mr. Keates will be required to renew the registration every five years.

Ontario law prohibits a proposed business name from being too similar to the name of any existing organization. To comply with this law, a NUANS report should be completed prior to registering a name; NUANS is a computer-based search engine that compares proposed names with existing company names.

Ontario business owners can register their business name with the *Ministry of Government Services*. The form required for registering a business name is available at http://www.mgs.gov.on.ca.

- Figure 12.13   Form 1: Registration under the Business Names Act—Sole Proprietorship/Partnership

FIGURE 12.13 Form 1: Registration under the Business Names Act—Sole Proprietorship/Partnership

---

Ontario

| Ministry of Government Services | Ministère des Services gouvernementaux | **Registration Form 1** under the *Business Names Act* - Sole Proprietorship / Partnership **Enregistrement Formule 1** en vertu de la *Loi sur les noms commerciaux* (Entreprise personnelle / société en nom collectif) |

Print clearly in CAPITAL LETTERS /
Écrivez clairement en LETTRES MAJUSCULES

1. Registration Type /
Type d'enregistrement

Page_____ of / de _____

If B, C, or D enter "Business Identification Number" /
En cas de B, C ou D, inscrivez le n° d'identification de l'entreprise.

A ☑ New / Nouvel B ☐ Renewal / Renouvellement C ☐ Amendment / Modification D ☐ Cancellation / Révocation

BIN Business Identification No./
NIE le n° d'identification de l'entreprise

2. Business Name / Nom commercial

M I L L B R O O K   B O W L I N G   C E N T R E

3. Mailing Address of Registrant/ L'Adresse postale de Registrant

Street No./ N° de rue — Street Name / Nom de la rue — Suite No. / Bureau n°
3 QUEEN ST BOX 267

City / Town / Ville — Province / Province — Postal Code / Code postal
MILLBROOK ONTARIO   L0A 1G0

Country / Pays
CANADA

4. Address of principal place of business in Ontario *(P.O. Box not acceptable)* /
Adresse de l'établissement principal en Ontario *(Case postale non acceptée)*   ☑ Same as above / comme ci-dessus

Street No. / N° de rue	Street Name / Nom de la rue	Suite No. / Bureau n°	City / Town / Ville
3	QUEEN ST	BOX 267	MILLBROOK
Province / Province	Country / Pays		Postal Code / Code postal
ONTARIO	CANADA		L0A 1G0

5. Give a brief description of the ACTIVITY being carried out under the business name./
Résumez brièvement le genre d'ACTIVITÉ exercée sous le nom commercial.

B O W L I N G ,   S N A C K   B A R ,   L L B O

6. Type of Registrant /
Type de personne enregistrée

A ☑ Sole proprietorship / Entreprise personnelle   B ☐ Partnership / Société en nom collectif   ☐ More than 10 Partners: records at business address / Plus de 10 associés : dossiers à l'adresse d'affaires

7. Registrant Information /
Renseignements sur la personne enregistrée

| Last Name / Nom de famille | First Name / Prénom | Middle Initial / initiale 2e prénom |
| KEATES | LAWRENCE | R |

8.
Street No. / N° de rue	Street Name / Nom de la rue	Suite No. / Bureau n°	City / Town / Ville
10	QUEEN ST		MILLBROOK
Province / Province	Country / Pays		Postal Code / Code postal
ONTARIO	CANADA		L0A 1G0

Additional Information. Only complete if the registrant is not an individual. See instructions 7/8 on the form. /
Renseignements supplémentaires. À remplir uniquement si la personne enregistrée n'est pas un particulier. Voir les instructions 7 et 8 sur le formulaire.

Ont. Corporation No. / *(For Corporate Partners Only)*
N° matricule de la personne morale en Ontario *Pour les personnes morales associées seulement*

7.
| Last Name / Nom de famille | First Name / Prénom | Middle Initial / initiale 2e prénom |
| | | |

8.
Street No. / N° de rue	Street Name / Nom de la rue	Suite No. / Bureau n°	City / Town / Ville
Province / Province	Country / Pays		Postal Code / Code postal

Additional Information. Only complete if the registrant is not an individual. See instructions 7/8 on the form. /
Renseignements supplémentaires. À remplir uniquement si la personne enregistrée n'est pas un particulier. Voir les instructions 7 et 8 sur le formulaire.

Ont. Corporation No. / *(For Corporate Partners Only)*
N° matricule de la personne morale en Ontario *Pour les personnes morales associées seulement*

9. Print name of person authorizing this registration / *(either the sole proprietor, a partner or a person acting under a power of attorney)*
If the person is a corporation, complete **additional information** below only. /
Indiquez en lettres majuscules le nom de la personne autorisant l'enregistrement *(propriétaire unique, associé, ou personne habilitée en vertu d'une procuration).* (Si c'est une personne morale qui autorise l'enregistrement, compléter les **renseignements supplémentaires** ci-dessous.)

| Last Name / Nom de famille | First Name / Prénom | Middle Initial / initiale 2e prénom |
| KEATES | LAWRENCE | R |

If person authorizing the registration is not an individual (eg. corporation, trust, syndicate), print name below and do not complete last, first and middle names above. / Si la personne qui autorise l'enregistrement n'est pas un individu (c'est-à-dire une personne morale, un trust ou syndicat) ne pas remlir le nom de famille, prénom et 2e prénom.

| Additional Information / Renseignements supplémentaires | MINISTRY USE ONLY - RÉSERVÉ AU MINISTÈRE |
| | |

It is the responsibility of the applicant(s) to ensure the accuracy of the information submitted. It is an offence under section 10 of the *Business Names Act* to submit false or misleading information. / Il incombe aux demandeurs de veiller à l'exactitude des renseignements présentés. Le demandeur qui fait une déclaration fausse ou trompeuse commet une infraction en vertu de l'article 10 de la *Loi sur les noms commerciaux.*

07219 (2009/10)   © Queen's Printer for Ontario, 2009 / © Imprimeur de la Reine pour l'Ontario, 2009

Incorporation of a Business

Law in Practice: Business incorporation

Kelly MacDonald wishes to incorporate her interior design business. There are three shareholders: Kelly holds 50% of the shares and the other two shareholders, Gabby Nicks and Ryelan Edwards, each hold 25% of the shares. Kelly wants to incorporate the business in the name of CAY DESIGNS INC.

Businesses in Ontario are incorporated under the *Business Corporations Act*. To initiate the process of incorporation, the following forms are completed and filed with the Ministry of Consumer and Government Services. The forms are available at http://www.ontario.ca/en/business/STEL02_163189. Note that a NUANS report (described on page 441) will need to be completed and submitted to the Ministry of Consumer and Government Services with the articles of incorporation.

- Figure 12.14   Form 07116E: Article of Incorporation

- Figure 12.15a   Form 07117: Consent to Act as a First Director—Kelly MacDonald

- Figure 12.15b   Form 07117: Consent to Act as a First Director—Gabby Nicks

- Figure 12.15c   Form 07117: Consent to Act as a First Director—Ryelan Edwards

- Figure 12.16   Form 07200: Ontario Corporation Initial Return/Notice of Change

FIGURE 12.14 Form 07116E: Articles of Incorporation

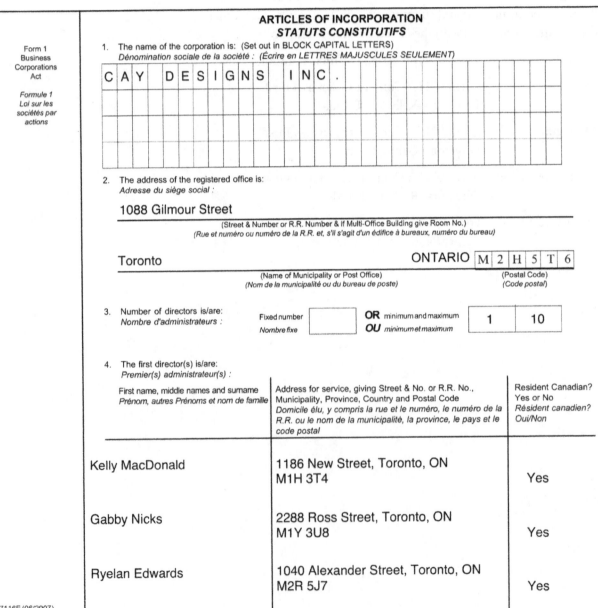

FIGURE 12.14   Continued

2

5.   Restrictions, if any, on business the corporation may carry on or on powers the corporation may exercise.
Limites, s'il y a lieu, imposées aux activités commerciales ou aux pouvoirs de la société.

NONE

6.   The classes and any maximum number of shares that the corporation is authorized to issue:
Catégories et nombre maximal, s'il y a lieu, d'actions que la société est autorisée à émettre :

1. One Class of common shares of unlimited number, to be known as Class A shares.

2. One Class of preference shares of unlimited number, to be known as Class B shares.

3. One Class of preference shares of unlimited number, to be known as Class C shares.

FIGURE 12.14 Continued

3

7. Rights, privileges, restrictions and conditions (if any) attaching to each class of shares and directors authority
with respect to any class of shares which may be issued in series:
*Droits, privilèges, restrictions et conditions, s'il y a lieu, rattachés à chaque catégorie d'actions et pouvoirs des
administrateurs relatifs à chaque catégorie d'actions qui peut être émise en série :*

1. The holders of the Class A shares, which shares shall be designated as common shares, shall be entitled:

(a) to vote at all meetings of shareholders, said vote to be based on one vote for each Class A share held; and

(b) to receive the remaining property of the Corporation upon dissolution.

2. The holders of the Class B shares shall be entitled:

(a) to a cumulative dividend of Two dollars ($2.00) per share per year, to be paid on the 30th day of September in each year; and

(b) upon the liquidation or winding up of the corporation, to repayment of the amount paid for such shares, plus any unpaid dividends, in priority to the Class A shares;

(c) the holders of the Class B shares shall not be entitled to vote at meetings of shareholders except as specifically provided in the Business Corporations Act.

3. The holders of the Class C shares shall be entitled:

(a) to a dividend as fixed by the board of directors, provided that if within six (6) months following the fiscal year end, the board of directors shall not have declared a dividend on the Class C shares for such fiscal year, then the rights of the holders of the Class C shares to such dividends for that fiscal year shall be forever extinguished;

(b) upon the liquidation or winding up of the corporation, to repayment of the amount paid for such Class C shares, plus any declared plus any unpaid dividends, in priority to the Class A and Class B shares;

(c) to redemption to the amount paid for such shares, together with any declared and unpaid dividends, at the option of the corporation. The corporation shall exercise this option by giving notice by mail to each Class C shareholder whose shares are to be redeemed at the last address registered by that shareholder with the corporation. The notice shall specify the date upon which redemption shall take place, and the details concerning the deposit of the shares in exchange for payment of the amount to be paid. From and after the payment by the corporation of the redemption price for the Class C shares redeemed, the shareholder thereof shall have no further right to receive dividends or exercise any rights of the shareholders in respect thereof; and

(d) to vote at all meetings of shareholders, said vote to be based on one vote for each Class C share held.

FIGURE 12.14 Continued

4

8. The issue, transfer or ownership of shares is/is not restricted and the restrictions (if any) are as follows:
L'émission, le transfert ou la propriété d'actions est/n'est pas restreint. Les restrictions, s'il y a lieu, sont les suivantes :

The right to transfer shares of the corporation shall be restricted in that no shareholders shall be entitled to transfer any share or shares without the resolution passed at a meeting of the board of directors or by resolution in writing signed by all of the directors.

07116E (06/2007)

FIGURE 12.14 Continued

5

9. Other provisions if any:
   Autres dispositions, s'il y a lieu :

1. The number of shareholders of the corporation, exclusive of persons who are in the employ of the corporation and exclusive of persons, who, having been informally in the employ of the corporation, were, while in that employment, and have continued after the termination of that employment to be shareholders of the corporation, is limited to not more than fifty (50), two (2) or more persons who are joint registered owners of one or more shares being counted as one shareholder.

2. Any invitation to the public to subscribe for securities of the corporation is prohibited.

3. The corporation may purchase any of its issued shares.

FIGURE 12.14 Continued

10. The names and addresses of the incorporators are:
    Noms et adresses des fondateurs :

6

First name, middle names and surname or corporate name *Prénom, autres prénoms et nom de famille ou dénomination sociale*	Full address for service or if a corporation, the address of the registered or head office giving street & No. or R.R. No., municipality, province, country and postal code *Domicile élu au complet ou, dans le cas d'une société, adresse du siège social ou adresse de l'établissement principal, y compris la rue et le numéro ou le numéro de la R.R., la municipalité, la province, le pays et le code postal*
Kelly MacDonald	1186 New Street, Toronto, ON M1H 3T4
Gabby Nicks	2288 Ross Street, Toronto, ON M1Y 3U8
Ryelan Edwards	1040 Alexander Street, Toronto, ON M2R 5J7

These articles are signed in duplicate.
Les présents statuts sont signés en double exemplaire.

Full name(s) and signature(s) of incorporator(s). In the case of a corporation set out the name of the corporation and the name and office of the person signing on behalf of the corporation
Nom(s) au complet et signature(s) du ou des fondateurs. Si le fondateur est une société, indiquer la dénomination sociale et le nom et le titre de la personne signant au nom de la société

Kelly MacDonald

Signature / signature

Kelly MacDonald

Name of incorporator (or corporation name & signatories name and office)
Nom du fondateur (ou dénomination sociale et nom et titre du signataire)

Gabby Nicks

Signature / signature

Gabby Nicks

Name of incorporator (or corporation name & signatories name and office)
Nom du fondateur (ou dénomination sociale et nom et titre du signataire)

Ryelan Edwards

Signature / signature

Ryelan Edwards

Name of incorporator (or corporation name & signatories name and office)
Nom du fondateur (ou dénomination sociale et nom et titre du signataire)

Signature / signature

Name of incorporator (or corporation name & signatories name and office)
Nom du fondateur (ou dénomination sociale et nom et titre du signataire)

07116E (06/2007)

FIGURE 12.15a Form 07117: Consent to Act as a First Director—Kelly MacDonald

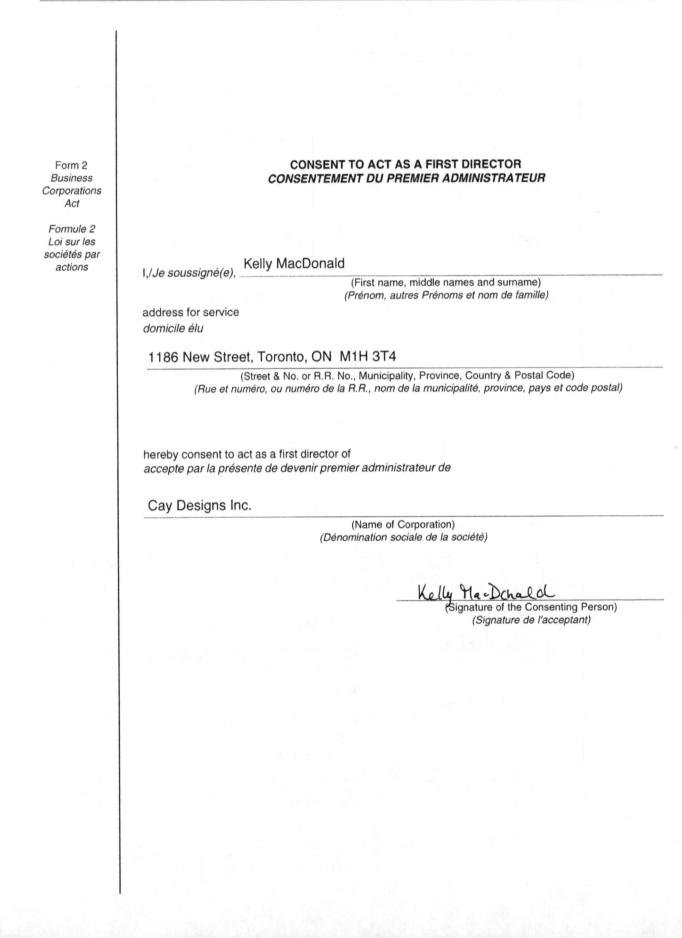

Form 2
*Business
Corporations
Act*

*Formule 2
Loi sur les
sociétés par
actions*

CONSENT TO ACT AS A FIRST DIRECTOR
CONSENTEMENT DU PREMIER ADMINISTRATEUR

I,/*Je soussigné(e),* ___Kelly MacDonald___
(First name, middle names and surname)
(Prénom, autres Prénoms et nom de famille)

address for service
domicile élu

___1186 New Street, Toronto, ON M1H 3T4___
(Street & No. or R.R. No., Municipality, Province, Country & Postal Code)
(Rue et numéro, ou numéro de la R.R., nom de la municipalité, province, pays et code postal)

hereby consent to act as a first director of
accepte par la présente de devenir premier administrateur de

___Cay Designs Inc.___
(Name of Corporation)
(Dénomination sociale de la société)

___Kelly MacDonald___
(Signature of the Consenting Person)
(Signature de l'acceptant)

FIGURE 12.15b   Form 07117: Consent to Act as a First Director—Gabby Nicks

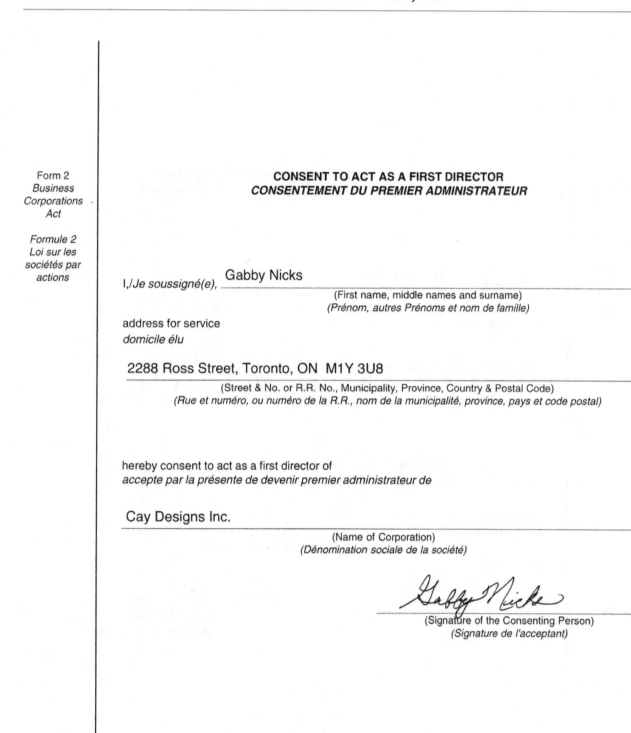

Form 2
Business
Corporations
Act

Formule 2
Loi sur les
sociétés par
actions

CONSENT TO ACT AS A FIRST DIRECTOR
CONSENTEMENT DU PREMIER ADMINISTRATEUR

I,/*Je soussigné(e)*,   Gabby Nicks

(First name, middle names and surname)
(Prénom, autres Prénoms et nom de famille)

address for service
domicile élu

2288 Ross Street, Toronto, ON M1Y 3U8

(Street & No. or R.R. No., Municipality, Province, Country & Postal Code)
(Rue et numéro, ou numéro de la R.R., nom de la municipalité, province, pays et code postal)

hereby consent to act as a first director of
accepte par la présente de devenir premier administrateur de

Cay Designs Inc.

(Name of Corporation)
(Dénomination sociale de la société)

(Signature of the Consenting Person)
(Signature de l'acceptant)

FIGURE 12.15c   Form 07117: Consent to Act as a First Director—Ryelan Edwards

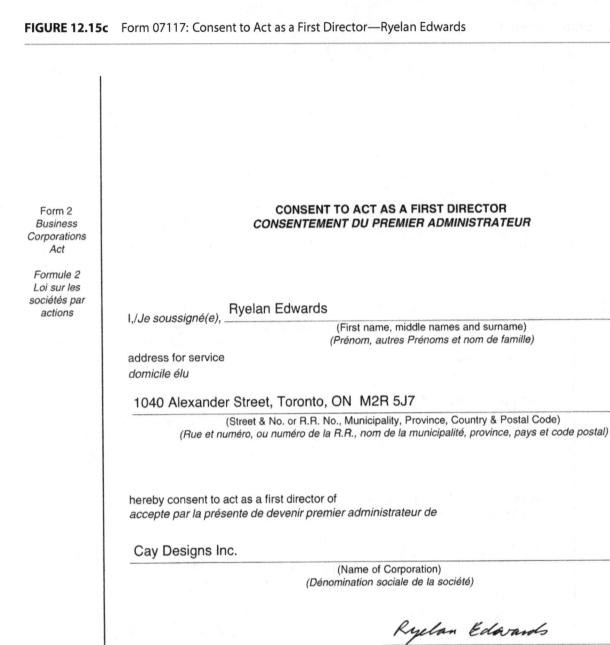

Form 2
*Business
Corporations
Act*

*Formule 2
Loi sur les
sociétés par
actions*

CONSENT TO ACT AS A FIRST DIRECTOR
CONSENTEMENT DU PREMIER ADMINISTRATEUR

I,/*Je soussigné(e),*   Ryelan Edwards
(First name, middle names and surname)
(Prénom, autres Prénoms et nom de famille)

address for service
domicile élu

1040 Alexander Street, Toronto, ON M2R 5J7
(Street & No. or R.R. No., Municipality, Province, Country & Postal Code)
(Rue et numéro, ou numéro de la R.R., nom de la municipalité, province, pays et code postal)

hereby consent to act as a first director of
accepte par la présente de devenir premier administrateur de

Cay Designs Inc.
(Name of Corporation)
(Dénomination sociale de la société)

Ryelan Edwards
(Signature of the Consenting Person)
(Signature de l'acceptant)

FIGURE 12.16 Form 07200: Ontario Corporation Initial Return/Notice of Change

---

Ontario

Ministry of Government Services	Ministère des Services gouvernementaux	For Ministry Use Only / À l'usage du ministère seulement
Central Production and Verification Services Branch 393 University Ave, Suite 200 Toronto ON M5G 2M2	Direction des services centraux de production et de vérification 393, av University, bureau 200 Toronto ON M5G 2M2	Page/Page 1 of/de 3

Form 1 - Ontario Corporation Initial Return / Notice of Change
Formule 1 - Personnes morales de l'Ontario Rapport initial / Avis de modification
Corporations Information Act / Loi sur les renseignements exigés des personnes morales

Please type or print all information in block capital letters using black ink.
Prière de dactylographier les renseignements ou de les écrire en caractères d'imprimerie à l'encre noire.

1.
Notice of Change
	Initial Return / Rapport initial	Avis de modification
Business Corporation/ Société par actions	✓	
Not-For-Profit Corporation/ Personne morale sans but lucratif		

2. Ontario Corporation Number
Numéro matricule de la personne morale en Ontario

130930402

3. Date of Incorporation or Amalgamation/
Date de constitution ou fusion

Year/Année	Month/Mois	Day/Jour
2011	02	03

For Ministry Use Only / À l'usage du ministère seulement

4. Corporation Name Including Punctuation/Raison sociale de la personne morale, y compris la ponctuation

Cay Designs Inc.

5. Address of Registered or Head Office/Adresse du siège social

c/o / a/s

Street No./N° civique: 1088 Street Name/Nom de la rue: Gilmour Street Suite/Bureau:

Street Name (cont'd)/Nom de la rue (suite)

City/Town/Ville: Toronto **ONTARIO, CANADA**

Postal Code/Code postal: M2H 5T6

For Ministry Use Only/ À l'usage du ministère seulement

6. Mailing Address/Adresse postale

✓	Same as Registered or Head Office/ Même que siège social
	Not Applicable/ Ne s'applique pas

Street No./N° civique

Street Name/Nom de la rue Suite/Bureau

Street Name (cont'd)/Nom de la rue (suite)

City/Town/Ville

Province, State/Province, État Country/Pays Postal Code/Code postal

7. Language of Preference/Langue préférée

English - Anglais ✓   French - Français

8. Information on Directors/Officers must be completed on Schedule A as requested. If additional space is required, photocopy Schedule A./Les renseignements sur les administrateurs ou les dirigeants doivent être fournis dans l'Annexe A, tel que demandé. Si vous avez besoin de plus d'espace, vous pouvez photocopier l'Annexe A.

Number of Schedule A(s) submitted/Nombre d'Annexes A présentées **2** (At least one Schedule A must be submitted/Au moins une Annexe A doit être présentée)

9. (Print or type name in full of the person authorizing filing / Dactylographier ou inscrire le prénom et le nom en caractères d'imprimerie de la personne qui autorise l'enregistrement)

I/Je **Kelly MacDonald**

certify that the information set out herein, is true and correct.
atteste que les renseignements précités sont véridiques et exacts.

Check appropriate box
Cocher la case pertinente

D) ✓ Director/Administrateur

O) ☐ Officer /Dirigeant

P) ☐ Other individual having knowledge of the affairs of the Corporation/Autre personne ayant connaissance des activités de la personne morale

Note/Remarque : Sections 13 and 14 of the *Corporations Information Act* provide penalties for making false or misleading statements or omissions. Les articles 13 et 14 de la *Loi sur les renseignements exigés des personnes morales* prévoient des peines en cas de déclaration fausse ou trompeuse, ou d'omission.

07200 (2011/06) © Queen's Printer for Ontario, 2011 / © Imprimeur de la Reine pour l'Ontario, 2011 Page 1 of/de 3

FIGURE 12.16 Continued

Form 1 - Ontario Corporation/Formule 1 - Personnes morales de l'Ontario
Schedule A/Annexe A

For Ministry Use Only
À l'usage du ministère seulement
Page/Page **2** of/de **3**

Please type or print all information in block capital letters using black ink. Prière de dactylographier les renseignements ou de les écrire en caractères d'imprimerie à l'encre noire.	Ontario Corporation Number Numéro matricule de la personne morale en Ontario 130930402	Date of Incorporation or Amalgamation Date de constitution ou fusion Year/Année Month/Mois Day/Jour 2011 02 03

DIRECTOR / OFFICER INFORMATION - RENSEIGNEMENTS RELATIFS AUX ADMINISTRATEURS/DIRIGEANTS
Full Name and Address for Service/Nom et domicile élu

Last Name/Nom de famille	First Name/Prénom	Middle Names/Autres prénoms
MacDonald	Kelly	

Street Number/Numéro civique: 1186   Suite/Bureau:

Street Name/Nom de la rue: New Street

Street Name (cont'd)/Nom de la rue (suite):

City/Town/Ville: Toronto

Province, State/Province, État	Country/Pays	Postal Code/Code postal
Ontario	Canada	M1H 3T4

*OTHER TITLES (Please Specify)
*AUTRES TITRES (Veuillez préciser)
Chair / Président du conseil
Chair Person / Président du conseil
Chairman / Président du conseil
Chairwoman / Présidente du conseil
Vice-Chair / Vice-président du conseil
Vice-President / Vice-président
Assistant Secretary / Secrétaire adjoint
Assistant Treasurer / Trésorier adjoint
Chief Manager / Directeur exécutif
Executive Director / Directeur administratif
Managing Director / Administrateur délégué
Chief Executive Officer / Directeur général
Chief Financial Officer /
Agent en chef des finances
Chief Information Officer /
Directeur général de l'information
Chief Operating Officer /
Administrateur en chef des opérations
Chief Administrative Officer /
Directeur général de l'administration
Comptroller / Contrôleur
Authorized Signing Officer /
Signataire autorisé
Other (Untitled) / Autre (sans titre)

Director Information/Renseignements relatifs aux administrateurs

Resident Canadian/ ✓ YES/OUI ☐ NO/NON   (Resident Canadian applies to directors of business corporations only.)/
Résident canadien   (Résident canadien ne s'applique qu'aux administrateurs de sociétés par actions)

	Year/Année	Month/Mois	Day/Jour		Year/Année	Month/Mois	Day/Jour
Date Elected/ Date d'élection	2011	02	03	Date Ceased/ Date de cessation			

Officer Information/Renseignements relatifs aux dirigeants

	PRESIDENT/PRÉSIDENT			SECRETARY/SECRÉTAIRE			TREASURER/TRÉSORIER			GENERAL MANAGER/ DIRECTEUR GÉNÉRAL			***OTHER/AUTRE**		
	Year/Année	Month/Mois	Day/Jour	Year/Année	Month/Mois	Day/Jour	Year/Année	Month/Mois	Day/Jour	Year/Année	Month/Mois	Day/Jour	Year/Année	Month/Mois	Day/Jour
Date Appointed/ Date de nomination	2011	02	03												
Date Ceased/ Date de cessation															

DIRECTOR / OFFICER INFORMATION - RENSEIGNEMENTS RELATIFS AUX ADMINISTRATEURS/DIRIGEANTS
Full Name and Address for Service/Nom et domicile élu

Last Name/Nom de famille	First Name/Prénom	Middle Names/Autres prénoms
Nicks	Gabby	

Street Number/Numéro civique: 2288   Suite/Bureau:

Street Name/Nom de la rue: Ross Street

Street Name (cont'd)/Nom de la rue (suite):

City/Town/Ville: Toronto

Province, State/Province, État	Country/Pays	Postal Code/Code postal
Ontario	Canada	M1Y 3U8

*OTHER TITLES (Please Specify)
*AUTRES TITRES (Veuillez préciser)
Chair / Président du conseil
Chair Person / Président du conseil
Chairman / Président du conseil
Chairwoman / Présidente du conseil
Vice-Chair / Vice-président du conseil
Vice-President / Vice-président
Assistant Secretary / Secrétaire adjoint
Assistant Treasurer / Trésorier adjoint
Chief Manager / Directeur exécutif
Executive Director / Directeur administratif
Managing Director / Administrateur délégué
Chief Executive Officer / Directeur général
Chief Financial Officer /
Agent en chef des finances
Chief Information Officer /
Directeur général de l'information
Chief Operating Officer /
Administrateur en chef des opérations
Chief Administrative Officer /
Directeur général de l'administration
Comptroller / Contrôleur
Authorized Signing Officer /
Signataire autorisé
Other (Untitled) / Autre (sans titre)

Director Information/Renseignements relatifs aux administrateurs

Resident Canadian/ ✓ YES/OUI ☐ NO/NON   (Resident Canadian applies to directors of business corporations only.)/
Résident canadien   (Résident canadien ne s'applique qu'aux administrateurs de sociétés par actions)

	Year/Année	Month/Mois	Day/Jour		Year/Année	Month/Mois	Day/Jour
Date Elected/ Date d'élection	2011	02	03	Date Ceased/ Date de cessation			

Officer Information/Renseignements relatifs aux dirigeants

	PRESIDENT/PRÉSIDENT			SECRETARY/SECRÉTAIRE			TREASURER/TRÉSORIER			GENERAL MANAGER/ DIRECTEUR GÉNÉRAL			***OTHER/AUTRE**		
	Year/Année	Month/Mois	Day/Jour	Year/Année	Month/Mois	Day/Jour	Year/Année	Month/Mois	Day/Jour	Year/Année	Month/Mois	Day/Jour	Year/Année	Month/Mois	Day/Jour
Date Appointed/ Date de nomination				2011	02	03									
Date Ceased/ Date de cessation															

07200 (2011/06)

FIGURE 12.16 Continued

Form 1 - Ontario Corporation/Formule 1 - Personnes morales de l'Ontario
Schedule A/Annexe A

For Ministry Use Only
A l'usage du ministère seulement
Page/Page 3 of/de 3

Please type or print all information in block capital letters using black ink. Prière de dactylographier les renseignements ou de les écrire en caractères d'imprimerie à l'encre noire.	Ontario Corporation Number Numéro matricule de la personne morale en Ontario	Date of Incorporation or Amalgamation Date de constitution ou fusion
	130930402	Year/Année 2011 Month/Mois 02 Day/Jour 03

DIRECTOR / OFFICER INFORMATION - RENSEIGNEMENTS RELATIFS AUX ADMINISTRATEURS/DIRIGEANTS
Full Name and Address for Service/Nom et domicile élu

Last Name/Nom de famille	First Name/Prénom	Middle Names/Autres prénoms
Edwards	Ryelan	

Street Number/Numéro civique: 1040 Suite/Bureau:

Street Name/Nom de la rue: Alexander Street

Street Name (cont'd)/Nom de la rue (suite):

City/Town/Ville: Toronto

Province, State/Province, État: Ontario   Country/Pays: Canada   Postal Code/Code postal: M2R 5J7

*OTHER TITLES (Please Specify)
*AUTRES TITRES (Veuillez préciser)
Chair / Président du conseil
Chair Person / Président du conseil
Chairman / Président du conseil
Chairwoman / Présidente du conseil
Vice-Chair / Vice-président du conseil
Vice-President / Vice-président
Assistant Secretary / Secrétaire adjoint
Assistant Treasurer / Trésorier adjoint
Chief Manager / Directeur exécutif
Executive Director / Directeur administratif
Managing Director / Administrateur délégué
Chief Executive Officer / Directeur général
Chief Financial Officer /
Agent en chef des finances
Chief Information Officer /
Directeur général de l'information
Chief Operating Officer /
Administrateur en chef des opérations
Chief Administrative Officer /
Directeur général de l'administration
Comptroller / Contrôleur
Authorized Signing Officer /
Signataire autorisé
Other (Untitled) / Autre (sans titre)

Director Information/Renseignements relatifs aux administrateurs

Resident Canadian/Résident canadien: ✓ YES/OUI ☐ NO/NON

(Resident Canadian applies to directors of business corporations only.)/
(Résident canadien ne s'applique qu'aux administrateurs de sociétés par actions)

Date Elected/Date d'élection: Year/Année 2011 Month/Mois 02 Day/Jour 03
Date Ceased/Date de cessation: Year/Année __ Month/Mois __ Day/Jour __

Officer Information/Renseignements relatifs aux dirigeants

	PRESIDENT/PRÉSIDENT Year/Année Month/Mois Day/Jour	SECRETARY/SECRÉTAIRE Year/Année Month/Mois Day/Jour	TREASURER/TRÉSORIER Year/Année Month/Mois Day/Jour	GENERAL MANAGER/DIRECTEUR GÉNÉRAL Year/Année Month/Mois Day/Jour	*OTHER/AUTRE Year/Année Month/Mois Day/Jour
Date Appointed/Date de nomination			2011 02 03		
Date Ceased/Date de cessation					

DIRECTOR / OFFICER INFORMATION - RENSEIGNEMENTS RELATIFS AUX ADMINISTRATEURS/DIRIGEANTS
Full Name and Address for Service/Nom et domicile élu

Last Name/Nom de famille	First Name/Prénom	Middle Names/Autres prénoms

Street Number/Numéro civique: Suite/Bureau:

Street Name/Nom de la rue:

Street Name (cont'd)/Nom de la rue (suite):

City/Town/Ville:

Province, State/Province, État: Country/Pays: Postal Code/Code postal:

*OTHER TITLES (Please Specify)
*AUTRES TITRES (Veuillez préciser)
Chair / Président du conseil
Chair Person / Président du conseil
Chairman / Président du conseil
Chairwoman / Présidente du conseil
Vice-Chair / Vice-président du conseil
Vice-President / Vice-président
Assistant Secretary / Secrétaire adjoint
Assistant Treasurer / Trésorier adjoint
Chief Manager / Directeur exécutif
Executive Director / Directeur administratif
Managing Director / Administrateur délégué
Chief Executive Officer / Directeur général
Chief Financial Officer /
Agent en chef des finances
Chief Information Officer /
Directeur général de l'information
Chief Operating Officer /
Administrateur en chef des opérations
Chief Administrative Officer /
Directeur général de l'administration
Comptroller / Contrôleur
Authorized Signing Officer /
Signataire autorisé
Other (Untitled) / Autre (sans titre)

Director Information/Renseignements relatifs aux administrateurs

Resident Canadian/Résident canadien: ☐ YES/OUI ☐ NO/NON

(Resident Canadian applies to directors of business corporations only.)/
(Résident canadien ne s'applique qu'aux administrateurs de sociétés par actions)

Date Elected/Date d'élection: Year/Année __ Month/Mois __ Day/Jour __
Date Ceased/Date de cessation: Year/Année __ Month/Mois __ Day/Jour __

Officer Information/Renseignements relatifs aux dirigeants

	PRESIDENT/PRÉSIDENT Year/Année Month/Mois Day/Jour	SECRETARY/SECRÉTAIRE Year/Année Month/Mois Day/Jour	TREASURER/TRÉSORIER Year/Année Month/Mois Day/Jour	GENERAL MANAGER/DIRECTEUR GÉNÉRAL Year/Année Month/Mois Day/Jour	*OTHER/AUTRE Year/Année Month/Mois Day/Jour
Date Appointed/Date de nomination					
Date Ceased/Date de cessation					

07200 (2011/06)

Residential Tenancies

Law in Practice: Rent increase

Olivia Taylor and Emily Campbell commenced their tenancy at 378 Hunter Street West, Apt. 7, Peterborough on January 1, 2010. The tenants signed a one-year lease agreeing to pay $800.00 including heat and hydro on the first day of each month.

The landlord, Paul Moore, who resides at 210 Reid Street, Peterborough, wishes to increase the tenants' rent on the anniversary date of when the tenancy commenced. Mr. Moore researched the *Residential Tenancies Act* to determine when the rent can legally be increased and by how much. According to s. 119(1) of the RTA, he may increase the rent by the guideline amount each 12-month period from when a tenant begins a tenancy or from the time of the last rent increase. After reviewing the Landlord and Tenant Board website, Mr. Moore was able to determine that the guideline percentage for 2011 is 2.1%. He is required to give the tenants 90 days' notice and, subsequently, he would like the rent increase to take effect on the anniversary date of their occupancy.

The landlord signed the Form N1 Notice of Rent Increas (figure 12.17) and delivered it to the tenants the day before the notice period began.

Residential tenancies in Ontario are governed by the *Residential Tenancies Act* (RTA). The RTA sets out the rights and responsibilities of landlords and tenants who rent residential properties. Tenants are protected from unfair rent increases and illegal termination of their tenancy. The required forms are listed below; forms and instructions are available at http://www.ltb.gov.on.ca/en/index.htm.

- Figure 12.17   Form N1: Notice of Rent Increase

FIGURE 12.17   Form N1: Notice of Rent Increase

Notice of Rent Increase
Form N1

Read the instructions carefully before completing this form.

To: (Tenant's name and address)	From: (Landlord's name and address)
Olivia Taylor and Emily Campbell 378 Hunter Street West, Apt 7 Peterborough, Ontario, K9J 6Z8	Paul Moore 210 Reid Street Peterborough, Ontario, K9H 3V8

Address of the Rental Unit:

378 Hunter Street West, Apt 7
Peterborough, Ontario, K9J 6Z8

Your New Rent

On ___01/01/2011___ , your rent will increase to $ ___816.80___
    (day/month/year)

per ___month___ .
    (month, week, etc.)

This rent includes the basic rent for your rental unit, plus any amount you pay separately to your landlord for services.

Explanation of the Rent Increase

This is a rent increase of: $ ___16.80___ per ___month___ or ___2.1___ %.
                                                   (month, week, etc.)

Shade one of the following:

☒ This rent increase is less than or equal to the rent increase guideline and does not need approval by an order under the *Residential Tenancies Act*.

OR

☐ This rent increase is more than the rent increase guideline, but:

1. ☐ The rent increase has been approved by an order under the *Tenant Protection Act* or the *Residential Tenancies Act*.

2. ☐ The rent increase must be approved by an order under the *Tenant Protection Act* or the *Residential Tenancies Act*. I have applied to the Tribunal or the Board for a Rent Increase Above the Guideline.

FIGURE 12.17 Continued

Important Information About the Law	1. The landlord must give the tenant this notice at least 90 days before the date of the rent increase. A landlord may increase the rent if at least 12 months have passed since the last rent increase or since a new tenant moved into the rental unit. No Notice of Rent Increase is required where the landlord and tenant have signed an Agreement to Increase the Rent Above the Guideline (Form N10).

2. A tenant does not have to sign a new lease when a fixed term tenancy ends. If the tenant decides not to sign a new lease, the tenant does not have to move, but the tenancy becomes "month-to-month".

If a tenant plans to move, the tenant must notify the landlord on Form N9 (Tenant's Notice to Terminate the Tenancy) at least 60 days before the lease expires if the tenant has a fixed term of tenancy or 60 days before the end of a monthly or yearly rental period. The tenant must notify the landlord on Form N9 at least 28 days before the end of a weekly rental period.

3. If the rent increase needs approval by an order under the *Tenant Protection Act* or the *Residential Tenancies Act,* the tenant is not required to pay more than the guideline increase until the order is issued. If the tenant only pays the guideline increase, the tenant may owe the landlord once the order is issued.

4. If you have any questions about the law related to rent increases and how it applies to this notice, you can contact the Landlord and Tenant Board at **416-645-8080** or toll-free at **1-888-332-3234**. Or, you may also visit the Board's website at **www.LTB.gov.on.ca** for further information.

Signature   ☒ Landlord   ☐ Agent

Name of Person Signing Paul Moore	Phone Number 705 748 4255
Signature	Date October 2nd, 2010

Agent Information   (if applicable)

Name		Company Name (if applicable)	
Mailing Address			Phone Number
Municipality (city, town, etc.)	Province	Postal Code	Fax Number

Law in Practice: Notice of termination for non-payment of rent

The tenants, Evan Davis and Julie Anderson, have resided at 408 Lake Street, Peterborough since October 1, 2007. Their lease was for a period of one year and they paid $950.00 including heat and hydro on the first day of each month. The tenants paid a last month's rent deposit of $950.00 as well as first month's rent on October 1, 2007 when they received keys for the apartment. Each 12-month period, the landlord gave the tenants the last month's rent deposit interest. The tenants have never received a rent increase.

The landlord, Rob Smith, resides at 97 Rink Street, Peterborough. Up until May of 2010, the tenants had paid their monthly rent on time. On May 1, 2010, the tenants contacted the landlord to inform him that they would have to pay their rent on the 15th of the month because of a recent job change. Since the tenants normally paid on time, the landlord did not serve them with an N4 Notice to End a Tenancy Early for Non-payment of Rent (figure 12.18). On May 20th, the tenants had failed to pay the monthly rent to the landlord and instead contacted Mr. Smith and told him they would pay the outstanding amount along with June's rent payment on June 1st. On June 3, 2010, the rent moneys were not received. The landlord prepared, signed, and served an N4 Notice for Non-payment of Rent for the months of May and June. The landlord, as required by law, dated the termination date 14 days after serving.

As of the termination date, the tenants had made one payment of $200.00. Mr. Smith attempted to contact the tenants by telephone, but was unsuccessful. The following day, the landlord prepared the L1 Application (figure 12.19), corresponding with the N4 Notice, and sent both by fax to the Landlord and Tenant Board. The landlord requested the Notice of Hearing to be sent to his fax number and intends to serve the tenants with the Notice of Hearing and L1 Application on the day the Notice is received.

- Figure 12.18 Form N4: Notice to End a Tenancy Early for Non-payment of Rent

- Figure 12.19 Form L1: Landlord's Application to Evict a Tenant for Non-payment of Rent

FIGURE 12.18   Form N4: Notice to End a Tenancy Early for Non-payment of Rent

---

Notice To End a Tenancy Early For Non-payment of Rent

Form N4

To: (Tenant's name)	**From:** (Landlord's name)
Evan Davis and Julie Anderson	Rob Smith

This is a legal notice that could lead to you being evicted from your home.

Address of the Rental Unit

Street Number   Street Name
`4` `0` `8` `   ` `L` `A` `K` `E`

Street Type (e.g. Street, Avenue, Road)   Direction (e.g. East)   Unit/Apt./Suite
`S` `T` `R` `E` `E` `T`

Municipality (city, town, etc.)   Province   Postal Code
`P` `E` `T` `E` `R` `B` `O` `R` `O` `U` `G` `H`   `O` `N`   `K` `9` `J`   `2` `H` `2`

This information is from your landlord:

I am giving you this notice because I believe you owe me $ `1` , `9` `0` `0` . `0` `0` **in rent.**

See the table on the next page for the details about how I calculated this amount.

I can apply to the Landlord and Tenant Board to have you evicted if you do not:

- **pay this amount* by** `1` `7` / `0` `6` / `2` `0` `1` `0`   This date is called the **termination date**.
  dd   mm   yyyy

or

- **move out by the termination date**

* If another rent payment comes due on or before the date you make the above payment to your landlord, you must also pay this extra amount.

WHAT YOU NEED TO KNOW
The following information is provided by the Landlord and Tenant Board

The termination date	The date that the landlord gives you in this notice to pay or move out must be at least: • 14 days after the landlord gives you the notice, if you rent by the month or year, or • 7 days after the landlord gives you the notice, if you rent by the day or week.
What if you agree with the notice	If you agree that you owe the amount that the landlord is claiming, you should pay this amount by the termination date in this notice. If you do so, this notice becomes void and the landlord cannot apply to the Board to evict you. If you do not pay the amount owing, and the landlord applies to the Board to evict you, you will likely have to pay the landlord's filing fee of $170.00, plus what you owe. **If you move out** by the date in this notice, your tenancy will end on the termination date. However, you may still owe money to your landlord. Your landlord will not be able to apply to the Board but they may still take you to Court for this money.
What if you disagree with the notice	If you disagree with what the landlord has put in this notice, you do not have to move out. You could talk to your landlord. You may also want to get legal advice. If you cannot work things out, and the landlord applies to the Board, you will be able to go to a hearing and explain why you disagree.

10101

Version. 15/10/2009   This form has been approved by the Landlord and Tenant Board   Page 1 of 2

FIGURE 12.18   Continued

| How you will know if the landlord applies to the Board | The earliest date that the landlord can apply to the Board is the day after the termination date in this notice. If the landlord does apply, the Board will schedule a hearing and send you a letter. The landlord must also give you a copy of the Notice of Hearing and the application. |

| What you can do if the landlord applies to the Board | • Get legal advice immediately; you may be eligible for legal aid services.
• Talk to your landlord about working out a payment plan.
• Go to the hearing where you can respond to your landlord's claims; in most cases, before the hearing starts you can also talk to a Board mediator about mediating a payment plan. |

| How to get more information | For more information about this notice or about your rights, you can contact the Landlord and Tenant Board. You can reach the Board by phone at **416-645-8080** or toll-free at **1-888-332-3234**. You can also visit the Board's website at **www.LTB.gov.on.ca**. |

This table is completed by the landlord to show how they calculated the total amount of rent claimed on page 1:

Rent Period From: (dd/mm/yyyy)	To: (dd/mm/yyyy)	Rent Charged $	Rent Paid $	Rent Owing $
01/05/2010	31/05/2010	,950.00	,0.00	,950.00
01/06/2010	30/06/2010	,950.00	,0.00	,950.00
/ /	/ /	,.	,.	,.

Total Rent Owing $ 1,900.00

Signature   ☒ Landlord   ☐ Agent

| Signature | Date (dd/mm/yyyy)

03/06/2010 |

First Name

R O B

Last Name

S M I T H

Company Name (if applicable)

Mailing Address

9 7   R I N K   S T R E E T

Unit/Apt./Suite

Municipality (city, town, etc.)   P E T E R B O R O U G H

Province   O N

Postal Code   K 9 J   3 K 9

Phone Number   (7 0 5) 7 4 9 1 8 7 3

Fax Number   (7 0 5) 7 4 9 7 9 8 2

E-mail Address

10101

FIGURE 12.19 Form L1: Landlord's Application to Evict a Tenant for Non-payment of Rent

---

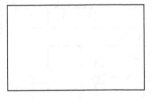

Landlord
and
Tenant
Board

Ontario

Application to evict a tenant for non-payment of rent and to collect rent the tenant owes
FORM L1

Information for the Tenant from the Landlord

I am applying to the Landlord and Tenant Board for an order:

- **to evict you because you owe rent, and**
- **to collect the money you owe me.**

I believe that you owe me a total of $ | | 1 | , | 8 | 7 | 0 | . | 0 | 0 | **as of** | 1 | 8 | / | 0 | 6 | / | 2 | 0 | 1 | 0 |
dd   mm   yyyy

This amount includes the filing fee for this application ($170.00). You may also owe me any new rent that comes due after I file this application. To see how I arrived at this amount, go to page 4.

Information for the Tenant from the Landlord and Tenant Board

IF YOU AGREE with the amount the landlord claims you owe:

If you agree with the amount the landlord claims you owe, you can do one of the following. But read all three options before you decide. You may want to get legal advice first.

Pay everything you owe

If you pay all the rent you owe plus the landlord's filing fee before the Board issues an order about this application, the landlord will not be able to evict you for not paying the rent. The Board usually issues an order after holding a hearing. For information about the hearing, see the attached Notice of Hearing.

The amount you have to pay includes:

- the amount of rent the landlord is claiming in this application (go to Part 4, Section 1 on page 4), plus
- any new rent that has come due after the application was filed, plus
- the landlord's $170.00 filing fee.

You can pay these amounts to the landlord directly, or to the Board in trust. If you pay everything to the landlord, be sure to get a receipt.

Once you have paid everything, you should contact the Board to make sure the hearing has been cancelled. If it has not been cancelled, you will need to go to the hearing.

Work out a payment plan

If you cannot pay everything you owe right now, you can contact your landlord to see if they are willing to work out a payment plan.

If you and the landlord reach an agreement, you or your landlord can file a copy of your written agreement with the Board. The Board can issue a consent order based on the payment plan you have agreed to. If the Board issues a consent order, you will not have to attend the hearing.

If you and the landlord cannot reach an agreement, you will need to go to the hearing.

The Landlord and Tenant Board collects the personal information requested on this form under section 185 of the *Residential Tenancies Act, 2006.* This information will be used to determine applications under this Act. After an application is filed, all information may become available to the public. Any questions about this collection may be directed to a Customer Service Representative at **416-645-8080** or toll-free at **1-888-332-3234.**

For Office use only : File Number: | | | | — | | | | | |

10101

FIGURE 12.19 Continued

Go to the hearing	The date, time and location of the hearing are shown on the Notice of Hearing that is attached to this application.
	At the hearing, you can explain why you think you should not be evicted and you can ask the Board for more time to pay the money you owe. You will also be able to raise other issues such as maintenance problems or harassment. It is important that you bring evidence to support your case.
	If you would like to resolve this application by mediation instead of the formal hearing process, in most cases you can speak to a Board mediator on the day of your hearing.
	After the hearing the Board will make a decision and issue an order that will be sent to you by mail. The order will tell you what you have to pay. You should read the order to be sure it is correct and that you understand it.

IF YOU DO NOT AGREE with the amount the landlord claims you owe:

If you do not agree with the amount your landlord claims you owe, you can talk to your landlord to see if both of you can agree on a different amount. You may want to get legal advice.

If you and your landlord agree on a different amount	If you and your landlord can reach an agreement about the amount you owe, read the options above called **Pay everything you owe**, **Work out a payment plan** and **Go to the hearing**. You can follow one of those options, but use the different amount you and your landlord have agreed on.
If you and your landlord cannot agree on a different amount	You will need to go to the hearing. The date, time and location of the hearing are shown on the attached Notice of Hearing.
	At the hearing, you can explain why you disagree with the amount the landlord claims you owe and why you think you should not be evicted. If the Board decides that you owe money, you can ask for more time to pay it. You will also be able to raise other issues such as maintenance problems or harassment. It is important that you bring evidence to support your case.
	If you would like to resolve this application by mediation instead of the formal hearing process, in most cases you can speak to a Board mediator on the day of your hearing.
	After the hearing the Board will make a decision and issue an order that will be sent to you by mail. The order will tell you what you have to pay. You should read the order to be sure it is correct and that you understand it.

For more information:

You can contact the Landlord and Tenant Board at **416-645-8080** or toll-free at **1-888-332-3234** or visit the Board's website at **www.LTB.gov.on.ca**.

10101

FIGURE 12.19 Continued

THE LANDLORD'S APPLICATION

Parts 1 to 7 of this application have been completed by the landlord.

Read the Instructions carefully before completing this Form. Print or Type in Uppercase.

Part 1: RENTAL UNIT COVERED BY THIS APPLICATION

Street Number
`4` `0` `8`

Street Name
`L` `A` `K` `E`

Street Type (e.g. Street, Avenue, Road)
`S` `T` `R` `E` `E` `T`

Direction (e.g. East)

Unit/Apt./Suite

Municipality (city, town, etc.)
`P` `E` `T` `E` `R` `B` `O` `R` `O` `U` `G` `H`

Province
`O` `N`

Postal Code
`K` `9` `J` `2` `H` `2`

Related Applications
List the file numbers of any other applications to the Board that relate to the same rental unit.

File Number 1

File Number 2

Part 2: TENANT NAMES AND ADDRESSES

Tenant 1: First Name (If there are more than 2 tenants, complete a Schedule of Parties form and file it with this application)   ☒ Male   ☐ Female
`E` `V` `A` `N`

Tenant 1: Last Name
`D` `A` `V` `I` `S`

Tenant 2: First Name   ☐ Male   ☒ Female
`J` `U` `L` `I` `E`

Tenant 2: Last Name
`A` `N` `D` `E` `R` `S` `O` `N`

Mailing Address   (if different from rental unit address above)

Unit/Apt./Suite

Municipality (city, town, etc.)

Province   Postal Code

Day Phone Number
( )

Evening Phone Number
( )

Fax Number
( )

E-mail Address

Part 3: REASON FOR THIS APPLICATION

I am applying for an order to end the tenancy and evict the tenant and to collect:

☒ the rent the tenant owes me up to the date they move out of the rental unit, and

☐ an amount for charges related to NSF cheques the tenant gave me.

Is the tenant still in possession of the rental unit on the date this application is filed with the Board?   ☒ Yes ☐ No

The tenancy agreement requires the tenant to pay rent by the ☐ week ☒ month ☐ other(specify) _____

The amount of rent currently on deposit: $ `   ` , `9` `5` `0` . `0` `0`

The date the rent deposit was collected: `0` `1` / `1` `0` / `2` `0` `0` `7`
dd   mm   yyyy

The last period for which interest on the rent deposit was paid: `0` `1` / `1` `0` / `2` `0` `0` `7` to `3` `0` / `0` `9` / `2` `0` `1` `0`
dd   mm   yyyy   dd   mm   yyyy

10101

FIGURE 12.19   Continued

Part 4: DETAILS OF THE LANDLORD'S CLAIM

Section 1. Rent Owing

I have calculated the amount of rent the tenant owes me as follows:

Rent Period From: (dd/mm/yyyy)	Rent Period To: (dd/mm/yyyy)	Rent Charged $	Rent Paid $	Rent Owing $
0 1 / 0 5 / 2 0 1 0	3 1 / 0 5 / 2 0 1 0	, 9 5 0 . 0 0	, 0 . 0 0	, 9 5 0 . 0 0
0 1 / 0 6 / 2 0 1 0	3 0 / 0 6 / 2 0 1 0	, 9 5 0 . 0 0	, 2 0 0 . 0 0	, 7 5 0 . 0 0
/ /	/ /	, .	, .	, .
			Total Rent Owing $	1 , 7 0 0 . 0 0

Section 2. NSF Cheque Charges

I have calculated the amount of NSF cheque charges and related administration charges the tenant owes me as follows:

Cheque Amount $	Date of Cheque dd/mm/yyyy	Date NSF Charge Incurred dd/mm/yyyy	Bank Charge for NSF Cheque $	Landlord's Administration Charge $	Total Charge $
.	/ /	/ /	.	.	.
.	/ /	/ /	.	.	.
.	/ /	/ /	.	.	.
.	/ /	/ /	.	.	.
.	/ /	/ /	.	.	.
				Total NSF Related Charges Owing $	, .

Attach additional sheets if necessary.

Part 5: TOTAL AMOUNT OWING

Total rent owing:	$	1 , 7 0 0 . 0 0
Total NSF cheque charges owing:	$	, .
Application filing fee:	$	1 7 0 . 0 0
Total:	$	1 , 8 7 0 . 0 0

10101

FIGURE 12.19 Continued

Part 6: LANDLORD'S NAME AND ADDRESS

First Name   (If there is more than 1 landlord, complete a Schedule of Parties form and file it with this application)   ☒ Male   ☐ Female   ☐ Company

`R O B`

Last Name

`S M I T H`

Street Address

`9 7   R I N K   S T R E E T`

Unit/Apt./Suite   Municipality (city, town, etc.)   Province   Postal Code

`P E T E R B O R O U G H`   `O N`   `K 9 J   3 K 9`

Day Phone Number   Evening Phone Number   Fax Number

`( 7 0 5 ) 7 4 9   1 8 7 3`   `(        )`   `( 7 0 5 ) 7 4 9   7 9 8 2`

E-mail Address

If the person who signs this application is an agent or an officer of a corporation, you must provide the following information:

First Name

Last Name

Company Name (If applicable)

Mailing Address

Unit/Apt./Suite   Municipality (city, town, etc.)   Province

Postal Code   Phone Number   Fax Number

`(      )`   `(      )`

E-mail Address

10101

FIGURE 12.19   Continued

Part 7: SIGNATURE

Landlord's/Agent's Signature   ☒ Landlord   ☐ Agent

Date

| 1 | 8 | / | 0 | 6 | / | 2 | 0 | 1 | 0 |

dd   mm   yyyy

Information for the Landlord and the Tenant

1. The landlord has to give the tenant(s) a copy of this application and the Notice of Hearing at least ten days before the hearing.

2. The landlord has to give the Board a Certificate of Service showing how and when they gave the tenant(s) a copy of this application and the Notice of Hearing, within five days of when they served these documents.

3. It is an offence under the *Residential Tenancies Act* to file false or misleading information with the Landlord and Tenant Board.

4. The Board can order either the landlord or the tenant(s) to pay the other's costs related to this application.

5. The Board has Rules of Practice that set out rules related to the application process and Interpretation Guidelines that explain how the Board might decide specific issues that could come up in an application. You can read the Rules and Guidelines on the Board's website at **www.LTB.gov.on.ca** or you can buy a copy from your local Board office.

10101

FIGURE 12.19 Continued

Landlord and Tenant Board
Ontario

L1 Payment and Scheduling Information Form

Part 1: Application Fee

The application fee is **$170**. Select how you are paying the application fee:

☐ **Cash**   ☐ **Debit Card**   ☐ **Money Order**   ☐ **Certified Cheque**

Money orders and certified cheques must be made payable to the "Minister of Finance"

Credit Card: ☒ Visa   ☐ MasterCard   ☐ American Express

Credit Card Number
| 8 | 7 | 2 | 5 | 4 | 2 | 9 | 5 | 2 | 4 | 2 | 0 | 0 | 0 | | | | |

Expiry Date
| 0 | 9 | / | 1 | 4 |
mm   yy

Cardholder's Name
| R | O | B | | S | M | I | T | H | | | | | | | | | | | | | | | | | | | |

Cardholder's Signature:

Important: The information you fill in under Part 1 is confidential. It will be used to process your application, but will not be placed on the application file.

Part 2: Information Required to Schedule the Hearing

When you file your application, the Board will use your answers to the following questions to schedule a hearing and prepare a Notice of Hearing. The Board will give you an application package that you will have to give to the tenant(s). The application package includes a copy of your application and the Notice of Hearing.

How do you want the Board to give you the application package? Select one of the following:

☐ **Pickup at Board or ServiceOntario Office** | | / | | / | | | dd / mm / yyyy   **Which office?** | | | | | | | | | | | | | | | | |

☐ **By Mail**   ☒ **By Fax** (| 7 | 0 | 5 |) | 7 | 4 | 9 | | 7 | 9 | 8 | 2 |

Will you give the application package to the tenant(s) on the date you receive the package from the Board?

☒ Yes   ☐ No   **If no**, on what date will you give the package to the tenant(s)? | | / | | / | | | | dd / mm / yyyy

How will you give the application package to the tenant(s)?

☐ **By Mail**   ☐ **By Courier**   ☒ **By Another Method**

Part 3: Interpretation Services Required

Shade in whether you require either of the following services at the hearing:

☐ **French language services**   ☐ **Sign language services**

Note: You must live in an area designated for French language services

FOR OFFICE USE ONLY:

HRM Code | | | | | | |

HR Date | | / | | / | | | | dd / mm / yyyy

Time | | : | | | hr : min   am/pm

OA ☐   AD ☐

F L | | |

Delivery Method: ☐ In Person   ☐ Mail   ☐ Fax   ☐ Courier   ☐ Email

10101

Law in Practice: Notice of termination for interfering with the reasonable enjoyment of other tenants

A tenant, Bradley Collins, has resided at 2206 Parkhill Road West, Unit 4, Peterborough since August 1, 2010. His lease is for a one-year period. Bradley's rent is $750.00 per month, including heat and hydro. Rent is payable on the 1st day of each month. The tenant paid a last month's rent deposit of $750.00 as well as first month's rent on August 1, 2010 when he received keys for the apartment.

The landlord hired a property management company that manages the building at 2206 Parkhill Road West as well as the other buildings he's owned since April 2006. ABC Property Management is operated by Richard Lesley and is located at 860 Aylmer Street, Peterborough.

On September 4, 2010, one of Bradley's neighbours contacted ABC Property Management with regard to a noise complaint. According to the neighbour, the tenant had been playing his music from 8 p.m. until 3 a.m. the night of the September 4th. The neighbour added that she politely asked the tenant to lower the volume, but this request was ignored. Richard Lesley is surprised because this is the first complaint against the tenant. On the same day as the complaint, Mr. Lesley responded by drafting, signing, and serving an N5 Notice (figure 12.20) for interfering with the reasonable enjoyment of other tenants. Mr. Lesley served the documents under Bradley Collins's door.

On September 7, 2010, the same neighbour contacted ABC Property Management regarding a second complaint. The neighbour explained that the tenant had guests over and they were quite loud. The tenant had been playing music from 10 p.m. until approximately 4 a.m. The neighbour eventually called the police to enforce the noise bylaw.

The tenant was served a second N5 Notice (figure 12.21) under his door by Mr. Lesley on the 8th of September. Upon serving the tenant this notice, the landlord prepared an L2 Application (figure 12.22) and sent it as well as the corresponding N5 Notices by fax to the Landlord and Tenant Board. The property manager requested the Notice of Hearing to be sent to his fax number and intends to serve the tenant with the Notice of Hearing and L2 Application the day they are received.

- Figure 12.20   Form N5: Notice to Terminate a Tenancy Early

- Figure 12.21   Form N5: Second Notice to Terminate Tenancy Early

- Figure 12.22   Form L2: Application to Terminate Tenancy and Evict a Tenant

FIGURE 12.20 Form N5: Notice to Terminate a Tenancy Early

Notice to Terminate a Tenancy Early
Form N5

Read the instructions carefully before completing this form.

To: (Tenant's name and address)	**From:** (Landlord's name and address)
Bradley Collins 2206 Parkhill Road West, Unit 4 Peterborough, Ontario K9H 7Z6	Andrew Wilkins c/o ABC Property Management 860 Aylmer Street Peterborough, Ontario K9J 2G5

Address of the Rental Unit:

2206 Parkhill Road West, Unit 4
Peterborough, Ontario K9J 7Z6

Termination Date

You must move out of the rental unit identified above on or before ___24/09/2010___
(day/month/year)

Part A

Reasons for this Notice

I am giving you this notice because:

☐ 1. You, your guest or another occupant of the rental unit has wilfully or negligently damaged the rental unit or the residential complex.

☒ 2. You, your guest or another occupant of the rental unit has substantially interfered with:
- the reasonable enjoyment of the residential complex by the landlord or another tenant, or
- another lawful right, privilege or interest of the landlord or another tenant.

☐ 3. The number of people living in the rental unit is more than permitted by health, safety or housing standards.

Part B

Details About the Reasons for this Notice

The landlord must provide details about the events that led to giving you this notice, including information about the dates and times these events occurred.

On September 4th, 2010, our office received a complaint that you had been playing music from 8 p.m. until 3 a.m. the night of September 3rd.

This activity interferes with the reasonable enjoyment of other tenants.

40501

FIGURE 12.20 Continued

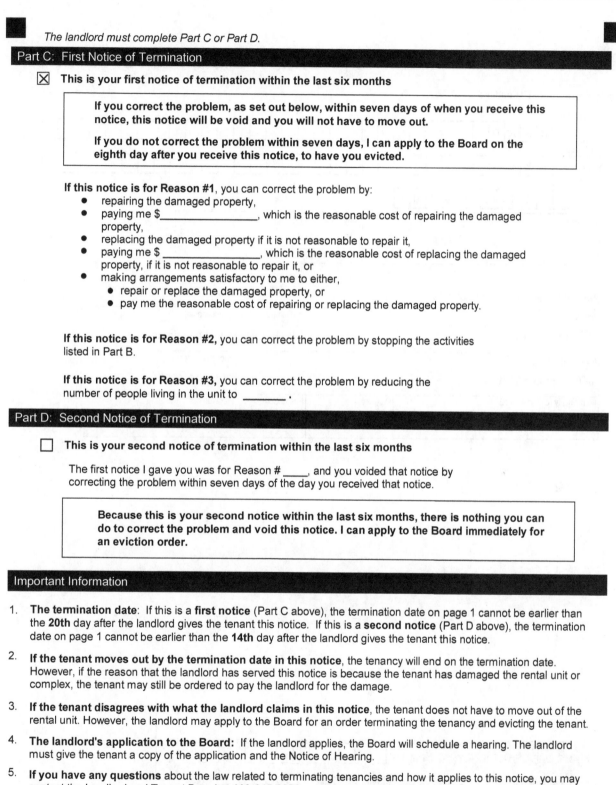

The landlord must complete Part C or Part D.

Part C: First Notice of Termination

☒ **This is your first notice of termination within the last six months**

> **If you correct the problem, as set out below, within seven days of when you receive this notice, this notice will be void and you will not have to move out.**
>
> **If you do not correct the problem within seven days, I can apply to the Board on the eighth day after you receive this notice, to have you evicted.**

If this notice is for Reason #1, you can correct the problem by:
- repairing the damaged property,
- paying me $_____, which is the reasonable cost of repairing the damaged property,
- replacing the damaged property if it is not reasonable to repair it,
- paying me $ _____, which is the reasonable cost of replacing the damaged property, if it is not reasonable to repair it, or
- making arrangements satisfactory to me to either,
  - repair or replace the damaged property, or
  - pay me the reasonable cost of repairing or replacing the damaged property.

If this notice is for Reason #2, you can correct the problem by stopping the activities listed in Part B.

If this notice is for Reason #3, you can correct the problem by reducing the number of people living in the unit to _____ .

Part D: Second Notice of Termination

☐ **This is your second notice of termination within the last six months**

The first notice I gave you was for Reason # ____, and you voided that notice by correcting the problem within seven days of the day you received that notice.

> **Because this is your second notice within the last six months, there is nothing you can do to correct the problem and void this notice. I can apply to the Board immediately for an eviction order.**

Important Information

1. **The termination date**: If this is a **first notice** (Part C above), the termination date on page 1 cannot be earlier than the **20th** day after the landlord gives the tenant this notice. If this is a **second notice** (Part D above), the termination date on page 1 cannot be earlier than the **14th** day after the landlord gives the tenant this notice.

2. **If the tenant moves out by the termination date in this notice**, the tenancy will end on the termination date. However, if the reason that the landlord has served this notice is because the tenant has damaged the rental unit or complex, the tenant may still be ordered to pay the landlord for the damage.

3. **If the tenant disagrees with what the landlord claims in this notice**, the tenant does not have to move out of the rental unit. However, the landlord may apply to the Board for an order terminating the tenancy and evicting the tenant.

4. **The landlord's application to the Board:** If the landlord applies, the Board will schedule a hearing. The landlord must give the tenant a copy of the application and the Notice of Hearing.

5. **If you have any questions** about the law related to terminating tenancies and how it applies to this notice, you may contact the Landlord and Tenant Board at **416-645-8080** or toll-free at **1-888-332-3234**. Or, you may visit the Board's website at **www.LTB.gov.on.ca** for further information.

40501

FIGURE 12.20   Continued

Part E: Signature

Signature   ☐ Landlord   ☒ Agent

First Name

| R | I | C | H | A | R | D | | | | | | | | | | | | | | | | | | | | | | |

Last Name

| L | E | S | L | E | Y | | | | | | | | | | | | | | | | | | | | | | | |

Phone Number

(7 0 5) 7 4 5 6 7 0 8

Signature	Date (dd/mm/yyyy)
	04/09/2010

Agent Information (if applicable)

Name	Company Name (if applicable)
Richard Lesley	ABC Property Management
Mailing Address		**Phone Number**
860 Aylmer Street		705-745-6708

Municipality (city, town, etc)	Province	Postal Code	Fax Number
Peterborough	ONTARIO	K9J 2G5	705-745-8787

FOR OFFICE USE ONLY: File Number ☐☐☐ – ☐☐☐☐☐ F L ☐☐

Delivery Method : ☐ In Person ☐ Mail ☐ Fax ☐ Courier ☐ Email

40501

FIGURE 12.21 Form N5: Second Notice to Terminate Tenancy Early

	Notice to Terminate a Tenancy Early **Form N5**

Read the instructions carefully before completing this form.

To: (Tenant's name and address)	**From:** (Landlord's name and address)
Bradley Collins 2206 Parkhill Road West, Unit 4 Peterborough, Ontario K9H 7Z6	Andrew Wilkins c/o ABC Property Management 860 Aylmer Street Peterborough, Ontario K9J 2G5

Address of the Rental Unit:

2206 Parkhill Road West, Unit 4
Peterborough, Ontario K9J 7Z6

Termination Date

You must move out of the rental unit identified above on or before <u>22/09/2010</u>
(day/month/year)

Part A

Reasons for this Notice

I am giving you this notice because:

☐ 1. You, your guest or another occupant of the rental unit has wilfully or negligently damaged the rental unit or the residential complex.

☒ 2. You, your guest or another occupant of the rental unit has substantially interfered with:
- the reasonable enjoyment of the residential complex by the landlord or another tenant, or
- another lawful right, privilege or interest of the landlord or another tenant.

☐ 3. The number of people living in the rental unit is more than permitted by health, safety or housing standards.

Part B

Details About the Reasons for this Notice

The landlord must provide details about the events that led to giving you this notice, including information about the dates and times these events occurred.

On September 7th, 2010, our office received another complaint that you had guests over and they were quite loud. We were also told that you were playing music from 10 p.m. until approximately 4 a.m.

This activity interferes with the reasonable enjoyment of other tenants.

40501

FIGURE 12.21 Continued

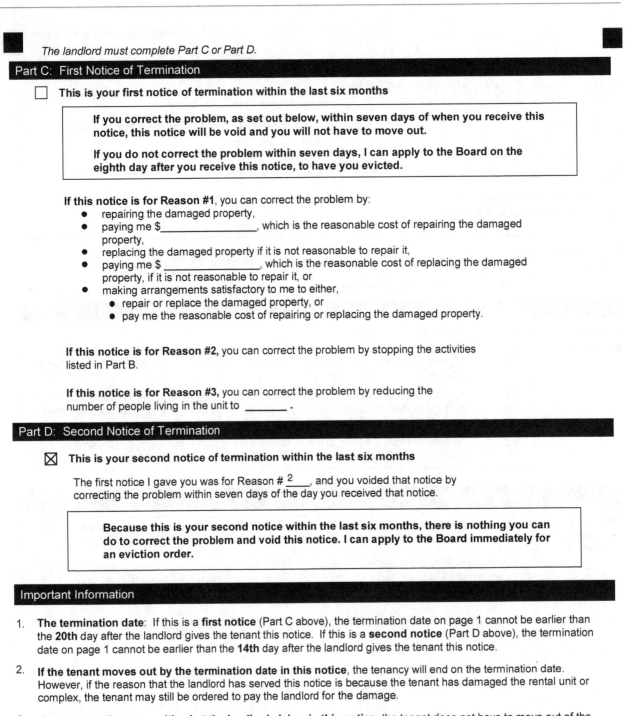

The landlord must complete Part C or Part D.

Part C: First Notice of Termination

☐ **This is your first notice of termination within the last six months**

> **If you correct the problem, as set out below, within seven days of when you receive this notice, this notice will be void and you will not have to move out.**
>
> **If you do not correct the problem within seven days, I can apply to the Board on the eighth day after you receive this notice, to have you evicted.**

If this notice is for Reason #1, you can correct the problem by:
- repairing the damaged property,
- paying me $_____, which is the reasonable cost of repairing the damaged property,
- replacing the damaged property if it is not reasonable to repair it,
- paying me $ _____, which is the reasonable cost of replacing the damaged property, if it is not reasonable to repair it, or
- making arrangements satisfactory to me to either,
  - repair or replace the damaged property, or
  - pay me the reasonable cost of repairing or replacing the damaged property.

If this notice is for Reason #2, you can correct the problem by stopping the activities listed in Part B.

If this notice is for Reason #3, you can correct the problem by reducing the number of people living in the unit to _____ .

Part D: Second Notice of Termination

☒ **This is your second notice of termination within the last six months**

The first notice I gave you was for Reason # 2___, and you voided that notice by correcting the problem within seven days of the day you received that notice.

> **Because this is your second notice within the last six months, there is nothing you can do to correct the problem and void this notice. I can apply to the Board immediately for an eviction order.**

Important Information

1. **The termination date**: If this is a **first notice** (Part C above), the termination date on page 1 cannot be earlier than the **20th** day after the landlord gives the tenant this notice. If this is a **second notice** (Part D above), the termination date on page 1 cannot be earlier than the **14th** day after the landlord gives the tenant this notice.

2. **If the tenant moves out by the termination date in this notice**, the tenancy will end on the termination date. However, if the reason that the landlord has served this notice is because the tenant has damaged the rental unit or complex, the tenant may still be ordered to pay the landlord for the damage.

3. **If the tenant disagrees with what the landlord claims in this notice**, the tenant does not have to move out of the rental unit. However, the landlord may apply to the Board for an order terminating the tenancy and evicting the tenant.

4. **The landlord's application to the Board:** If the landlord applies, the Board will schedule a hearing. The landlord must give the tenant a copy of the application and the Notice of Hearing.

5. **If you have any questions** about the law related to terminating tenancies and how it applies to this notice, you may contact the Landlord and Tenant Board at **416-645-8080** or toll-free at **1-888-332-3234**. Or, you may visit the Board's website at **www.LTB.gov.on.ca** for further information.

40501

FIGURE 12.21 Continued

Part E: Signature

Signature ☐ Landlord ☒ Agent

First Name

R	I	C	H	A	R	D																									

Last Name

L	E	S	L	E	Y																										

Phone Number

(7 0 5) 7 4 5 6 7 0 8

Signature	Date (dd/mm/yyyy)
	08/09/2010

Agent Information (if applicable)

Name	Company Name (if applicable)
Richard Lesley	ABC Property Management

Mailing Address		Phone Number
860 Aylmer Street		705-745-6708

Municipality (city, town, etc)	Province	Postal Code	Fax Number
Peterborough	ONTARIO	K9J 2G5	705-745-8787

FOR OFFICE USE ONLY: File Number ☐☐☐ – ☐☐☐☐☐ F L ☐☐

Delivery Method : ☐ In Person ☐ Mail ☐ Fax ☐ Courier ☐ Email

40501

FIGURE 12.22   Form L2: Application to Terminate Tenancy and Evict a Tenant

---

Landlord
and
Tenant
Board
Ontario

Application to Terminate a Tenancy and Evict a Tenant
Form L2

Read the Instructions carefully before completing the Form. Print or Type in Uppercase.

Part 1: General Information

Landlord's Name and Address   (if there is more than 1 landlord, complete a Schedule of Parties form and file it with this application)

☐ Male   ☐ Female   ☒ Company

First Name
| A | N | D | R | E | W | | W | I | L | K | I | N | S | | | | | | | | | | | | | | | | |

Last Name
| C | O | | A | B | C | | P | R | O | P | E | R | T | Y | | M | A | N | A | G | E | M | E | N | T | | | | |

Street Address
| 8 | 6 | 0 | | A | Y | L | M | E | R | | S | T | R | E | E | T | | | | | | | | | | | | | |

Unit/Apt./Suite
| | | | | | | |

Municipality (city, town, etc.)
| P | E | T | E | R | B | O | R | O | U | G | H | | | | | | |

Province   Postal Code
| O | N | | K | 9 | J | | 2 | G | 5 |

Day Phone Number   (7 0 5) 7 4 5 6 7 0 8

Evening Phone Number   (___) ___ ___

Fax Number   (7 0 5) 7 4 5 8 7 8 7

E-mail Address
| | | | | | | | | | | | | | | | | | | | | | | | | | | | | |

Rental Unit Covered by this Application

Street Number
| 2 | 2 | 0 | 6 | |

Street Name
| P | A | R | K | H | I | L | L | | | | | | | | | | |

Street Type (e.g. Street, Avenue, Road)
| R | O | A | D | | | | | |

Direction (e.g. East)
| W | E | S | T | |

Unit/Apt./Suite
| U | N | I | T | | 4 | | | | | |

Municipality (city, town, etc.)
| P | E | T | E | R | B | O | R | O | U | G | H | | | | | | |

Province | O | N |

Postal Code | K | 9 | J | | 7 | Z | 6 |

Tenants' Names and Addresses   (if there are more than 2 tenants, complete a Schedule of Parties form and file it with this application)

☒ Male   ☐ Female

Tenant 1: First Name
| B | R | A | D | L | E | Y | | | | | | | | | | | | | | | | | | | | | | | |

Tenant 1: Last Name
| C | O | L | L | I | N | S | | | | | | | | | | | | | | | | | | | | | | | |

☐ Male   ☐ Female

Tenant 2: First Name
| | | | | | | | | | | | | | | | | | | | | | | | | | | | | |

Tenant 2: Last Name
| | | | | | | | | | | | | | | | | | | | | | | | | | | | | |

Mailing Address **(if different from rental unit address above)**
| | | | | | | | | | | | | | | | | | | | | | | | | | | | | |

Unit/Apt./Suite
| | | | | | |

Municipality (city, town, etc.)
| | | | | | | | | | | | |

Province   Postal Code
| | | | | | | |

Day Phone Number   (___) ___ ___

Evening Phone Number   (___) ___ ___

Fax Number   (___) ___ ___

E-mail Address
| | | | | | | | | | | | | | | | | | | | | | | | | | | | | |

Related Applications
List the file numbers of any other applications to the Board that relate to the same rental unit.

File Number 1 | | | | - | | | | |

File Number 2 | | | | - | | | | |

10201

For Office use only : File Number: | | | | - | | | | |

Version. 06/04/2009

FIGURE 12.22   Continued

Part 2: Reasons for Your Application

The following are the reasons for making this application. For a further explanation of each reason, see the instructions to this form.

A. Termination of Tenancy

I am applying for an order terminating the tenancy and evicting the tenant because:

☒ **1. The tenant has been given the following notice of termination:**

☐   Notice to Terminate a Tenancy Early (Form N5)

Is this application based on the first or the second Form N5 notice?

☐ First N5 notice

☒ Second N5 notice

If this application is based on the first Form N5 notice, did the tenant correct the problem within 7 days of receiving the notice?

☐ Yes   **If yes**, then the notice is void and you cannot apply to terminate the tenancy for this reason.

☒ No   **If no**, or if this application is based on the second Form N5 notice, then you can apply to terminate the tenancy for this reason.

☐   Notice to Terminate a Tenancy Early - Illegal Act or Misrepresentation of Income (Form N6)

☐   10-Day Notice to Terminate a Tenancy Early (Form N7)

☐   Notice to Terminate a Tenancy at the End of the Term (Form N8)

☐   Notice to Terminate a Tenancy at the End of the Term for Landlord's or Purchaser's Own Use (Form N12)

☐   Notice to Terminate a Tenancy at the End of the Term for Conversion, Demolition or Repairs (Form N13)

The termination date set out on the Notice to Terminate a Tenancy is: ☐☐ / ☐☐ / ☐☐☐☐
dd   mm   yyyy

Documents you must attach: There are documents that you must attach to the application. See the instructions for further information.

☐ **2. The tenant has abandoned the rental unit.**

> Explain why you believe the tenant has abandoned the rental unit. A rental unit will not be considered to be abandoned if the tenant is not in arrears of rent.

☐ **3. The tenant occupies the superintendent's unit and the tenant's employment as superintendent has ended.**

The tenant's employment ended on: ☐☐ / ☐☐ / ☐☐☐☐
dd   mm   yyyy

FIGURE 12.22   Continued

Part 2: Reasons for your Application (cont'd)

B. Compensation for Overholding Tenant

☐   I am applying for an order requiring the tenant to pay compensation for each day the tenant remains in the rental unit without paying after the termination date set out in the notice or the agreement to terminate the tenancy.

Current rent charged to the tenant: $ ☐☐ , ☐☐☐ . ☐☐

The amount of the rent currently on deposit: $ ☐☐ , ☐☐☐ . ☐☐

The date the rent deposit was collected: ☐☐ / ☐☐ / ☐☐☐☐
                                                                           dd   mm   yyyy

The last period for which interest on the   ☐☐ / ☐☐ / ☐☐☐☐   to   ☐☐ / ☐☐ / ☐☐☐☐
rent deposit was paid: dd   mm   yyyy   dd   mm   yyyy

NSF cheque charges and related administration charges: If you are applying for an order for compensation, and you wish to claim charges related to NSF cheques the tenant gave you, provide the following details:

Cheque Amount $	Date of Cheque DD/MM/YYYY	Date NSF Charge Incurred DD/MM/YYYY	Bank Charge for NSF Cheque $	Landlord's Administration Charge $	Total Charge $
☐☐☐☐.☐☐	☐☐/☐☐/☐☐☐☐	☐☐/☐☐/☐☐☐☐	☐☐☐.☐☐	☐☐☐.☐☐	☐☐☐.☐☐
☐☐☐☐.☐☐	☐☐/☐☐/☐☐☐☐	☐☐/☐☐/☐☐☐☐	☐☐☐.☐☐	☐☐☐.☐☐	☐☐☐.☐☐
☐☐☐☐.☐☐	☐☐/☐☐/☐☐☐☐	☐☐/☐☐/☐☐☐☐	☐☐☐.☐☐	☐☐☐.☐☐	☐☐☐.☐☐
☐☐☐☐.☐☐	☐☐/☐☐/☐☐☐☐	☐☐/☐☐/☐☐☐☐	☐☐☐.☐☐	☐☐☐.☐☐	☐☐☐.☐☐
☐☐☐☐.☐☐	☐☐/☐☐/☐☐☐☐	☐☐/☐☐/☐☐☐☐	☐☐☐.☐☐	☐☐☐.☐☐	☐☐☐.☐☐
☐☐☐☐.☐☐	☐☐/☐☐/☐☐☐☐	☐☐/☐☐/☐☐☐☐	☐☐☐.☐☐	☐☐☐.☐☐	☐☐☐.☐☐
☐☐☐☐.☐☐	☐☐/☐☐/☐☐☐☐	☐☐/☐☐/☐☐☐☐	☐☐☐.☐☐	☐☐☐.☐☐	☐☐☐.☐☐
☐☐☐☐.☐☐	☐☐/☐☐/☐☐☐☐	☐☐/☐☐/☐☐☐☐	☐☐☐.☐☐	☐☐☐.☐☐	☐☐☐.☐☐
☐☐☐☐.☐☐	☐☐/☐☐/☐☐☐☐	☐☐/☐☐/☐☐☐☐	☐☐☐.☐☐	☐☐☐.☐☐	☐☐☐.☐☐
☐☐☐☐.☐☐	☐☐/☐☐/☐☐☐☐	☐☐/☐☐/☐☐☐☐	☐☐☐.☐☐	☐☐☐.☐☐	☐☐☐.☐☐

Total NSF Related Charges Owing $ ☐ , ☐☐☐ . ☐☐

FIGURE 12.22   Continued

Part 2: Reasons for your Application (cont'd)

C. Payment of Money

You can apply for either of the following reasons regardless of whether you are also applying to terminate the tenancy. However, you cannot apply for these reasons if the tenant has moved out of the rental unit.

Is the tenant still in possession of the rental unit?   ☐ Yes   ☐ No

If yes, shade either of the following that apply:

☐   I am applying for an order requiring the tenant to pay $ ☐☐ , ☐☐☐ . ☐☐ for damage caused by the tenant, their guest or another occupant of the rental unit.

> Describe the damage to the property that requires repair or replacement and explain how you calculated the above amount:

*If you did not provide information about the rent deposit under Part 2(B), you must provide the information in this part:

Current rent charged to the tenant: $ ☐☐ , 7 5 0 . 0 0

The amount of the rent currently on deposit: $ ☐☐ , 7 5 0 . 0 0

The date the rent deposit was collected: 0 1 / 0 8 / 2 0 1 0
                                            dd   mm   yyyy

The last period for which interest on the   ☐☐ / ☐☐ / ☐☐☐☐ to ☐☐ / ☐☐ / ☐☐☐☐
rent deposit was paid: dd   mm   yyyy   dd   mm   yyyy

☐   I am applying for an order requiring the tenant of a Rent-Geared-to-Income unit to pay $ ☐☐ , ☐☐☐ . ☐☐ for the additional amount that the tenant would have been required to pay had the tenant not misrepresented their income or that of other family members living in the unit.

10201

FIGURE 12.22 Continued

Part 3: Signature

Landlord's/Agent's Signature ☐ Landlord ☒ Agent

Date 0 8 / 0 9 / 2 0 1 0
dd mm yyyy

If you are an agent or an officer of a corporation, you must provide the following information:

First Name
R I C H A R D

Last Name
L E S L E Y

Company Name (if applicable)
A B C   P R O P E R T Y   M A N A G E M E N T

Mailing Address
8 6 0   A Y L M E R   S T R E E T

Unit/Apt./Suite

Municipality (city, town, etc.)
P E T E R B O R O U G H

Province
O N

Postal Code
K 9 J   2 G 5

Phone Number
(7 0 5) 7 4 5   6 7 0 8

Fax Number
(7 0 5) 7 4 5   8 7 8 7

E-mail Address

Important Information

1. If the landlord gave the tenant a notice of termination, the landlord must file this application no later than 30 days after the termination date set out in the notice.

2. Once the landlord files this application with the Board, the Board will give the landlord a Notice of Hearing. In most cases, the landlord must give the tenant a copy of this application and the Notice of hearing at least **ten** days before the hearing. However, where the application is for any of the following reasons, the landlord must give the tenant these documents at least **five** days before the hearing:
   - impaired safety (Form N7, Reason #1)
   - damage (Form N7, Reason #2)
   - misuse of premises (Form N7, Reason #3)
   - interfering with landlord's reasonable enjoyment (Form N7, Reason #4)
   - illegal act involving drugs (Form N6, Reason #1)
   - superintendent's unit (no notice of termination required)

   Once the landlord has given the tenant a copy of the application and Notice of Hearing, the landlord must file a Certificate of Service with the Board showing how and when the landlord gave the documents to the tenant, within five days of when they served these documents.

3. It is an offence under the *Residential Tenancies Act* to file false or misleading information with the Landlord and Tenant Board.

4. The Board can order either the landlord or the tenant to pay the other's costs related to the application.

5. The Board has Rules of Practice that set out rules related to the application process, and Interpretation Guidelines that explain how the Board might decide specific issues that may arise in an application. You can purchase a copy of the Rules and Guidelines from your local Board office or view them online at **www.LTB.gov.on.ca**.

6. You may contact the Landlord and Tenant Board at **416-645-8080** or toll-free at **1-888-332-3234.** Or, you may visit the Board's website at **www.LTB.gov.on.ca** for further information.

10201

Page 5 of 5

FIGURE 12.22   Continued

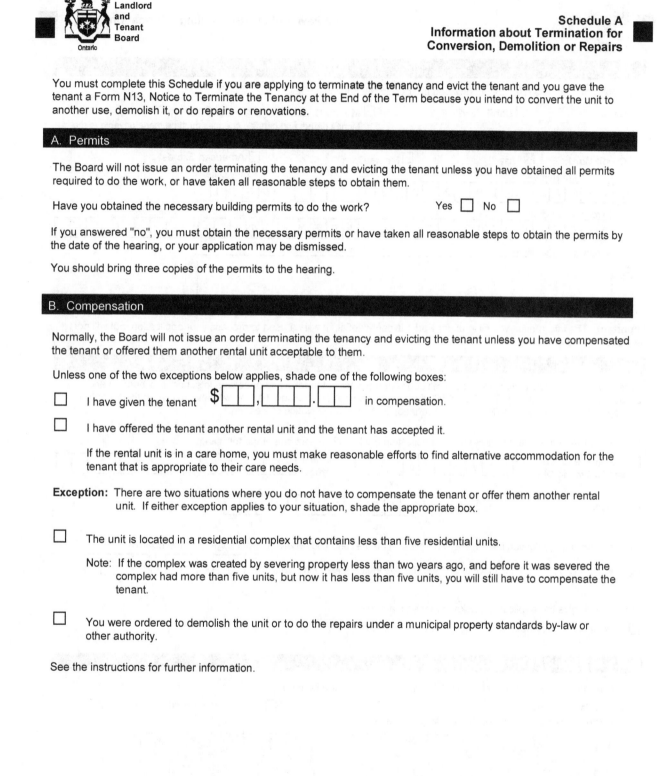

Landlord
and
Tenant
Board

Ontario

Schedule A
Information about Termination for
Conversion, Demolition or Repairs

You must complete this Schedule if you are applying to terminate the tenancy and evict the tenant and you gave the tenant a Form N13, Notice to Terminate the Tenancy at the End of the Term because you intend to convert the unit to another use, demolish it, or do repairs or renovations.

A. Permits

The Board will not issue an order terminating the tenancy and evicting the tenant unless you have obtained all permits required to do the work, or have taken all reasonable steps to obtain them.

Have you obtained the necessary building permits to do the work?   Yes ☐   No ☐

If you answered "no", you must obtain the necessary permits or have taken all reasonable steps to obtain the permits by the date of the hearing, or your application may be dismissed.

You should bring three copies of the permits to the hearing.

B. Compensation

Normally, the Board will not issue an order terminating the tenancy and evicting the tenant unless you have compensated the tenant or offered them another rental unit acceptable to them.

Unless one of the two exceptions below applies, shade one of the following boxes:

☐   I have given the tenant $☐☐,☐☐☐.☐☐   in compensation.

☐   I have offered the tenant another rental unit and the tenant has accepted it.

If the rental unit is in a care home, you must make reasonable efforts to find alternative accommodation for the tenant that is appropriate to their care needs.

Exception: There are two situations where you do not have to compensate the tenant or offer them another rental unit. If either exception applies to your situation, shade the appropriate box.

☐   The unit is located in a residential complex that contains less than five residential units.

Note: If the complex was created by severing property less than two years ago, and before it was severed the complex had more than five units, but now it has less than five units, you will still have to compensate the tenant.

☐   You were ordered to demolish the unit or to do the repairs under a municipal property standards by-law or other authority.

See the instructions for further information.

10201

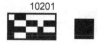

FIGURE 12.22 Continued

Landlord
and
Tenant
Board
Ontario

L2 Payment and Scheduling Information Form

Part 1: Application Fee

The application fee is **$170**. Select how you are paying the application fee:

☐ **Cash** ☐ **Debit Card** ☐ **Money Order** ☒ **Certified Cheque**

Money orders and certified cheques must be made payable to the "Minister of Finance"

Credit Card: ☒ Visa ☐ MasterCard ☐ American Express

Credit Card Number
| 8 | 7 | 4 | 7 | 5 | 0 | 0 | 1 | 9 | 7 | 2 | 2 | 8 | 7 | 3 | 0 | | | | |

Expiry Date
| 0 | 6 | / | 1 | 3 |
mm   yy

Cardholder's Name
| A | B | C | | P | R | O | P | E | R | T | Y | | M | A | N | A | G | E | M | E | N | T | | | | | | | | | |

Cardholder's Signature:

Important: The information you fill in under Part 1 is confidential. It will be used to process your application, but will not be placed on the application file.

Part 2: Information Required to Schedule the Hearing

When you file your application, the Board will use your answers to the following questions to schedule a hearing and prepare a Notice of Hearing. The Board will give you an application package that you will have to give to the tenant(s). The application package includes a copy of your application and the Notice of Hearing.

How do you want the Board to give you the application package? Select one of the following:

☐ **Pickup at Board or ServiceOntario Office** [ ] / [ ] / [   ] **Which office?** [   ]
dd   mm   yyyy

☐ **By Mail** ☒ **By Fax** (| 7 | 0 | 5 |) | 7 | 4 | 5 | | 8 | 7 | 8 | 7 |

Will you give the application package to the tenant(s) on the date you receive the package from the Board?

☒ **Yes** ☐ **No** **If no**, on what date will you give the package to the tenant(s)? [ ] / [ ] / [   ]
dd   mm   yyyy

How will you give the application package to the tenant(s)?

☐ **By Mail** ☐ **By Courier** ☒ **By Another Method**

Part 3: Interpretation Services Required

Shade in whether you require either of the following services at the hearing:

☐ **French language services** ☐ **Sign language services**
Note: You must live in an area designated for French language services

---

FOR OFFICE USE ONLY:

HRM Code [   ]   HR Date [ ] / [ ] / [   ]   Time [ ] : [ ] [ ]   OA ☐ AD ☐
dd   mm   yyyy   hr   min   am/pm
F L [ ]

Delivery Method: ☐ In Person ☐ Mail ☐ Fax ☐ Courier ☐ Email

10201

Your Future

Follow your own star!
—Dante Alighieri

13

Introduction

If you are studying this text, your eventual goal is presumably to secure a career in the field of law. After you've attained the education and skills required, it's time to begin your job search and let the world know what you're capable of. This chapter will guide you through the employment process, from placement requirements to a successful interview and a job in your chosen field. We will discuss how to identify potential careers for yourself, how to promote yourself to prospective employers, and how to continue growing professionally within your chosen career.

Program Placements

Don't be intimidated by the fact that, as a student, you only have limited practical experience in the field of law. Most college legal programs offer placement opportunities to help you gain practical experience and learn to apply your skills outside the classroom.

While specific placement arrangements vary according to college, students usually either attend their placement part time over several semesters while taking other classes, or attend their placement full time for one semester. At some colleges, students attend their placement at the end of the school year. You will likely begin the placement process by meeting with your program coordinator to discuss your interests and strengths. Together, the two of you will define the type of work best suited to you. After this, you may choose to seek out prospective employers yourself, based on your coordinator's recommendations, or you may draw directly on your coordinator's wealth of professional relationships with key employers. Court services, police services, municipal offices, community agencies, and law firms of all kinds—these are organizations that routinely accept placement students.

Most placements are unpaid, but they remain the best way to establish contacts and references in the industry. They are also a great opportunity to gain feedback and experience in the real world. Quite often, at the end of the placement, the employer will provide you with a formal evaluation. You may also be asked by your program coordinator to keep an activity log and perform a self-evaluation. These assessments are not only vital to the learning process, but will also help steer you in the direction you want to go in your career.

Don't worry if after your first placement you still feel lost and unsure. Placements are excellent for exploring what's out there, but it still takes time to find your true calling. Figure 13.1 lists some common career choices in the legal field, along with some less common ones.

FIGURE 13.1 Potential careers for legal assistants

Bank and trust company loans officer	Legal secretary
Community legal worker (clinics)	Legal software consultant
Corporate clerk	Legal software sales trainer
Court and tribunal agent	Litigation clerk
Court employee	Office management instructor
Courtroom clerk/reporter	Office manager
Government legal department employee	Paralegal
Insurance company employee	Parliamentary assistant
Law clerk	Patient advocate
Law firm receptionist	Provincial offences agent
Lawyer (with further education)	Provincial offences prosecutor
Legal assistant	Research assistant
Legal procedures instructor	

Organizing Your Job Search

When beginning your job search, treat the process like any other major project. Organize your efforts in a way that gives you quick, easy access to all the documents you will need, including cover letters, applications, resumés, reference letters, job ads, response letters from prospective employers, portfolio contents, and lists of contacts. Use either binders with dividers, or file folders or accordion-style folders to separate different types of paperwork.

Next, develop a strategy for seeking out the available jobs. Figure 13.2 provides a sampling of the many resources you will find useful in this regard.

FIGURE 13.2 Job search resources

Newspaper classified ads	A common and simple resource. However, many employers no longer consider this an effective means of recruitment.
Internet websites	Many Internet organizations have developed websites for connecting employers and potential employees. http://www.gojobs.gov.on.ca http://www.ontariomunicipaljobs.com http://www.jobbank.gc.ca http://www.gojobs.gov.on.ca http://www.workopolis.com http://www.jobs-emplois.gc.ca http://jobsinlaw.ca http://www.wowjobs.ca http://findjobontario.com http://www.monster.ca http://www.ospreycareers.com http://www.indeed.ca
Networking	Finding a job is not as simple as the old adage that says, "It's not what you know, but who you know." However, it is good to have a well-cultivated network of colleagues, peers, associates, and personal contacts. A valuable network includes resources from the past and present and can be an inside source for information on upcoming positions. Always inform your network when you are looking for a job.
Signs	Signs are not a common form of advertising for the types of positions you're looking for, but occasionally some employers will use them.
Human Resources and Skills Development (HRSD) Canada	With offices in most urban areas, HRSD Canada maintains job-posting boards and electronic listings for public access.
Field journals	Legal magazines (e.g., *Canadian Lawyer*) and other law field newsletters and small papers sometimes advertise for legal office assistance.
Broadcast letters	A broadcast letter is a general letter sent to numerous potential employers indicating your interest in a relevant position and requesting an interview. By their nature, these letters are not job-specific and may not be received by a potential employer when it is actually hiring. Broadcast letters therefore may not garner much response, but are still worthwhile trying.
Hidden market	The "hidden market" is based on knowledge of business expansions, company relocations, and social trends. It is available to everyone but is generally untapped. Accessing this market requires research, alertness, and the help of your network.
Employment agencies	Specialized agencies match up employers with people seeking positions. Registering with these agencies can secure you interviews, and even provide experience through temporary positions.
Job fairs	Job fairs are becoming more popular with large companies, especially when the company is setting up in a new city. Usually there are a number of available positions for which candidates go through a screening exercise, complete an application, and leave a resumé. A job fair is a good way to learn about companies and obtain some experience in job searching.

Researching the Employer

Let's say you've found a job listing that looks interesting. Now you need to let the prospective employer know that you're capable and available.

To market yourself effectively, you must first know your audience. Research the hiring firm or company. Learn their history and their key areas of operation and potential growth. Then research the position. What are the dynamics of the office? How many employees do they have? Why is the position vacant? (Is someone off on maternity leave, for example, or is it a newly created position?) What is the potential for your advancing in the firm? What is its level of technology? The more you know about the firm, the better equipped you are to understand its needs and to address them. What a prospective employer is looking for is a candidate who demonstrates initiative, enthusiasm, and knowledge about the position, and also has the practical ability to do the job.

Cover Letters

Some companies require job applicants to complete an application form, but in most cases you will be submitting a resumé with a one- or two-page cover letter.

The cover letter introduces you and explains how you are suitable for the position, linking your resumé to the particular position advertised. (Think of it as a reader's guide to understanding your resumé.) It should draw attention to the relevant strengths of your resumé, convey your enthusiasm about the position, and highlight those qualifications that make you suitable for the job. The most important objective of the cover letter, however, is to obtain an interview in person.

Like any other letter, the cover letter has an introductory paragraph, a body, and a closing paragraph. It should be professional, should have a pleasant and enthusiastic tone, and should entice the employer into wanting to know more.

Make sure you address all the requirements in the job posting. Technology has been introduced into the area of recruitment, and some companies now use scanners to search for key words in cover letters. For example, a

---

PRACTICE TIP

Your cover letter and resumé must be completely error-free. You should put the same care and attention into your resumé that you put into your professional correspondence. Consider reviewing chapter 8, Legal Correspondence, and referring to the Writing Guide appendix at the end of this text, both before and after you prepare your cover letter and resumé.

Surface errors—that is, errors in spelling, grammar, or punctuation—are the types of errors most easily detected by the reader, and the first to be noticed. No matter how perfect you may be for the position you're applying for, errors in your cover letter will invariably reflect poorly on you, suggesting to the reader that you cannot be relied on even to write your own correspondence. Thankfully, surface errors are also easily correctable, requiring only attention and care. So proofread, proofread, proofread!

recruiter may scan for such terms as "PCLaw," "organization," or "legal procedures." If your letter contains the key words or phrases, your application moves to the next stage of the process. Without them, your application will be screened out, your resumé will be overlooked, and you will lose the opportunity for an interview.

The Address

Address the letter to the person and department identified in the job ad as the one recruiting. If no one is identified there, go the extra mile and obtain the person's name by some other means. If you are unable to locate the name, be careful to ensure that your salutation is all-inclusive; don't assume that the recruiter is one gender or the other. For example, rather than "Dear Sir" or "Gentlemen," use "Dear Sir or Madam" or "Dear Selection Committee Members." The inside address should be exactly as indicated in the job posting. The reference or subject line of your letter should quote the name of the position and any file number listed.

The Introductory Paragraph

The introductory paragraph of your cover letter should be short and to the point. It should state why you are writing and should refer to the details of the position. You might write the following, for example: "Please accept this letter as my application for the position of law clerk with Woodrow & Perry." An alternative would be the following: "I am writing in response to your ad in *The Peterborough Examiner* requesting applications for the position of law clerk in your firm." This first sentence clearly indicates the reason for your letter. A final sentence in the opening paragraph can introduce the rest of your letter. You might write the following, for example: "This position is in my trained field and I am quite interested in this opportunity." The introductory paragraph need only be a sentence or two. It sets up a context for the information that will follow.

The Body Paragraphs

The body of your letter is where you promote your skills. Ensure that the letter has a natural and orderly flow to it. An effective arrangement is to begin with your current job (if any) and the number of years you have worked in the field, followed by a statement outlining your education. After providing this basic information, refer directly to the job ad and ensure that, in your account of yourself, you refer to all the qualifications they are seeking. It may be helpful at this point to refer to your college course outline, since it contains details about your areas of study as well as the key skills you have developed.

You can use more than one paragraph in this section, but be succinct. Keep your sentences broad in meaning and use key words and language. Your resumé is the place to fully detail your experience, skills, and abilities; the body of the cover letter should show your initiative and potential value to the employer. Include a statement to demonstrate that you have researched the company and that you can offer what they need. You could write the following, for example:

> I am interested in civil litigation law, particularly medical malpractice and personal injury. I understand that your firm of Collis & Collis, LLP is well regarded in this field. I plan on moving to the Peterborough area immediately upon graduation. I will be available for an interview any time after April 2, 20--.

Such statements lead nicely into the resumé's more detailed presentation of your particular skills and abilities.

The Conclusion

The closing paragraph of your letter should reaffirm your suitability for the position, thank the recruiter for her time, and request an interview. The following would be appropriate:

> As outlined above, I have gained the necessary experience and skills to successfully perform in this position. For your reference, I have attached my resumé, and request the opportunity for a personal interview where I can further demonstrate my suitability for the position of law clerk in your firm. Thank you for your time and consideration. I anxiously await your response.

The closing of your letter should be the standard one of business correspondence. It needs to include a complimentary closing (such as "Yours truly"), space for your signature, your name (typewritten), and enclosure notations. Be sure that you sign your letter and indicate that there is a resumé attached.

Other Details

To make your application look professional, choose a high-quality paper for your cover letter and your resumé. Be conservative in your choice of colour—off-white or sand is much better than purple. Keep in mind that letters and resumés will likely be photocopied or faxed, and many colours and patterns can make these copies difficult to read. Select a standard letter format (as detailed in chapter 8, Legal Correspondence) and an appropriate business font (such as Times New Roman or something similar). Figures 13.3 and 13.4 show cover letters that are effectively written and organized.

When you are applying by email, don't copy and paste your resumé into the body of the message unless the prospective employer requests it; the formatting of your resumé may become scrambled and difficult to follow when the recipient prints it. However, you may enter your cover letter information into the body of an email and include your resumé as an attachment to the email. Another option, as shown in figure 13.5, is to have a basic message in your email, with both your cover letter and resumé included as attachments. (For more information on covering letters, see Sharyn Borovoy, *Getting Ready for Work* (Toronto: Emond Montgomery, 2010), chapter 1.)

FIGURE 13.3   Sample cover letter: Student seeking placement

Julie Anne Lynn Carpenter

705-739-1091
905-760-2194 (cellular)
julcarpenter1221@maddox.ca

10 Port Road
Peterborough, ON K9J 2B0

March 22, 20--

Wilkins & Meadus, LLP
1392 King Street
Peterborough, ON K2P 2E4

Attn: Doug Wilkins

Dear Mr. Wilkins:

RE: Law Clerk Placement

As a student in the final semester of the Law Clerk program at Sir Sandford Fleming College in Peterborough, I am required to complete a 100-hour placement component in order to graduate from the program. I am interested in legal issues related to landlord and tenant relationships. I understand your firm of Wilkins & Meadus is well respected in this area. I plan on moving to Peterborough on April 1, 20--, and will be available for an interview any time after that date.

During my academic studies at Sir Sandford Fleming I have developed key skills and abilities in the following areas:

- Identifying the legal issues that can arise in landlord and tenant relationships and applying the appropriate legal principles.
- Preparing the legal documentation needed to enforce the rights of both landlords and tenants.
- Preparing other relevant documentation.
- Interviewing clients or witnesses and accurately recording relevant information.
- Gathering, organizing, and presenting evidence to a tribunal.
- Researching legal issues relating to landlord and tenant matters.

As you will note from my enclosed resumé, Sir Sandford Fleming College has provided me with a thorough understanding of law office practices and procedures. In addition to the training that I have received through Sir Sandford Fleming College, I have had several prior jobs that have helped me excel in customer service. As indicated on my enclosed resumé, I worked as a manager at New York Fries. In this position I learned quickly that customer satisfaction is a key element in almost any career. I believe that this will be an asset if I receive the opportunity to have a position with your office.

I take an active role in my education at Sir Sandford Fleming College. I am the class representative for my program, which involves meeting with the faculty and contributing my opinion. I believe that my educational and employment experience, combined with my dedication and enthusiasm, enables me to make an immediate and valuable contribution to your firm.

I would appreciate the opportunity to meet with you and discuss my interest in a placement position with your office. I am available by phone any time after 2:00 p.m. Monday to Thursday and any time Friday.

Thank you in advance for your time and consideration.

Yours truly,

Julie Anne Lynn Carpenter

Encl.: resumé

FIGURE 13.4 Sample cover letter: Candidate with experience

Julie Anne Lynn Carpenter

705-739-1091
905-760-2194 (cellular)
julcarpenter1221@maddox.ca

10 Port Road
Peterborough, ON K9J 2B0

March 22, 20--

Collis & Collis, LLP
294 Queen Street
Peterborough, ON K3N 1X6

Attn: Diana Collis

Dear Ms. Collis:

RE: Law Clerk Position, Competition #LC-12

It is with great interest that I submit my resumé to you in response to the posting in *The Peterborough Examiner*, on Monday, March 20, 20--, for a law clerk position with your firm.

You stated in your advertisement that you are looking for someone with experience in the area of medical malpractice. As you can see from my resumé, I have been employed with a law firm in Peterborough since March 2005. I have primarily been involved with civil litigation matters, including medical malpractice and personal injury. I have experience drafting pleadings, affidavits, and other documents that are filed with the court. I have also been involved in some estate and collection matters, as well as criminal and family law.

As outlined above, I have gained the necessary experience and skills to successfully manage the needs of your office.

For your reference, I have attached my resumé, and request the opportunity for a personal interview where I can further demonstrate my suitability for the position of law clerk in your firm. Thank you for your time and consideration. I anxiously await your response.

Sincerely yours,

Julie Anne Lynn Carpenter

Encl.: resumé

FIGURE 13.5 Sample email cover letter: Basic message

File   Edit   View   History   Bookmarks   Tools   Help

flemingc.on.ca Go to a Web Site

Mail Message

Send | Save | Cancel | Address Book | Change To ▼ | Check Spelling ▼ |

Mail | Attachments | Send Options

From: Julie Anne Lynn Carpenter   CC:
To: dcollis@collisandcollisllp.com   BC:
Subject: Job Posting PL-2890-11
Attachments: Cover Letter Job Posting PL-2890-11.docx, Resume Job Posting PL-2890-11.docx

Plain Text ≪ | Font ▼ Size ▼ B I U

Dear Ms. Collis:

Please find attached my cover letter and resumé with respect to the above-noted posting found on http://www.jobsinlaw.ca.

Yours truly,

Julie Anne Lynn Carpenter
julcarpenter1221@maddox.ca

This email and any files transmitted with it are confidential and intended solely for the use of the individual or entity to whom they are addressed. If you have received this email in error, please notify the system manager. This message contains confidential information and is intended only for the individual named. If you are not the named addressee, you should not disseminate, distribute or copy this email. Please notify the sender immediately by email if you have received this email by mistake, and delete this email from your system. If you are not the intended recipient, you are notified that disclosing, copying, distributing or taking any action in reliance on the contents of this information is strictly prohibited.

Resumés

A resumé is a tool for promoting your skills to a prospective employer. Compared with the cover letter, a resumé is detailed and specific. It spells out everything you want the recruiter to know about you.

Before sitting down and writing your resumé, you should have a plan. Decide on all aspects of the presentation: content, order, style, and format. Working from a plan or outline will make the actual task of preparing your resumé that much easier.

Top-Five Resumé Tips

1. Your resumé is about your future, not your past.

2. It is not a confessional. In other words, you don't have to "tell all." Stick to what's relevant and marketable.

3. Don't write a list of job descriptions. Write achievements!

4. Promote only skills you enjoy using. Never write about things you don't want to repeat.

5. Be honest. You can be creative, but don't lie.

Source: http://susanireland.com/resume/how-to-write/tips.

Three Types of Resumés

There are three types of resumé formats: chronological, functional, and combination. The chronological format, shown in figure 13.7, is self-explanatory. Your employment history is outlined in reverse chronological order from the current or most recent job, to the furthest in the past. A functional resumé, shown in figure 13.8, places more emphasis on responsibilities and accomplishments by having them precede your employment history. And the combination format, as the name suggests, is a blend of the chronological and functional resumé formats (see figure 13.9).

Chronological resumés used to be the norm. They simply listed all past employment in date order and noted the duties performed. When it became more popular to customize a resumé for a specific, advertised position, the functional resumé came into its own. Now, the most common resumé format is the combination. This format allows for more diversity in style, in the information included, and in the order in which information is presented. All of these options together allow you to personalize your resumé.

Elements of a Resumé

The typical elements of a resumé are the following: the resumé heading, personal information, career objective (optional), education, skills and abilities, employment history, accomplishments, volunteer history (optional), and references.

Resumé Heading and Personal Information

You may choose to include your personal information (name, address, and contact information) at the top of the first page, somewhat like letterhead. Alternatively, this information could appear as the first category in your resumé. No personal data need be included beyond name, address, and contact information. Be mindful that your telephone and email are now available for professional as well as personal purposes, and that the tone of voicemail greetings and of email addresses and signatures should be tempered accordingly (avoid, for example, addresses such as dreamboat@hotmail.com).

Career Objective

A career objective (an optional inclusion) is a statement at the beginning of your resumé that succinctly identifies the type of position and kind of work you are ultimately seeking. When writing an objective statement, don't be vague. A well-written objective statement can emphasize to the reader the position you are seeking. Remember that it is important to customize the objective statement for each position sought. Do not write an objective statement where there are many potential positions that you are qualified for, you cannot be specific about your targeted job, or you are using the resumé at a job fair.

Education

In reverse chronological order, list the name of your educational institution; the program you studied; the certificate, diploma, or degree you attained; your dates of attendance; and any special awards or achievements. If you have a university degree or college diploma, it is not always necessary to include high school information. Use your judgment in this regard. If you studied business or administration in high school, this information may be worth mentioning.

In addition to describing your formal education, list the relevant seminars, workshops, and training courses you have attended.

Skills and Abilities

Your skills and abilities are specific talents you have acquired either through formal training or through your work experience. Generally, these items are merely listed in some type of bullet format, with the most relevant appearing first. These skills are sometimes referred to as "hard skills." Complementary and intangible skills are known as "soft skills." Examples of soft skills include initiative, leadership, and decision-making ability. Soft skills are usually developed through experience rather than through formal training.

> Ultimately, your resumé is a promotional self-portrait. Ensure that this self-portrait is done exactly as you would like.

Employment History

Where you include your employment history depends on the style of your resumé. If you have chosen a chronological format, employment history would appear before skills and abilities and accomplishments. In a functional style, employment history takes a back seat to practical skills and competencies. Regardless of its placement in the resumé, employment history should outline the name of your employer, the title of the position you held, the dates of your employment, and your most important duties and responsibilities. When describing the work you performed, focus on those aspects that are most relevant to the position you are seeking.

Accomplishments

A list of accomplishments became an element of the resumé relatively recently. As the title implies, this list describes your specific accomplishments in the workplace. For example, if your previous employer had an abysmal filing system before you arrived, and through your work and expertise you created an efficient and streamlined system, you should mention this achievement in your list of accomplishments. Even if your experience is limited to part-time work, you can identify ways in which you excelled at your duties. For example, were you always punctual? Did your register consistently balance when you cashed out? Did your manager frequently turn to you as the go-to person? These details can be either highlighted in the list of accomplishments or embedded in your employment history.

Volunteer History

Your volunteer history is another optional element in your resumé. But do not underestimate prospective employers' interest in this information. Many volunteer positions require the same skills and abilities as financially compensated work. For example, if you have held a position on the board of directors for a non-profit organization, you may have gained valuable experience and demonstrated significant practical ability. Apart from the practical experience you may have gained, these volunteer experiences also tell your prospective employer about you as a person: your dedication, your contribution to the community, and your willingness to share your strengths.

References

References have become a critical part of the hiring decision. Employers want testimonials to your past work performance and specific opinions on your ability to meet previous employers' expectations. It is generally preferred that references not be listed on your resumé, but simply noted as "Available on request." You should then compile a separate list of references and their contact numbers, to be provided as necessary. However, if a particular reference has assisted you in obtaining an interview, you should include their information in the References section of your resumé.

Choose your references carefully. Their comments can make or break an application. References should be as relevant as possible to your prospective employment. It is usually expected that your current employer will be listed as a reference, unless your job search is confidential. Select people who you know think highly of you and your work.

If you have limited experience and are just entering the workforce, you have fewer options. In this case, choose people who can attest to your character: your values, your dedication, your capabilities. For example, college instructors are qualified to comment on the abilities you have acquired. Parents of children you have looked after for many years, or a family friend that you have assisted in an informal way by typing letters or assisting with the organization of various functions, may be excellent character references.

NOTES:

Always ask permission to use a person as a reference before providing their name to a prospective employer. To help the person give you a good reference, provide them with a copy of the job ad and with your cover letter and resumé, and perhaps with a listing of the key areas you think are important for them to mention. People asked to give references are often grateful for a draft letter outlining the key points to mention. While they will choose to add or subtract from this draft as they deem appropriate, it will help to refresh their memory and to enlighten them about what you consider to be your strengths.

Organizing and Presenting Your Resumé

How you organize and present the mass of information in your resumé will depend on the type of position you are seeking. It is recommended that you develop more than one resumé if you are looking for different types of positions. For example, a resumé for a courtroom clerk position should be written differently from a resumé for a legal research position. Each position has unique requirements, and job applicants must emphasize different aspects of their skills.

Above all, resumés should be simple, clear, concise, easy to follow, aesthetically pleasing, and completely without error. Your language should be appropriate to the position you're applying for, and free from jargon or stylistic inconsistency. For example, choose either bullet points or full sentences for the descriptive portions of your resumé. Rather than using uninteresting, passive verbs, select strong action verbs, such as those listed in figure 13.6, to bring life to your sentences. When proofreading your resumé, carefully check for consistent verb tenses. Do not write some sentences in the present tense and others in the past. (Note, though, that descriptions of current employment are logically set in the present tense, regardless of the tense of other descriptions.) Be careful not to overuse verbs such as "demonstrated" or "utilized."

Recent years have seen the emergence of companies that provide resumé-writing services and the like, but nothing stands out and grabs a recruiter's attention like a personalized resumé. Just put yourself in the recruiter's shoes: a typical job competition may elicit hundreds of resumés, all of which must be reviewed by one or two recruiters. Very soon these applications will start looking alike, and only the most distinguished ones will be noticed. There is nothing wrong with referring to other resumés and resources while creating your own, and in fact it is recommended. But these external models should only provide ideas. Your personal resumé should be just that: personal.

One note of caution: the resumé is not a place for modesty. Do not understate your skills and accomplishments. Be honest, but not humble. Keep in mind that many skills and abilities are transferable. This means, for example, that if you have been a cashier at Wal-Mart, you have experience working with the public and handling cash. These skills are useful in a law office, and employers should be reminded of this.

FIGURE 13.6 Sample action verbs

Use action verbs whenever possible in describing your skills and accomplishments. They create a stronger picture of your abilities. Be careful, though, not to use the same word too many times.

Accelerated	Communicated	Filed	Proofread
Achieved	Compiled	Forecasted	Published
Acted	Completed	Formatted	Purchased
Adapted	Composed	Generated	Recognized
Addressed	Computed	Guided	Reconciled
Administered	Conducted	Illustrated	Recorded
Advised	Constructed	Implemented	Reduced
Aided	Consulted	Improved	Referred
Analyzed	Contributed	Increased	Renewed
Applied	Controlled	Initiated	Reorganized
Appraised	Copied	Inspired	Reported
Approved	Corrected	Installed	Represented
Arbitrated	Created	Instructed	Researched
Arranged	Customized	Integrated	Restored
Assembled	Debated	Justified	Restructured
Assessed	Defined	Maintained	Retained
Assigned	Delegated	Managed	Reviewed
Assisted	Demonstrated	Modified	Revised
Attained	Designed	Motivated	Scheduled
Attended	Detailed	Negotiated	Screened
Attracted	Developed	Observed	Selected
Balanced	Devised	Obtained	Simplified
Booked	Diagrammed	Operated	Solved
Briefed	Dissected	Ordered	Standardized
Budgeted	Documented	Organized	Summarized
Built	Drafted	Performed	Supervised
Calculated	Edited	Planned	Surveyed
Charted	Ensured	Prepared	Taught
Clarified	Established	Presented	Trained
Classified	Evaluated	Prioritized	Updated
Coordinated	Examined	Produced	Validated
Coached	Expanded	Programmed	Wrote
Collated	Explained	Projected	
Collected	Facilitated	Promoted	

Resumé Length

The ideal length of a resumé has always been the subject of disagreement. Ultimately, you decide what to include in the resumé, and thereby determine its length. By including only the most important information and presenting it as concisely as possible, you will have written an effective resumé. It is generally agreed, however, that a resumé should not exceed two pages. This is a reasonable guideline, especially for students just entering the workforce who have limited work experience and accomplishments.

As your career progresses, you will acquire experience, and with it a wider set of skills, abilities, and accomplishments. It may become difficult to present all this relevant information in only two pages. At this point, three pages should become your maximum length, and you should make every effort to fit your resumé onto two pages. Not only is it more effective to be concise, but lengthy resumés may simply be too demanding on busy recruiters. (For more information on resumés, see Sharyn Borovoy, *Getting Ready for Work* (Toronto: Emond Montgomery, 2010), chapter 1.)

Portfolios

A portfolio provides an account of you as an employee that is more detailed and personal than the one a resumé provides. It presents a comprehensive illustration of your relevant history, allowing you to expand on your achievements and experiences.

By allowing scope for concrete examples of your skills and accomplishments, the portfolio enables you to draw attention to specific abilities you may have gained through volunteer work and other experiences not central to your working life.

Usually the portfolio is presented to prospective employers at the interview stage. Because it is still a relatively new and seldom-used marketing tool, it can often help set you apart from other interviewees.

NOTES:

FIGURE 13.7 Chronological resumé

Julie Anne Lynn Carpenter

705-739-1091
905-760-2194 (cellular)
julcarpenter1221@maddox.ca

10 Port Road
Peterborough, ON K9J 2B0

Profile

- Enthusiastic, motivated, dedicated, reliable, determined to succeed
- Great people person, work well as part of a team or independently
- Very professional, with strong office etiquette skills; well organized, able to multitask effectively
- Trustworthy, hard-working, respectful, and courteous
- Able to learn new skills quickly and effectively
- Work well under pressure

Relevant Employment Experience

March 14, 2009–Present   Woodrow & Perry   Peterborough, ON
Law Clerk

- Law Clerk under Solicitor/Office Manager
- Reception: answer phones, deal with clients, take payments, send faxes and emails, handle new client intake calls, perform general reception duties
- Open new client files under LegalPro and PCLaw
- Draft various court documents including affidavits of documents, affidavits of service, statements of claim, affidavits, notices of motion, trial records, statutory declarations, and orders, as well as other documents
- Draft various correspondence and memoranda; familiar with dicta machine
- Preparation for discovery: set up discoveries with opposing counsel, book reporting services, draft notice of examinations, prepare affidavit of documents, satisfy undertakings given at discoveries
- Request various kinds of information such as medical, employment, income tax, insurance, police records/information, and other documentation
- Book medical/legal appointments with doctors; compose and provide medical briefs
- Attend courthouse for issuing and filing purposes, and to gather information
- Use the Internet for various research purposes
- Enter time dockets using PCLaw
- Prepare pre-bills, statements of accounts
- Perform various office duties: supply ordering, banking, photocopying, binding, running errands outside the office
- Respond to miscellaneous requests made by lawyers

January 2008–April 2008   Brealey Library (SSFC)   Peterborough, ON
Student Staff

- Ran circulation desk
- Stacked shelves
- Organized library processes
- Worked under minimal supervision

… /2

Page 2
Julie Anne Lynn Carpenter

January 2007–April 2008　Sir Sandford Fleming College　Peterborough, ON
Note Taker
- Responsible for providing clear and legible handwritten/computer-generated notes for students with learning disabilities
- Solicited feedback from instructors on the quality of note taking

Summer 2004–2007　Wayfarer/Elite Insurance　Beaverton, ON
Receptionist
- Answered telephones
- Input data into computer system using Microsoft Word and in-house programming
- Performed front-desk duties, including dealing with the public
- Processed invoicing and mailing, acted as courier
- Became knowledgeable in office procedures

Computer Skills
- Trained with Microsoft Word and Corel WordPerfect
- Excellent typing skills
- Strong research skills using the Internet
- Familiar with database software, also used in accordance with the Rules of Civil Procedure
- Trained with PCLaw, LegalPro, DivorceMate, Quicklaw, Teraview, and Conveyancer
- Highly knowledgeable in Microsoft Outlook
- Familiar with Palm Pilot software

Co-operative Placement Program
April 2009–May 2009　Hogget and Guerin　North York, ON
Completed 100 hours of placement with the criminal law firm Worsoff, Silver
- Answered phones, filed, kept dates organized using Palm Pilot software, performed front desk duties, dealt with clientele and courts
- Created affidavits of service, Charter motions, notices of application, discovery requests, stay applications, books of authorities, and bail variations

Education
September 2007–April 2009　Sir Sandford Fleming College　Peterborough, ON
- Successfully completed the law clerk program with diploma
- Completed 100 hours of placement with criminal law firm of Worsoff, Silver
- Awarded letter of excellence

September 2002–June 2006　Brock High School　Cannington, ON
- Achieved OAC level with honours
- Achieved honour roll

REFERENCES AND REFERENCE LETTERS AVAILABLE UPON REQUEST

FIGURE 13.8 Functional resumé

Julie Anne Lynn Carpenter

705-739-1091
905-760-2194 (cellular)
julcarpenter1221@maddox.ca

10 Port Road
Peterborough, ON K9J 2B0

Interpersonal Skills
- Work well independently and as part of a team
- Excellent communication skills
- Interact well with others
- Results oriented
- Learn new skills quickly
- Adapt easily to new situations
- Innovative thinker
- Excel under pressure
- Excellent time-management and organizational abilities
- Able to adapt to changing environments and new ideas

Administrative Skills
- Able to open new client files under LegalPro and PCLaw
- Draft various court documents including affidavits of documents, affidavits of service, statements of claim, affidavits, notices of motion, trial records, statutory declarations, orders, and others
- Draft various correspondence, memoranda; familiar with dicta machine
- Preparation for discovery: set up discoveries with opposing counsel, book reporting services, draft notices of examination, prepare affidavit of documents, satisfy undertakings given at discoveries
- Request various kinds of information including medical, employment, income tax, insurance, and police records/information
- Book medical/legal appointments with doctors; compose and provide medical briefs
- Attend at courthouse for issuing and filing purposes and to gather information
- Use the Internet for various research purposes
- Enter time dockets using PCLaw
- Prepare pre-bills, statements of accounts
- Perform reception duties: answer phones, deal with clients, take payments, send faxes and emails, handle new client intake calls
- Perform various office duties: supply ordering, banking, photocopying, binding, running errands outside the office

Legal Skills
- Able to conduct legal research in Common Law and Statute Law
- Familiar with the *Criminal Code* of Canada and the rules of evidence
- Knowledgeable about procedures and rules for Family Law and for Wills and Estates
- Experienced with Property Law and with conducting title searches
- Familiar with Corporate Law, Business Law, and Contract Law
- Acquainted with Alternative Dispute Resolution and Small Claims Court practices
- Understand Civil Law and the Rules of Civil Procedure
- Knowledgeable about Debtor and Creditor Law and Construction Liens

... /2

Page 2

Julie Anne Lynn Carpenter

Technological Skills

- Utilize Microsoft Word and Corel WordPerfect
- Research case law and statutes using Quicklaw and the Internet
- Familiar with database software, used in accordance with the Rules of Civil Procedure
- Production of relevant documents using PCLaw, LegalPro, DivorceMate, Quicklaw, Teraview, and Conveyancer

Employment Experience

March 14, 2010–Present   Woodrow & Perry   Peterborough, ON
Law Clerk
Provide administrative support for two lawyers

April 2009–May 2009   Hogget and Guerin   North York, ON
Law Clerk, Placement (100 hours)

January 2009–April 2009   Sir Sandford Fleming College   Peterborough, ON
Student Staff
Stacked shelves
Helped students locate required texts in library

January 2008–April 2009   Sir Sandford Fleming College   Peterborough, ON
Provided clear and legible handwritten/computer-generated notes

Summer 2005–2008   Wayfarer/Elite Insurance   Beaverton, ON
Receptionist
Provided front-line client service

Education

Law Clerk Program, Sir Sandford Fleming College
Brealey Drive, Peterborough, ON
September 2002–2004
Dean's Honour List Graduate

Grade 12 Diploma, Kenner Collegiate Vocational Institute
Monaghan Road, Peterborough, ON
Received Math Award for highest achievement
Member of School's General Operations Committee

Volunteer Activities

Fairhaven Long-Term Care Facility
Operated Tuck Shop one Saturday per month for residents and their guests: food preparation, sales, waited on tables, assisted residents, stocked supplies, etc. (2001–2002)

Five Counties Children's Centre
Participated in silent auction: assisted with planning, solicited donations, and operated auction on event night (December 2000)

REFERENCES AND REFERENCE LETTERS AVAILABLE UPON REQUEST

FIGURE 13.9 Combination resumé

Amelia Hoggett

1-705-745-5796
Ahoggett@flemingc.on.ca

12 Leo Avenue
Peterborough, Ontario K9K 1R6

OBJECTIVE

A challenging position in a busy law firm where my academic training is utilized to its fullest extent

EDUCATION	2008–2011	Sir Sandford Fleming College, Peterborough ON Law Clerk Program
	2004–2008	Ajax High School, Ajax ON Grade 12 graduate

SKILLS AND ABILITIES

Legal Skills

- Basic legal research on a topic of interest to a client or an employer
- Use Microsoft Word to format and edit standard legal correspondence, including memorandums of law, memos, and letters
- Understand and apply the Rules of Civil Procedure
- Knowledge and understanding of rules, statutes, and regulations governing the Ontario Court of Justice and the Superior Court of Justice
- Knowledge of relevant court jurisdictions and the functions of various court levels

Administrative Skills

- Answer phones and direct client inquiries appropriately
- Check, transcribe, and forward phone messages to appropriate people
- Assist with the logging of disbursements for billing
- Send, receive, and log faxes
- Photocopy and file correspondence
- File client records
- Format court documents in accordance with the formats prescribed in the Rules of Civil Procedure
- Type, format, and edit correspondence
- Prepare correspondence for mailing and produce mailing labels

Technological Skills

- Computer competency in Windows XP, Microsoft Word, Quicklaw, Conveyancer, email
- Document preparation using Conveyancer, Teraview, E-reg, Estate-a-base, DivorceMate
- Research using Quicklaw and the Internet
- Billing using PCLaw

... /2

Page 2
Amelia Hoggett

INTERPERSONAL SKILLS
- Excellent interpersonal and organizational skills
- Detail-oriented, hard-working, dependable, and effective team member
- Trustworthy, flexible, energetic, and highly self-motivated
- Strong ability to multitask in a fast-paced environment

EMPLOYMENT EXPERIENCE
Shane Hadwyn, Barrister and Solicitor, Peterborough, Ontario   2010
Law Clerk, Placement (100 hours)

The Brick, Peterborough, Ontario   2008–2010
Customer Service Representative

OTHER EDUCATION/TRAINING PROGRAMS
- Conflict Resolution and Confrontation Skills   2010
- Effective Business Writing Skills   2010
- Customer Services Training   2008
- St. John Ambulance First Aid Training   2005

ACCOMPLISHMENTS
- Received Letter of Academic Achievement each semester at
  Sir Sandford Fleming College

VOLUNTEER ACTIVITIES
Advisory Committee Member, Law Clerk Program   2009–Present
Sir Sandford Fleming College
Peterborough, Ontario
- Provide advice on the appropriateness of new programs in relation to employment demands
- Help define the body of knowledge, competencies, and skills required by graduates
- Suggest opportunities for field placement locations

REFERENCES
Available on request

Elements of a Portfolio

The elements of a portfolio vary from person to person and from job to job. Typically, for a young legal assistant, a portfolio includes the following:

- table of contents

- resumé

- letters of recommendation or references

- official transcript of your academic record

- list of courses taken and course descriptions

- educational certificates, diplomas, and degrees received

- special awards or acknowledgments

- employment evaluations

- placement evaluations

- samples of program-related assignments showing experience (ideally) in each area of law

- work samples created from various legal software programs.

These components should be combined in a logical format.

Focus on those areas of your expertise that the employer is seeking. For example, if the position will involve preparing documents for matrimonial matters, include a section providing samples of your work in this area and describing the relevant documents you have prepared and what software you have used. Include sample separation agreements, marriage contracts, and divorce and support documents. You may also want to include any related billing documents.

When outlining the relevant experiences you have had, ensure that you convey what you did, when you did it, why, how, with whom, the results, and most important, how exactly all of this relates to the position you're applying for. This is the time to be as specific as possible.

The Portfolio's Objective

Your portfolio should be geared specifically for the advertised job, should provide relevant information, and should convince the prospective employer that you possess the necessary skills for the position. It should go one step further than this if possible, and display you in a broad perspective as a positive and valued employee.

Other Details

Put pride and creativity into your portfolio. Quality counts. Choose high-grade paper, create all text on a computer, be consistent in format, and consider using sheet protectors. Select a professional-looking font and use it consistently. Provide high-quality copies of the documents you include. Maintain the originals for your records. Select a conservative, standard binder. Zippered binders are best for preventing frayed pages. Divide your portfolio into sections with tabs. There are many products on the market that make possible custom-created tab labels and colour coding. Pay attention to detail. The recruiter will try to gain an understanding of your work habits and standards by examining your portfolio.

Do not send your portfolio with your application. It should be reserved for the interview stage (unless it's requested in advance). Instead of waiting to be asked, take the initiative and present the portfolio to your interviewer. Offer to guide them through it. And bring a duplicate copy that you can leave with them.

Aside from the self-marketing function of your portfolio, it does have other benefits. During its preparation, you will be examining your history, your goals, and your accomplishments. This can help you determine where you really want to go and how far you have come. It helps you reflect on and analyze your career. If updated regularly (even when you are not job searching), it serves as a living record of your employment history.

Ultimately, the objective of self-marketing material is simply that— to promote yourself. Fashion your portfolio to reflect your history and to suggest your future capabilities. Doing this will bring you one step closer to securing your position of choice.

Interviews

Getting an interview is the objective of all your work to this point. Your research, cover letter, and resumé have brought you this far. Now you need to make the most of this opportunity. It is not enough to simply sit back and wait for interview day. This is where the hard work begins.

The Initial Phone Call

When you receive the phone call inviting you to an interview, there are questions you can and should ask. For example, ask for the names and titles of the members on the selection committee. Request a copy of the detailed job description and other reference or orientation material (if available). Such materials may include information about the office's particular legal focus, about the company's philosophy or mission statement, and about its organizational structure. Such materials will not necessarily be available, but your requesting them reflects well on your initiative and interest in the position.

During this initial telephone conversation, ask about the format of the interview. Is it simply an oral question-and-answer process? Will you be asked to make any formal presentations to the committee? Will there be any written or technical components to the interview? These are all appropriate questions for you to ask, and will aid in your interview preparation.

Be mindful of general telephone etiquette. For example, your phone voice should be clear, confident, professional, courteous, and enthusiastic. Through your questions you should convey your knowledge of and interest in the position. If you are offered a choice of time for the interview, consider your own best time of day, and what is likely to be theirs. It is usually considered advantageous to be either the first candidate of the day, the first candidate after the lunch break, or the last interview of the day. These are the times when candidates receive the most attention from recruiters and when you can make the most impact.

Confirm the time and place of the interview. Obtain the caller's name and phone number; you may need to call them back for more information. Finally, thank them for the call.

Preparing for the Interview

Having arranged the details of the interview, you can now begin to prepare. Thorough preparation will be evident to the selection personnel and will create a positive impression that may separate you from other candidates. Your goal is to be remembered by the interviewers as they reflect on the day's candidates.

In a job interview, you may be up against nine competitors. Be ready to state your focus more clearly than your nine rivals. Know your focus or get beaten by the competition who knows theirs.

—Alan Fox

First, understand the needs of the employer. Continue the research you began when preparing your cover letter. The more you know about the company, the better you'll understand what to emphasize in the interview. Approach the interview as your best opportunity to promote yourself.

The key to preparing is to study, study, study. The better prepared you are, the better your chance of success. After you finish your research on the company, focus on the position itself. Review the job posting and description. This is where you will find valuable information about what precisely the employer is looking for. As you go over the posting, highlight the specific requirements listed, mark the sections you need to research further, and identify to yourself how your qualifications meet these requirements.

Figure 13.10 shows the basic elements in the interview process and how to deal with them. Keep in mind that there are significant differences between public sector and private sector interviews. Public sector interviews are standardized, present the same questions to each candidate, generally involve a selection panel of three to five members, and typically involve a scoring system, with candidates given a certain number of points depending on the quality of their answers.

An interview is not a one-way street. Though the interviewer may be leading the meeting and assessing you, this is also your opportunity to learn more about the position and whether it would suit you, and whether it meets your expectations.

Private sector interviews are much less predictable. The interview could simply be one-on-one with you and the employer. Questions are much less formal and may vary from candidate to candidate. You often find more personal, open-ended questions leading to general discussion about skills and past experiences. The interview can go off on tangents, and the final decision may be based on your personality and your "fit for the job."

FIGURE 13.10   Elements of the interview

Where	Refer to your telephone notes to confirm the time and place of the interview. If you are not completely familiar with the location, do a drive-by the day before in order to avoid the stress of having to find the office and suitable parking on the day of the interview.
When	Do not be late. Always arrive 5 to 15 minutes early for the interview. Some public sector job interviews provide questions or reference material for you to review while waiting. This is also the time when you will generally be asked to provide your references' names and contact information, and perhaps to sign a consent form for a criminal records check.
What to bring	Bring a copy of your resumé, your cover letter, your portfolio, the job ad or job specification, and questions to ask. While waiting to be escorted to your interview, review this material.
Welcome	The chair of the selection panel will generally open the door to invite you in.
Introductions	The chair will introduce themselves by name and title. They will then introduce you to each member of the panel.
Panel	The selection panel can vary in size. In private sector jobs, it is not uncommon to be interviewed by only one or two people. The standard in public sector jobs is three people, sometimes as many as five.
Handshake	As you are introduced to each member, approach them and shake their hand. Initiating the handshake always makes you appear more confident and professional. The handshake should be firm.
Names	People like to hear their own names. Try to remember the names of panel members as they are introduced to you. Repeat their name as you shake their hand.
Eye contact	It is important to make a strong initial impression on the panel members. As you shake their hands and use their names, look them in the eye. This again shows confidence and sets the stage for a more personal, relaxed environment.
Format	Before the questioning actually begins you will be advised of the interview format: the number of questions and who will ask the questions. You may be told how long the interview will last. (Expect it to last 30 to 60 minutes, depending on the nature and level of the position.)
Supplies	You are usually provided with a pad of paper, a pen, and water. Use them. The water will make you more comfortable when speaking and make your voice clearer. Use the pen and paper to make notes. As each question is asked, jot down its key points. A quick glance at your paper can help you focus on your answer. This note-taking process is particularly useful when you are faced with complex, multi-faceted questions.
Reference materials	In many cases you will be provided with a copy of the job specification and invited to refer to it before and/or during the interview. These materials can be helpful, but do not depend on them. You need to demonstrate your own understanding of the position.
Questions	Listen carefully to all questions. Misunderstanding a question can work against you. If you're uncertain about a question's meaning or simply need time to develop your answer, it is acceptable to ask that the question be repeated.

Attitude	The interview panel will be observing your attitude. Enthusiastic answers will convey your interest in the job.
Body language	Body language communicates strong messages. You should sit straight in your chair, leaning slightly toward the panel in front of you with both feet on the ground. Do not slouch, cross your arms, or fiddle with pens or paper. Smile. It is contagious and sends a strong positive message. It also makes your voice sound more pleasant.
Dress	Dress as though you already have the position being applied for. In most cases your dress should be business formal. If you've had the opportunity to observe how employees at this office normally dress, you can go one step further. Professional images are generally the safest bet. Grey tones are said to demonstrate a calm and balanced attitude.
Voice	Your voice should be forceful but not aggressive. Do not speak too quickly or too slowly. Sound enthusiastic and vary your tone of voice to maintain the panel's interest. Do not end sentences hesitantly or with an interrogative inflection. Avoid fillers such as "um."
Conclusion	When the interviewer or interview panel has asked all their questions, they will give you the opportunity to question them. You should take advantage of this offer. Have two or three questions prepared. They should be questions that indicate your long-term interest in the position and show that you are familiar with both the position and the firm. Do not ask questions about such things as vacation time, sick time, and salary, since this will make you appear self-serving. Such matters can be negotiated once you are offered the position.
Exit	At this point, the chair will thank you for attending and stand up as a signal for you to leave. Retrieve your belongings, stand up yourself, and thank the board for their time. Shake each member's hand, with eye contact, and use their name if you can remember it.

Interview Checklist

As you prepare for your interview, ensure that you:

- Plan to dress appropriately.
- Allow yourself enough time to get there on time.
- Have a copy of your resume with you.
- Have a list of references and contact information.
- Carry a portfolio and pen.

You need to predict interviewers' questions, and plan your responses. When studying the job advertisement and formal job specification, try to interpret what is important to the employer, what is their primary focus, and what extras would impress them.

Foreseeing possible questions can help to relieve the pressure you're feeling: it is the unknown that is stressful. If you feel confident and prepared, you will be less nervous and better able to deliver superior answers. List likely questions and prepare detailed answers.

In addition to reading, researching, and studying for the interview, you can prepare yourself by rehearsing your answers in front of others or in the mirror. Perhaps you can find someone accustomed to interviewing who could put you through a mock interview. This can be particularly beneficial.

Remember that confidence is convincing. To make your interviewer believe you are qualified and capable for the job, you must believe this yourself. Develop a positive mental attitude by being prepared for anything. (For more information on preparing for an interview, see Sharyn Borovoy, *Getting Ready for Work* (Toronto: Emond Montgomery, 2010), chapter 2.)

The Interview

There are a number of interview methods or styles. Understanding each style can help you to see what a prospective employer is actually seeking in an answer.

Situational questions are the traditional type for employment interviews. According to this method, employers ask interviewees what they would do in a specific work situation. This method tests your knowledge and skills in a basic way. Be concise and specific. Try not to hesitate. Follow up your answer by relating the hypothetical situation to the position you're applying for and, if possible, to your past work experiences. These are questions that, with proper preparation, should not be difficult. Understanding the job and what the employer needs will assist you in giving a well-thought-out answer.

Open-ended questions put the ball in your court. This is an opportunity for you to answer the question but also to expand your answer and provide further information. Open-ended questions are broad and do not have a right or wrong answer. Often, the employer is determining how well you think on your feet. This is an appropriate place for you to demonstrate your general knowledge as well as those skills and abilities that would help you manage the suggested situation. If your answers are too short, you miss a valuable opportunity to sell yourself to the firm or company. Short answers, in this situation, give the employer less basis to judge you. On the other hand, very lengthy answers can seem rambling and can cause the panel to lose interest. This is a place where the panel is also evaluating your communication skills.

Behaviour-based interviews are relatively new on the job market, but are becoming increasingly popular. The purpose of this interview method is to determine what you have done in the past, the assumption being that your past will foreshadow your future actions. Instead of asking general questions about what you would do, the employer in this case asks specific questions about what you have done. To successfully answer behavioural questions you need to be able to recall an instance of your having done what they are asking about, how you did it, why you did it, and what the results were. This is obviously another opportunity to relate your past accomplishments to the current position. If you have never done what the interviewer is asking you about, say so, but try to follow up with an experience from your past that is comparable and that required the same abilities.

Another type of interview is based on factual questions. Factual questions are simply that. They are meant to elicit specific information, and they have a right or wrong answer. These questions are often used in an internal competition where job expertise is the goal and candidates need to have a certain level of knowledge. These questions are also used when an employer is trying to determine your basic knowledge. This can be more challenging for an outside candidate, but this is where your research and preparation can make the difference.

As you can see in figure 13.11, these different methods of questioning are all after, essentially, the same answer. The key is to take advantage of the question, regardless of style, and deliver a well-rounded, informative, and positive answer. Figure 13.12 shows some examples of typical interview questions.

Just before the conclusion of the interview you will likely be asked if you have any questions for the panel. You should. Prepare beforehand two or three questions that demonstrate your understanding and interest in the position and in the firm. Suitable topics include opportunities for advancement in the firm, the general makeup or dynamics of the office, and what they see as the most important aspect of the job. Do not ask self-serving questions concerning such matters as salary, vacation time, and sick time. These are questions that should be addressed during the negotiation process if you are offered the position.

Top Interview Tips

- *Always answer questions in a positive spirit.* Even if you are describing a negative situation, spin the answer by focusing on something you learned from the situation. Do not speak negatively about a former boss or supervisor.

- *Never answer a question with a simple yes or no.* Never waste an opportunity to sell your skills, abilities, and experience. Even if questions appear only to require yes or no, there is always room for some form of expansion.

- *Avoid using statements that minimize you or your job performance and responsibilities.* Starting off sentences with phrases such as "I only" or "I just" is self-defeating.

- *Admit when you do not know the answer to a question.* It is better to be honest than to fumble your way through an answer and have the panel see you fumbling. If you're asked about a situation you've never had to confront, admit it, but then tell the employer how you would go about confronting that situation, given the opportunity.

- *Always relate your past experience to the position at hand.* If, for example, you were responsible for petty cash in a previous job, but the job you're applying for involves no such responsibility, you might try saying that your ability to manage a petty cash account will help you handle client accounts. The better you relate your skills and experiences to the potential job, the more you will convince the hiring committee that you are suitable.

- *Highlight other desirable features as you answer questions.* In addition to seeing how you handle the direct questions, the panel will be evaluating your soft skills, including your capacity for initiative, conflict resolution, communication, problem solving, sound judgment, common sense, adaptability, and leadership.

FIGURE 13.11 Types of interview questions

Style	Sample Question	How to Answer
Situational	What would you do if you had multiple tasks to perform with competing deadlines?	Answer in a way that demonstrates your knowledge about such things as prioritizing and using scheduling tools. An expanded answer would also mention that this situation is one you are used to dealing with.
Open-ended	Do you work well under pressure?	Answer "yes." But be specific about how you do this, and emphasize that you have done it successfully in the past.
Behavioural	Tell us about a specific time when you had to work under pressure to meet competing deadlines. What were the circumstances? What did you do? Why did you do it that way? What were the results?	Answer this question with specific details. Make note of the various parts of the question so as not to overlook anything. Refer to an actual instance when you faced this situation. Give a detailed account of the circumstances. And always find a way to conclude by referring to a positive result.
Factual	What causes pressure in a working environment?	Answer with a list of circumstances that cause pressure, such as difficult clients and time deadlines. After answering the basic question, relate how you have dealt successfully with these pressures.

FIGURE 13.12 Sample interview questions

- Tell me about yourself.
- What are your strengths and weaknesses?
- How do you ensure that you meet deadlines?
- How do you handle conflicting priorities?
- Tell me how your past experiences and skills make you the best candidate for this position.
- What initiatives have you made in previous jobs that were successfully implemented?
- Why should we hire you?
- Do you prefer to work on a team or independently?
- What would be the first thing you would do on the job if you were the successful candidate?
- How would you deal with a subordinate's performance shortcomings?

- What is your working style?
- How do you organize yourself? Others?
- Why do you want to work for our organization?
- What do you think would be your main challenge in this position?
- What do you like best about your current or your last job? What did you like least and why?
- Tell us about a specific achievement that you are proud of.
- What education and training qualify you for this position?
- What do you feel are the three most important characteristics of a good supervisor/manager?
- What are the elements of a good team?
- Tell me about a time you had an angry customer. What did you do? What was the result?

- What are your plans for the future?
- Tell us about a time you made an error. What did you do to correct it? What was the end result?
- What would you do if your boss called in sick, no one was in charge, and time-sensitive matters needed to be dealt with?
- How would you handle a conflict with a co-worker?
- Why do you want this job?
- Define the following legal terms: *sine die, pro bono, ex parte,* application, motion.
- What are the necessary steps in opening a client file?
- Describe your computer experience.

Following those questions, you may be asked whether you have anything further to say. This is an ideal time to conclude the interview with a "30-second commercial." This is a very brief overview of you, your skills and experiences, and what you can bring to the firm. It summarizes your responses to their interview questions and further emphasizes your enthusiasm and confidence. With this, rise and thank each person for their time; shake hands, making eye contact; and leave with a positive bearing. (For more information on the interview process, see Sharyn Borovoy, *Getting Ready for Work* (Toronto: Emond Montgomery, 2010), chapter 3.)

The Follow-up to the Interview

At your first opportunity after leaving the interview, take the time to write down the questions you can remember being asked. These will serve you well for future interviews. You may also want to jot down how you answered, or what you wish you had mentioned. This information will be valuable in the future.

One final opportunity after the interview to put your name back before the panel comes with the thank-you letter. It is professional, considerate, and beneficial to write and send a thank-you letter to the panel as soon as possible. A thank-you letter is brief but can bear weight. Ensure that you have the full names and titles of those on the interview panel. Address the letter to them personally, and follow standard letter format procedures. Three short paragraphs are generally all that is required. The introductory statement merely thanks them for their time, identifies the position applied for, and lists the date of the interview. The second paragraph includes a few sentences recapping the interview, reiterating your interest, expressing your suitability for the job, and so on. The final paragraph need only state that you enjoyed meeting them and discussing the job opportunity, and that you would be happy to provide them with any further information they might want. It tells them how to contact you and reiterates that you are seriously interested in this job. A sample thank-you letter is shown in figure 13.13.

If you have not had any contact from the interview panel in more than a week, and they did not specify when they would make a decision, it is appropriate to make a follow-up phone call. If handled well, such a call can yield information about the competition while reaffirming your interest in the position. In some cases, particularly in large firms or companies, the job application process involves a second round of interviews. Where this system is in place, the first round tends to be viewed as an initial perception and screening process, whereas the second interview is the occasion for real probing and evaluating. If a second round of interviews is planned, you will usually be told this at the beginning of the competition process. A different panel usually conducts second interviews.

While awaiting the decisive phone call, you ought to have decided whether you wish to accept the position if it is offered to you. Though it is acceptable to request further time to consider the offer, this is the

FIGURE 13.13   Sample thank-you letter

Julie Anne Lynn Carpenter

705-739-1091
905-760-2194 (cellular)
julcarpenter1221@maddox.ca

10 Port Road
Peterborough, ON K9J 2B0

April 21, 20--

Collis & Collis, LLP
294 Queen Street
Peterborough, ON K3N 1X6

Attention: **Ms. Diana Collis**

Dear Ms. Collis,

RE: Law Clerk Position, Competition #LC-12

I am writing to formally thank you for the interview held yesterday (April 20, 20--) for the position of law clerk in your firm.

I enjoyed discussing this opportunity with you and was excited to hear that your firm is expanding in the area of medical malpractice. As we discussed, this is my particular field of interest and an area in which I have gained considerable experience. After hearing more about your law clerk position, and your firm, I am very interested in working with you.

Should you have any further questions for me, I can be reached at the number noted above. Thank you for your time and consideration during this process. I enjoyed meeting you and hope to hear from you soon.

Sincerely yours,

Julie Anne Lynn Carpenter

time usually reserved for discussing terms of employment. If the position is offered to you, the terms of employment should be outlined to you: salary, review dates, benefits, start date, and training. It is here that you may ask the self-serving questions you have been waiting to ask.

Hope for the best, but prepare for the worst. Realistically, you will receive more rejections than employment offers. There is stiff competition out there, and rejections do not necessarily reflect poorly on you. If you are not successful in a particular competition, consider requesting feedback (also known as a post-board interview). This is a meeting between you and the chair of the interview panel to discuss the areas where you did not measure up to other candidates, the areas where you could improve, and what your strong attributes are. It is not always a lack of skills and experience that loses you the job; sometimes it is your presentation of them. Take this opportunity to learn from the process and improve for the next one.

Figure 13.14 summarizes the job search process, from identifying a career objective to following up on the job interview.

Professional Development

Your education should not end once you land a job. Professional growth and development keep your skills relevant and enhance your chances of career progression. To ensure that you remain competitive, you must continually expand your skill base and experience.

Keep a record and have a plan. Set goals and objectives, create timelines, and work out how you are going to achieve what you want. Your career plan should include a summary of your strengths and weaknesses to help you focus. Keep a list of your transferable skills and abilities. And always maintain a current resumé and portfolio.

Enhance your chances of being remembered for future opportunities by maintaining and nurturing your network contacts. These people will still be helpful in the future. Join groups related to your field. Keep your ears open and keep abreast of major career trends and demands.

To develop yourself further in your career, take courses and seminars regularly that will help you progress to the next level. Pay attention to continuing education courses offered through local colleges, and review new course calendars each term. Law societies often offer courses and seminars on specific aspects of the law, and these are usually run by local experts and lawyers. Conferences are another excellent way to build your expertise and expand your network.

Other ways of developing yourself professionally are to accept temporary opportunities and to job-shadow people in other positions. These types of strategies open you to new processes and procedures, further developing your skills and abilities and increasing your marketability.

Keep your current employer aware of your desire for progress. Take on extra responsibilities such as participating in or leading a work-related committee, contributing to new initiatives, or helping co-workers. These actions will demonstrate your abilities and your eligibility for progress. Current conduct can limit or enlarge future opportunities. Always protect your future.

FIGURE 13.14 Finding and securing your position of choice

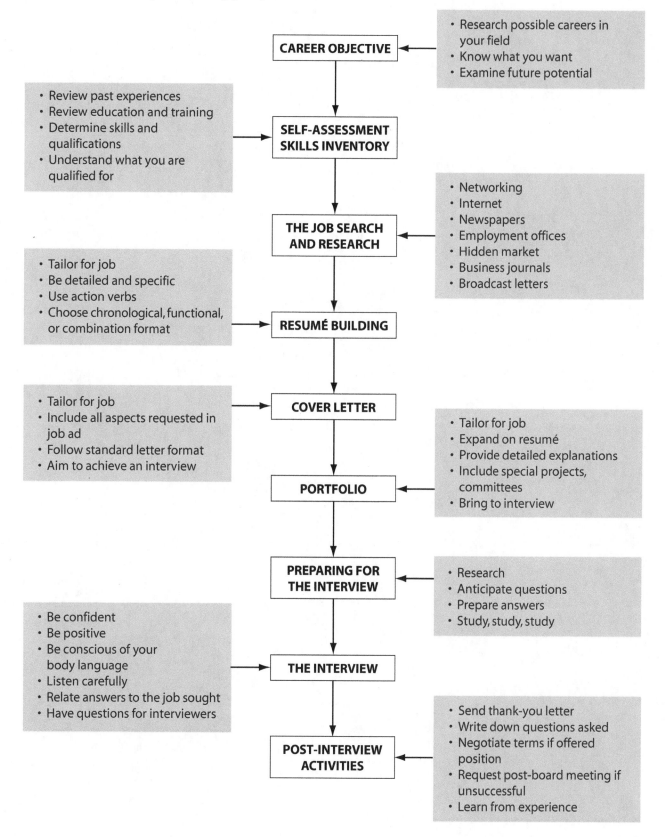

REVIEW QUESTIONS

1. What is the purpose of a placement?

_____

_____

_____

_____

_____

_____

_____

_____

2. What is the primary goal of a cover letter?

_____

_____

_____

_____

_____

_____

_____

_____

_____

3. How is a resumé used?

_____

_____

_____

_____

_____

_____

_____

_____

4. List and describe the different types of resumés.

_____

_____

_____

_____

_____

_____

_____

_____

_____

_____

_____

_____

5. Why would you include your volunteer history in a resumé?

_____

_____

_____

_____

_____

_____

_____

_____

6. Describe a portfolio and its use.

_____

_____

_____

_____

_____

_____

_____

7. At what point in the application process do you discuss specific employment details such as remuneration and vacation pay? Why then?

_____

_____

_____

_____

_____

_____

_____

8. How do you prepare for an interview?

_____

_____

_____

_____

_____

_____

_____

_____

_____

9. List and describe the different methods of interview questioning.

_____

_____

_____

_____

_____

_____

_____

_____

_____

_____

_____

10. Explain the difference between soft and hard skills.

_____

_____

_____

_____

_____

_____

_____

11. Choose three elements of a basic interview structure and explain the importance of each element.

_____

_____

_____

_____

_____

_____

_____

_____

_____

_____

_____

_____

_____

12. What do you feel is the key to securing a job? Why?

_____

_____

_____

_____

_____

_____

_____

_____

_____

_____

ACTIVITIES

1. Find a job posting related to your area of study. Complete the following chart by matching your skills to what the position requires.

Position title	
Skills required	
Your relevant skills or experience	

2. a. Once you find an appropriate posting, draft a cover letter using one of the examples provided in this chapter. Your instructor may provide you with alternative models.

   b. Once your draft is complete, get feedback from a classmate or from your instructor.

   c. Create your final version for submission.

3. a. Now it is time to create your resumé. Determine the type of resumé that best suits your skill set and the position you are applying for. Review the samples in this chapter. Create a draft version of your resumé. Remember to tie your cover letter, your resumé, and the requirements of the position together.

   b. Once your draft is complete, have a classmate or your instructor comment on it.

   c. Create your final version for submission.

4. Review the section of this chapter dealing with portfolios. Follow the criteria set out there and create an employment portfolio. Your instructor may have further specifications.

5. Choose three of the sample interview questions listed in figure 13.12. Prepare a response to each of the questions. Each response should be at least one page in length and should tie your skills and abilities to the position you are seeking.

APPENDIX
Writing Guide

Introduction

Before learning the essential steps of editing and proofreading, you should know what to look for. This Writing Guide explains the essentials of punctuation, grammar, and style. Learning the following rules and applying them in all of your writing will result in clearer, more professional correspondence. In addition to the sections below, make sure you have access to a good dictionary, whether online or in hard copy; the *Canadian Oxford Dictionary*, 2d ed., is an excellent resource. Another text that will serve you well throughout your career is *The Elements of Style*, 4th ed., by William Strunk Jr. and E.B. White.

Punctuation Rules

The proper use of punctuation may not seem at first like an important aspect of writing. However, the placement of punctuation can affect readability and comprehension, and even change the meaning of a sentence.

Commas

The comma is one of the most misused punctuation marks. Without it, readers are left to fend for themselves as they try to navigate a tangle of information. Notice how you feel, for example, as you read this sentence:

> When the lawyer submitted his documents to the court the presiding justice Mr. Justice Jones indicated that the matter should be set to July 5 20-- when the court would be available to hear this case on the basis of the material filed including a statement of facts a casebook an affidavit and a motion on a Charter issue all of which will be heard that day presuming sufficient time on the docket the

seized judge's schedule and the availability of courtroom staff and all concerned parties.

Now, see how the addition of commas changes the sentence—and your grasp of it:

When the lawyer submitted his documents to the court, the presiding justice, Mr. Justice Jones, indicated that the matter should be set to July 5, 20--, when the court would be available to hear this case on the basis of the material filed, including a statement of facts, a casebook, an affidavit, and a motion on a Charter issue, all of which will be heard that day, presuming sufficient time on the docket, the seized judge's schedule, and the availability of courtroom staff and all concerned parties.

The simple addition of commas provides pauses in the flow of the sentence, allowing the reader to absorb information in a structured way. However, this revised sentence is still too long, and really should be broken down into two or three sentences for ease of reading. For example:

The lawyer submitted his documents to Mr. Justice Jones, the presiding judge. The material filed included a statement of facts, a casebook, an affidavit, and a motion on a Charter issue. Justice Jones set July 5, 20-- as the hearing date for dealing with all the issues, presuming sufficient time on the court docket, the seized judge's schedule, and availability of all concerned parties and court staff.

The omission of commas can also change the intended meaning of a sentence. For example:

John can file type and answer the phone at the same time.

This sentence makes it sound as if John can "file type," which is an odd and probably unintentional phrasing. The addition of commas clarifies the meaning:

John can file, type, and answer the phone at the same time.

The omission of a comma can also introduce serious ambiguity into a sentence. For example:

Mr. Buckle attended court with Mrs. MacDonald and Ms. Burgis and Mr. Atkinson did not show up.

With whom did Mr. Buckle attend court—Mrs. MacDonald, or Mrs. Macdonald and Ms. Burgis? And who did not show up—Ms. MacDonald and Mr. Atkinson, or just Mr. Atkinson? The judicious use of a comma eliminates the ambiguity:

Mr. Buckle attended court with Mrs. MacDonald and Ms. Burgis, and Mr. Atkinson did not show up.

The box below summarizes the various uses and rules of the comma.

Comma	

Comma
 	
a,
	1. The comma is used before the "and/or" in a series when there are at least three elements.
	
	    The printer holds letter, legal, and tabloid size paper.
	    You can drive a car, ride a bike, or take public transit.
	
	2. A comma follows the introductory clause in sentences beginning with certain words, including *although, despite, because, before, should, unless, until, where, when, while, for, after, on, as, if,* and *in.*
	
	    Unless you have proofread the letter, do not send it out.
	
	3. A comma follows transitional words such as *however* and *therefore.*
	
	    However, once you have proofread the letter, please send it immediately.
	
	4. The comma is used to distinguish parts of a sentence that are not essential to the overall meaning.
	
	    The office, which is located on the sixth floor, employs more than 40 legal assistants.
	
	5. Commas introduce a quotation.
	
	    Aristotle said, "The law is reason, free from passion."
	
	6. Commas separate the names of cities and provinces, and the day and year in a written date.
	
	    Our office is located in Peterborough, Ontario.
	    The trial was set for January 3, 2012.
	
	7. Commas are used in numerical figures of one thousand or more.
	
	    $2,564.00
	    As of 2001, Canada had a population of 30,007,004.

Apostrophe

Like the comma, the correct use of the apostrophe presents a challenge for many writers. Before outlining the rules for using the apostrophe, it is worth mentioning two of the most common errors involving the apostrophe:

1. *It's/Its*

   The words "it is" and "it has" form the contraction *it's*, with the apostrophe indicating the missing letters. The word *its*, without the apostrophe, is the possessive form of "it."

   > It's time to send a reminder.
   > Please ensure that each item is in its proper place.

2. *Plurals*

   The apostrophe is *not* used to form plurals. See Rule 1 in the box below, and see the discussion of plurals and possessives later in this chapter.

The rules for the correct use of the apostrophe are outlined below.

Apostrophe	1. The apostrophe is used to form the possessive form of nouns and pronouns.
	Cindy's father, Don, will meet you at 70 Simcoe St., Peterborough.
	2. The apostrophe is used to form contractions—words that are shortened or combined. Contractions are often used in informal writing, but are generally avoided in formal writing, such as client correspondence.
	gov't (government)
	don't (do not)
	3. The apostrophe is used as a quotation mark within a quotation.
	The woman said to the student, "I ask that the envelope be marked 'confidential' to ensure that only the recipient opens it."
	4. The apostrophe is the accepted abbreviation for "foot" or "feet" in measurements.
	The prisoner's cell was 6' by 8'.
	5. The apostrophe is used to take the place of omitted numbers in abbreviated dates.
	They graduated from college in '94.
	6. The apostrophe is also used to indicate the plural form of single letters or acronyms, but only where confusion could result if an apostrophe were not used.
	Be sure to dot your i's and cross your t's.
	I bought three new CDs on Saturday.

Colons and Semicolons

Like the apostrophe, colons and semicolons present a challenge for many writers, and are frequently used incorrectly. Ensure that you understand the following rules.

Colon	1. The colon is used between independent clauses where the second part is an explanation or illustration of the first part.
	You can't drive there: you don't have a licence.
	2. The colon is also used preceding a list of words or phrases.
	I need to stock up on supplies: paper clips, staples, and pens.
	File contents are to be organized as follows: correspondence, legal documents, research, and billing.
	3. The colon is also used in time representations and in ratios.
	2:00 p.m.
	2:1
	4. The colon is sometimes used after formal salutations.
	Dear John:
	To Whom It May Concern:
	5. The colon is used after the word "Note," followed by a statement beginning with a capital letter.
	Note: File number identifiers are changed to Year, Lawyer/Paralegal, numerical sequence format.

Semicolon	1. The semicolon is used to separate two independent clauses when the conjunction is omitted. If the clauses are not closely related, two sentences (separated by a period) are preferred.
	When he was seven, he wore short pants and short hair; when he was seventeen, he wore long pants and long hair.
	2. If the items in a series themselves include commas, the semicolon is used to distinguish the separate elements.
	Today I revised an affidavit, two contracts, and five invoices; typed a lot of letters; and called three clients.
	3. Transitional words such as "therefore" and "however" are usually preceded by a semicolon; as noted above, they are always followed by a comma.
	It's raining; however, I'll still go running. The court agreed with his argument; therefore, the case was decided in his favour.

Other Punctuation

Period	1. The period is used at the end of declarative and imperative sentences, indirect questions, and polite requests that resemble a statement.
	The lawyer prepared her case well. Don't forget to call him back. The question is whether we need a new system. Would you please photocopy this for me.
	2. The period is also used with initials and abbreviations.
	Mr. J.A. Smith Ms. M. Hanley Cody Carpenter Jr.
	3. The period is also used with decimal figures.
	$6.23 45.6 percent
Question mark	1. The question mark is used at the end of direct questions or to emphasize polite requests that resemble a question.
	Did you have a good weekend? Will you review this invoice, please?
	2. It is also appropriate to place a question mark in parentheses when you are not certain of a fact.
	He was born in 1964(?).
Exclamation point	1. The exclamation point should be used sparingly. It is often used in advertising copy to draw one's attention.
	Buy now and get a free widget!
	2. The exclamation point is properly used to reflect enthusiasm, surprise, disbelief, or urgency of strong feeling.
	Let's donate our time and help these people out! I can't believe he said that!

Hyphen
 	
a-
	1. The hyphen is used primarily to indicate end-of-line word division and to form compound words. Note that word-processing software does not divide words over lines, so end-of-line division does not apply.
	
	    Words should be divided only between syllables. Words pronounced as one syllable should never be divided. Consult a dictionary, such as the *Canadian Oxford Dictionary*, 2d edition, for word divisions. (Note that word division style varies somewhat from dictionary to dictionary. Choose one source and follow it.)
	
	2. The hyphen is also used to form compound words such as multi-word adjectives in order to clarify the meaning of the words or to avoid confusion.
	
	    an up-to-date report (*but* a report that is up to date)
	    a light-blue coat (indicating colour)
	    a light, blue coat (indicating weight and colour)
	
	3. The hyphen is also used with some prefixes.
	
	    semi-private
	    re-admit

Dash **a——a** *or* **a--a**	1. The dash often replaces other forms of punctuation, such as commas or semicolons, where you want to emphasize the separation. Regulatory issues—for example, broadcasting restrictions—may need to be considered. 2. The dash is represented by a longer hyphen on some keyboards. Where this keystroke is not available, two hyphens together (without a letter space) substitute for the dash. (Most word-processing programs can automatically convert two hyphens to a dash.)

Parentheses
 	
(a)
	1. Parentheses, like the dash, separate elements within a sentence, but the elements separated by parentheses are usually non-essential to the meaning of the sentence.
	
	    The office manager referred the new hire to HR (human resources).
	
	2. Parentheses are also used for reference purposes.
	
	    There are too many expenses this month (see the report attached).

Brackets
 	
[a]
	1. Brackets (often called "square brackets" to distinguish them from parentheses) are used to represent corrected or inserted phrases within a quotation.
	
	    "The teacher told us the matter was due on April 30 [a Sunday] and that it needed to be 5,000 words."
	
	2. Brackets are also used within a sentence where parentheses are already used.
	
	    The form (which must be submitted to the Canada Revenue Agency [CRA]) must specify all sources of income, including investments.

Quotation marks " a "	1. Quotation marks enclose direct quotations (the exact words of a speaker). Indirect quotations (references to something someone said but not in their exact words) do not require quotation marks. He said, "I started work last September." He said he started work last September. 2. Quotations marks are also used to highlight or emphasize a word within a sentence. "Irregardless" is not a word. The box was marked "fragile." 3. Periods and commas are always placed inside the closing quotation mark. Other punctuation marks are placed inside the closing quotation mark only where they are part of the quoted material; most commonly, they are placed outside. The label read "Open here," so I opened it. She asked, "Don't you believe me?" He had the temerity to accuse me of "malingering"! 4. When a direct quotation is longer than one sentence, quotation marks are used only at the beginning and end of the entire quoted material, not at the beginning and end of each sentence. Direct quotations that are very lengthy may be separated from the main text and indented and/or set in a smaller type size. Where direct quotations are separated from the main text in such a way, quotation marks are not necessary. The titles of articles, chapters, essays, songs, reports, and so on are enclosed in quotation marks.
Ellipsis ● ● ●	An ellipsis represents the omission of words from a direct quotation. The judge delivered his decision by saying, "Mr. Smith … is hereby found guilty as charged." (The omitted words were, "of Peterborough County is charged with theft under $5,000, and on the basis of the evidence before me.")
Asterisk a *	An asterisk is used primarily as a footnote indicator. The asterisk is placed immediately after a word or sentence (and generally after all punctuation except dashes). At the bottom of the page, the asterisk appears again, with the footnote text. The whole footnote is usually set in a smaller type size. (Where many footnotes are used, asterisks are usually abandoned in favour of superscripted numbers.)
Diagonal a /	A diagonal slash (typed without spaces before or after) is used to separate alternatives or to represent the words "per," "or," and other commonly accepted abbreviations. km/h (kilometres per hour) he/she (he or she) c/o (in care of)
Underscore a —	1. The underscore in handwritten and typewritten text is equivalent to italics in word-processed text. Specific words within a sentence can also be underscored as an alternative to quotation marks. 2. Underscores or italics are required for the titles of published materials such as books, magazines, and newspapers, and for the titles of artistic works such as plays, musicals, and movies.

Grammar

Grammar refers to the system and structure of language. The improper use of grammar in speech or writing can act as a barrier to communication and reflect poorly on the sender. In addition, the receiver of your message may become frustrated with the communication.

Plurals and Possessives

A noun is any person, place, or thing (e.g., Paul, office, book). The rules for forming the plural form of a noun are set out in the table below. Remember that an apostrophe is *not* used to indicate a plural form, but is used to indicate possession.

Non-Possessive Plural Forms of Nouns	
Rule	**Example**
Plural forms of a noun not ending in an "s" add an "-s."	The criminal law files are red. The junior paralegals are at a Law Society training session this afternoon.
Plural forms of nouns ending in "s, z, ch, sh, and x" add "-es."	The boxes are stored in the basement. The plaintiff was accosted in the bushes.
Plural forms of nouns ending in "y" add "ies."	The families of the three accused men were sitting in the front row. **Exception:** attorney ➡ attorneys

The possessive form of a noun indicates a type of relationship, often ownership, through the use of an apostrophe. Possessives are formed differently depending on whether the noun is singular or plural, and the letter in which it ends. Ensure that you understand the following rules, and pay special attention to errors in this area whenever you proofread.

Possessive Forms of Singular and Plural Nouns	
Rule	**Example**
Singular and plural nouns that do not end in "s" add an apostrophe and an "s."	Stephen's files are accurate and up to date. The lawyer's desk is well organized. The judge's office is at the back of the building. The children's laughter echoed loudly.
Nouns that end in an "s" add an apostrophe only.	Lawyers' conflict of interest responsibilities are regulated by law societies across Canada.
Nouns that are hyphenated and compound nouns add an apostrophe and an "s" to the end of the hyphenated word or compound noun.	Janice's mother-in-law's office is located at 599 Brealey Drive, Peterborough.
Where shared ownership is indicated, add an apostrophe "s" to the final noun.	Sarah and Tanya's file is located in the far left filing cabinet.
Where individual ownership is indicated, add an apostrophe "s" to each noun.	Will's and Shane's files are both in the far left filing cabinet.

Subjects and Verbs

The subject of a sentence is the who or what that the sentence is about, or that carries out an action. The subject and verb must always "agree," as explained in the rules below.

Rule	Example
If a subject is singular, its verb must also be singular.	*He is* going to come in with his retainer money this afternoon.
If a subject is plural, its verb must also be plural.	*They are* going to finish drafting the pleadings this afternoon.
If there are two subjects referring to one person, the verb is singular.	The *paralegal and office manager is* Sarah Carpenter.
If two subjects are joined by the word "and" the verb is usually plural.	*Allicia and Kelsey are* coming in at 3:00 p.m. to sign the papers.
If one of these words comes before the subject, the verb is singular: one (of), each, every, neither, either.	*No* eating or drinking *is* permitted in the courtroom. *Every* person on the court list *is* required to check in. *Each* officer *is* scheduled to write the exam at 9:30 a.m.
When using either/or and neither/nor, the verb takes the same form of the subject (singular or plural). If the subject has singular and plural items, the verb agrees with the nearest element.	*Either* Allicia *or* Kelsey *is* going to attend. *Neither Allicia* nor her *associates are* able to attend. *Neither* her *associates* nor *Allicia is* able to attend.
If one of these words comes before the subject, the verb is plural: both, several, others, few, many.	<u>Several</u> new law clerks <u>were</u> hired by the firm last June. <u>Few</u> of them <u>have</u> left since then.

NOTES:

Style

Like the other rules described above, the rules governing capitalization and numbers are followed in order to aid comprehension and make the experience of reading easier on your reader.

Capitalization

Rule	Example
Capitalize the first word of a sentence.	I will head over to the office at 10:00 a.m.
Capitalize the first word of a quotation.	The paralegal asked, "Do you want to adjourn this matter to the 27th of May?"
Capitalize the first word of a salutation and a complimentary closing.	Dear Ms. Gleadow, Regards,
Capitalize names of individuals.	Jennifer Collis
Capitalize the word "I."	I am going to court today.
Capitalize professional designations and titles.	Professor Paul Atkinson Doctor Patrick Kilmartin Prime Minister Pierre Trudeau Senator Michael Kirby Chief Justice Beverley McLachlin
Capitalize the names of countries, provinces, territories, cities, towns, etc.	Canada Province of Ontario City of Peterborough
Capitalize names of streets, parks, schools, and churches.	Wallace Point Road Little Lake Park Lord Durham School
Capitalize the names of government departments and boards.	Ministry of Education Liquor Control Board
Capitalize federal, provincial, and territorial courts.	The Supreme Court of Canada The Superior Court of Ontario The Provincial Court of British Columbia The Supreme Court of the Northwest Territories

Numbers

Rule	Example
Spell out numbers from one to ten; use numerals for numbers greater than *ten*. Numbers are often typed as words and then included as figures in brackets. Hyphenate all compound numbers from twenty-one through ninety-nine.	Please make seven copies of the disclosure statement. Please make 24 copies of the disclosure statement. Please remit one hundred and twenty-nine dollars ($129.00) to our office within seven (7) days. The invoice is for one thousand, eighty-two dollars and eighty-four cents ($1,082.84).
Write out a number if it begins a sentence.	Twelve people are sitting on the jury.
Dates may be written in words, numerals, or both.	The disclosure meeting is scheduled for September 25th. The meeting is scheduled for the twenty-fifth of September.
When two words next to each other in a sentence are numbers, spell one out and write one as a number.	There were ten 65-year-olds at the opening of the seniors' residence.
Use numerals with the time of day when exact times are being emphasized or when using a.m. and p.m.	Court begins again at 9:30 a.m.
Use numerals when representing statistics or measurements.	The licensees received a 2-year licence. The office is approximately 50 km from here.

NOTES:

Frequently Misspelled Words

To find the correct spellings of uncommon or difficult words, use your dictionary. Below is a list of words that are often misspelled; learn them now so you don't need to look them up later.

a lot	competent	inaccuracy	prejudice
absence	compulsory	independence	privilege
accessible	conquer	judgment	recommend
accidentally	conscientious	licence (n.)	referred
accommodate	courteous	license (v.)	seize
achieve	deceive	loneliness	separate
acquaint	deficiency	mischievous	sergeant
acquire	defendant	negligence	succeed
address	dependant (n.)	noticeable	suppress
advisable	dependent (adj.)	occasionally	susceptible
all right	eighth	occurrence	tenant
attendance	embarrassed	omitted	tendency
bookkeeper	endeavour	pastime	unaccustomed
boundary	exaggerate	permissible	undoubtedly
bulletin	extraordinary	perseverance	valuable
bureau	grammar	possession	
calendar	harass	practice (n.)	
commission	hindrance	practise (v.)	

NOTES:

Frequently Misused Words

A number of words are often used incorrectly. These words may have the same spelling as other words but different meanings; the same pronunciation but different spellings and meanings; similar meanings; or the opposite meaning.

Words	Correct Usage
accept, except *Accept* is a verb meaning to receive. *Except* is usually a preposition meaning to exclude or leave out.	I will accept all of the witness statements, except Ms. Moyle's.
access, excess *Access* is a noun meaning a way into something or somewhere. *Excess* is a noun meaning more than needed.	Ted has access to the client files. Ted's rearrangement of the files is in excess of our expectations.
adapt, adept *Adapt* is a verb meaning to change. *Adept* is an adjective meaning skilled.	Jennifer will adapt to the new office procedures for dealing with incoming client files. Natasha is very adept at writing legal briefs and legal memorandums.
advice, advise *Advice* is a noun meaning an opinion or suggestion. *Advise* is a verb meaning to inform or to give advice.	Because you asked for my advice, I advise you to proceed to trial.
affect, effect *Affect* is a verb meaning to influence. *Effect* is usually a noun meaning result.	The witness statement did not affect the final outcome of the trial, but did have an adverse effect on the defence.
a lot, alot, allot *A lot* is an adverb meaning much or a large amount. It can also refer to a piece of property. *Alot* is not a word, but is a common misspelling of "a lot." To *allot* is a verb meaning to share or distribute.	A lot of money was spent on the furniture for the new office. He bought a lot on the east side of the river. Tyren will allot Ayden a cubicle in Ryder's office to do the Law Society audit.
among, between *Among* is a preposition meaning surrounded by or in the company of several or more things. *Between* is a preposition that refers to the position of being bounded by two things.	The envelope was misplaced among all the papers. Between you and me, this doesn't look right.
appraise, apprise *Appraise* is a verb meaning to evaluate. *Apprise* is a verb meaning to inform someone of something.	The interviewer will appraise your suitability for the job. We will keep you apprised of our progress.

Words	Correct Usage
capital, Capitol *Capital* is an adjective meaning important. It is also a noun that refers to money or other resources, or to the city where the legislature meets. *Capitol* is a noun meaning the building where the US legislature meets.	That is a capital idea. Camden plans to invest $10,000 in capital funds to Cody's expansion. The capital city of Canada is Ottawa. The Capitol building has been renovated over the last several years.
complement, compliment *Complement* is a verb meaning to enhance or a noun meaning an enhancement. *Compliment* is a verb meaning to praise and a noun referring to a piece of praise.	Your compliments are a nice complement to the other feedback I received.
counsel, council *Counsel* is a verb meaning to give advice or instruct, or advocate. It can also be used as a noun. *Council* is a group of people that manage, advise, deliberate, or legislate.	Bob counselled Trevor on his best course of action. Trevor listened to Bob's counsel on the options put before him. The local council was not willing to bend on its decision to rezone the west end of the city.
discrete, discreet *Discrete* is an adjective meaning separate and distinct. *Discreet* is an adjective meaning careful, especially to gain an advantage or to avoid offence.	There are several discrete points to discuss. Our questions were discreet, and not overheard.
elicit, illicit *Elicit* is a verb meaning to bring out or to extract. *Illicit* is an adjective meaning illegal.	The Crown was unable to elicit information from the defendant about the illicit drug cocaine.
emigrate, immigrate *Emigrate* is a verb meaning to leave one country or area to settle in another. *Immigrate* is a verb meaning to come into another country or area to reside there.	Abi Adeusi emigrated to Canada from England. Amy Maycock will immigrate to Portugal when she retires.
fewer, less *Fewer* is an adjective meaning a smaller number and is used with countable things. *Less* is an adjective used with mass nouns, measurements, and things that cannot be counted.	There were fewer people at the meeting than we expected. Despite our estimate, the research took less than an hour to complete.
irregardless, regardless *Irregardless* is not a word. *Regardless* is an adverb meaning in any event.	We carried on regardless of the difficulties involved.

Words	Correct Usage
it's, its *It's* is the contraction of "it is." *Its* is the possessive form of "it."	It's time to send a reminder. Please ensure that each item is in its proper place.
principal, principle *Principal* is a noun meaning a person in authority, the head of a school or lead of an organization, or an amount of money. It is also an adjective meaning primary. *Principle* is a noun meaning a basic truth or law.	The principal of Lord Durham school is a man of principle. The principal amount of the loan will be paid off in five years. The principal witness came forward a week before trial. The principles of honesty and fairness were discussed in detail with the class.
than, then *Than* is a conjunction and a preposition used to show comparisons. *Then* is an adjective or adverb denoting time or point in time.	Allicia decided that ten client files are more than enough to satisfy the Law Society's requirements for an audit. Kelsey went to the bank to deposit the trust money, then went to the courthouse to pick up the disclosure statement from the Crown's office.
there, their, they're *There* is an adverb that refers to a place or position, or that indicates the fact or existence of something. *Their* is a possessive adjective that means "belonging to them." *They're* is a contraction of "they are."	There are too many files to review in an hour. Their transcription machines in the office are not working properly. They're going to be late for court today.
whether, weather *Whether* is a conjunction used to indicate a choice between two or more options. *Weather* is a noun meaning atmospheric condition.	Whether we walk or drive depends on the weather.
whose, who's *Whose* is the possessive form of "who." *Who's* is a contraction of "who is."	Whose files are those? Who's going to sign this form on his behalf?
your, you're *Your* is the possessive form of "you." *You're* is a contraction of "you are."	Have you taken your lunch break yet? You're just the person I was looking for!

Index

Credits

Figure 2.1: Courtesy of Troy Woodland. Figure 2.2: Copyright © Supreme Court of Canada. Figures 3.8, 5.2, 5.8, 5.16, 5.17, 6.4, 6.5, 6.10, 6.11, 6.15, 6.17, 6.18, 6.23, 11.13: Reprinted with permission of LexisNexis, a division of Reed Elsevier Inc. All Rights Reserved. Figure 5.3: Courtesy Amicus Attorney. Figure 5.4; Adapted from Laurence Olivo and Mary Ann Kelly, *Civil Litigation*, 2d ed. (Toronto: Emond Montgomery, 2009). Figures 5.18, 5.19: Reprinted by permission of Do Process Software LP. Figures 5.20, 5.21: Courtesy of DIVORCEmate Software Inc. Figure 5.23: Copyright 2011, The Law Society of Upper Canada. All rights reserved. Reprinted with permission of The Law Society of Upper Canada. Figure 6.21: Courtesy of The Law Foundation of Ontario. Figures, 9.5, 9.6, 9.7: Published with the permission of Canada Post. Figure 11.43, Reprinted by permission of the Ontario Teachers' Pension Plan Board. Figures 11.9, 12.1 to 12.12 and 12.15 to 12.22: © Queen's Printer for Ontario, 2011. Figures 12.13, 12.14: Reproduced from Preparation of Wills and Powers of Attorney: First Interview to Final Report, Fourth Edition, by Mary L. MacGregor with the permission of Canada Law Book, a division of Thomson Reuters Canada Limited (1-800-387-5351, http://www.canadalawbook.ca). Figure 11.10: Canadian Legal Information Institute. Statutes and Regulations of Ontario. Figures 11.11, 11.12: Canadian Legal Information Institute. Cain v. Peterson, 2005.